# Fate and Honor, Family and Village

# Fate and Honor, Family and Village

*Demographic and Cultural Change in Rural Italy since 1800*

## Rudolph M. Bell

The University of Chicago Press

Chicago and London

The University of Chicago Press, Chicago 60637
The University of Chicago Press, Ltd., London

Library of Congress Cataloging in Publication Data

Bell, Rudolph M
  Fate and honor, family and village.

  Includes index.
  1. Peasantry—Italy.   2. Rural families—
Italy.   3. Italy—Rural conditions.   I. Title.
HN475.B38     301.44′43′0945     79–11011
ISBN 0–226–04208–1

RUDOLPH M. BELL is a professor of history at Rutgers
University. He is the author of *Party and Faction
in American Politics*.

For Tara Cristina

# Contents

# TABLES

## FIGURES

# Acknowledgments

Suspicion and bureaucracy reinforce each other to thwart access to the the types of materials used in this study. The researcher who asks at the Municipio to see, transcribe, and photocopy its rows of registers is met with friendly but persistent refusal. Writing to higher authorities is useless, since law is on the side of those who can see no reason to allow an outsider to look at personal information about generations of villagers. Fortunately there is the countervailing influence of *la famiglia*, and enough remains of *onore* that one does not deny easily the needs of even a remote cousin. The present study would not have been possible at all without the networks of people named below. My understanding of rural Italy has been shaped by their friendship, assistance, and encouragement.

My brother-in-law's wife, Ilde Zecca Tomici, and her parents, Linda Orsi and Renato Zecca, introduced me to the village of Albareto (Emilia-Romagna) and to the community of Albaretesi in America. For fifteen years I have learned from them. Linda Orsi's brother, Don Agostino, secured permission in 1972 for us to copy the village's manuscript census schedules and all its vital records (registers of births, marriages, and deaths) dating back to 1780. Then, and again in 1974, several clerks and *comune* officials assisted us in every possible way: Mayor Marco Botti, Secretary Raffaela Galiana, Giuseppe Bertorelli, Ernesto Grilli, and especially Piero Parenti, an amateur historian who in the town hall attic uncovered complete military conscription records for the entire nineteenth century. To Sheriff Guido Varacchi I am indebted for sharing with me his intimate knowledge of the *partigiani* struggle.

The late Dr. Nicholas Iannotti, my parents-in-law's family physician and the first postfascist democratically elected mayor of Castel San Giorgio, had lost close touch with his native town. But his brother-in-law, Prof. dott. Carmine Antonio Vesce of Naples, is a good friend of Prof. Antonio Corvino, currently vice-mayor. Thus the mayor graciously allowed us to photocopy and transcribe the town's demographic records. For their interest and willingness not only to be interviewed at great length but also to provide family clippings and various memorabilia, I wish to thank Luigi Cuomo, Angelo Ianniello, and Mario Guerrasio.

My colleague Professor Remigio Pane, upon learning of my research interests, secured permission through his brother-in-law Armando Talarico, a senior official in the prefecture, for us to examine the vital records of the town of Rogliano (Calabria). Mr. Talarico's son Rinaldo made us instantly welcome, overcame all remaining bureaucratic obstacles, and shared with us his incisive analysis of the Calabrian spirit. My understanding of the region was greatly enhanced by Ercole Rizzuto, Pietro Fusco, Cesare and Gina Bruni, Michelina Naccarato, Nella Provenzano, and especially Rosa Runco, who shared her poetry and her insights.

Salvatore Di Fazio, a student in one of my undergraduate courses, volunteered that his "Uncle" Nino was the mayor of a village in Sicily and would gladly help. As it turned out, Sal's mother's cousin was not only the mayor but also a member of the national chamber of deputies. His honor, dott. Antonio Buttafuoco, put the staff of the Municipio at our disposal, opened all its records, entertained our young daughter, and in every way made us part of Nissoria. These villagers are now friends, and if occasionally in the chapters that follow I appear to be a bit insistent in questioning concepts such as Banfield's "amoral familism," it may well be because the Nissorini have captured my affection and respect. Don Benedetto Pernicone allowed us to copy the parish registers, which antedate those of the Municipio. For their frankness and insight I am particularly indebted to Antonino Lombardo, Salvatore Ciaramidaro, Nunzio Rinaldi, Rita Pantò, Orazio Pantò, and Don Benedetto.

In other aspects of the research I was greatly aided by the assistance of librarians at Enna, Catania, Cosenza, the Alessandrina Library in Rome, Florence, Genoa, and Trieste. Professor Aldo Russo of the University of Florence and Paula Casinelli assisted in the compilation of sex ratios from early census reports. A grant from the Fulbright-Hays Exchange Program made possible the initial fieldwork conducted between July 1971 and June 1972. Assistance from the Rutgers University Research Council allowed us to do intensive field study in the South from May to September 1974. During a year when I was director of the Rutgers College Junior Year in Italy Program, 1976–77, the students' mature handling of "culture shock" gave us an opportunity to complete brief return visits to the sites of our earlier fieldwork. For their comments on various aspects of the work I am indebted to Michael Adas, Joseph Chierici, Peter Stearns, Traian Stoianovich, and Edward Thompson. Warren I. Susman, a friend, displayed all the virtues and none of the vices of il padrone, and Donald Weinstein has been a sustaining force. V. Susan Fox did a splendid job with the graphic art work.

Laura Tomici Bell is the source of my world view about the Italian peasantry. In addition to sharing the dreary task of copying all the vital records and transcribing them into machine-readable format, she conducted most of the interviews. Unlike my interviews, hers were conversations. The dedication is to my elder daughter, who has been a constant source of joy in some out-of-the-way places.

# 1
# Introduction

Vogliamo un mondo fatto per la gente,
di cui ciascuno possa dire "È mio"!
dove sia bello lavorare e far l'amore,
dove il morire sia volontà di Dio.

"25 aprile 1945"

Tragic, backward, hopeless, downtrodden, static, passive: such adjectives dominate scholarly literature on the Italian peasantry (see app. A for definition) even to the present day. Although there is some truth in all these words, they fail to capture the self-image and world view of rural Italians. Vigorously and occasionally successfully, the Italian peasantry responded to a bewildering variety of innovations over the past two centuries. Many of these innovations, linked to what all too casually is called modernization, were imposed from without; the impetus for other changes, however, came from within villages, towns, and hamlets. In these rural communities individuals and, more often, families applied time-tested values in an effort to make sense of the volatile realities of life. Villagers made no sharp distinction between traditional and modern; rather, like Dilsey, they endured. And if alterations of their surroundings were largely beyond their control, had it not always been that way?

Four words capture the essence of the Italian peasant's response to life: *fortuna, onore, famiglia,* and *campanilismo.* Because so much of the past was beyond human understanding, because the present was uncontrollable, and because the future was unpredictable except for those with magical powers, fatalism *(fortuna)* dominated the peasantry's world view. When a southern Italian *contadino* remarked that "fatalism is our religion; the church just supplies the pageantry of life," he used the word "fatalism" in two different senses. The concept of fate as preordination or cosmic determination emerges at all levels of speculation on what the species is about, and judged in terms of theological debate on God and man, peasant attitudes may be characterized as poorly articulated and gloriously ambivalent. Only partially related to fate as predestination is the concept of fatalism as a "generalized sense of powerlessness" and a major dimension of alienation. Indeed, for

1

most students of modernization (and its students all too easily become its advocates), fatalism is the bête noire that explains resistance to change or, in the view of a recent scholar working with data on Latin America, that allows post hoc rationalization of individual and societal failure.

My own use of the term "fatalism" to describe in part the world view of Italy's peasantry involves neither philosophical questions of predestination nor value judgments about responses to change. Rather, I refer to the sum total of all explanations for outcomes perceived to be beyond human control. Fatalism begins with the mysteries of God, Mary, and the saints, but it goes well beyond Roman Catholic doctrine. It explains why one man is a day laborer and another a shoemaker or a landowner. It accounts for outbreaks of typhoid fever and malaria, crop failures, abundant rainfall, the success of immigrants to America or Argentina, and even the refusal of aged and burdensome parents to die. Confronted with the assertion that becoming a shoemaker is a matter of individual effort and the control of malaria a result of improved knowledge of disease transmission, the peasant nods wisely and readily concedes that fate works in myriad ways.

Above all, the persistence of fatalism in rural Italy until virtually our own time, especially in southern Italy (the Mezzogiorno), reflected an accurate assessment of that society's inability to control or even to explain life and death. The clustering of deaths in seasonal cycles, and of births and marriages as well, gave a structural rhythm to life. But this pattern, regular for the village as a whole, encompassed a series of uncontrollable events for the individual and the family. Only with the conquest of unpredictable death, until "passing away" became something that happened mostly to old people who had lived their full measure of time, did *contadini* act as if they might usefully and knowingly measure and plan the future.

*Onore* (honor, respect, dignity) has meaning only within the context of *fortuna* and *famiglia*. Fate determines how much hunger a family suffers, how many of its infants and children die, whether its efforts will result in good situations for its marriageable members. But the villager does not sit idly by to await the uncontrollable outcome of fate. For every happening some response is required, and it is the pattern of such responses that establishes *onore*. The shame suffered by the Sicilian family whose unmarried daughter becomes pregnant is no mere cinema cliché. The loss of *onore*, which extends even to the girl's second cousins, arises not from fate but from a human failing—their families did not properly chaperone the young couple—and therefore it can be rectified by family action: the children must marry. Villagers will snicker and attribute the weakness to a vague genetic failing, but the *onore* of both families is nonetheless restored. The struggle to maintain *onore* in the area of sexual behavior may make excellent cinema script, but it is only a small part of the total effort required. Respect and dignity come with continued support of one's immediate family at a level appropriate to one's station in life. For women especially, respectability means devout attendance at mass without becoming a *bizzocca* (house nun); it means strictly observing mourning customs, accepting fully the request to be a godparent, and, above all, responding to the sudden needs of the extended family.

*La famiglia* is at the center of Italian life; it is not only a convenient way to provide for the proper raising of children but also the society's basic mode of organization. The individual without family is anomic; groups larger than *la famiglia* are secondary. In politics, in work, in the economy, in religion, in love, indeed in all of life, perceptions exist and decisions are made primarily in terms of family. In a political struggle the well-organized family sees to it that it has members in the opposing factions. Thus, when the outcome is determined, at least one member will be on the winning side and in a position to shield other members from possible retaliation. Although not always worked out in a cold and calculated manner, this system aided many families in the bitter partisan struggle in the aftermath of the Second World War.

*Campanilismo*, the unity of everyone who lives within the sound of the village church bell, is secondary only to family in the code of rural Italy. In some cases *campanilismo* involves specific and highly valued rights—for example, to the allocation of firewood from communal forests or to the gathering of mushrooms, chestnuts, and berries. In most cases, however, communal landholding gave way centuries ago to private plots, and village unity rests upon less tangible factors. Nonetheless, and despite the increasing intrusion of regional and even national government in education, public safety, road building and the like, loyalty to place of birth remains strong. Often this loyalty is expressed in sharply negative characterizations of nearby places. The natives of a Sicilian village describe five surrounding towns as, respectively, (1) struck by evil spirits, (2) mentally backward, (3) filled with cuckolds, (4) perfumed, and (5) a haven for gangsters. *Campanilismo* finds positive expression in high rates of marriage between local boys and girls and in the tendency of immigrants in distant lands to establish enclaves restricted to fellow villagers or townsmen.

Together these four values served to define the peasant's self-identity and to circumscribe his behavior. The transition from peasant to rural proletarian, I shall attempt to demonstrate, involved transformations in each of these values. Spatial self-identity (*campanilismo, Gemeinschaft*) gave way to class and to national perception (*irredentismo, Gesellschaft*). Action taken in terms of family came into conflict with individualism. Interpersonal relations became defined less by honor and reciprocal obligation than by legal codes and cash transfers. Fatalism yielded to anthropomorphism. Fate, honor, family, and village are more than cultural codes but less than universal psychological realities. The chapters that follow trace the impact of demographic change upon rural Italian culture primarily, though not exclusively, through these four values.

In the introduction to his recent fine study, *A History of Italian Fertility during the Last Two Centuries*, Massimo Livi-Bacci expressed a deeply felt need "to link the results of demographic analysis with the pace and patterns of the cultural modifications in the Italian society. Unfortunately," he continued, "we have done little more than acknowledge a need for a higher level of knowledge in this field." I hope that the present study contributes to fulfilling precisely this need. Because the main focus is on culture, there are some organizational decisions about the following chapters that may confuse or even dismay historical demographers. Findings on natality, nuptiality, and mortality are not grouped as such. Instead, they appear arrayed in various chapters according to the cultural question under consideration. For example, data on mortality appear as part of an analysis of changing perceptions of time and again in a chapter on work. Perhaps the index will help.

Nor is the organization strictly chronological and periodized from 1800 to 1970. Rather, I have tried to capture at least partially the rural view of history, of what has happened in the Italian countryside over the past two centuries. This history, then, begins with the immutable, with matters perceived to be beyond human control: wind, rain, soil, and stones. The following chapter, "Past," forgoes a full narrative history of each of the four communities under intense study in order to concentrate on peasant perceptions of the past as a determinant of the present and future. Chapter 4 presents the basic demographic data and links these to seasonal agricultural rhythms of time. Beginning with the chapter on family and continuing with the one on work, the main focus is on human institutions perceived as mutable and even as agencies of change but that for the most part have functioned in quite the reverse way. The next two chapters, on space and on migration, deal with behavior which peasants view as fundamentally initiative, controllable, and of their own doing. The final chapter finds the future in the past.

Before proceeding to the study proper, some readers may wish to know a bit more about the research base upon which it rests. Thus far I have made no reference to regional, climatic, and cultural distinctions. Italy is a highly varied land, as are its people; I hope to give this variety due attention by distinguishing developments in different regions. Specifically, my analysis deals with four villages or rural towns: Albareto in Emilia-Romagna, Castel San Giorgio in Campania, Rogliano in Calabria, and Nissoria in Sicily (see fig. 1). These four communities

Fig. 1
Italy: locations of Albareto, Castel San Giorgio, Nissoria, and Rogliano

in no sense constitute a random sample of all Italy, and several interesting regions are excluded entirely. Reasons for my choices are made clear in the acknowledgments; in essence, I took what I could get.

The problem, then, is the relationship between these four villages and "rural Italy" or the Italian peasantry.

Would that I could beg the question by dismissing "rural Italy" as a stylistic shorthand to avoid repeating four hard-to-remember names. (One of my students had the good sense to dissuade me from using the computer-processing acronym that still haunts me—NARC.) No, when I write "rural Italy" I mean to state a conclusion based on primary research on four communities and not contradicted (unless otherwise noted) by the preponderance of scholarly work on other parts of rural Italy. I do, with many historians and a fairly strong consensus of anthropologists, believe further that rural Italian culture, at least to the line of the olive trees, should be viewed as Mediterranean. Albareto is north of this line and serves throughout this study as a reminder of the complexity of the Italian versus Mediterranean distinction. Of course the conclusions are tentative, set forth within a paradigm not because that paradigm is proven or even provable but in order to make sense of things. Four villages are only a start; the fifth, sixth, and nth are to be welcomed.

Finally, a note is in order concerning levels of evidence. Although I do not share fully the notion of a "hierarchy of reliability" set forth by those distinguished cliometricians Robert Fogel and Stanley Engerman, there are varying kinds of evidence in the chapters that follow. Often, seemingly stronger evidence exists on less interesting or consequential points and vice versa. For example, data on age at first marriage are abundant and highly reliable; findings from one community may be compared against another and changes over time may be traced and studied. Thanks to Livi-Bacci's work, it is relatively easy to place local findings—how "typical" they are—within the national scene. Calculation of standard tests of statistical significance is straightforward, although interpretation is made problematic since the communities do not constitute random samples. Nonetheless, I am confident about the accuracy of the age at first marriage data graphed herein. But there are more tantalizing questions: what impact did changing marital ages have on modes of choosing a spouse, on familial relationships, parental authority, household economy, and conception control? Statistical findings often show what is to be explained or yield perimeters of what is possible, results that are useful but limited. Wherever it has seemed appropriate, I have gone beyond numerical findings and asked questions for which the evidence is literary, oral, or visual. Local proverbs, several familial stories passed through four generations, and a government report on declining parental authority support, but hardly constitute certain proof for, my contention that rising female nuptial ages reflected a shift from familial to individual marital choice. Partly as a matter of style, but more importantly because I reject the idea that historical evidence is strictly hierarchical, findings based on non-statistical material are not relegated to the subjunctive, the conditional, or the ubiquitous "perhaps." No one recognizes better than an author just how tentative many conclusions must be.

More than a decade ago a scholar writing about the Italian South asked, "How Would You Like to be a Peasant?" Such rhetorical questions, sympathetic though their intention may be, reflect a limitation in many academic approaches to understanding the peasantry. A peasant is born, not trained, elected, or chosen. Not until the last generation or two was it possible for more than a few peasants to decide successfully to become something else. Only the nostalgic arrogance of weekend farmers and the well-intentioned bungling of developmental planners are served by acting as if nonpeasants might be what thay are not and as if peasants ought not to be what they are. The question for peasants was not contentment but survival, not self-fulfillment but familial obligation, not advancement but stability. Within admittedly narrow constraints, however, peasants struggled to master their world or at least to function within it. Antonio Gramsci's wry comment in his ninth prison notebook captures well one essence of peasant history.

Prima tutti volevano essere aratori della storia, avere le parti attive, ognuno avere una parte attiva. Nessuno voleva essere "concio" della storia. Ma può ararsi senza prima ingrassare la terra? Dunque ci deve essere l'aratore e il "concio." Astrattamente tutti lo ammettevano. Ma praticamente? "Concio" per "concio" tanto valeva tirarsi indietro, rientrare nel buio, nell'indistinto. Qualcosa è cambiato, perchè c'e chi si adatta "filosoficamente" ad essere concio, chi sa di doverlo essere, e si adatta.

My study, then, concerns not the ploughmen of history but its fertilizer.

# 2
# Setting

Ai nostri monti ritorneremo,
L'antica pace ivi godremo.

Azucena, *Il Trovatore*

Rural Italians quite readily and properly identify themselves not only by the names of their birthplaces but also topographically. They are inhabitants of the mountain or of the plain; they live in a nucleus of high density or in scattered houses spread along a valley floor. Climatological factors condemn one place to arid summers while another enjoys abundant rainfall. Temporal distance to markets, ancient prerogatives of separate judicial proceedings, the presence of a monastery—all these and more are closely related to geographic circumstances. Variations in altitude, climate, soil condition, and physical accessibility affect every aspect of rural Italians' lives and cause discernible fluctuations in rates of birth, marriage, and death.

The legal unit most appropriate to the study of Italian demography at the local level is the *comune* or municipality. However, *comuni* vary in population from a few hundred residents to a million and more. Even for the four municipalities under intensive study some distinctions are necessary, although their populations vary only from about 3,000 to 9,000 (see table 1 for the relevant data). The most useful distinction is between a village and a town (since none of the four is a city). Forming this distinction, which ought not to be treated as a rigid dichotomy, are a number of related criteria, most but not all of which will be fulfilled in any single case. A village has only one large piazza, one church, no regular school (in the nineteenth century) or *liceo* (in the twentieth), and only one principal thoroughfare. It has no hotel or inn, since it expects no overnight strangers, and probably no public restaurant either. Its population is generally under 3,000 or 4,000; it may be served by no resident medical doctor or pharmacist and certainly not by more than one of each. Few crafts are practiced, and most shops are rendered unnecessary, since local artisans work only to fill orders. Produce for export from the village is marketed elsewhere. Each resident is able to recall, and often behaves in terms of, kin relationships with a substantial portion of the total population. Controversies, feuds, and political contests turn more upon family and residence than upon class and status. Most villagers are peasants; most townspeople are not. The placement of Albareto, Castel San Giorgio, Nissoria, and Rogliano along a continuum from village to town requires a brief description of each.

## ALBARETO
### (Emilia-Romagna Region)

Albareto consists of a center, of the same name, plus a series of eleven outlying residential clusters (*frazioni*) administratively integrated with the center to form one *comune*.[1] Throughout the nineteenth century about one-fifth of the total population resided in the center, a portion that rose to one-quarter by 1931 and that approaches one-half today. The most populous outlying *frazione*, Monte Groppo, counted 541 residents in 1871 (when 750 people lived in Albareto center) but has declined steadily since then. None of the other *frazioni* housed more than 500 or less than 100 people until after World War II, when a general exodus from the countryside resulted in the virtual abandonment of some hamlets. In both the center and the outlying clusters a substantial portion of the population has always resided in dispersed housing rather than nucleated settlements. The definitions employed in Italian censuses (*centro* or *nucleo* vs. *case sparse*) changed from decade to decade. Between 1871 and 1881, for example, the percentage of Albaretesi living in so-called *case sparse* declined from 54 to 35, whereas by 1911

TABLE 1  **Resident Population from Census Returns**

| Year | Albareto | Castel San Giorgio | Nissoria | Rogliano |
|------|----------|--------------------|----------|----------|
| 1861 | 3,905 | 4,963 | 2,555 | 4,888 |
| 1871 | 3,733 | 4,694 | 2,653 | 4,893 |
| 1881 | 4,003 | 5,099 | 2,957 | 5,235 |
| 1901 | 3,939 | 5,335 | 3,406 | 5,730 |
| 1911 | 4,860 | 5,475 | 2,821 | 6,057 |
| 1921 | 4,544 | 5,962 | 3,019 | 6,378 |
| 1931 | . . .[a] | 6,103 | 3,121 | 12,706[b] |
| 1936 | . . .[a] | 6,690 | 2,776 | 9,136[c] |
| 1951 | 4,162 | 8,069 | 3,438 | 7,173 |
| 1961 | 3,472 | 8,658 | 3,115 | 7,092 |
| 1971 | 2,484 | 9,004 | 3,032 | 6,135 |
| Land Area (Hectares) | 10,398 | 1,363 | 6,162 | 4,136 |

[a]Albareto was joined with Borgotaro from 1928 to 1946.
[b]Includes surrounding villages of Mangone, Manzi, Parenti, and San Stefano di Rogliano.
[c]Includes Manzi and San Stefano di Rogliano.

fully 62 percent were so classified. From my observation of extant structures and discussion with older residents about building usage, I estimate that about 40 percent of structures intended for human dwelling were "dispersed" and that these housed slightly over half the population. These figures probably held with only minor variations throughout the nineteenth century, certainly until 1880, then declined gradually with emigration from more isolated mountain areas and fell off sharply after World War II, when returning migrant pensioners clustered into Albareto center. (The building boom of the 1970s, fueled by Milanesi industrialists searching for pastoral retreats, may bring a return to nineteenth-century patterns.) Numbers aside, the Albaretesi are closer to their mountains and pastures than they are to each other.

The *comune*'s nearest neighbor is the town of Borgotaro, about seven kilometers from Albareto center in a northeasterly direction and more than twice as large. Much of the history of Albareto concerns its struggle to maintain independence against the encroachments of its neighbor. The contest involves a great deal more than legal formalities; two-thirds of Albareto's 10,000 hectares of pasture and woodland are held communally. From 6,000 hectares of forest an elected town commission to this day allocates how much firewood each household may cut. An ample zone of chestnut trees provides residents with an important dietary supplement, and in times of crop failure and war, chestnuts were the major source of nutrition. The Taro Valley is famous throughout the world for the quality of its mushrooms, and these too villagers always have gathered freely.

Water is usually available throughout the year, either as rainfall or from mountain streams. Nevertheless, in 1879 a complete absence of precipitation between March and October ruined crops, dried pasture lands, and forced the sale of many dairy animals. Usually the problem is the opposite; torrential rains swell numerous winding streams. These overflow, flood, and change course, leading to incessant litigation over land boundaries and water rights. So unpredictable are the streams that as late as 1893 there was no bridge across the Gotra (a stream no wider than ten meters) connecting Albareto to its hamlet of San Quirico, nor was there a bridge spanning the Taro River to Borgotaro.

Albareto is situated in a valley deep in the Apennine mountains slightly above 500 meters elevation. The center is just off the traditional roadway from Parma through the Centocroci pass and eventually to the Ligurian coast. Although the easiest movement for Albaretesi is along the Taro River toward Parma, historically they have gone in the opposite direction: for trade, for marriage, and in times of war. A series of three mountain ranges, reaching heights up to 1,800 meters, separates them from the coastal cities of Genoa and La Spezia. But the Albaretesi are mountain people, with keen sight for mushrooms, able to catch trout in cold streams barehanded, and well aware that the best prices for their cheeses are to be had at the sea.

Thus, while Albareto is in the region of Emilia-Romagna, it shares little in common with the intensive agriculture of the Po Valley and the grinding poverty of the *braccianti* in the farm districts around Bologna. Instead, we are dealing with a relatively inaccessible string of mountain hamlets situated midway between Genoa and Parma and at about an equal distance (sixty-five kilometers) south from Piacenza. Slopes rising upward from the valley allow the growing of vegetables that are nearly all consumed by the family. Winter snows isolate Albareto for as long as weeks at a time, but in the spring they feed fast-rushing streams laden with fish. Hunting, gathering from the woods, and transporting goods through the mountains add to the means of livelihood. The village's land tenure pattern is highly fractionalized, with little use of sharecroppers or wage laborers. It has no industry, and local craftsmen do not sell their wares to larger towns.[2]

Within the summary typology provided in table 2 (q.v. for summary of all settings), Albareto is classified as mountain (rather than coastal, plateau, or plain). It is a village, not a town, and its residential pattern is dispersed. The village is isolated rather than integrated, a distinction based on communication networks that are discussed at length in the chapter on space. I take an "isolated" community to be one with a low level of penetration by urban economy and culture at least until 1945.

## CASTEL SAN GIORGIO
### (Campania Region)

As with Albareto, Castel San Giorgio is the legal center for a string of distinct population clusters. Unlike Albareto, however, it is not the largest cluster, and only since 1860 has it included all its present *frazioni*. The legal arrangement is not one that entirely pleases the outlying clusters. One of these, Lanzara, is both older and more populous than Castel San Giorgio center, and prior to 1860 Lanzara kept its own vital records. Also unlike Albareto, the separate clusters are very compact hamlets of high density; never has more than 10 percent of the population been classified in the official census as living in dispersed housing. *Campanilismo* here extends only to the local nucleus and even today political contests revolve less around party than around precise place of residence. It is assumed, with good reason, that, once elected, the mayor will divert precious water for irrigation from the other hamlets to his own.

The political contest usually follows a fundamental geographic split between the mountain clusters to the east and the western nuclei situated on the plain. The center of Castel San Giorgio itself is located

TABLE 2  Summary Classification of Settings

| | Albareto | Castel San Giorgio | Rogliano | Nissoria |
|---|---|---|---|---|
| Region | Emilia-Romagna | Campania | Calabria | Sicily |
| Province | Parma | Salerno | Cosenza | Enna |
| Community type | Village | Town | Town | Village |
| Terrain | Mountain | Plain | Mountain | Plateau |
| Water supply | Ample | Inadequate | Limited | Limited |
| Settlement pattern | Dispersed | Nuclear | Nuclear | Nuclear |
| Urban penetration | Isolated | Integrated | Integrated | Isolated |
| Land tenure | Small and moderate holdings | Smallholdings, tenant farming | Large holdings | Smallholdings, *latifondi* |
| Major crops | Dairy | Vegetables | Fruits, grain, animal products | Wheat |
| Supplements | Mushrooms, game, fish, chestnuts | … | Chestnuts, fish | … |
| Industry | … | Crafts, extractive | Crafts, agric. middlemen | … |
| Mode of exchange | Cash | Cash | Cash | Kind |
| Other characteristics | Communal land | Mountain hamlets | Bureaucratic subcenter | Sulfur mining |

precisely between the two, with the houses on the east side of its main street built into a steep hill. Across the road and spilling outward for about 300 meters are shops and town dwellings, beyond which extend intensively cultivated fields. Further west on the plain is a semicircle of five nucleated clusters, each with its territorial boundaries carefully noted, since the land provides no natural breaks.[3] The mountain settlements to the east are less accessible, reached only by narrow winding roads leading nowhere else. Boundaries among them are formed by streams and by shallow but unmistakable ravines.[4]

The nuclei that comprise Castel San Giorgio range in altitude from seventy meters on the plain to 600 meters in the hills. They are situated along the road from the mountain cities of Benevento and Avellino through the interior market town of Mercato San Severino, then through Castel San Giorgio to the main road from Salerno to Naples. Trade from Avellino to Salerno skirts Castel San Giorgio, but traffic to Naples must pass through the town. Indeed, contracts recorded in the mountain *frazione* of Aiello as early as the seventh century indicate that it contained a toll station for goods coming from the southeast toward Naples. The town, historically and in the present day, is within the periphery of Naples. Castel San Giorgio's fortunes rose and fell with those of its giant neighbor, merely forty kilometers across a fertile plain. Its vegetable produce, its tufa, and its marble found their way to the towns and cities of the coast. There developed a contest between Salerno, about twenty kilometers from Castel San Giorgio, and Naples over economic and political control of the region, a contest reflected in a variety of documents recorded in the Municipio. In the conflict Castel San Giorgio was a pawn, having no influence on the outcome but itself very much shaped by its location within the direct geographic sphere of two powerful cities.

Agriculture on the western plain consists of intensive produce farming. Fertile soil and a long hot summer assure abundant crops so long as water can be diverted from nearby mountain streams. But there is not enough water to irrigate the plain fully, and every planting is a gamble. Planting and harvesting of various crops go on year around, since there is no danger of frost. A parliamentary inquiry in 1882 (the famous Jacini inquiry) found such a maze of different crop rotation schemes in use in the area that it despaired of reporting any "standard" patterns. Given the range of produce widely grown in the region—garlic and onions, citrus fruits, broccoli, cauliflower, figs, fennel, grain, mulberries, jujube, maize, parsnips, peppers, tomatoes, turnips, olives, wine, and squash—smallholders undoubtedly made two plantings annually on the same plots and at best rotated grains with legumes. Again from the Jacini inquiry, we learn that most *contadini* regularly sent their children ten kilometers or more to town with a cart to gather fertilizer consisting of human waste left in the streets. The investigators stayed precisely to the task at hand in reporting only that such fertilizer turned out to be of varying quality.[5]

The detailed *catasto* of 1929 provides a good snapshot of agricultural labor patterns in Castel San Giorgio. Among 2,696 agriculturists it reports only 785 as owning any land at all (or 155 of 529 families), with most of the remainder holding rent contracts of one sort or another. As one would expect in a zone of intensive culture and varied produce, most rents were in cash or cash and kind; sharecropping was very infrequent. Spring wheat, maize, garlic, onions, tomatoes, potatoes, and tobacco were now the major crops grown for sale. The mean holding was 1.24 hectares (3 acres), an amount sufficient to support and provide work for a family. However, only a minority held a "mean" farm. The 320 smallest holdings averaged only one-quarter of a hectare, not enough to live on even if no rent or taxes of any kind had to be paid. Another 319 owned or rented farms that averaged .75 hectares, not enough to support a family. Surely better off, but hardly prosperous, were the 219 holders of 1.6 hectares each. The remaining 25 holdings ranged from 3 to 150 hectares. Even allowing for multiple holdings (883 holdings and 529 families headed by an agriculturist), the majority of the agricultural population, if its only income had been from these holdings, would have been hungry in the best of years and would have starved in the lean ones. The alternatives were day work in town or countryside, wage labor by women and children, chronic indebtedness, a journey to Naples to merge with the urban poor, or emigration. These options will be examined in subsequent chapters. All evidence indicates that the plight of peasants in Castel San Giorgio was even greater throughout the nineteenth century than it had become by 1929. And it is not that much better today.[6]

Mountain settlements to the east followed a different pattern to produce an equally poverty-ridden labor force. Agriculture was limited to the gathering of nuts and the tending of vines. The wine of the region was not distinguished for quality; viticulture involved little more than choosing the day when the grapes were fullest, quickly pressing the purple clusters, and selling in *barili* of 25 liters to be consumed as early as two months after harvest. There were no large holdings among the wine growers. Mean production in 1873 was under 20 quintals (2,000 liters), with only 5 percent producing more than 49 quintals and the two largest holders responsible for no more than 80 quintals.[7] In the nineteenth century the eastern hills were also the scene of limited mining operations for tufa and bituminous products. In addition there were some marble quarries. These gave rise to a stone-cutting industry practiced by individual craftsmen employing no more than an apprentice or two. In Castel San Giorgio itself townspeople engaged in a wide variety of trades. Goods and services were consumed not only by local residents but also by visitors and traders from nearby towns, especially those to the east who stopped in Castel San Giorgio on their way to Naples.[8]

Summary classification of Castel San Giorgio is tenuous at best. The dominant factor, in my judgment, is proximity to Naples; this proximity fostered a high level of integration, considerable skill diversity among town residents, numerous shops and trading facilities, and a well-developed cash economy long before the advent of industrialization. With due note of its more isolated village hamlets in the eastern hills, Castel San Giorgio as a whole will be categorized as plain, town, nucleated, and integrated; it differs substantially from the village of Albareto.

## ROGLIANO
### (Calabria Region)

Rogliano, built as a fortress into the crest of a hill overlooking the Savuto River valley, lies deep in Calabria, nineteen kilometers south from Cosenza and along the main interior road to Catanzaro. The town's central piazza stands at the gateway to the Sila Piccola, a major plateau of remarkable alpine beauty and verdant pasturage. In this position it serves as a gathering point for the people and produce of the plateau, secure against any invasion from the valley below. At the point where a narrow road begins its twisting course into the Sila arise the town hall and the prefecture, so hard upon the road that their balconies hang over it. Here in earlier times the rulers of Rogliano exacted tribute and meted justice to the plateau above.

Although the military significance of Rogliano is but a distant tradition, its development as a tertiary bureaucratic center shaped its recent history. *Campanilismo* assured that surrounding villages and towns would despise the Roglianesi and resent their overbearing pretensions. Nevertheless, under the Kingdom of the Two Sicilies and again with the unification of Italy, Rogliano was a seat of justice, the place where permits were to be obtained, where lawyers met, where major transactions took place. Its market day is Sunday, when even now merchants come from surrounding towns and from the plateau to sell their wares and produce. Thus throughout the week outsiders came to Rogliano, either to transact legal business or to carry on trade. The town was economically and politically integrated with the surrounding region and with urban culture as far away as Naples, but unlike the way station of Castel San Giorgio, Rogliano was a regional center, albeit a subsidiary one.

Within the town's walls there developed two economies. One consisted of artisans and highly specialized craftsmen, notable for fashioning wooden utensils and furniture. These were sold primarily during Rogliano's three fair days on the first Sundays of July, August, and September. Buyers came not only from surrounding mountain towns but also from Tyrrhenian coastal settlements as far north as Paola and from interior centers across the Sila, even including San Giovanni in Fiore. The other major economic activity arose from the agricultural sector and consisted of the weighing, grading, packing, transporting, and selling of wine, grain, oil, fruits, and animal products. Owing to its bureaucratic functions, Rogliano captured a major share of the intermediary sector in agricultural production, not only for its own lands but also for surrounding towns and the Sila plateau.

Peasants gained little from either economy. To be sure, nearly four-fifths lived within the thick defensive walls that circumscribed a few thousand meters around Rogliano's central piazza.[9] But their work, or more often their vain search for any employment at all, took them daily to the countryside. Until the agricultural reforms of the past two decades, most of the countryside belonged to a handful of wealthy town-resident families. As late as 1929 Baron Ricciulli owned 10 percent of all the arable land in Rogliano; prominent names such as Morelli, Schettini, and Clausi, families closely linked by marriage, held an additional 40 percent. On these lands worked the *braccianti*, hired laborers densely crowded in town dwellings and condemned to poverty not only by low wages but even more so by the infrequency of calls to work. Although not precisely comparable to the classic *latifondi* of Sicily, large holdings in Rogliano also tended to inhibit the development of labor-intensive agriculture. The *catasto* of 1929 reports 6,000 of 11,000 hectares as forest, land held not for communal benefit, as in Albareto, but for private gain. Another 1,000 hectares consisted of orchards, mostly such less labor-intensive items as figs, mulberries, and apples rather than wine and olives. About the same hectarage is listed as permanently devoted to pasturage and an equal amount as fallow or uncultivated, leaving roughly 2,000 hectares divided 7 to 1 in favor of grains over vegetables.[10]

The overall pattern was one of production for outside markets at the expense of landless peasants. Extensive pasturage and woodland provided for 600 cows, 2,500 pigs, and 4,600 sheep and goats, but the *contadino's* diet rarely included meat or cheese, and animal husbandry practices offered scant employment opportunities. Fruit picking gave work even to women and children, but only for brief periods and at very low wages—fifty centesimi per day in the 1880s plus one meal consisting of corn meal and legumes. The net annual profit to the owner of a hectare of fig trees (which require very little attention throughout the year), by way of example, was about 200 times the labor cost for harvesting. Rogliano could not produce enough to keep its peasantry from chronic malnutrition but provided substantial crops for export.[11]

Landholding patterns exacerbated a configuration that would have been difficult for peasants anyway. Although rainfall generally is abundant in the autumn and early winter, fast runoff and dry summers require careful planning and some irrigation to shift land from pasture and orchard to higher calories-per-acre crops requiring more labor hours. This problem became devastatingly clear when the 1951 land reform gave small plots of former pasture land to *braccianti* willing to move to the countryside with their families and to become faithful, politically Christian farmers. They ploughed; they planted; they watched helplessly as their crops withered in the summer sun and hot southern wind; they left for Germany. The subsoil, mostly limestone and sandstone, is infertile, and steep hills promote erosion of the thin topsoil and inhibit use of machinery. Only a small minority of peasants, surely fewer than one in four, ever controlled any land in Rogliano either as owners or renters, and three-fourths of all owners earned less than fifty lire annually, according to an 1883 report. At that time just one hectare of average land planted with grain yielded a net profit of 245 lire, and women who worked only 100 days at wages earned fifty lire annually. Rogliano had a *monte frumentario* to lend seed (at 15 percent interest) to smallholders, but only until 1877, when the town council joined the wave of the future by selling all the grain and converting the warehouse into a public kindergarten.[12]

Within the typology of the following chapters Rogliano is mountain, nuclear, integrated, and town. It is treated as a town despite the fact that a narrow numerical majority of the population were peasants. As will be shown in subsequent chapters, some of Rogliano's demographic characteristics resemble a village more closely, but on balance government, trade, and artisanal sectors dominated the town's economy and culture. The land tenure pattern was concentrated and devoted to cash crops with labor supplied by landless hired help. Middlemen, artisans, and bureaucrats played a prominent role in the town's life.[13]

## NISSORIA
### (Sicily Region)

The village of Nissoria is situated in the northcentral plateau of Sicily, at an altitude of 670 meters. Located nearly forty kilometers northeast from the ancient fortress city of Enna, it is bisected by the old mountain road to Catania, the one along which Garibaldi marched from Palermo. Unlike many Sicilian agrotowns, including its immediate neighbors, Nissoria is not built on the crest of a hill for defensive purposes. The village was founded only in the eighteenth century, when it was expanded from a former mule station. Nevertheless, all the houses press tightly around the central square, as if to stay within imaginary walls. Despite its location along the road from Palermo to Catania, Nissoria remained isolated. For items not produced locally, Nissorini would have had to go to Leonforte, a much larger town seven kilometers to the west. But except for a small burgher class and a handful of landowners, no one had any cash or goods with which to trade. The nature of the economy reinforced *campanilismo* to a far greater degree than was true even in Castel San Giorgio.

The lands outside the village for centuries have been devoted to wheat, with the exception of small home garden plots and a few hundred hectares of grapevines and olive trees. There is no danger of frost on Nissoria's hillsides; however, the absence of spring and summer rainfall render the area suitable only for winter wheat in a three- or five-year rotation cycle. But whereas late nineteenth-century grain production in the fertile plain of Catania averaged over fourteen hectolitres per hectare, the figure for nearby plateau areas such as Nissoria was under 10. Land usage reported in the *catasto* of 1929 (1,481 hectares hard wheat, 496 barley and oats, 1,415 beans, chickpeas, and lentils, and 497 fallow or pasture) confirm the prevalence in Nissoria of two different rotation systems.[14] Substantial holders employed a five-year rotation: wheat, wheat, beans, beans, fallow. In essence, the fallow year allowed two successive grain plantings, with diminished but nonetheless profitable returns in the second year. Smallholders could not afford the luxury of a fallow year and planted in a three-year cycle: wheat, barley or oats, and beans. There is every reason to believe that, even before government reports came to the same conclusion, smallholders understood that a three-year cycle with no fallow led to soil exhaustion and consistently lower yields, but there was no way for peasants to order their stomachs to take a year of repose. In addition to being caught in a cycle of chronic malnutrition and decreasing crop yields, smallholders faced the danger of *la lupa* (literally "she-wolf" and idiomatically "ravenous hunger"). This was the local name given to broom-rape, a weed parasitic to bean plant roots which remains dormant in the soil until the plants begin to mature and then spreads rapidly to wipe out an entire field before anything can be harvested. *La lupa* was endemic to the area, in more ways than one.[15]

Much more clearly than the other three communities under intensive study, Nissoria's economy was of a classic peasant type. Whereas some scholars might characterize the Albaretesi as alpine mountain people, the Castelsangiorgesi as hinterland truck farmers, and the Roglianesi as rural proletarians, most Nissorini were "peasants" as, say, Eric Wolf defines the term: cultivators who control their land and what is raised on it, who produce primarily for subsistence but also for market, and who live in a system where dominant groups aided by the state control the distribution of surpluses acquired from cultivators. Further, Nissoria's economy is an excellent example of what Wolf terms the paleotechnic (reliance on human and animal energy) Mediterranean (dry farming, shallow ploughing, cereal production) ecotype.[16]

The Jacini inquiry's multivolume study on agriculture in Sicily reports for the Nicosia district (of which Nissoria was one of twelve *comuni*) that 80 percent of family heads owned at least some land, that medium- and smallholders prevailed, and that sharecropper and rental contracts were relatively long term, two to nine and three to six years respectively. These general conclusions for the 1880s are confirmed by the detailed *catasto* of 1929, which reports for Nissoria 1,077 agriculturists and 869 holdings divided as follows:

| Hectarage | Number of Holdings |
|---|---|
| <0.26 | 37 |
| 0.26– 0.50 | 61 |
| 0.51– 1 | 100 |
| 1.01– 3 | 271 |
| 3.01– 5 | 171 |
| 5.01–10 | 173 |
| 10.01–20 | 52 |
| 20.01–50 | 3 |
| 150 | 1 |
| | 869 |

Relative equality of landholding (compared with the *latifondi* of western Sicily or the pattern described for Rogliano), however, meant only that most peasants had to seek additional work on land belonging to others. Smallholders (less than three hectares surely could not support a family), concluded the Jacini inquiry, "should be considered as proletarians, not landowners, since with the former they have in common exhausting work, inadequate food, and unhealthy living conditions."[17]

Landless and land-poor peasants appear in Nissoria's demographic records as *villici*. These men and women, and their families, lived in crude dwellings outside the village center and in far off *comuni*, near the fields they tended. Once a year, in August, they presented themselves in the piazza before the local *gabellotti* to seek a contract for the next growing season. These avaricious leaseholders might grant them the same plot, a different one many kilometers away, or none at all. The arbitrary nature of the whole procedure, in the absence of continuous supervision, guaranteed that even the best *villici* did nothing to improve the land. The original contract called for delivery of a certain quantity of grain (rent in kind rather than *mezzadria*), an amount set at a high floor and then bid up even further by desperately competing *villici*. Their drive for subsistence forced these "temporary" laborers to exploit the land, to sow on nearby plots designated to remain fallow, and to emphasize quantity over quality. The *gabellotti* shunned close supervision, road and building improvements, and experimentation with advanced agricultural techniques as means to increase their profits; it was much simpler and safer to steal from the peasantry. Far removed from the details of exploitation were the *baroni* and *civili* who actually owned the estates leased to *gabellotti*. The civilized ones were dons, not capitalists; their goal was prestige, not profit.

Economic pressure sent other Nissorini to work in the sulfur mines. These were at some distance from the village, and so miners were absent from their families for months at a time. In the 1880s pay ranged from 1.40 to 1.70 lire daily, about double the prevailing wage for male agricultural workers, but against these sums were subtracted charges for overpriced and poor quality food, for broken tools, and for the "right" to have what they mined brought to the surface. In a year, a Nissorino who went to the sulfur mines at Piazza Armerina might expect to return home with about 100 lire, about half the average profit from one hectare of land; enough both to avoid hunger and to guarantee the necessity of returning to the mines next year.[18]

In sum, Nissoria is classified as village, nuclear, isolated, and plateau. About two-thirds of its land (in the nineteenth century) was fractionalized into holdings too small to support a family; the remainder consisted of wheat *latifondi*. Many Nissorini had to work as agricultural laborers on a crop rent basis or at wages, and a significant minority left the village, temporarily they always vainly hoped, to seek employment as miners. No local crafts developed except for shoemakers and the like who served only the village.[19]

# 3
# Past

> ...Novelties attract us only when they are dead, incapable of arousing vital currents; that is what gives rise to the extraordinary phenomenon of the constant formation of myths which would be venerable if they were really ancient, but which are really nothing but sinister attempts to plunge us back into a past that attracts us only because it is dead.
>
> Fabrizio Corbera, Prince of Salina,
> *The Leopard*

In rural Italian communities harsh present realities and a pervasive sense that the future was immutable beckoned society to live for the past. The mythical past offered a world without exploitative landlords and hungry mouths, a world of miraculous saintly healing and glorious military victory. The traditions of an idyllic past, or at least one shorn of poverty and injustice, became true by their very assertion generation after generation. Of prophets there were many, but each lasted only until future became present. Storytellers, and every villager was a storyteller, perpetuated myths without fear of possible contradiction. History and myth became one.

That the past was not what rural Italians believed it to be is relatively unimportant; the significance of historical perception is crucial. The landed aristocracy's attempt to create a world that stood still is better documented in fictional masterpieces such as *The Leopard* than in the works of social scientists. More widely studied, but perhaps less fully understood, has been the tendency for rural worker movements of protest to hark back to a mythical golden age. (The peasantry is probably equally motivated by the past when not engaged in protest, but documentation is harder to come by.) Even sympathetic observers characterize such movements as "primitive" or "archaic," while for other writers the "backwardness" and "impracticality" of the protesters is alone sufficient to explain their failures.[1] Both commit the fallacy, pointed out in a slightly different context by Herbert Butterfield, of writing history from the perspective of the winners.[2] In this case the winner is a future that the participants knew nothing of and cared not to predict. And insofar as scholars attempt to explain *why* people behaved as they did, they may tend to get things backward.

Our academic understanding of rural societies, including Italy's, is encumbered with words such as "preindustrial," "precapitalist," "pre-political," and "premodern." The prefix (it seems inescapable) is the culprit. While it may be highly useful as part of a classification scheme, the prefix "pre" cannot help us to understand why protesters who looked to the past acted as they did. Even as senstive an observer as Eric Hobsbawm sidesteps the essential thrust of the collective actions he studies when he concludes that, taken together, they form "a sort of 'pre-historic' stage of social agitation."[3] In no sense was Hobsbawm overly ambitious in attempting to analyze traditional protest movements as more than individual curiosities. But by assigning these movements to an early point in a spectrum leading to modern collective social action, he emphasized an ideological breakthrough external to the protests themselves at the expense of coming to grips with the motivational forces behind early social agitation.

The effort in Nissoria to change its patron saint is a case in point. When Prince Rodrigo founded the village, he named its church for Saint Gregory of Armenia. Gregory (d. ca. 1010) rose from middling origins to become bishop of Nicopolis, where he attained great reputation for miraculous healing. Fearful that adulation would lead to vainglory, Gregory left for Italy, then moved on to Orléans in France, where he led a life of seclusion and severe fasting. Once more, however, his healing powers attracted wide attention. Through connections with a noble local woman, he again became a bishop. His wonder working continued after his death.[4] The drive in the early 1850s to switch to a different patron began with the ordinary folk of Nissoria, who apparently ceased to believe in Saint Gregory's powers[5] and stopped participating in feast day activities in his honor. (These took place inconveniently on March 16, a time when food and wine supplies were running low and the fields demanded long hours of labor.) The prince of Paternò took up their complaint and, against the wishes of the local *civili*, obtained Rome's permission to rededicate the church, this time to Saint Joseph. Despite Saint Gregory's reputation as a healer, he had been notably ineffective when called upon to halt epidemics that raged in the 1840s and reached a peak in 1852. Surely the husband of the Blessed Virgin, herself the patron of all Italy, would have greater influence. Moreover, Gregory had attached himself to petty nobility; his story was one of middle-class success dear to the hearts of the local ruling group so despised by the peasants, whereas Joseph always had been the special protector of manual laborers. Finally, Gregory was a foreigner whose life had been entwined with those of Sicily's conquerers from the west and the east. Joseph was a universal saint who, by reputation, found time to listen to the prayers of even a remote village. In 1854 the movement succeeded; all celebration of Gregory ceased and the peasants instituted their own festival for Saint Joseph. Although the "correct" day for commemorating Joseph also fell in March, the prince approved a three-day celebration beginning on the first Sunday in August, when the wheat had been harvested. For the feast, a committee chosen informally by the laity instructed village millers to set aside a portion of the wheat harvest *before* allotting leaseholders and landlords their shares. Shopkeepers and craftsmen contributed in kind and according to ability. Then, with even the lowly *villici* back in the village, communal loaves, wine, and provisions were distributed according to need and desire. The church and the local ruling group played little part in this annual festival of *campanilismo*, abundance, and equality.

(To this day the festival continues, and although cash contributions have replaced grain allotments, the poorer folk rule the day. Emigrants working in northern Italy and Germany make every effort to return for the celebration.)

Now in all this there is ample evidence for what Hobsbawm terms a "primitive" and "pre-political" movement: class conflict, with an alliance between the nobility and peasantry against the rising bourgeoisie; the beginnings of class consciousness in the selection of a patron saint; stirrings toward casting out foreign rulers in favor of a unified and independent Italy; revolt against church authority in switching festivals from official calendar days to postharvest times. Indeed, the movement has significant parallels with the "night of the knives" six years later, when Nissorini responded to the aspirations raised in the wake of Garibaldi's march across Sicily by attempting to kill (successfully in six cases) every male member of the locally powerful Squillaci family. But the "night of the knives" belongs to the future; to understand accurately the contest over its patron saint, we must look not to Nissoria's future but to its past.

Designating certain behavior in the village of Nissoria (and in the other communities in this study as well) traditional is not merely another way of labeling it premodern or nonmodern. The category "traditional" is meaningful only if limited to choices in which tradition is a primary motivational force. And tradition takes on this role only when the past, however much mythologized, is the radix for human behavior. The mere repetition of a ritual, a pattern of behavior, a response to adversity does not constitute "tradition" no matter how rigorously quantifiers may plot such outcomes. Tradition is not a synonym for mindless acquiescence, resistance to change, or stubborn backwardness; and any correlation between "traditional societies" and "underdeveloped nations" is largely incidental or periphrastic. Traditional behavior, then, refers to actions taken with conscious reference to the past, usually but not always in terms of a positive assessment of the way things are believed to have been in earlier times. Obviously any action not totally determined by genetic or ecological factors involves some reference to the past, and even the most traditional behavior results in outcomes that necessarily occur in the future. A commonsense approach is in order.[6] When the Nissorini changed their patron saint, villagers still believe, they did so less because they expected a rosier future than because in their present misery they looked back to a (mythical) time when things had been better.

Much of the intellectual confusion surrounding the concept of tradition arises from its linkage with modernity. Two social scientists working on India state the problem in a way that is highly relevant here: "The assumption that modernity and tradition are radically contradictory rests on a misdiagnosis of tradition as it is found in traditional societies, a misunderstanding of modernity as it is found in modern societies, and a misapprehension of the relationship between them."[7] One source of such misapprehension is crude Marxism. It is true that Marx himself likened peasants to a sackful of potatoes, a mass not a class, and that he generally counterposed traditional/primitive to modern/mature. Such a sharp polarization turned out to be wrong. The other major locus of misapprehension is modernization theory, whose perpetrators perhaps stand less far removed from Marx's errors than they would wish. The theory never developed independently of global power concerns and in many respects is less a theory than a post hoc rationalization of the dominant world position which North American and northern European nations forged for themselves in the nineteenth century. Whatever its origins, modernization theory perpetuates intellectually invalid dichotomies: we versus they, light versus dark, superior versus inferior, desirable versus disdained. Yet much can be salvaged from all this error and confusion. A limited structural mode of analysis is useful, and some categorization is always in order. Building upon the work of the two social scientists quoted above and introducing Eric Wolf's distinction between paleotechnic and neotechnic peasant ecotypes make possible a working model for analyzing changes in rural Italian culture.[8]

At one end of a continuum, an ideal type ("traditional") consists of agricultural workers using only the power of their own bodies and a limited number of animals. Total productive capacity is such that a majority of the society's potential labor power must be devoted to direct agriculture. Human fertility and mortality rates are high. The level of material life is precarious, and networks of communication are limited. Past outcomes constitute goals rather than experiences upon which to base calculations for the future. Fate, honor, family, and village dominate decision making and have great explanatory power. At the other end of the continuum is an ideal type ("modern") in which vast amounts of inorganic energy are harnessed for food production, thereby releasing three-fourths or more of the society's potential labor power from the soil. Birth and death rates are low. Levels of material life increase sharply, and provisions are made for the routine acquisition of growing amounts of permanent or semipermanent possessions other than land. People calculate how present behavior will affect future outcomes and behave accordingly. Knowledge, law, individual, and nation take the places of fate, honor, family, and village. The real continuum flanked by these ideal types is a dialectical process.

One important signal of movement from traditional toward modern is the emergence of a sense of developmental, directional, predictive history in which human agency is primary as opposed to a repetitive, cyclical, and often mythical history in which fate is dominant. The irony is that, as history separates from and ultimately supersedes myth, concern for the past gives way to an ahistorical and even antihistorical emphasis on present and future. But the process is never complete or unidirectional. Indeed, the retention and reemergence of tradition as a force in modern rural Italy is crucial to understanding phenomena that range from a high birth rate to the appeal of fascism to agitation over a super roadway.[9] And tradition may be a potent force for change, as illustrated in the histories of Albareto, Castel San Giorgio, Nissoria, and Rogliano.

An Italian village's creation of its past (and I use the word "creation" with care) often begins with a search for links with ancient Rome. Castel San Giorgio's claims went back further, to an assumed Greek settlement and, in recent years, to the Etruscans. But even in Castel San Giorgio the starting point for popular local history was Rome. It is doubtful whether townspeople read much of Livy. Nevertheless, local tradition captured fully both his romance with the past and his glorification of ultimate triumph over a foreign enemy. When Livy wrote, "I shall find antiquity a rewarding study, if only because, while I am absorbed in it, I shall be able to turn my eyes from the troubles which for so long have tormented the modern world,"[10] he gave expression to something the Castelsangiorgesi also felt deeply. When he described the courageous resistance of Nuceria to Hannibal's attack in 216 B.C. and the deep fidelity of its townspeople to Rome even after their homes had been sacked and burned, he immortalized a factual thread to which Castel San Giorgio attached itself.[11] Nuceria (now Nocera) borders Castel San Giorgio to the northwest, and with so much activity in the area, local tradition easily created a role for the Castelsangiorgesi's distant ancestors. The common belief was that, owing to *fortuna* (in this case a geographic location slightly east of the main road), Castel San Giorgio avoided the full wrath of Hannibal's army and saved its property and its honor. Isolation and avoidance of resistance to conquerors played a key role in the town's past, a past that motivated its responses to the present as recently as the Second World War. Reminding townspeople explicitly of how their forebears had helped to defeat Hannibal at no cost to themselves, local officials organized the Castelsangiorgesi on September 8, 1943, to line the town's main street and offer platters of newly harvested grapes to German troops occupying the land after Mussolini's defeat. Local antifascists, all of whom came from the mountain hamlets, were persuaded to stay home and keep silent. The Germans stayed only a brief while, and even during this time their major concern was the coastal defense of Salerno and Naples. Guns could be heard in the distance, but there was no local firing. Fortunately, the traditional shrewdness of the Castelsangiorgesi inspired them again to be ready with platters of grapes when English troops drove out the Germans and marched in on September 22. This time antifascists were invited to the town center to help welcome the "liberators." And best of all, the English did not eat the grapes, and so wine making went on that year as usual.

The historically dated founding of Nissoria by the prince of Paternò in 1746 made it impossible for villagers to assert direct links with antiquity. All the same, a recent local written history optimistically records a series of facts based on oral legend and now randomly supported by archaeological finds. Possibly Nissoria is the site of the ancient city of Imakara mentioned by Cicero, or going back yet further (tombs recently discovered date to the ninth century B.C.), upon its hills may have been situated Pikinos, a settlement destroyed in the wars between Syracuse and Carthage in 440 B.C. The latter possibility fits well with current antagonisms; Assoro (the neighboring town that Nissorini believe is struck by evil spirits) alone had allied itself with victorious Syracuse. Assoro's success in 440 B.C. explains why even today it dominates, especially in matters of *fortuna,* the surrounding plateau.[12] The concern to establish Nissoria's antecedents is not restricted to a few amateur local historians. Villagers believe that their current isolation stems directly from their lack of a great past. Hopes for a railway connection with the Palermo-Catania line in the nineteenth century were disappointed. An even more devastating blow came in 1920, when rail connections were granted to neighboring Leonforte and Assoro but not to Nissoria. Villagers believe, quite correctly, that pressure and influence helped to decide where railroads would stop in Sicily. Assoro won because it had more power, power rooted primarily in the glories of its antiquity. In the last decade Nissorini again dreamed of a transportation link, this time with the Catania-Palermo *autostrada.* But this hope also "went up in smoke." One villager stated the matter with exquisite simplicity: "Senza un passato non c'e futuro" (Without a past there is no future).

Along with the glorious deeds of ancient ancestors, local creation of a past usually assigns a major role to nature. Oral histories frequently mention diluvial rains, strange hot winds, and puzzling temporary soil infertility. Such occurrences often were explained as the result of human failings, God's punishment of the wicked. The story of Rogliano's great earthquake in 1638 is not untypical. Inscribed in the outer wall of the Duomo is the extent of destruction: more than 1,200 persons killed (about one-third of the population), the church and all the houses destroyed. For fifteen years preceding the earthquake intense popular religious outpourings occurred in the Sila region. Encouraged by the zealous archbishop of Cosenza and by a woman named Isabella of Urso, these expressions took on heretical qualities, at least according to a later official church version. The outpourings involved a reemergence of Waldensianism, once prevalent in the area, combined with the explicitly Calvinist polemics of Valentino Gentile from nearby Scigliano. (Gentile emigrated to Geneva, but his ideas remained influential in Calabria.) Against all heresy stood Antonio Ricciulli, bishop of Umbriatico and a member of the baronial Ricciulli family noted in the preceding chapter as the largest landowner in Rogliano. The bishop, and his nephew of the same name who succeeded him in 1660, ardently defended noble privilege and church wealth by actively inquiring into the theology of the archbishop of Cosenza and later of his followers. The earthquake of 1638 immeasurably aided Ricciulli's efforts. Among the few houses not leveled by the disaster was none other than his family's town palace. With this certain sign that God approved his work, Antonio Ricciulli himself ascended to the archbishopric of Cosenza in 1641, a position from which his campaign against heresy reached new heights of success and, ultimately, allegiance from the masses.

Written histories of Rogliano, as well as oral versions, uniformly cite the great earthquake as a turning point, as the cause of all that followed. God's blessing on the Ricciulli family paved the way for their later success. The movement of whole mountains enhanced Rogliano's geographic position as an impregnable gateway to the Sila. The flurry of construction activity attracted government officials who established bureaucratic quarters there. The building of new roads encouraged agricultural produce to move through Rogliano. Finally, the failure of surrounding towns to recover as fully from their earthquakes (which occurred episodically from the tenth to the nineteenth century), proved to the Roglianesi their superiority. No other town had responded so effectively to *fortuna*.[13]

In all the history of rural Italy, from defeating Hannibal to surmounting earthquakes, *campanilismo* permeates both legend and fact. The unity of village and tradition becomes most complete, however, in a village such as Albareto, where maintenance of communal rights is essential to economic survival. However varied the particulars, the central theme of events remembered or written down by the Albaretesi is defense of access to woods and pasture. The origin of these rights is obscure, but even elderly villagers who are only moderately literate "know" that at Parma exist documents which mention wood-gathering privileges for the settlements along the Gotra. These existed under the noble Fieschi family before the twelfth century, when the Fieschi were counts of Lavagna and before they had been forced to become citizens of Genoa. Lavagna's coastal position is important, as is the fact that Albareto's communal rights were anterior to the great rise of Genoa and Milan. The village saw these giant city-states, and their chronic warfare from the eleventh to the fifteenth century, as a threat to the community itself and to its relatively free access to the sea. In 1202 Albareto passed from the count of Lavagna to the republic of Piacenza, a transfer that imperiled local rights and drew the village's economic activity into the more competitive and less profitable orbit of Milan. (From Lavagna and the Ligurian coast Albareto represented nearest access to dairy products, and its economy prospered. But from the interior centers—Milan, Piacenza, and Parma—Albareto was at the outer perimeter of cheese production; transportation costs made just enough difference to reduce Albareto's economy to bare subsistence.) The Fieschi ultimately regained the Taro Valley, but at the expense of Albareto's independence. In order to defend the area, they established a stronghold at Borgotaro and placed all the surrounding countryside under its dominion. Lombardy and Genoa continued to contest the area until 1731, when the territory passed to the Spanish Bourbons. Under Bourbon rule it remained until 1859, except for a brief but important period when it was held by France and then by Maria Luigia, archduchess of Austria. Under the Fieschi, the Farnese, and later the Bourbons, Albareto resumed its economic ties with the coast and engaged in a continual and moderately successful effort to deny use of its communal lands to Borgotaro.

In the village's collective version of its complex past, the year 1799 is crucial. In the spring of that year, as Austrian and Prussian forces pressed deep into Lombardy and attempted to surround Genoa, French troops moved through Centocroci, a major mountain pass from Liguria to the Po Valley. One night a high-ranking officer was slain in Albareto, less than a kilometer from the central village square. Although probably innocent of the crime (which seems to have been the work of highwaymen) the villagers, fearful of retribution, fled with their possessions and animals to the mountains, leaving behind only the local priest. He negotiated the village's safety in exchange for two of its finest bulls, a contract that satisfied everyone and, the Albaretesi believe, paved the way for French recognition in 1805 of Albareto (under the new name Comune of Valdena) as an independent community with full rights to its communal property. This arrangement was upheld in 1814, when the duchess of Parma decreed Albareto a separate *comune* and included the same eleven hamlets it controls today.

For the Albaretesi the meaning of the events of 1799 is clear. The maintenance of communal rights is an arduous and sometimes dangerous responsibility. It may require negotiation, as in 1799, or military service, as in 1806 when Napoleon instituted universal conscription. And the past shows that the effort will ultimately triumph. Defense of traditional local rights shaped the actions of Albaretesi as late as the Second World War. In 1927, for reasons of administrative efficiency, a decree from Rome abolished Albareto as a *comune* and placed it under Borgotaro. While the arrangement may have been more efficient, it denied meaning to centuries of struggle in this mountain village. Resentment remained beneath the surface until the fall of Mussolini in 1943, when many Albaretesi became *partigiani* and the former municipal building was converted into a hospital (a particularly dangerous step since the Allies were pinned down south of Florence and German troops repeatedly attacked the "hospital" in the hope of locating wounded partisan leaders). We shall examine this struggle in detail in chapter 9, but it is important to note at this point that the contest, in the eyes of the Albaretesi who joined it, involved a powerful combination of tradition with such highly modern concerns as democracy, class consciousness, and international antifascism. Albareto's partisans fought consciously against a regime that had "stolen" their village and for the reassertion of control over woods, pastures, and streams. They did no more than their forebears would have done in a similar situation.[14]

In his perceptive study of a central Italian town, Feliks Gross ascribes a crucial catalytic role to changing views of the past. In explaining rapid modernization between 1957 and 1969, Gross cites not only water, electricity, and roads, but also history:

> In 1957 the Bonagentesi looked back: "In the past [before the war] it was better, more work and order" they usually said. In 1969, when asked the same question, most answered: "It is far better now." Their perception of the past has begun to change, and they look toward the future with more hope.[15]

The traditional villager acted in terms of the past; history gave vigor to the concepts of *fortuna, onore, famiglia,* and *campanilismo.* Oral histories, as well as sporadic efforts to gather local stories in written form, were consistently concerned with factual presentation. Names and dates were neither forgotten nor blurred into legends, ballads, and fairytales. Indeed, emphasis on accuracy often led to acrimonious debate over whether Rogliano's earthquake began in morning or evening, or whether Hannibal's march from Capua brought him east or west of the hamlet of Santa Maria a Favore (part of Castel San Giorgio). But the traditions, replete though they were with precise names and dates, remained myth. They enhanced a belief system, a set of values. It was history in the Hebraic-Christian sense: an uncritical and often antianalytical reliance on the past as an alternative to a dismal present. It was history that offered no developmental explanation of how things had come to be the way they were. (A casual survey of America's bicentennial celebrations gives ample proof that selective "history" is not unique to Italian peasants.) But it had its uses.

The traditional past was a chronicle of *fortuna*. For generation upon generation it reinforced the view that major changes occurred (as Clio in purest form would have it) for reasons not fully intelligible to man and certainly owing to forces beyond human control. Nature set the broad limits—Nissoria's isolation and Castel San Giorgio's integration were the consequences of geography—but within these limits fate ran its uneven course. Heavy rains and swollen streams defeated the Italians at Fornovo in 1495 and delayed unification for 400 years. A duke without heirs died in 1731, and Albareto passed to Spanish control. In a *frazione* of Castel San Giorgio the intercession of Saint Biagio miraculously revived a child choked with a fishbone, and the larger neighboring town of Nocera, impressed by this heavenly sign, allowed the hamlet to remain independent. A prince inexplicably decided to establish a village where before there had been only a mule station and hunting preserves; Nissoria was born, and thereby the myth of the good king gained new strength. A stream of such events, all documented with painstaking care, formed a village's history. Flashbacks, episodes linked by invisible threads of fate, produced a kaleidoscopic past in which *fortuna* rearranged a handful of static elements into fortuitous patterns, outcomes beyond human comprehension. Even such symmetry as we expect of a kaleidoscope came less through invention of a past than through the selective quality of tradition. Thus the structure of the past was static, while its content remained dynamic. Moreover, the greater the precision in detailing an event, the more surely its cause came to be ascribed to fate.

Intertwined with *fortuna*, the traditional past served as a record of collective and individual *onore*. Dignity in the face of fate did not come merely by riding out history's tempests (although a conscious decision to do so often had proved to be the best way to maintain *onore*). Rural Italians seldom spoke of achieving or acquiring honor (as one might do in the case of wealth). *Onore* always existed in some dim past; it turned the present into a contest for preservation. A family lacking honor might indeed act with dignity, but the resulting *onore* would not be recognized before the generation of its grandchildren's children. In the case of a whole village, the process took centuries. Time, measured over several lifetimes, was an essential part of honor, and this required that the present become a servant of the past. How long will it be before the Nissorini cease to regard a neighboring town as filled with cuckolds? Will the Roglianesi ever lose the greater dignity that arose with their effective response to the earthquake of 1638? Can the Albaretesi voluntarily give up their communal lands? In a traditional society the answers are clear, but the role of history is more obscure. Certainly the precise recollection of events was an obligation for the family or the village of honor. But if, as was likely, the record was a mixed one—a military defeat here or an illegitimate child there—some adjustments had to be made. The most obvious choice was to drop an unfortunate episode from the collective tradition, but often this proved difficult. A neighboring town or a feuding family was all too likely to perpetuate the episode, complete with minute details. The more subtle choice was to ascribe the episode to *fortuna*, thereby making it irrelevant as a matter of *onore*. This was simple enough: rain, not lack of courage, caused a defeat; the child's father eventually married the unwed mother (or else he died as he hastened back home to do so). The shifting of dishonorable outcomes to *fortuna* served both to enlarge its significance and to create an overwhelmingly negative role for fate. This, of course, explained an uncertain future, a brutal present, and a glorious past when fate had not yet taken its full toll.

Thus far there has been little opportunity to examine the role of history in maintaining the primacy of *la famiglia*. Although this will be treated more fully in chapter 5, some note may be made here of the great attention paid to family history. As Feliks Gross points out, collective tradition establishes "family identification not only in space but also in time."[16] The peasant identifies some fellow villagers not merely as *paesani* but as *cugini*. The literal translation "cousin" is not intended; rather, the term designates a kinship tie of significance. Kin who are less close, and especially relatives through marriage, are referred to with the phrase "siamo parenti" (we are related). The choice of "siamo parenti" or "mio cugino" is a sure indicator of the depth of attachment to the person mentioned. Frequently the choice violates genetic distance in order to take into account an important historical event. A family feud reduces even a brother to *parente*, whereas acceptance of the role of godparent, perhaps even several generations earlier, raises a third cousin by marriage to a *cugino*. A complex network, learned from early childhood as part of evening storytelling (called *firozzi* in Albareto) and reinforced by patterns of attendance at weddings, funerals, and feasts, circumscribes every individual's action. This network, rooted in genetic relationships but nourished by history, determines responses to requests for aid, offers of assistance, and proposals of marriage. Respected heads of families so linked strive only to maintain a sense of continuity by acting as tradition informs them their ancestors did. There is *onore* in maintaining a "justified" historical feud but not in becoming a peacemaker. (If the feud is not deemed "justified," then the participants have lost *onore* anyway.) In sum, history serves to blunt the potential of *la famiglia* to become a present-minded vehicle for change. Under the weight of the past, marriage is less an alliance for the future than a way to perpetuate traditional relationships. A family cannot look to its advantage as a nuclear unit without denying its extended past, and to reject tradition is to reject the force that gives meaning to the present.

Finally, the traditional past reinforces *campanilismo*. More than words in a book about some distant place, history is oral communication, face to face, the telling of events that happened on the very ground where the storyteller stands. Unity of space integrates then with now; past and present are one, linked by the land and the village. Tied firmly to his plot and to his social condition, the peasant nonetheless may traverse centuries. Traditionalism superficially appeared to fix rural Italians in a static and subordinate position; at another level it allowed the poorest *contadino* to conquer time itself.

At the beginning of this chapter I set forth the proposition that the harshness of present reality forced peasants to turn to the past, to create a path, the only possible path, away from the misery surrounding them. Whatever the practicality of the solution of traditionalism, which admittedly did little to improve material conditions and may even have retarded the growth of a consciousness ready to demand effectively a fairer share of the present, it served to make life bearable and occasionally even joyful. If the original proposition is correct, it follows that dramatic improvement in the rural workers' standard of living should have caused a change in the force of traditionalism. This indeed has happened. Improved sanitary conditions in the late nineteenth century, forced order and moderate property redistribution under Mussolini, together with apparent prosperity in the postwar years (made easier because rural depopulation left fewer mouths to feed), freed rural Italians from immediate threats of starvation, disease, and early death. The *contadini* now have electricity, indoor plumbing, household appliances including a television set, and perhaps a Fiat. They predict or at least hope for a future that will be even better.

Vastly improved material conditions paved the way for a new value system as well, but one deeply related to the old. I have attempted to show that in traditional societies the past is the radix of human behavior; and so it remains for the peasants who now vote in such large numbers for Italy's Communist Party (PCI). The reasons why rural workers do not uniformly respond to communism need not detain us at this point. Far more interesting is the success of the PCI, virtually unique among Western democratic systems, in appealing to and even helping to shape rural class consciousness. The PCI's role in the liberation from fascism, great though it was, does not explain its subsequent success. Three of the communities in the present study developed no partisan movement of consequence, and in all four a nostalgic favorable recollection of Mussolini is evident. Nor can the PCI's success be due to its promises of a fairer distribution of wealth, at least not in a crass and immediate sense. Rural Italians are fabled, correctly, for their cynicism about political promises, and in any event the Christian Democratic party, which is in power and therefore occasionally delivers something, promises more than the communists. Superior organization is also not the explanation.

The key to the Communist Party's appeal lies in Antonio Gramsci's subtle adaptation of Marx's dialectical analysis of history. Gramsci understood, indeed he felt intensively, the crucial role of the past in traditional rural Italy. His ideas, admittedly filtered through lesser officials in terms of local needs, turned traditionalism on its head. The past remained a glorified radix, but rather than being a goal forever sought and never attained, it became the essential and inexorable means, literally the root, toward the new goal of a "better" life. Gramsci did not call upon peasants to reject the past; on the contrary, he saw the past as the necessary period of *sacrificio* borne by the *contadini*'s forefathers. And tradition made it an obligation, a matter of *onore*, we may say, to give purpose to centuries of penitential sacrifice by working to assure ultimate triumph. The PCI appeals to *il destino*, a word that evokes the old power of *fortuna*. Peasant communists believe they are destined to succeed; the outcome is beyond human control; history is on their side. And if contradictions seem to emerge, they may be only in the mind of an outsider. When I asked an ardent communist in Nissoria why he regularly attended mass, he explained that this made his wife happy and, in any event, he always dedicated his rosary during the mass to Marx, Lenin, Gramsci, "e tutti i nostri santi."[17] Thus, even in the present, the past controls the future.

# 4
# Time

—Oh! benedette voi che siete morte!—esclamò—Oh!
benedetta voi, Vergine Santa! che mi avete tolto la mia
creatura per non farla soffrire come me!

"Nedda"

Agrarian cultures tend to perceive time as a cyclical alternation of paired
opposites in accordance with the regular passing and return of the
seasons, of occasions for commemoration, of life and death.[1] In rural
Italy this cyclical perception is aptly expressed in the wheel-of-time
image. With a fixed perimeter and no end points, the wheel has spokes
radiating outward from its center and punctuating the rim. The spokes
are the times when society pauses to plant or to harvest, to gather or to
go separate ways, to sell or to buy, to mourn or to celebrate, to curse or
to pray. Time turns upon itself, beyond human control.[2]

In contrast to the wheel-of-time image is that of a line. Linear time
emerges as a significant perception in cultures that see historical process as developmental and purposeful, headed for a final outcome or at
least in a particular direction.[3] Ironically, instruments based on a cyclical image of time, the calendar and the clock, find special favor among
measurers of linear time who need a way to divide off precise and equal
units. But the idea of breaking time into repeated segments of hours,
days, months, and years is logically absurd and of little practical value
in a paleotechnic agrarian society. Only when time itself becomes a
commodity do such measurements make sense, and this did not occur
in western Europe until the eighteenth and early nineteenth centuries.[4]
Even then, the idea of trading upon time did not penetrate deeply into
rural Italy (or, for that matter, into other areas of western Europe and
the Mediterranean noted by social scientist Immanuel Wallerstein as
"semiperipheral" to the commercial/industrial core concentrated along
northern Atlantic waters). "Stopping the clock," "working against
time," and "time running out" are phrases meaningful only in
economies that have harnessed vast amounts of inorganic energy to the
productive process. Wasting time, in these economies, means nonuse
of energy; time is an enemy of energy to be captured so that it then may
be bought and sold.

Even limited acceptance of linear time as a commodity involved the *contadini* in a process of interaction with outside forces. Mussolini, it is said, made the trains run on time, and the driver of a Fiat may get from here to there at an appointed hour. Electricity overcame the day/night cycle as energy flowed through meters calibrated to calculate the exact purchase price of light. Mechanized farming reduced the communal experience of sowing/harvesting from seasons to days, and irrigation banished the dry season. Above all, the conquest of unpredictable and untimely death, until "passing away" became something that happened mostly to old people who had lived their "full time," allowed the *contadini* to begin to believe that they might usefully measure and plan the future. By the end of the nineteenth century Italian peasants in massive numbers decided to emigrate temporarily to the New World, to trade upon a year or two of *their* time in exchange for the possibility of returning to buy land.[5]

Clifford Geertz's observation on the Balinese calendar's demarcation has wider applicability: "They don't tell you what time it is; they tell you what kind of time it is."[6] In the Italian countryside a related viewpoint prevailed. The formal documents used to register births, marriages, and deaths required the *contadini* to record their lives in the day/month/year format useful in a linear time culture. But from these documents it is possible to reconstruct the *kind* of time it was and thereupon to build an explanation or at least a better understanding of the cyclical perception of time that permeated rural culture. Demographic data are the main resource; nevertheless, lengthy series of statistical calculations should not obscure an underlying reality: the "events" being summarized were central to the evolution of rural Italian culture.

## THE SEASONS

Summer, the time of harvest, of dryness, of heat, was a time of death, especially for children. Figure 2 portrays data indicating the kind of time summer was in the Sicilian village of Nissoria (space precludes the presentation in graphic form of data for the other three communities, where patterns are similar but less pronounced. These data are provided in tabular form in app. B). The figure, based on all recorded deaths between 1810 and 1973, is drawn so as to set aside for the moment the problem of change over time in order to concentrate on death at various ages[7] and on the seasonal pattern. In using the past tense I mean to indicate that this pattern no longer holds, and in the last section of this chapter I shall examine how it changed.[8]

The numbers (ranging from 20 to 240) along the side of each part of figure 2 show the percentage of "expected" deaths which occurred in the months shown along the bottom of the figure. By "expected" is

meant the number of deaths that would have occurred in a given month
if deaths were equally likely in all months. For example, in Nissoria
there were 1,552 deaths recorded for one-year-olds, yielding an "expected" frequency of 129 (1,552÷12) each month; but actual deaths in
August numbered 256, which is 199 percent of "expected" frequency.
This is the number plotted on the graph.[9]

An excessive number of infants born during the preceding spring and
winter died in July and August. What caused the deaths of so many
infants between the ages of two and eleven months? Why did they die
during the summer? What did their fathers and mothers feel? How did
the community respond? Unfortunately, the evidence that has survived, rich though it is as a source for showing a cyclical pattern, does
not yield as full an answer to these more important questions.
Nevertheless, the cold reports contain hints which allow at least tentative judgments. Although the documents do not list cause of death, they
do indicate something of the surrounding circumstances—whether a
priest was called before the child actually died (a sign that infanticide

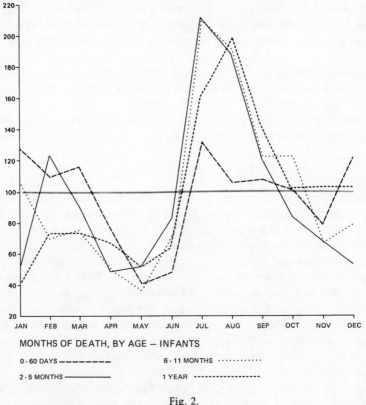

MONTHS OF DEATH, BY AGE — INFANTS

0 - 60 DAYS ─ ─ ─ ─ ─ ─ ─          6 - 11 MONTHS  · · · · · · · · · · ·

2 - 5 MONTHS ──────────          1 YEAR  - - - - - - - - - - - - - - - - -

Fig. 2.
Infants

was not involved), whether the child died during the night while sleeping with its parents (smothering, accidental or otherwise, a clear possibility), whether the child died suddenly, was feverish, or changed color. Other notes tell of parents returning home from the fields to find a child dead in its cradle or of accidents involving animals or of "weakness" from birth.[10]

Certain statistics allow further insights into the necessarily irregular patterns that emerge from these notes. In only 2.8 percent of all deaths recorded in Nissoria (and 2.6 percent in Castel San Giorgio) was the father reported as unknown, a rate of illegitimacy consistent with figures derived from birth and marriage registers.[11] The percentages are far below the 17 percent illegitimacy rate determined, for example, from

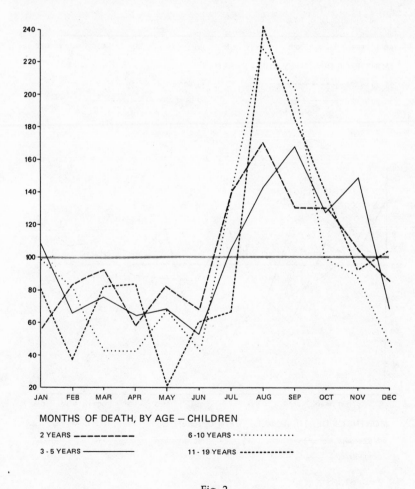

MONTHS OF DEATH, BY AGE – CHILDREN

2 YEARS ‒‒‒‒‒‒‒‒‒‒    6 -10 YEARS ················

3 - 5 YEARS ────────    11 - 19 YEARS ‒‒‒‒‒‒‒‒‒‒‒‒‒

Fig. 2.
Children

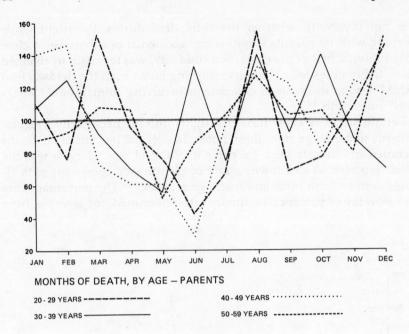

MONTHS OF DEATH, BY AGE — PARENTS

20 - 29 YEARS  ------------        40 - 49 YEARS  ················

30 - 39 YEARS  ──────────        50 -59 YEARS  ----------------

Fig. 2.
Parents

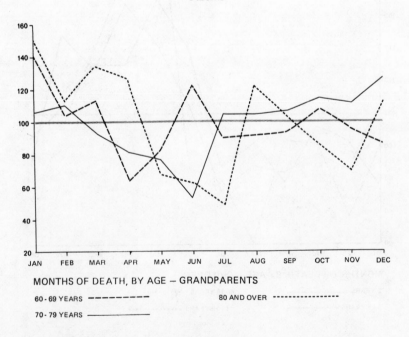

MONTHS OF DEATH, BY AGE — GRANDPARENTS

60 - 69 YEARS  ------------        80 AND OVER  ----------------

70 - 79 YEARS  ──────────

Fig. 2.
Grandparents

death reports for children under age six in urban Italy in 1881.[12] Unmarried women may have conceived in the countryside, but they gave birth in the city. These statistics, taken together with the infrequency of reports of infants found dead, indicate that rural parents did not abandon their children to die of starvation or exposure. A special section of an 1886 health report gives evidence of steps taken to aid foundlings. Provisions varied greatly from one province to another: 100 lire premium in Parma (Albareto) to the foster parents of a foundling who by age thirteen had learned to read and write, 2.55 lire for diapers in Nicosia (Nissoria), six years of maintenance payments for boys and eight for girls in Cosenza (Rogliano). All in all, by the late nineteenth century regional government offered at least enough support for foundlings that rural parents who abandoned their infants did so by placing them in designated *ruote*.[13] Religious houses earlier served this purpose, though it is impossible to judge how effectively.[14]

Infanticide by any means appears to have been infrequent. Government figures for 1886, which indicate a rate of 10.1 per 1 million inhabitants, reflect only how little the government knew. Still, infanticide did not reach major proportions in the countryside. The horror with which a prefect reported one case (the offspring of an incestuous coupling) in a town adjacent to Nissoria suggests the infrequency of such killings.[15] Whatever the true number, no pattern emerges similar to those found by historians of other societies in which infanticide is suspected to have been frequent.[16] In particular, circumstantial evidence for infanticide usually includes a highly imbalanced sex ratio, most often showing "too many" male children.[17] But, as table 3 reveals, infant males appeared in death registers more often than did females; overall mortality to age ten shows sex ratios in accord with differences at natality and probable impact of diseases and accidents. In sum, the demographic record indicates that rural Italians did not practice infanticide on a significant scale.

TABLE 3   **Sex Ratio of Reported Deaths (N Males per 100 Females)**

| Age | Albareto | Castel San Giorgio | Nissoria | Rogliano |
|---|---|---|---|---|
| 0–60 days | 144 | 122 | 140 | 143 |
| 2–5 months | 103 | 132 | 123 | 102 |
| 6–11 months | 98 | 107 | 116 | 98 |
| 1 year | 105 | 102 | 93 | 105 |
| 2 years | 92 | 100 | 98 | 92 |
| 3–5 years | 92 | 94 | 96 | 92 |
| 6–10 years | 97 | 98 | 138 | 97 |
| Overall | 102 | 109 | 113 | 102 |

Inadequate care due to ignorance and poverty, however, surely contributed to high mortality rates. Most accounts tell us that Sicilian
women stayed home and did not work in the fields,[18] and indeed,
married women generally did not engage in agricultural wage work.
However, the wheat harvest of late June and July was the one time in
the year when labor was in short supply, and peasants easily found
work for cash on large estates. Husbands spent several weeks away
from home to earn cash while their wives and older children went out to
reap on the family's small holdings. This task took women away from
home before dawn to return only after sunset. To take their infants with
them to lie under the hot sun, with scythes ripping the air and a mule
hobbling about, would have been dangerous; nor is it possible to reap
while toting a baby. Therefore, infants were left at home in less experienced or less capable hands, hands not able to do field work. Even in
the best of circumstances such an arrangement endangered the infant,
who had to be taken from the nourishment of the mother's breast and
given some form of pabulum (usually animal's milk mixed with grain).
Although infants were fed *pappa* as early as their third week, sole reliance on it for fourteen hours or more greatly increased the likelihood
that the infant would suffer gastroenteritis, diarrhea, or constipation.
The mixture had to be baked until thickened; then the guardian used
her fingers to feed the infant. But some guardians, out of stupidity or in
order to conserve fuel if there was any, did not bother to bake the
mixture, and none would have done more than to wash her hands in
cold water. Moreover, the infant was swaddled, wrapped around and
around with long narrow bands of cloth. If the sitter changed the
swaddling at all, there was the danger of crushing the infant by wrap-
ping too tightly or of leaving the bands so loose that the baby pried
them to its neck and choked. Most mortality reports are silent, but those
that do explain circumstances surrounding the death give ample testimony to the perils that faced infants whose mothers had to leave them
for their work away from home. Part of the great peak in infant mortality in July, unfortunately we cannot say precisely how much, resulted
from poor care by mother substitutes.[19]

Confirmation of the importance of maternal absence as a factor in
infant mortality comes from the Albareto and Rogliano data (see app.
B). The surges in deaths among six- to eleven-month-olds in Rogliano
in August and November parallel the times when women went in large
numbers to harvest figs and olives, respectively. In Albareto the best
time to gather mushrooms was between mid-August and mid-
September, when bright sunshine followed a rainy day. Before dawn
the women of Albareto were deep in the forests, wearing high boots to
protect against snakebites, for gathering mushrooms was a job they did
better than the men. They did not start for home, often hours away, until

the woods were totally dark. August to September was the time in Albareto when infants died.

Summer heat brought other dangers as well.[20] Some mothers of infants less than a year old were pregnant and therefore did not breast feed. Their infants, especially in July, suffered the dangers of both malnutrition and contamination of food. Even sterile milk contains saprophytic bacteria, and if milk is left standing in warm weather counts rise very rapidly to more than 1 million per milliliter. One group of these bacteria causes the souring of milk, which is harmless, but other strains evoke vomiting and diarrhea. Even when death did not follow, the standard treatment of providing the infant with no food until it recovered served to weaken further its resistance to a variety of infectious diseases. July was also the month when cereals and other foods were most scarce in Nissoria. Resort to less digestible and more contaminated food supplies, if these were available, increased the probability of gastrointestinal disorders.[21]

Infectious diseases also struck hard in the summer. Infants born in regions where malaria is endemic or hyperendemic, as in nineteenth-century southern Italy, are passively immune (from placental transfer) to the disease, but only through repeated infection and active disease can active immunity be acquired. All four malarial strains produce in children fevers ranging to 41°C, with severe enlargement of the liver and spleen, often leading to fatal malarial cachexia. Although malaria as an immediate cause of death occurred primarily in the fall ("aestivo-autumnal fever"), weakness resulting from the intermittent fever of tertian strains, which left the infant apparently healthy one day and seriously ill the next, caused significant mortality as early as late June. Another major contributor to the peaks of death in July was undoubtedly bacterial meningitis. Many varieties have been identified, but in the absence of diagnosis (a pathology of upper respiratory infection followed by continuous fever and listlessness gave inadequate clues) and treatment, mortality among infants must have approached 100 percent. In addition to endemic diseases such as malaria and meningitis, young children fell victim to epidemic outbreaks of cholera, smallpox, and typhoid. Although the episodic occurrence of such outbreaks contributed primarily to a long-term cyclical perception of time, the fact that they peaked in summer or early fall simultaneously reinforced the association of death with seasonality. In sum, the hot months took a frighteningly high toll among children in their first year.[22]

From figure 2 it is evident that there was no abatement in this pattern among one-year-olds. Gastrointestinal diseases probably remained the major reason for a peak of summer deaths,[23] owing to food scarcity in the preharvest months (and the substitution of inferior alternatives), the absence of mothers who left home to help with the harvest, the tendency not to cook foods in the hot months, and the spread of infection with growth of the insect population. Moreover, greater contact with other villagers, which began in May and continued through August, multiplied exposure to diseased persons and to healthy carriers of diphtheria, tuberculosis, measles, and a variety of bronchial and pulmonary infections.

Among children between the ages of two and five and in an even sharper configuration among those between six and nineteen years of age, the clustering of deaths in summer remained dramatically evident in Nissoria, whereas for the other three communities (see app. B) seasonal differentiation abated somewhat with age, especially in Castel San Giorgio. Those who survived early perils in Castel San Giorgio, thereby gaining at least partial immunity to a variety of fatal diseases, enjoyed slightly better nutrition than the children of Nissoria. Castel San Giorgio's integrated position in the hinterland of Naples, its mixed agriculture with emphasis on vegetables, the opportunities for employment for its artisans, and the smaller size of its families made it easier to acquire the bare essentials of nutrition. In particular, the mixing of crops meant that freshly harvested foods were available through much of the year, thereby attenuating the concentration of child mortality in the summer. In Nissoria, on the other hand, virtually everything combined to increase danger in the hot months. Sole reliance on wheat and fava beans led to chronic food shortages from late May until August. Geographically and culturally the village was isolated; its economy lacked crafts; its inhabitants had to trade in kind and without credit; they suffered high absolute temperatures, an absence of rainfall (forcing them to use polluted water), and high density in the village nucleus; they lacked means of disposing of their wastes. Viewed with studied indifference by the *civili* and the *baroni*, everything condemned peasant children to an annual summer of malnutrition, disease, and death.[24]

For adults death came in two seasons. Except for the anomalous thirty to thirty-nine age group (an anomaly not present in the other three communities), figure 2 for parents portrays a healthy time beginning with the dry warm days of April, concentrated death in August, low mortality in the fall, then death in the winter. With variations due to climate, as in Albareto's late cold and wet spring, the pattern holds elsewhere. Neither the August nor the December peak was as sharp as in the case of children, but both were ample enough to command the peasantry's attention. In August mothers and fathers succumbed along with their children to epidemic outbreaks of cholera and typhoid. In December adults died of pneumonic infections.[25]

Seasonal patterns of mortality, twin-peaked for adults and massively concentrated for children, reinforced one kind of cyclical time: the regular alternation of dry and wet, heat and cold, death and life closely linked to agricultural work rhythms. But rural culture also responded to another cycle, one that was devastating and unpredictable, natural and irregular. Some children, many children, died every summer, and so the hot season and harvest came to mean death. (Village elders recall that one was payment for the other.) But the village's collective sense of time also marked prominently those special seasons when "everyone" died or by a stroke of fate barely escaped. As with the famine of *la lupa*, it was easy enough to remember the last such time and perhaps even to explain why the devastation had occurred, but no one dared to predict the next outbreak.

Consider, for example, the experience of Francesco Rinaldi, one of eighty-five babies born in Nissoria in 1825.[26] Mortality rates were "normal" during the next few years (forty-one of eighty-five surviving to age six) until 1831. In that hot season eight of Francesco's playmates (born in 1825) died, one of every five children born that year. Among the dead was the daughter of a carpenter (who also lost a two-year-old daughter in the same epidemic), but the other seven were, like Francesco, *contadini*. Although the epidemic peaked in August, when twenty-four Nissorini of all ages died, it continued to rage into early October. Among the dead were seven mothers, ranging in age from twenty-three to forty, one of whom was Francesco's. The ages of the victims, the substantial presence of nonagriculturists among the dead, the seasonal course of the disease (beginning when water supplies were low and ending with the fall of rains), and the absence of any diagnostic hints other than high fever all suggest typhoid as a probable cause of this epidemic. Elsewhere in Italy 1831 was not a year of unusually high mortality,[27] but for Nissorini of Francesco's generation it turned childhood into a time of fear.

The year 1840, when six teenagers died, was another bad time, as were the five years following Francesco's 1850 marriage, the time when Nissorini responded to the horrifying death rate by agitating successfully for a more effective patron saint. Through all these seasons Francesco and his wife Lucia survived, but many of their children, relatives, and neighbors did not. The Rinaldis knew everyone in Nissoria and shared the collective experience of a funeral procession, on average, every three days, much more often in the summer. Only after 1904, the last year in which the death rate in Nissoria exceeded fifty per 1,000 per year and the year in which Francesco died, did the absolute number of annual deaths remain consistently below 100 (in a population of about 3,000). Throughout the nineteenth century every year, especially every summer, took its toll; from the statistics it is evident that the cholera

years of 1866 and 1886 were particularly bad. The disease struck in July
and continued into September, a month in which more than one Nissorino died each day. The years 1878, 1879, 1890, 1894, and 1895 were
also bad times. In the latter years, when the incidence of deaths in the
summer was no higher than usual (one every other day), winter outbreaks of diphtheria, probably the highly contagious pharyngeal type,
along with whooping chough, influenza, and pneumonitis turned formerly healthy months into times of death.

Francesco Rinaldi, along with his fellow Nissorini, experienced the
events which here are depicted only as a series of graphs and numbers.
How did the Nissorini respond to the reality of death here described as
a statistical pattern? The clues are all too few, but those that exist point
to the likelihood that mortality, its unpredictability and its apparent
irrationality, shaped the lives of these villagers. Although death obviously was a frequent occurrence, it does not follow that it thereby lost
meaning.[28] From the official registers, which always indicated the name
of the person reporting a death and his relationship to the deceased, it
is clear that, even in the case of infants, fathers took time out to appear
before the clerk and report the death. If the father had migrated or died,
one of his brothers or other male kin by blood usually made the report.
Custom held that mothers were too grief stricken to appear in public
except during the funeral ceremony. Besides, procreation was a matter
of *onore* for the husband and "his" family (parents and brothers); the
death of a child, especially a boy, took from the father a portion of his
"respect," his standing in the community. A man without heirs had no
*interesse* beyond the short term; this automatically made him untrustworthy, a poor risk in a society in which so much depended on
*onore* and *onore* depended on reciprocity. Even the death of a daughter
denied the father a chance to strengthen his family through a future
marriage alliance. Report of the death was a formal announcement to
the community that fate had intervened to deal a blow to *la famiglia*.
When more than half of all children died (and disease transmission and
class differentials meant that one death increased the likelihood of
another in the same family), every death threatened to leave the family
without heirs. While children were perceived as organic parts of *la
famiglia* rather than as persons, their mortality required an appropriate
and dignified response from its head. Even in the case of adults, an
ego-familial pattern of reporting deaths continued: a wife's death by
her father, brothers, or sons if they were grown; a husband's by his
father, brothers, or grown sons.

The significance of death as a denial of the cyclical continuation of *la
famiglia* is also evident in the choosing of names. Children received the
names of their grandparents; a first son was baptized with his father's
father's name. If the offspring died, the next born of the same sex

carried the name. It may be, as argued by psychoanalytic historian Lloyd deMause, that such naming is part of a "reversal reaction" in which parents see their own parents reborn in the child (with clearly harmful consequences for the offspring).[29] My own judgment is that with sufficient evidence for such an assertion lacking, for rural Italy the force of familial continuity is adequate to explain naming patterns. In any event, death denied *la famiglia* the means of its perpetuation; for this reason alone, mortality even among infants deeply affected the Nissorini.

Appeal to spiritual intervention also shows that these villagers never became inured or indifferent to death. Resort to a *mago* involved a combination of pseudoscience and supernaturalism. In addition to incantations and exorcism, the *mago* was an expert in the mixing of herbs. Given all the wrong actions taken by distraught parents (such as starving a child suffering from a gastrointestinal disorder and failing to replace body fluids), the *mago*'s preparations usually did little harm and occasionally aided recovery. Prayer to a special saint offered an even more powerful source of potential cure. Saints Francesco di Paola, Filippo Neri, and Antonio di Padova, all of whom had wide reputations as wonder workers, were generally held to be most responsive to appeals for healing. Members of *la famiglia* now residing with God also were believed to be ready to intercede. That such efforts were always made indicates that, while frequent and inexplicable death reinforced a sense of fatalism, it did not lead to resignation. The Nissorini fought against death with every weapon at their disposal.

When a member of *la famiglia* died despite all efforts to deny fate its victim, the family initiated an elaborate funeral ritual. The body was transferred to or kept in the matrimonial bed, which had been covered with the best spread. Candles burned all night as *la famiglia* kept watch, the frequency, loudness, and emotion of its wailings an indication of its *onore*, its defiance of *fortuna*. In the morning, the corpse (from which any gold had been removed) was transferred to a plain coffin for the procession on foot past the deceased's family's residence (that of a husband's or wife's parents, whether or not they were alive, or, in the case of a child, that of the paternal grandparents). As the procession moved along to the burial ground, often taking a circuitous route in order to pass the home of a favorite uncle or an important cousin, other mourners joined the march. In contrast to the wailing of the night before, this was done in complete silence, a public and communal display of inner strength. But upon the lowering of the coffin the widow or mother attempted to join her loved one in the grave, restrained only by force;[30] then the *grida forti* began again, as one and all shouted their hatred of fate. The cries of friends and observers spurred the membes of the family to even greater lamentations in a contest to determine who cared the most. Gradually, and in aimless contrast to the carefully considered and silent walk to the cemetery, the mourners recessed in small groups to the home of *la famiglia*. They joked, gossiped, and openly expressed joy that fate had chosen someone else this time. Once at the doorstep a more somber mood prevailed, and a recounting began of all the good things the deceased had done in his lifetime or, in the case of a child, might have lived to do. This went beyond the usual funeral oration. What was said became the basis, witnessed as it was by all who cared about the deceased, for the "history" of this particular member of *la famiglia*. Moreover, in the case of an adult, especially one who possessed *onore*, the recalling of favors granted became a list of reciprocal debts still owed to *la famiglia*. And a debt openly acknowledged was to be repaid. After a time a near relative, but not a member of *la famiglia*, brought to the house a *gran pranzo*. Persons outside the family customarily stayed, often sharing a glass of wine, but they did not partake further in the ritual meal.

The next day signs appeared on the doors of all persons related to the deceased indicating the nature of the relationship and the fact of bereavement. The signs remained for at least one year; in the case of a widow they might remain forever. Similarly, a widow of *onore* continued to wear black for the remainder of her life, while for widowers the accepted period of public mourning was three years, and during the first year men did not shave. Mourning periods for dead children were considerably shorter, usually about three months. The phrase used most often by elderly interviewees to recall communal and parental responses to infant and child mortality was "un dolore accettato." Such deaths were "accepted" (not *acceptable*) as inevitable but important points in the cycle of life. The significance of the event, beyond an emotional response that simply cannot be quantified, varied with the child's age, sex, and number of siblings. The death of an only son, even if his parents had not passed the childbearing stage, threatened *la famiglia* in the most fundamental way, but the response to other deaths differed only in degree.[31]

Seasonal mortality reinforced a cyclical image of time in rural Italy and defined forcefully the kind of time it was. Nevertheless, the villagers' actions in the face of death were essentially responsive; they tried to react with honor to events beyond their control. In the matter of marriage, on the other hand, the community played an initiative role in perpetuating a cyclical mode for measuring time. The church calendar, which also marks off kinds of time (Advent, Lent, Ordinary Time, and so forth), set the basic seasonal pattern of marriage. But beyond such official prohibitions and encouragements, rural folk maintained a variety of strictures about marriage at certain times. Figure 3 portrays the seasonality of marriage patterns in all four communities. As in the

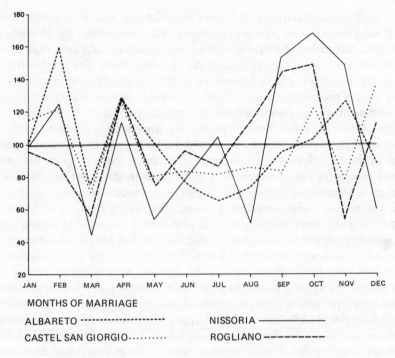

MONTHS OF MARRIAGE

ALBARETO ----------------------     NISSORIA ——————

CASTEL SAN GIORGIO··········     ROGLIANO ---------

Fig. 3.

previous figure on deaths, the data include all events between 1810 and
1973; the months are represented horizontally and the vertical set of
numbers (ranging from 40 to 180) shows the percentage of "expected"
marriages in each month. The general pattern is one of few marriages in
March, May, and the summer months and a large number of marriages
in April and in several months after the harvest. The shortage of marriages in March is due to church regulations aimed at avoiding nuptial
celebrations during Lent. However, the effectiveness of these "rules"
has been far from consistent or universal over the past century; in
Rogliano, for example, the portion of March marriages dropped from 7
percent between 1820 and 1849 to 4 percent between 1920 and 1949, but
in Nissoria exactly the reverse occurred, as March marriages rose from 3
percent to 7.5 percent for the same decades.

The avoidance of marriage in May is even more irregular and subject
to highly localized custom. Throughout Italy (and the northern hemi-
sphere generally) May is a month of rebirth, a time when nature bursts
forth, when it is neither too hot nor too cold, when the rainy season is
over, when the first fairs are held, when deaths are fewer, when sexual
mores may be relaxed temporarily. It is a time of joy, of hope for a good
crop, of a full but not oppressive work pace. The graph shows that the

May decline in marriages in Castel San Giorgio and in Albareto may well have been part of a larger summer hiatus; moreover, the absence of any traditional lore touching upon May nuptials indicates that these communities did not specifically ban or avoid them. For Rogliano and Nissoria, however, figure 3 reveals a particular shortage of marriages in May that is reversed in June. There is a wealth of lore in each community explaining why people ought not to marry in May.

The Nissorini offer three superficially unrelated reasons to avoid a May marriage, two directed at would-be husbands and one at wives. May is the month of the mules, who are turned loose to graze on fresh green grass and who perform only light tasks in these preharvest days. A man who marries during the month of the mules risks being sterile, and the woman who would defy custom by taking him, in addition to remaining childless, is likely to find him more interested in eating than in working. Another admonition points out that May is the month of the ass (whose age is counted from May) and that he who marries in May will soon find himself cuckolded. Finally, May is the month of the Madonna, the special protector of all Italy and the patroness of maidenhood to whom young girls offer their devotions. To marry in Her month would be deeply offensive to the Virgin Mary. Most Nissorini believe that no one is quite that stupid, and therefore they assume that any woman who marries in May is not a virgin. (The parish priest dismisses this aspect of Marian devotion as superstitious nonsense, but his congregation does not marry in May.)

In a variety of ways these strictures are reflected in the nuptial records of Nissoria. An analysis of the remarriage dates of 264 widows, for example, reveals that 8 percent of them occurred in May; this is twice the rate for first marriages and indicates no avoidance of May by these nonvirgins. The cuckold admonition, it turns out, relates to another widespread belief in Nissoria—namely, that the neighboring town of Agira is filled with *cornuti*. The ninety-two men from Agira who married in Nissoria did so without paying any heed to the May admonition, whereas the eighty from nearby Assoro, a town noted for its evil spirits and practitioners of magic, avoided May marriages to a greater extent than did the Nissorini themselves. The "shortage" of May marriages, which began only in the 1880s, has been increasing steadily until, among 286 first marriages performed since 1965, not one has been in May. Not all Nissorini about to wed believe that May vows will lead to sterility, laziness, adultery, or insult to Mary (those who adhere to the Marian admonition are less concerned with the insult itself than with the probability that Mary will become less responsive to prayer), but even those who do not have many relatives who do. Why spoil a festive occasion by arousing the fears of a member of *la famiglia*?

The Roglianesi also avoid marrying in May, but not for any of the reasons given in Nissoria. In this Calabrian town belief in spiritual intervention remains a potent force, and there is frequent recourse to its several *maghi*. Although primarily called upon for their powers as herb healers and to ward off the evil eye (*il malocchio*), *maghi* also tell fortunes. In particular, they are consulted about the choice of day for an important event such as a marriage. Somewhere in May, many Roglianesi believe, there lurks an evil day; this *giornata maligna* shifts from year to year, and it is so powerful that not even a *mago* can divine when it will come. But every year it comes, and some tragedy or other occurs in May. It is far safer to avoid marrying or undertaking any important task in such a month. A further reason for the paucity of May vows is the widespread devotion to Saint Rita of Cascia, known as the "saint of the impossible" because of her many intercessions to rescue hopeless situations. Forced against her will to marry, Rita remained a model wife for eighteen years to a man who was brutal, dissolute, and adulterous. When he was killed in a vendetta, his sons vowed revenge; rather than see her sons commit murder, Rita prayed for their death. This God granted, after which Rita became a nun. A thorn from a crucifix embedded itself in her forehead during an ecstasy; the wound never healed, and its continuing, offensive suppuration forced Rita to live most of her remaining years as an austere recluse until she died of a wasting disease. All this and many other grim details are known to Saint Rita's devoted followers, who frequently use her image in a *brae* (a diamond-shaped amulet containing salt crystals and incense and worn in contact with the skin to protect against *il malocchio*). The roses of Saint Rita, which are blessed on May 22, remind those who believe in her power and know the misery of her life to choose some other month to marry. Between 1935 and 1973 only thirty-five of 2,300 marriages performed in Rogliano occurred in May.

In marked contrast to the supernatural factors associated with infrequent May nuptials, the equally great shortage of marriages in the summer is explained by rural folk in practical economic terms. Before the harvest food was too scarce for a proper feast, and then everyone was too busy, first with reaping and picking, then with the *vendemmia*. Several Nissorini explained the particular shortage in August by pointing out that since the entire village celebrated San Giuseppe that month anyway, there was little reason to schedule a second festive day during an already joyous time. Summer lows everywhere gave way to fall as a time for marriage, the peak coming first in wine-poor Rogliano and later in the cooler northern village of Albareto, where the agricultural season ended only in November when the threat of snow forced the removal of grazing animals to the Ligurian coast.

The November pattern varies greatly in these four communities. A month of rain and cold, it is also a month of death, heralded by the celebration of All Souls' Day. It marks the end of the annual cycle of planting and harvesting, the time for assessing the year's results and planning for the winter ahead. It is, for obvious reasons, a sensible time to marry and begin a new household. Supplies for a feast are at hand, work is less demanding, and, if good fortune prevails, before the next cycle is through the young couple will be celebrating their own procreation and the continuation of *la famiglia*. In Albareto and Nissoria this was what happened,[32] but in Castel San Giorgio and Rogliano November was actually a month of few marriages. It cannot be that the postharvest peak simply occurred earlier in these towns, since they experienced another upsurge in December. In Rogliano the need to pick olives may have accounted for reluctance to marry in November, but that still leaves Castel San Giorgio's pattern unexplained. The special remembrance of death in November is the reason given most often by the Castelsangiorgesi (and Roglianesi) for not marrying in that month. Castel San Giorgio and Rogliano, as noted in an earlier chapter, were integrated in the economy and culture of the surrounding region, whereas Albareto and Nissoria were more isolated villages. Integration apparently resulted in earlier and fuller adoption of the Catholic tendency to celebrate death in November. As shown in figure 2, this was not in fact a time when an extraordinary number of people died; ceremonial remembrance of departed souls in this particular month was not congruent with natural cycles of mortality. Religious observance in November stemmed from cultural centers outside the local community and therefore made greater inroads in integrated towns. The importance of such integration is further indicated by a yearly breakdown for Nissoria, which shows that since 1935 only forty-two of 1,158 marriages have been performed in November (only one of these after 1964). Earlier, before improved communication and transportation reached Nissoria, its residents had married frequently (92 percent above random distribution) in November. But as they embraced the practices of urban culture, and as mortality became less seasonal, the Nissorini also began to avoid November nuptials.

Throughout this analysis of fluctuations portrayed in figure 3 emphasis has been on the valleys rather than the peaks, on the kind of time deemed inappropriate for marriage. In choosing this approach I have been guided by the results of interviews and by written references to the timing of wedding celebrations. These, in sharp contrast to, say, modern American beliefs about June weddings, give no evidence of concern for an auspicious time to marry; all the lore I could find or that I heard about dealt with times that boded ill for a marriage. This, it seems to me, is no accident. Setting a wedding date was a matter of choice, a human action, but as with so many peasant choices, one circumscribed by fate. Because so much of life was brutal, because peasants lived in a world of "total scarcity,"[33] because the mythical past offered an alluring respite from the unknown future, rural culture viewed fate with awe and fear. Good fortune was possible, but bad luck was probable. Believing, with reason, that they had little control over how long or prosperous their marriages would be, young couples carefully avoided setting a date deemed likely to tempt fate and make the future even more perilous.

Births—the third essential element of the demographic basis for a cyclical perception of time—appear to be less clearly related to seasonal rhythms. Figure 4 provides the data, summarized in the same manner as for earlier figures on death and marriage except that the scale of monthly fluctuations is much reduced (75–140). Everywhere there is a tendency for births to be fewer during the harvest season: the reaping of wheat in Nissoria in June/July, the September/October *vendemmia*

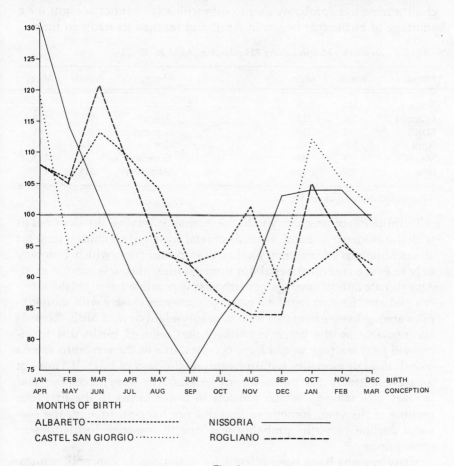

Fig. 4.

and mushroom and chestnut gathering in Albareto, the July/August vegetable crop in Castel San Giorgio, the late summer harvest in Rogliano. The pattern is most pronounced in Nissoria, where the monoculture of wheat resulted in a particularly concentrated harvest season.[34]

The birth rate among Nissoria's women was 22 percent lower between April and August than in the remainder of the year. One possible explanation for this seasonal decline is that, assuming for the moment that conceptions occurred about equally throughout the year, something caused an unusually large number of pregnancies to terminate prior to term during the dry season. But the available data suggest that this did not happen. Females of childbearing age did not die more frequently than males of the same ages, except in August, nor was the overall period April through August one of unusually high mortality for women (see table 4). An excess of August deaths among women of childbearing age (probably due to tuberculosis)[35] cannot account for a shortage of births that began in April and reached its nadir in June.

TABLE 4    Deaths by Month among 724 Nissorini Aged 20–45

| Month | Female | Male | Month | Female | Male |
|---|---|---|---|---|---|
| January | 110 | 115 | July | 85 | 90 |
| February | 103 | 121 | August | 160 | 118 |
| March | 92 | 115 | September | 103 | 96 |
| April | 100 | 71 | October | 107 | 100 |
| May | 74 | 49 | November | 82 | 112 |
| June | 67 | 80 | December | 114 | 133 |

NOTE.    Calculated as for fig. 2.

Termination of pregnancy with the woman surviving also does not fit with the evidence at hand. Records of fetal wastage (a technical term for all terminations of pregnancy other than parturition, which I employ only to evade controversies about prenatal life), of course, do not exist. An estimate of fetal wastage nevertheless is possible based on the modern pediatric finding that fetal wastage correlates closely with mortality rates among liveborn infants within twenty-eight days of birth. Records are available on the latter; it is likely that reduced births due to increased fetal wastage would have occurred one to three months after a month of high mortality within twenty-eight days of birth.[36] Times of greatest mortality for the newborn in Nissoria were December and January (see table 5), which projects to fewer births in the first four months of the year, something that did not happen. In sum, the seasonal decline in births probably was due to seasonal fluctuations in conceptions.

Many reasons have been offered for variations in conception rates:

TABLE 5   Deaths by Month among 824 Infants in Nissoria

| Month | Within 15 Days | 16–30 Days | | Month | Within 15 Days | 16–30 Days |
|---|---|---|---|---|---|---|
| January | 132 | 134 | | July | 118 | 122 |
| February | 118 | 120 | | August | 102 | 95 |
| March | 88 | 120 | | September | 125 | 120 |
| April | 72 | 82 | | October | 114 | 110 |
| May | 42 | 35 | | November | 76 | 73 |
| June | 56 | 54 | | December | 156 | 132 |

NOTE.   Calculated as for fig. 2 except that instead of using the actual number of deaths an adjustment has been made to reflect birth rate differentials by month.

parallel variations in marriage rates, fluctuations in frequency of intercourse, and changes in the probabilities of ovulation, fertilization, and implantation. These in turn may vary with climate, work and migration patterns, festivals, opportunities for privacy, discontinuation of lactation, and nutrition. A comparison of figures 3 and 4 reveals no parallels between seasonality of marriage and conception. Indeed, in the case of Nissoria a substantial portion of the September–November marriage time overlaps the period of fewer conceptions.

With regard to fluctuations in frequency of intercourse, even the theoretical underpinnings are ambiguous, and the evidence is necessarily circumstantial. Although some scientific studies report little or no relationship between increased frequency of intercourse and conception, common sense dictates acceptance of mathematical models showing that an increase in coitions in a given intermenstruum, say from five to twelve, results in an increased chance of conception, in this case from .16 to .20 or .32.[37] April and May in Nissoria, the months of most frequent conceptions, marked the end of the cool wet season. It was a time of fewer deaths; food supplies had not yet run out, and there was some slackening of the work pace, between weeding in March and reaping in June. It may have been a time with increased opportunities for privacy as children stayed longer out of doors. (One villager assured me that it was just the reverse; couples sought the privacy of open fields, now high with wheat and dried from the wet season.) The days after Easter, a time of rebirth, were a kind of season for celebrating nature, for the first fairs of the year, and for gossip about those suspected of being cuckolded. It may well have been a time not only when sexual banter increased but also when couples more frequently engaged in intercourse.

Circumstances during months of fewer conceptions, July–November, were far less conducive to conception. Obviously an excess of conceptions in the spring in itself reduced the number of pregnancies that might begin in the following months. Moreover, the pace of work was much harder in the summer; threshing in July was followed by the crowded and public gatherings of August (when, it may be recalled, even the *villici* came to the village, usually with no place to stay) and the *vendemmia* of the fall. High mortality in the July–September trimester, undoubtedly accompanied by increased morbidity generally, can only have decreased the frequency of sexual intercourse and the probabilities of ovulation, fertilization, and implantation. The same may be said for the aftereffects of malnutrition in the preharvest months and the high temperatures of July and August. All in all, it was a kind of time in which fewer children were conceived.

The contraceptive effects of breast feeding also contributed to seasonal variations in conception. A host of studies demonstrate that lactation and postpartum amenorrhea are related, something also known by villagers who made no scientific studies of the subject.[38] The relationship, however, is less than perfect; best estimates from controlled studies of individuals indicate that sixteen months' lactation yields an average of twelve months' amenorrhea. A shift from full to partial lactation (which customary practice in Nissoria encouraged even when the necessity of work did not require long periods of absence by the mother) doubles the probability of resumption of ovulation.[39] Weaning practices varied considerably in Nissoria, with the age of the child ranging from six to eighteen months. An infant of six months or more in the spring generally was at least partially weaned, due to greater availability of animal's milk and simultaneous shortage of foods to nourish the mother. A younger child would continue to be breast fed until the next spring, for a total of twelve to eighteen months. In short, despite considerable variation in practice, the customary time for reducing or ceasing lactation was spring. The consequent onset of ovulation is consonant with a rise in conceptions in May.

Another possible cause of seasonal variation in conceptions is that couples by some means tried to plan the births of their children. It is reasonable to assume that parents viewed the winter season as a more favorable time to give birth than the hot and busy summer. But this is an assumption, and one not supported by any local tradition or proverbial wisdom. If couples did choose to attempt to time the birth of an offspring, they had available two partially effective methods. One was *coitus interruptus* (now referred to locally as *marcia indietro*), which worked well whenever the practitioners had reason to expect it would. The other involved any of a number of vaginal washes and flushes, ranging from special herbs to wine vinegar; douching of this sort could have caused the levels of fluctuations in seasonal conception shown in figure 4. In sum, the Nissorini had at their disposal the means to limit births, albeit haphazardly, but evidence is lacking to show that they chose to do so.[40]

Reviewing briefly the less distinct patterns of the other three communities (see fig. 4), there appear to be no major inconsistencies with the Nissoria data. Conceptions peaked in June in the cooler mountain climates of Albareto and Rogliano, while in the Neapolitan plain town of Castel San Giorgio the zenith was a bit earlier, in April. Conceptions among Roglianesi were lowest in November and December, precisely the time when women were busiest with olive picking; while in Albareto a low point occurred in September, a month of mushroom gathering, *vendemmia*, and trips away from home to sell cheese and animals. Overall, seasonal fluctuations in conception among rural Italians occurred less because of conscious and specific planning (although the possibility cannot be eliminated entirely) than because lactation practices, work habits, celebration patterns, and nutrition combined to make spring a likely time for pregnancies to begin.

The cyclical passage of seasons involved changing kinds of time, times defined and shaped by the occurrence of events crucial to the lives of the rural folk of traditional Italy. Spring, a season of rebirth and festival, was a kind of time marked also by a peak in the inception of human life and by a relative paucity of deaths. It was a time of joy, a joy perhaps even more precious because it would not last. A reminder of the likelihood of ill fortune ahead came in the form of warnings against marriage in May. Threats of an evil day, sterility, adultery, and unanswered prayer were no light matters, especially as they affected the single most important and creative day of the *contadino*'s life. With the onset of summer came the expected but desperately unwanted time of death, especially of children. And in any year there was the added terror of not knowing how close to *la famiglia* the contagion would strike or how long it would rage. The community celebrated in August anyway, a defiant inversion of the spring pattern, and a promise that with the harvest over the village would survive; but only at the fall rains did death abate. Births and marriages now occurred in greater numbers, although weddings were suspended in November in communities that adopted the Catholic tradition of mourning institutionalized in the pre-Advent month. Midwinter, especially the Christmas season, saw another peak in births as the cycle begun the previous spring came full around.

## LINEAR TIME

In rural Italy the growth of a linear image of time took place only slowly and incompletely. The process involved interaction with urban centers which centuries earlier had begun to use calendars and clocks to measure time as a commodity. Additionally, a host of technological innovations lessened the force of natural seasonal fluctuations even among agriculturists. But along with these developments surely must be considered the impact of changes in the demographic patterns outlined earlier in this chapter. Among these the most significant is seasonal death, especially among children. Substantial improvement in child survival rates occurred in Italy (and in the Western world generally) toward the end of the nineteenth century. The improvement stemmed less from a technological breakthrough in any one area than from the convergence of several favorable and partially related factors: advances in medical knowledge of disease transmission, rising concern with public health, widespread pasturization of milk (which alone may have cut infant mortality from 150 per 1,000 to less than 100 per 1,000),[41] development of vaccination programs, and better nutrition due both to agricultural production increases and reduced population pressure resulting from emigration. Villagers did not perceive these factors as imposed from the outside. Knowledge of steps to improve public health, for example, appeared to come not from some distant program but from the local doctor or even the *mago*, who often displayed surprising flexibility in mixing incantations with sound advice on public health. Emigration, which in several ways improved the survival chances of those who remained, also appeared to the village to be an initiative act on its part. In short, rural Italians recognized improved health conditions and assigned to themselves a causal role in bringing about the change. Indeed, they came to believe that only the willful neglect of the central government prevented them from improving even more rapidly.[42] And just as the presence of widespread and unpredictable early death contributed mightily to fatalism, so also did better health pave the way for a belief in human agency.

Figure 5 portrays in five-year averages the course of mortality rates in the four communities since 1810. From these it is evident that the years 1830–90 constituted a long half-century of high mortality, with peaks occurring approximately thirty years apart at the beginning, middle, and end of the period. But it is also reasonable to visualize a full century of high mortality, extending to 1920 and punctuated by a deadly influenza epidemic in 1918; this is especially so for Castel San Giorgio. A "permanent" decline in mortality rates may be dated at 1885, as in Albareto, or 1890, as in Rogliano and Nissoria, or 1920, as in Castel San Giorgio.

Analysis of changing mortality rates, however, fails to capture fully the villagers' perception of death. In the summer of 1974, when we were actually copying out long rows of vital records in Nissoria, people often stopped by to ask why anyone would undertake such a dreary task in such an out-of-the-way place. (The mayor, an extremely astute politician, invariably intervened to explain that we had chosen his *comune* above all others in Sicily, just another sign of our wisdom and his power.) I drew a rough version of what is now figure 5 and used it to explain some of what we were up to. Several villagers rightly, I have come to believe, understood the calculations but dismissed "my" mortality rates as unrealistic. Their view was that, since everyone must die, the mortality rate is always 100 percent, sooner or later. This is the crucial point; a per annum (or, for that matter, per decade, century, or millennium) death rate is necessarily based on a linear image of time, and it is precisely this that the Nissorini dismiss as irrelevant. Their view of improved health, as usual a fundamentally correct understanding, was not that it could prevent death, thereby lowering a "meaningful" version of a mortality rate, but that it would extend the age to which people survived. They believed that the quantity of death (my calculations) was less important than its changing quality.

In order to portray, even if only partially, the demographic base for a changing perception of the quality of death, I have constructed figure 6. This figure begins with the villagers' assumption: everyone must die—the only question is when. The numbers at the left show the cumulative portion of deaths recorded in Nissoria at various ages. For example, among deaths in the 1780s, 7 percent came within sixteen days of birth, 12 percent within one month (therefore, by subtraction, 5 percent between sixteen days and one month), 29 percent within one

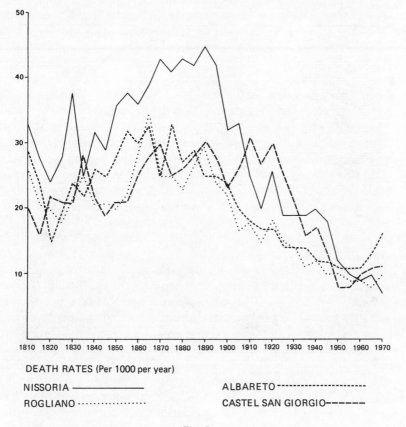

DEATH RATES (Per 1000 per year)

NISSORIA ——————                    ALBARETO ------------------

ROGLIANO ·················                    CASTEL SAN GIORGIO——————

Fig. 5.

year, 61 percent within six years, and so forth. Now a somewhat different picture emerges from that derived from figure 5. Perinatal mortality
(within one month), despite a peak in the 1880s, remained in the two
centuries until 1960 within a relatively narrow range, 7–16 percent of all
deaths. Infant deaths (age one to twelve months) show greater volatility
throughout: from a nineteenth-century low of 17 percent in the first
decade to an appallingly high 35 percent in the 1880s. In the first decade
of this century even this portion was exceeded, while between 1910 and
World War II the rate dropped to 13–18 percent, a level below most of
the nineteenth century but still high enough to make the first year of life
perilous. Death in childhood (ages one to nineteen years) also took a
high toll; as late as the 1890s, three-fourths of all deaths in Nissoria
meant the burial of someone under the age of twenty, 45 percent of
these occurring after infancy. Child deaths dropped substantially beginning in 1900, but only after 1950 did they constitute less than 5
percent of the total. Death also struck young adults and those in early

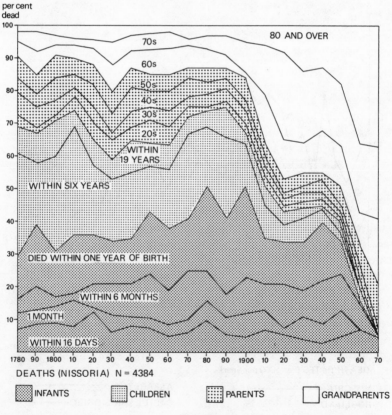

Fig 6.

middle age, the mothers and fathers of Nissoria. Burials involving people between the ages of twenty and fifty-nine declined from over 20 percent to nearly 10 percent during the nineteenth century as, throughout these years, death came just as often among villagers in their twenties and thirties as it did in the next two age groups. Survival chances between the ages of twenty and forty improved at the end of the nineteenth century but declined again between 1920 and 1950. The figures for people age sixty or older reveal greatly improved longevity beginning in 1900, a leveling off between 1920 and 1950, and then a rapid increase again until, in the early 1970s, nearly 60 percent of all deaths involved persons above the age of seventy, more than half of whom were over eighty.

Overall, the data portrayed in figure 6 permit the conclusion that a sense of fatalism, a sense that the future was beyond human control, was a realistic and functional cultural response to death. The quantity of death may have declined beginning in 1890 (although even this finding is irrelevant if we not only accept but also give primacy to the Nissorini's perception that the quantity of death is always equal to the population), but the quality of death, its unpredictable denial of the years a human being (the villagers would say "un cristiano") has a "right" to live, changed more slowly and unevenly. Perinatal mortality remains a problem; infant death by no means has been eradicated; child mortality reached low proportions only in the last two decades; the same is true among young adults. Barely one generation has watched its children grow without the constant and fearful expectation that 40 percent would die. Village elders still alert enough to convey their life memories were raised during a time when over seven of every ten burials involved a child. Nor was the experience of death better by very much in Albareto, Castel San Giorgio, and Rogliano (see table 6).

For rural Italy, then, the continuation of early and unpredictable death well into the present century served to reinforce both fatalism and a cyclical image of time. In part, the sharp seasonal fluctuations that characterized child mortality gave special nurture to a nonlinear perception of time. But even after summer peaking began to decline in the 1890s, the quality of death retained many of its older attributes. Villagers who all around them saw fate intervene to deny members of their families a full measure of time found incomprehensible and even absurd the notion that time was a commodity. For them time was not something they possessed or controlled; daily they faced the finiteness, discontinuity, and abrupt ending of time itself. A widow who spoke with me of "when my husband was alive" recalled not the passage of a certain number of years but a fundamentally different kind of time; she drew no causal and linear continuity between then and now. Only when death became a predictable event of one's old age did it prove meaning-

TABLE 6 Deaths Occurring at Different Ages, by Decade, in Albareto (A), Castel San Giorgio (C), and Rogliano (R) (%)

| | INFANCY | | | CHILDHOOD | | | AGE 20–59 | | | AGE 60 AND OVER | | |
|---|---|---|---|---|---|---|---|---|---|---|---|---|
| DECADE | A | C | R | A | C | R | A | C | R | A | C | R |
| 1810 | ... | 29 | 27 | ... | 13 | 16 | ... | 29 | 29 | ... | 29 | 28 |
| 1820 | ... | 37 | 31 | ... | 18 | 14 | ... | 22 | 28 | ... | 23 | 27 |
| 1830 | ... | 30 | 28 | ... | 14 | 22 | ... | 23 | 26 | ... | 33 | 24 |
| 1840 | ... | 33 | 26 | ... | 14 | 19 | ... | 22 | 29 | ... | 31 | 26 |
| 1850 | ... | 36 | 30 | ... | 15 | 21 | ... | 20 | 26 | ... | 29 | 23 |
| 1860 | ... | 40 | 25 | ... | 17 | 24 | ... | 19 | 27 | ... | 24 | 24 |
| 1870 | 40 | 28 | 23 | 16 | 21 | 23 | 22 | 14 | 25 | 22 | 37 | 29 |
| 1880 | 30 | 38 | 30 | 20 | 20 | 22 | 22 | 11 | 17 | 28 | 31 | 31 |
| 1890 | 33 | 40 | 31 | 16 | 14 | 16 | 20 | 15 | 17 | 31 | 31 | 36 |
| 1900 | 37 | 35 | 21 | 10 | 14 | 23 | 17 | 19 | 17 | 36 | 32 | 39 |
| 1910 | 28 | 20 | 19 | 17 | 18 | 16 | 23 | 30 | 25 | 32 | 32 | 40 |
| 1920 | 23 | 31 | 28 | 13 | 16 | 12 | 21 | 23 | 20 | 43 | 30 | 40 |
| 1930 | ... | 35 | 24 | ... | 10 | 13 | ... | 12 | 12 | ... | 43 | 51 |
| 1940 | 7 | 26 | 21 | 5 | 10 | 8 | 29 | 21 | 18 | 59 | 43 | 53 |
| 1950 | 5 | 22 | 12 | 2 | 2 | 4 | 18 | 21 | 17 | 75 | 55 | 67 |
| 1960 | 1 | 10 | 12 | 1 | 4 | 1 | 6 | 20 | 10 | 92 | 66 | 77 |
| 1970 | 0 | 2 | 9 | 0 | 3 | 2 | 19 | 19 | 14 | 81 | 76 | 75 |

ful to count ages carefully, to know not only how old one was but also how many years were "left," and therefore to avoid wasting time.

Thus far I have attempted to show that the demographic experience of rural Italians, at least until quite recently, certainly was congruent with and may well have nurtured both an attitude of fatalism and a perception of time as cyclical. The clearest demographic patterns are for Nissoria, a Sicilian village where most residents were peasants even by the strictest of definitions. The experiences of Albareto, Castel San Giorgio, and Rogliano, three rather diverse communities, confirm by the very differences in their particulars the general points raised about seasonality and the quality of birth, marriage, and death. Death did not come everywhere at the same time, but everywhere there was a time of death. Fatalism and a cyclical time image do not coexist in all rural cultures, although they do seem to prevail in the Mediterranean.[43] Indeed, the very regularity of seasonal cycles related to climate and agriculture implies an ability to forecast the future, to know that eventually the rains will come, that things will change. The relationship between cyclical time and fatalism in rural Italian culture is best characterized as symbiotic rather than causal, necessary, or hierarchical. Their symbiosis was rendered reinforcing by a mutual link to demographic experience. The predictable alternation of opposing pairs of kinds of time led not to plans but to prayers, not to resigned stupor but to defiant celebration, not to concerted offensives but to familial defenses, not to anthropomorphism but to supernaturalism.

In order to focus upon the long term, at least in the first three figures in this chapter, I ignored change over time. Now that the basic thesis is set forth, it is appropriate to examine briefly how seasonal concentration of births, marriages, and deaths varied by decade in each community between 1810 and 1973. Figure 7 portrays the data in terms of a plot of the "strength of seasonal concentration."[44] The numbers on the vertical axes should be interpreted as indices of relative magnitude. Consistent with earlier figures, the plots reveal that seasonal conception/birth cycles were far less concentrated than those associated with death. Strongest seasonal patterns occurred with regard to times of marriage; thus human intervention and action served not to attenuate or counteract the natural and less controllable birth/death basis of seasonality but, rather, to strengthen and expand the areas of life subject to a cyclical perception of time. Moreover, a closer examination of changes by decade shows no consistent trend away from a traditional and cyclical pattern toward a modern and linear one. That is, the strength of

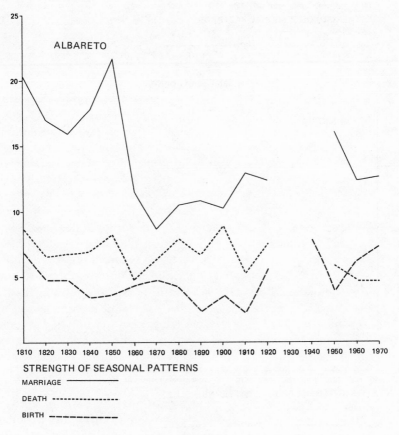

Fig. 7.
Albareto

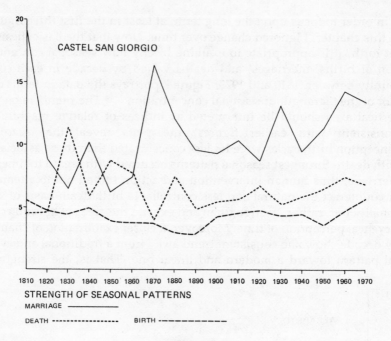

STRENGTH OF SEASONAL PATTERNS

MARRIAGE ————————

DEATH ·················· BIRTH ——————

Fig. 7.
Castel San Giorgio

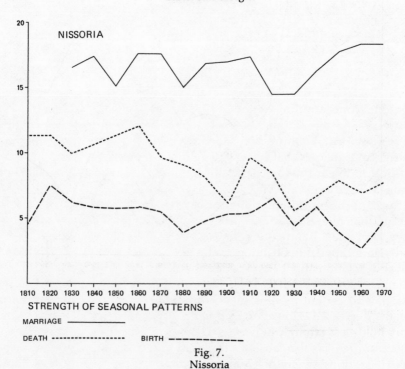

STRENGTH OF SEASONAL PATTERNS

MARRIAGE ————————

DEATH ·················· BIRTH ——————

Fig. 7.
Nissoria

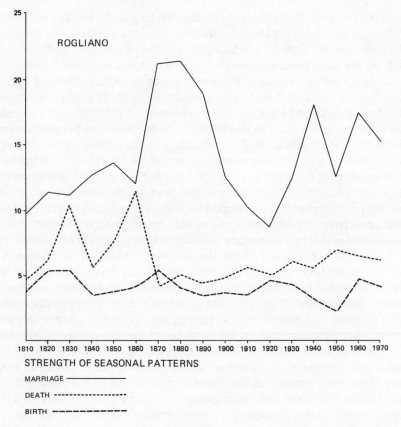

**Fig. 7.**
Rogliano

seasonal concentration, although it varies greatly among the four communities and across time, remains forceful even in the present day. If it is true that rural culture was functionally attuned to demographic experience, it follows that instead of a model of one great transition from cyclical to linear time, any transition must have been incomplete and, indeed, itself cyclical.

Perhaps the most important conclusion to be drawn from the graph is an obvious one: the various lines go in ambiguous and even contradictory directions. In any one community the seasonal strengths of births and deaths appear to be independent of each other, but there is a partial inverse relationship between death and marriage. Especially in Rogliano and Castel San Giorgio in the 1870s, the tendency to confine nuptials to certain months increased as the seasonal concentration of deaths decreased. However, in other places and decades this relationship holds less strongly or is even reversed. Consistency across different communities is also absent nearly as often as it is present. Any generalizations, therefore, must be made with qualifications and

treated as hypotheses subject to further testing and possible revision.
Enough of such caveats. Seasonality in births oscillates in forty- to
fifty-year cycles, four cycles being visible between 1810 and 1970. In
each of the four communities the 1810–30 period contains a peak, the
cause of which is probably the convergence of factors affecting spring
conceptions discussed earlier in connection with Nissoria. A second
but less pronounced peak is evident around the 1870s (except in Castel
San Giorgio) and a third in the 1920s. In both these decades postharvest
births increased substantially, indicating a rise in midwinter conceptions, probably due to the annual return of more and more migratory
workers during the slack season. (See chap. 8 for a fuller discussion of
these movements.) Finally there is the post–World War II peak, when
the return of laborers for an August vacation contributes to a rise in May
births and frequent elections in April/May bring emigrant workers home
to vote and result in a secondary peak of births in January and February.

The trend with regard to deaths is clearer: high levels of seasonal
concentration (say, an index number above 10) disappeared after the
1860s. Until that time, the clustering of deaths in the summer, especially
among infants and children, was greatest where temperatures were
most extreme and nutrition most inadequate (Nissoria). Better diet and
cooler weather meant that in the northern mountain village of Albareto
summer was never so fully experienced as a time of death. Between 1870
and 1910 or thereabout, the benefits of improving public health in rural
Italy attenuated somewhat the clustering of deaths in the summer; but
total health may have been worsening, and many children survived the
summer only to die of pulmonary infections in the cool and wet winter
months. During these decades the shifting of death's seasons from
summer to winter canceled each other out, thus creating the statistical
artifact that the strength of seasonal concentration decreased when in
reality it had become bipolar. Beginning in 1910–20 the reduction of
summer deaths reached a point sufficient to leave only winter as a time
of death. This pattern grew in strength as the proportion of deaths
occurring after the age of fifty-nine increased steadily. Older persons
always had died more frequently in the cold and wet months. But the
new pattern is less severe, not only in terms of a mathematical index
but, more importantly, because winter deaths now occur mostly among
people who are "expected" to die anyway after having lived a full life.

The timing of marriages reveals something quite different: greatest
seasonal concentration occurred at times of rapid and fundamental
societal change. In Albareto, for example, seasonality was strong during
the decade of Napoleon's downfall, when the town regained its communal rights under the Duchy of Parma; and again in the 1850s, when
the Albaretesi began in large numbers to migrate to the Ligurian coast,
Marseilles, Paris, and London, thus shattering the village's isolated
gathering economy; also during the decade of the Great War and again

in the 1950s, when Albareto entered another transitional phase, this time toward becoming a mountain resort for pensioners and summer tourists. In Rogliano the crisis of change occurred in the decade following the Risorgimento, as political power shifted to Cosenza and ultimately to Rome. The diminution of its bureaucratic functions, combined with the decline everywhere in the Western world of artisanal activities such as those practiced extensively in Rogliano, dealt a severe blow to this rural Calabrian town. On a lesser scale Castel San Giorgio underwent a transition at about the same time, due primarily to the inability of its local craftsmen to compete against goods imported under free trade agreements. Both towns experienced secondary transformations around the time of the Second World War, as Mussolini's war efforts spurred the economies of Cosenza and Naples to hire *pendolari* from Rogliano and Castel San Giorgio, respectively. These *pendolari*, essentially commuting workers, rode scheduled buses to the city where they worked for daily wages while retaining small landholdings or participating in the harvest at home. Full employment, previously unknown in either town, opened new possibilities, but fuller integration with urban culture may have been even more consequential. Most recently, the peak in the 1960s is congruent with the beginnings in the Mezzogiorno of the "new" economic miracle of Italy, one goal of which is to bring *modernità* to the southern countryside. The plot for Nissoria reveals seasonal nuptial peaks of less severity but greater duration, a pattern consistent with modes of change in this more isolated village. In sum, there is considerable congruence between decades of highly seasonal wedding dates and periods of rapid change and innovation.

Furthermore, the nature of villagers' perceptions about why they marry in one month rather than another suggests that seasonal concentration of marriage reflects a deliberate effort to lessen the impact of cultural penetration by outside forces. Recall the May taboos in Rogliano and Nissoria, which emerged only in recent decades and now have become totally effective. These arose not from the needs of a mechanized and technologically sophisticated society or from any official practice of church or state. Rather, ordinary rural folk maintain informal but powerful proscriptions linked solely and directly to supernaturalism. Peasants "know" as well as any social scientist that mules and donkeys have nothing to do with a husband's virility or a wife's adultery. Maybe there is not really an evil day lurking somewhere in May, and with all the changes going on in the church who can be sure that Saint Rita is still listening? But they enjoy their ways; their culture is not merely a pale and delayed imitation of what city folk do. In an analogous way, the avoidance of November nuptials, although superficially involving recognition of the official Catholic time of mourning, turns out not to be based on church rules at all. The priest would be glad to marry people in November, but young couples prefer to adhere to the advice of their families not to disturb or desecrate the dead (not merely the memory of the dead but the actual souls who may be in a position to intercede with a positive response to prayer) by celebrating in November.

In an important essay on symbolic representations of time, anthropologist Edmund Leach suggested that all aspects of human thinking about time derive from two basic experiences: (1) the repetition of natural phenomena and (2) the irreversibility of life change; this is to say, the nonlinear and linear modes discussed throughout the present chapter.[45] Leach's fundamental insight is his assertion of a link between the two which, as he points out, are not logically the same. Under the pressure of religious prejudice (or, according to the reader's preference, the psychological inability to deal with death), human beings attempt to deny a linear perception of time by equating or fusing it with an image of repetition. One of Leach's major concerns is to show that in many societies the repetitive image is pendular rather than cyclical, a distinction which in my judgment does not hold for rural Italy and is, in any event, less consequential than the basic division between nonlinear and linear. The linking, indeed the merging, of repetitive and irreversible time comes through the equating of death and birth, through the repudiation of death by the assertion of a new life to "replace" the deceased. Evidence of such linking is the practice of naming children after their grandparents; also suggestive is the doubled imagery of perceptions of kinds of time marked alternately by death/harvest and conception/sowing.

To Leach's insight about the demographic basis of a unified image of time must be added the impact of marriage. Apart from the dating of the event which, as demonstrated earlier, is highly subject to seasonal variation motivated by partially nonfunctional (at least in a strict economic sense) beliefs, marriage also involves a fusion of birth and death, repetition and irreversibility, beginning and ending, in the life of *la famiglia*. The end of active parenthood by one generation makes possible the birth of another, one that in a variety of ways may exhibit "solidarity" in opposition to the intervening parents.[46] The parents of the marrying couple simultaneously transfer control over their families' *onore*, placing it in new and uncertain hands. Moreover, the marriage serves to graft onto *la famiglia* a new set of persons, or at least to define them with additional and closer ties. The individual lives in irreversible time:

$$\text{birth} \rightarrow \text{marriage} \rightarrow \text{death}$$

but *la famiglia* is in its very essence cyclical—formation at marriage, expansion and growth, spin-off and death, formation at marriage. Its continuation involves a potentially endless series of fissions, units of temporal and spatial measurement setting off where and when it has been. But through fission is achieved fusion, and thereby the repetition of time itself.

# 5
# Family


Niétri Zecca semma chi da sempre, chi sa duman. . . .

Renato Zecca


In Albareto the Zecca family name has existed for centuries. It appears chiseled in marble on the municipal hall plaque commemorating those who died serving their country during the Great War and again among the civilian casualties in 1943. Although not so illustrious and prosperous as the Bosi family, the Zeccas are well regarded in the village as descendants of hard-working farmers holding modest parcels of land. Between 1820 and 1830 six *albaretesi* men named Zecca married and began families of their own. Here is what happened:

A. On November 22, 1824, Pellegro Zecca, a *contadino* aged sixty, took as his second wife Giacomina Opici, a thirty-nine-year-old *contadina* born in nearby Tombeto.

B. On February 22, 1825, Giuseppe Zecca, a *contadino* aged thirty-six, married Annunziata Orsi, a twenty-two-year-old native of Albareto. Her family was better off than his, especially through her mother, Maria Schiavetta, and she appears in the marriage register as a housewife, not a peasant.

C. On October 13, 1825, Domenico Zecca, a *contadino* aged twenty-four, married Rosa Tomaselli, a twenty-two-year-old *contadina* born in Albareto.

D. On October 24, 1825, Luigi Zecca, the twenty-four-year-old brother of Giuseppe (B above) married Maria Domenica Bottego, a twenty-two-year-old native of Albareto.

E. On April 29, 1828, Antonio Zecca, a twenty-four-year-old first cousin of Giuseppe (B above) and Luigi (D above), married Maria Caterina Maestri, a nineteen-year-old *contadina* from Albareto.

F. On November 20, 1830, Michele Angelo Zecca, a twenty-six-year-old *contadino*, married Giovanna Broglia, a twenty-two-year-old *contadina* from Tombeto.

Figure 8 summarizes the demographic history of these six marriages over the next four decades.[1] In the previous chapter I suggested that, despite very high mortality rates, rural Italians were not indifferent to death because for them every death threatened the family's continued existence. An alternative view, the one that I am questioning, is well expressed by François Lebrun in his study of seventeenth- and eighteenth-century Anjou. He concludes that people were resigned and at times indifferent to high mortality because of "le sentiment plus ou moins conscient de faire partie d'une lignée assurée de durer malgré le décès de tel ou tel de ses membres."[2] But among the six Zeccas, and I might have chosen any other of hundreds of names in Albareto or in southern Italy throughout the nineteenth century, the future was far from assured.

Pellegro married Giacomina (case A) when she was near the end of her childbearing years (and he was sixty), and perhaps they had little hope of raising a family. But the situation of the late-marrying female, though uncommon, was far from unique, as shown in table 7. As it turned out, Pellegro and Giacomina did have two children, a girl conceived in the third year of their marriage and a boy born four months after Pellegro's own death. The widow Giacomina, as was the custom in such circumstances, named the infant for her dead husband, but the boy was sickly from birth and died after five days.

TABLE 7   **Ages of Females at First Marriage (%)**

| Age Group | Albareto | Castel San Giorgio | Nissoria | Rogliano |
|---|---|---|---|---|
| Under 21 | 29 | 16 | 60 | 25 |
| 21–25 | 41 | 44 | 28 | 40 |
| 26–30 | 19 | 25 | 8 | 19 |
| 31–35 | 5 | 8 | 2 | 8 |
| 36–45 | 5 | 6 | 1 | 7 |
| Over 45 | 1 | 1 | 1 | 1 |
| N cases | 1,278 | 3,665 | 1,599 | 3,445 |

The situation of Giuseppe and Annunziata (case B) is perhaps more typical. Their first two sons died in infancy, and the third born cannot have brought them much hope. Angelo's military conscription record reveals that he was badly deformed from birth and could not walk; he never married. Their next two sons died in early childhood, and not until 1836, after eleven years of marriage, did Giuseppe and Annunziata have a healthy son, Francesco, who survived the perils of childhood. But he died young, a victim of typhoid at the age of twenty-seven. Two daughters also died before the age of two, leaving only Maria and Giuseppe among this couple's ten children. Both parents died before any grandchildren were born to continue the family name.

Domenico and Rosa (case C) lost four children (among nine live births) at very young ages, but Rosa's greatest tragedy was the death of

| (A) PELLEGRO & GIACOMINA | (B) GIUSEPPE & ANNUNZIATA | (C) DOMENICO & ROSA | (D) LUIGI & MARIA | (E) ANTONIO & MARIA | (F) MICHELE & GIOVANNA |
|---|---|---|---|---|---|
| | 4/29/1826 Marco<br>5/15/1826 Marco | 11/2/1826 Domenica | 8/8/1826 Marco | | |
| | | 2/5/1827 Domenica<br>12/6/1827 Giuseppe | | | |
| 3/9/1828 Maria | 3/28/1828 Antonio<br>9/2/1828 Antonio | | 6/6/1828 Antonio | | |
| | 9/29/1829 Angelo | | | 2/5/1829 Giovanna | |
| | | 3/19/1830 Luigi | 1/25/1830 Maria | | |
| 9/20/1831 PELLEGRO | | 11/7/1831 Luigi | 9/23/1831 Luigia | 9/12/1831 Caterina | 8/30/1831 Giovanni |
| 1/16/1832 Pellegro<br>1/21/1832 Pellegro | 7/25/1832 Luigi | 2/2/1832 Anna | 9/3/1832 Luigia | | |
| | 12/9/1833 Luigi | | 6/9/1833 Domenico | | |
| | 7/8/1834 Luigi | | 3/2/1834 Domenico | 10/6/1834 Luigia | 2/9/1834 Luigia<br>2/10/1834 Luigia |
| | | | 2/14/1835 Angela | | 1/4/1835 Luigi |
| | 5/29/1836 Francesco<br>11/13/1836 Luigi | | 11/9/1836 Angela | | |
| | | 5/1/1837 Andrea<br>5/12/1837 Andrea | 4/28/1837 Angelo | 1/22/1837 Luigia<br>5/3/1837 Luigi | 11/26/1837 xxxxx |
| | | 8/8/1838 Luigia | | | |
| | 5/9/1840 Maria<br>5/18/1840 Maria | | | 7/8/1840 Domenica | |
| | 4/9/1841 Domenica | 2/4/1841 Marianna | | | 7/6/1841 xxxxx |
| | | | 1/11/1842 Antonio<br>1/21/1842 Antonio | | 8/19/1842 Luigi |
| | 11/20/1843 Domenica | | 10/30/1843 Luigi | 10/14/1843 Celestina | |
| | 5/27/1845 Maria | 2/26/1845 Domenico | | | 2/3/1845 xxxxx |

4/27/1850 Maria=
Giovanni Tomaselli

1/22/1846 xxxxx
10/11/1848 Rosa
3/29/1849 Rosa

11/12/1846 Francesco

12/8/1850 Giuseppe

4/21/1849 Giovanna=
  Giuseppe Curà
11/4/1849 Veronica

9/6/1850 xxxxx
9/8/1850 GIOVANNA

1/28/1851 Francesco

11/4/1852 Francesco

11/20/1852 Giovanni

4/4/1854 DOMENICO
5/28/1854 Giuseppe

4/21/1855 Anna=
Giuseppe Bottego

12/2/1855 Maria=
Prospero Toscini

6/27/1857 Caterina=
  Giuseppe Delpippo
12/20/1857 Francesco

1/12/1858 GIUSEPPE

9/18/1858 Luigia=
Pietro Delpippo

11/29/1858 Marco=
  Rosa Bernieri (D1)
11/29/1858 Antonio=
  Maria Bernieri (D2)

10/14/1860 Domenica=
Francesco Curà

2/8/1860 Giuseppe (D1)
6/16/1860 Maria (D2)

6/4/1861 Francesco (D1)
6/22/1861 Francesco (D1)

1/30/1861 Luigi=
Maria Bernieri (E1)

4/16/1864 Francesco

10/7/1864 Marianna=
Marco Cacchioli

1/16/1864 xxxxx (D1)
11/6/1864 Marianna (D2)

2/18/1864 Marianna (E1)
4/9/1864 ANTONIO

2/24/1866 LUIGI

Fig. 8.
Six Zeccas

K E Y

Name: birth
Name: death
NAME: death of a parent
xxxxx: stillbirth
Name=Name: marriage

her husband and her eldest son in the spring of 1854. This left her with only one surviving son, nine-year-old Domenico; he probably died within the next decade (probably away from Albareto, as there is no death certificate for him), since his mother divided her property in 1865 among her three married daughters.

Luigi and Maria (case D) represent a somewhat more fortunate series of outcomes. Their two elder sons survived and were married in a double wedding ceremony to two sisters on November 29, 1858. Before that occasion, however, death had taken three of their children consecutively over a period of five years. Still, six children survived and one, Antonio, fathered three sons whose sons' sons' sons today play soccer in the schoolyard at Albareto.

Antonio and Maria (case E) also raised a son whose descendants remain in Albareto today. Four of Maria's daughters also survived and married, but two boys and a girl did not.

Michele and Giovanna (case F) were less fortunate. Both their sons died, one at the age of seven and another at twenty-one, when he hit his head on a rock while fishing in the Gotra and drowned. Giovanna was pregnant on at least five other occasions, but these resulted in four stillbirths and one daughter who died within hours. Giovanna herself died as a result of complications arising from her last stillbirth, and sometime thereafter her husband migrated from Albareto. Nothing survives in the village of this family.

Altogether, the six male Zecca marriages that occurred in the decade from 1820 to 1830 produced the following results: forty-eight term pregnancies yielding forty-three live births; of these eleven died in infancy, nine in childhood, and four in their twenties; thirteen survived to marry, one was a cripple, and on five there are no further records (which makes emigration likely). Now a variety of conclusions may be drawn from this summary profile, all of which might have statistical validity, of course assuming an adequate number of cases. The present data are not a large enough sample, but with the reader's indulgence, I wish to examine a bit further this portion of the Zecca family history before focusing upon the full data for all four communities. Interpretation of statistical results for the Zeccas alone, where one may see at the individual level what happened, should provide the framework for analysis of larger numbers.

The Zeccas replaced themselves (twelve marrying persons produced thirteen marrying persons) and may have contributed to an expanding population (if the five who probably emigrated are added to the thirteen who married). Three-fourths of live births survived the first year, and more than two-thirds of these reached the age of twenty. In an "average" family, consisting of eight or more children, the probability was that at least three would survive to adulthood. It is this sort of statistic that supports Lebrun's statement that the lineage would go on. But, as the Zecca example shows, within any statistical average may be concealed a great deal of variation: a decade of marriage after which no children survive, years of stillbirths, the death of a mature son, a widow left to raise young children, or too many survivors and a threat to the family's tenuous economic position. It is this variation, this uncertainty (despite the statistical averages), that made fatalism a realistic and functional attitude in traditional rural Italy.

The sharply differing outcomes of the six Zecca marriages summarized above illustrate well the rural folk view of *la famiglia:* it had continued endlessly, forming anew in generation after generation. From an individual's position looking backward into the past this indeed had to be the case, else the individual would not exist. One of the ironic and probably unintentional potential misrepresentations by social scientists of the societies we study is that invariably we diagram and analyze the family by beginning with some ancient paterfamilias and tracing his descendants over several generations, working as it were from then until now.[3] But the real people represented as triangles and circles in standard ideographic notation perceived family in precisely the opposite direction, that is, in terms of ancestors. From the vantage point of a present "I" the family's past was a cyclical series of births and marriages (death failing to break the cycle) extending back to some unknowable starting point through an unbroken male lineage. Thus, to make a small but crucial tense shift in Lebrun's conclusion, the present "I" is part of a lineage that, until now, has been assured. But this is no assurance that the family will continue into the future. Indeed, the positive view of the past, uncertainty about the present, and apprehension about the future characteristic of traditional rural Italy were strongly and continuously reinforced by the fear of failing to continue *la famiglia.* The present "I," knowing that his family had survived since time began, faced the burden of realizing that he alone, among all these ancestors, might be responsible for its demise. As we have seen, four of six Zeccas did not live to see any of their children marry.

Before turning to the full data, a brief digression may be in order to consider two important studies that differ significantly from this view of *la famiglia* as an endless process threatened by an abrupt ending. The first is Edward Banfield's *Moral Basis of a Backward Society,* wherein the author offers the hypothesis that in a southern Italian village people acted in accordance with the following rule: "Maximize the material, short-run advantage of the nuclear family; assume all others will do likewise."[4] Banfield concludes that behavior which might logically follow from adherence to this rule is evident and therefore that his hypothesis is correct. Thus the moral basis of this society is "amoral familism." In addition to having a penchant for choosing value-laden words in ways not justified by his data, Banfield falls into the logical fallacy of affirming the consequent.[5] The behavior he describes, even if it is accurately summarized, may arise from many possible hypotheses or a combination of several. For example, a negative view of participation in government to effect communal improvements, which according to Banfield arises from amoral familism, may equally well reflect a realistic assessment of government action vis-à-vis rural Italy. But my concern at present is less with the logical fallacies of Banfield's argument than with his use in the core of his hypothesis of the term "nuclear family."

The phrase is understandable enough in English as a technical term indicating parents and their children. It is, however, a jargon term, the nearest equivalent in popular usage being "immediate family." Even this phrase creates confusion and is susceptible of various interpretations and ambiguity about the inclusion of married children or offspring living under a separate roof. Although the term "immediate family" can be translated into Italian, it has little meaning. People prefer to use the vague word "famiglia" and, if more information is needed, to specify precise relationships: parents, siblings, children, and so forth. Even after only a few interviews, it became evident that the phrase "nuclear family" has no place in popular language for the very good reason that the concept it refers to is not a motivational reference point as such. People do act in terms of their relationships to parents, children, siblings, cousins, aunts, grandparents, and other members of la famiglia, but in varying ways. Often the "advantage" of a husband can be served only to the disadvantage of his children (in matters ranging from food allotments to land usage and emigration). How then does the wife/mother respond? Certainly not as an amoral nuclear familist. And even when the same action aids both husband and children, does it follow that the wife/mother's perception is that she is advancing her "nuclear" family? Without exception, studies of rural Italy assign a major role to la famiglia. It would seem useful, therefore, to employ the term in a way more congruent with the society's understanding of itself.

This brings me to the second study to which the following pages take at least partial exception, Peter Laslett's introductory essay in Household and Family in Past Time. Undoubtedly Laslett does an important service in bringing together a variety of conflicting usages in terminology by historians of the family, and there is much to be said for his plea that similar structures be called by similar names. The classification scheme he offers is internally consistent and would allow the tabulation of data for most families likely to be found in western Europe even without use of the residual "other multiple families" category.[6] Thus, two of the criteria for deciding to employ a related set of categories—mutual exclusivity and joint inclusivity—are met. But another criterion of equal importance is less fully realized, at least for application to rural Italy: utility for understanding how the subject under study operates or behaves. The shortcoming is due in part to the use of categories which, although reasonable in the abstract, are contrary to what rural Italian culture perceived. For example, Laslett classifies coresident siblings and coresident relatives of other kinds as two types within the category "No family." I suggest that this category might better be labeled P, Q, R, or S; anything but "No family," since all that we know of Italian society tells us that such persons do have a family. A sister who in 1972 emigrated from Rogliano to work in a German factory joined her brother there; she was allowed to go only because she thereby remained under the aegis of *la famiglia*. A spinster aunt who took in and raised her nephew when his parents died from cholera in 1866 certainly was part of a family. Other important types are ignored in Laslett's scheme. For example, a husband who remarried and raised under the same roof children from both marriages falls into the same category as a household involving only one marriage. Whether the distinction is important depends on the questions being asked, but for rural Italy it looms large in matters of inheritance, nutrition, migration, death rate, marital prospects, and in all likelihood familial tensions about which only hard evidence may be lacking.

A more fundamental difficulty in Laslett's scheme is that it is static when what it classifies is dynamic. This is the heart of the debate between Laslett and Lutz Berkner[7] over the stem family; it also partially explains the nonconforming terminology of several contributors to the Laslett collection.[8] Take the case of Rosa Tomaselli (the wife of Domenico Zecca in case C). Using Laslett's set of categories, her family structure, from her birth in 1803, was as follows:

married couple with child(ren) for sixteen years
widow with child(ren) for six years
married couple alone for thirteen months
married couple with child(ren) for three months
married couple alone for ten months
married couple with child(ren) for twenty-six years
widow with child(ren) for ten years
widowed solitary for two years
secondary unit DOWN for one year
secondary unit UP for four years

In her sixty-seven years in Albareto, Rosa's family structure (according to Laslett) changed ten times; a sufficiently large sample of people such as Rosa, preferably taken in different years, could tell us the typical household structure of her society and the frequency of less common types. But it would tell us very little about Rosa and her family. Indeed, the portion of different types that appeared according to Laslett's static scheme would be a function primarily of four factors: age at marriage, duration from marriage to first live birth, age-specific mortality rate, and inheritance practices (since the designation *capo famiglia* generally passed to the child only when the parent gave up ownership of his or her land). All these are important and have a decided impact upon family structure, but they are not family structure.[9]

Eugene Hammel, in an important contribution to the Laslett collection, deals with the *zadruga* (an extended or joint fraternal household once found with much frequency in Slavic societies) in a way that may serve to replace the overly static concepts of nuclear-, extended-, and mutiple-family types.

> What is most evident from all these data is that the zadruga is not a thing but a process. Separation of a process into snapshots of its behavior leads only to misinterpretation, and the computation of misleading indices, such as simple means of household size, frequency of division of households, or the size of the largest units.... The zadruga, as a process, is a set of rules operating within certain constraints that influence the rates at which persons are added to residential groups and that control the maximum size of these groups by introducing pressures for continued accretion or for division. The intensity of accretion is determined largely by demographic rates.

Hammel goes on to indicate a variety of pressures affecting the *zadruga* as process: soil fertility, land use, warfare, government intervention, outside opportunity, agricultural technique.[10]

Similarly, the family is a process, one that changes form over time within the constraints of demographic rates.[11] It varies from region to region as well, due to local ecology, regional opportunity, national policy, and even international economic developments. Family may be a strategy, a way of maximizing resources or of providing the bare requirements of nutrition. Family may be a vehicle to accumulation of wealth, retention of land, a job opportunity, or a chance to migrate. What one means by *la famiglia* varies with the context. A married woman in Albareto never forgets that the land she inherited from her mother belongs to *la famiglia*, which in this instance never includes her husband. At a wedding members of *la famiglia* include anyone with whom any kinship is believed to exist; the bride and groom introduce *each other's* families, aided by their parents, who may remember these matters more accurately. At the building of a house *la famiglia* includes those relatives who are willing to contribute their labor power or assist with the cooking. In a dispute over the furnishings left after a widowed mother's death, two daughters may curse their familial ties. Indeed, inheritance squabbles are a major factor in reducing the extent and import of *la famiglia*.[12]

Family as a process may be understood as a series of four spirals radiating outward from the present "I." One of these spirals connects the present "I" to his or her parents and through them to an endless past. Another spins out laterally to include siblings and then cousins; because these relationships are perceived as horizontal (rather than vertical through the parent or grandparent and then forward again to the sibling or cousin), they lack the endless quality of the parental connection. Lateral relationships begin at birth and end at death; they are relatively fragile, especially when strained by contests over benefits deriving from the parental connection. A third spiral is formed at marriage in a link to the spouse and thence to his or her family. From the perspective of the present "I" this connection is also temporary, lasting from marriage to death, and relationships with all members of the spouse's family are seen as lateral, with little regard for generations. Finally, there is the spiral extending from the present "I" to his or her children and possibly to their children. Alone among the four spiraled networks, this one remains to be forged, its extent to be determined, its fate to be made known. Alone among the four, its development may be aided or retarded by human action in the present. And if all goes well, death of the present "I" will mean the merging of the last spiral with the first; the endless will not be ended.[13]

(The reader will observe that the "nuclear or simple family" cuts across two and possibly three [to the degree that the present "I" perceives himself or herself to be part of the parental spiral] of the networks outlined here. It is for this reason that the phrase "nuclear family," in my judgment, lacks social reality and is not very useful in understanding rural Italy.)

Family as process means that these four spiraled networks do not exist in a static and hierarchical relationship with each other. In a contest against "outsiders," *la famiglia* easily embraces all four networks with little controversy. A foreman selecting laborers for olive picking in Rogliano gives work to all his relations before hiring any outsiders. But, more often, the needs and demands of members within *la famiglia* are in conflict, as in the years when the harvest is poor and there is not enough work to go around. Now the foreman must decide among members of his family; certainly he takes genetic distance into account, preferring a son to a brother to a cousin (but where will he place his wife's brother?), assuming other things are equal. But other things are not equal. The ability of the foreman's various kin to do the job well is a low-priority consideration; history and *onore* are not. The foreman's decision will be in terms of a pattern of reciprocal obligations, either in repayment of past favors or with an eye to future needs that may depend on another's good will. The future, however, is unpredictable, and the best gamble is to deal with kin who in the past have acted with *onore*. An important exception is a family member who lacks *interesse*, which is always the case with a relative who does not have children of his own (unless, for example, he is a priest who can influence the church to return the favor). People without a future, however uncertain it might be, have no *interesse* beyond the short run and therefore are untrustworthy. It is in this sense that Banfield's hypothesis about maximizing "the material, short-run advantage of the nuclear family" misses the point entirely by confusing means with ends. Particular decisions involving the short term are deeply linked through *onore* to the longest possible term, the endless cycle of *la famiglia*.

Consider the dilemma of a peasant family in Nissoria, perhaps around 1880, when epidemics took a high toll and three times in a decade *la lupa* ravaged the fava beans which were the main food source. Sickness, hunger, half a hectare or less of dry land, and no prospects for the future are the givens. A way out appears when a labor boss for the sulfur mines in Piazza Armerina stops by in the village and offers work for boys small enough to hunch along the narrow stairs and long corridors leading to the surface but strong enough to shoulder a sack weighing twenty kilos or more. The pay is not bad—85 centesimi at the least and as much as 1.25 lire for the very agile—although there will be deductions for food, medical care, and spillage. In order to show good faith, the labor boss (*partitante*) offers the child's family a *soccorso morto* (prepaid death benefit) of 80–150 lire, not enough to buy land but enough to feed a family until the next harvest. If the child dies, the family keeps the premium; if not, he gets to repay the *soccorso morto* by monthly deductions from wages. An 1866 law disallowed work in the mines for children under the age of ten, but the effort touched only those few who could have passed the twenty-kilo test at that age. In 1880 about 2,500 children worked in the mines within forty kilometers of Nissoria. For them and for their families any hypothesis that includes notions about maximizing anything is ludicrous, unless one accepts the mine owners' contention that prepayment against death was intended to assure good treatment.[14]

Precisely how the family as process operates depends on a variety of factors. Again it is useful to recall Hammel's analysis of the *zadruga*. As with that process, the family is shaped primarily by demographic rates. These rates, however, operate within and are at least partially determined by the pressures and constraints of ecological realities, political intervention, economic and technological developments, and cultural norms. All these have varied in the course of the past two centuries. Central to the model of family here outlined is marriage, the act by which a present "I" acquires a network of kin through the spouse and establishes the right of procreation.

## AGE AT MARRIAGE

Statistics on age at marriage are more easily calculated than explained; unfortunately, despite the range of factors reflected in nuptial ages, some researchers have stressed only the most obvious consequence of delayed marriage—lower fertility. If instead one begins by examining causes of variation in marriage age, the statistic appears to be more complex, involving a lengthy series of possibilities and reflecting upon a variety of issues related to a history of the family as process. In brief outline form these are (1) *economic*—economic structure, degree of occupational mobility, land tenure patterns, premiums placed on acquisition of wealth or education, and the tendency to migrate in search of work all affect the age at which people wish to marry and raise children; (2) *political*—military conscription requirements and especially long service during armed conflicts cause variations in nuptial ages, as do parental consent laws; (3) *social and cultural*—rigidity of class lines (which partially controls the size of the pool of potential partners), strictness in following norms such as siblings marrying in age order (especially among sisters), narrowness of "acceptable" age differences between spouses, frequency of premarital intercourse, conception control practices, modes for choosing partners, and geographic mobility all work to increase or decrease mean nuptial ages; and (4) *demographic*—mortality and birth rates not only define how may potential partners of varying ages are available but also establish what couples may expect in the future.

All these factors may be reflected in varying degrees in the data summarized in figure 9, which portrays mean ages of men and women marrying for the first time in all four communities by decade since 1810. Nuptial ages increased during the first half of the nineteenth century in Castel San Giorgio and Rogliano, although in the latter the rise was a decade later and substantially steeper, at least for males. There followed (after 1860) a steady decline toward a nadir fifty years later; the past half century has witnessed an increase in marriage ages (although not so great as the nineteenth-century peak) which ended in Castel San Giorgio after World War II and in Rogliano may now be over.[15] Despite its incompleteness, the graph for Albareto shows some consistency with Rogliano and Castel San Giorgio patterns, the exceptions being a peak in the 1870s (not 1860s) and a sharp temporary fluctuation during the Great War. Nissoria presents a very different situation: a small and gradual decrease in male ages and a slight increase in those of females over the entire period. The general trend, then, with Nissoria as the significant exception, was for marriage ages to increase during the period 1810–20 to 1860–70, then drop steadily until 1910–20, and then

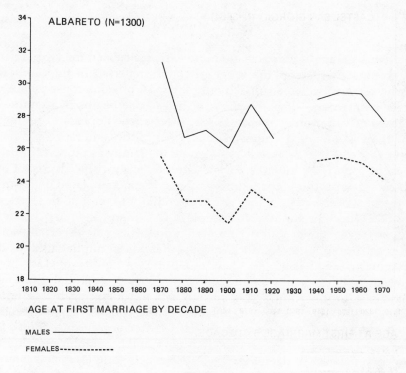

AGE AT FIRST MARRIAGE BY DECADE

MALES —————————

FEMALES ------------

Fig. 9.
Albareto

increase again until recently. Male and female nuptial ages usually moved in parallel fashion.

Before we proceed further, a note of caution is in order against exclusive consideration of mean age. This statistic tells us nothing about the spread of actual marriage ages about the mean. For example, figure 9 shows an increase in mean nuptial age for Rogliano females between the 1810s and 1820s from 23.6 to 24.2, a trend that appears to continue for several decades thereafter. A closer breakdown, however, reveals that the increase in the 1820s was due entirely to a jump in the number of women in Rogliano age forty or more who married for the first time; the portion of marriages involving females under age twenty actually increased during the 1820s from 17 percent in the previous decade to 25 percent. In both decades 65 percent of first marriages involved women under the age of twenty-five, a figure that dropped significantly only in the next decades, to 50 percent in the 1830s and 42 percent in the 1860s. Much of the analysis that follows is based not only on fluctuations in mean age but also on variation about arithmetic means. These the reader will find summarized by age group in appendix C.

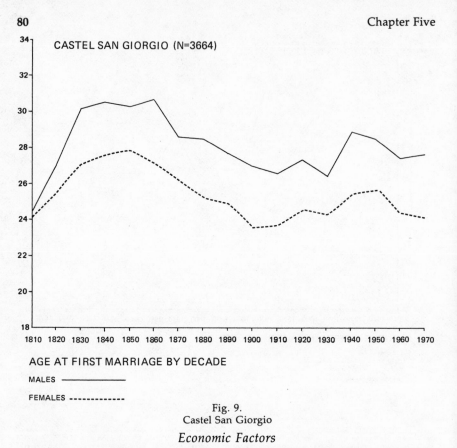

CASTEL SAN GIORGIO (N=3664)

AGE AT FIRST MARRIAGE BY DECADE

MALES ————————

FEMALES ------------

Fig. 9.
Castel San Giorgio

### Economic Factors

Table 8 sets forth data on the relationship between age at marriage and groom's occupation.[16] In all four communities landowning sons married two to three years later than did *contadini*. Generally, the more land involved, the older the groom at marriage; in Rogliano, for example, eleven *civili* (town elites such as the Ricciulli family, whose income derived from the leasing of very large holdings) married at a mean age of 35.6. This delay in marriage, however, cannot have stemmed from a desire to limit offspring and thereby avoid excessive subdivision of holdings because, as table 8 shows, the brides of propertied men were no older than the wives of peasants.

The apparent exception in Rogliano, upon closer examination, lends further support to the conclusion that delayed marriage did not result from an effort to reduce fertility. Among 111 marriages involving substantial landowners in Rogliano there are several among first cousins in the Ricciulli, Morelli, and Clausi families in which the bride was much older than the groom. In the most extreme case, a fifteen-year-old boy married his fifty-one-year-old first cousin in 1820 in order to assure that her inheritance (as the only surviving daughter) would not revert in part to her dead mother's nephews. The arrangement worked; the bride

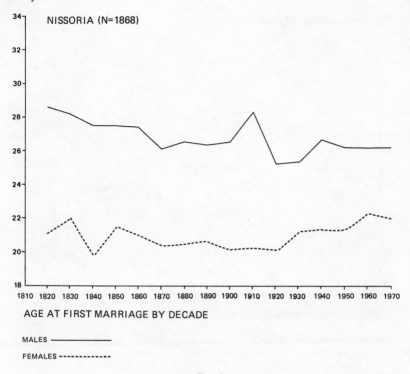

Fig. 9.
Nissoria

died, albeit twenty-one years later, and since the couple obviously had no children, her husband gained full control of the family's lands, which had originally belonged to their mutual grandfather on their

TABLE 8  **Occupation and Age at Marriage**

| Occupation | Albareto | Castel San Giorgio | Nissoria | Rogliano |
|---|---|---|---|---|
| Largeholders | 29.3 (23.1) | 30.5 (26.7) | 29.4 (20.9) | 30.7 (27.1) |
| Rural, middling | ...[a] | 30.1 (23.8) | ...[a] | 28.4 (27.3) |
| Peasants | 27.7 (23.5) | 28.3 (26.0) | 26.4 (20.9) | 27.4 (24.6) |
| Town, skilled | 28.2 (23.7) | 27.5 (24.4) | 26.0 (21.1) | 27.8 (24.0) |
| Town, less skilled | 30.3 (25.3) | 27.6 (24.7) | 27.3 (20.1) | 27.2 (23.1) |
| Town, unskilled | 30.6 (26.7) | 28.1 (25.0) | 24.2 (19.3) | 26.7 (24.1) |
| Lower service | 30.3 (24.4) | 29.2 (25.3) | 31.2 (21.8) | 27.8 (24.6) |
| Upper service | 29.9 (24.6) | 30.7 (25.9) | 29.3 (24.9) | 29.6 (25.3) |
| Business | 30.4 (26.5) | 28.8 (25.3) | 28.6 (22.1) | 30.2 (23.9) |
| Professional | 30.6 (25.1) | 30.1 (26.1) | 25.9 (22.5) | 29.1 (25.0) |
| N cases | 1,225 | 3,562 | 1,712 | 3,337 |

NOTE.  Mean male ages followed in parentheses by mean ages of brides according to their husbands' occupations.
[a]Too few cases for meaningful results.

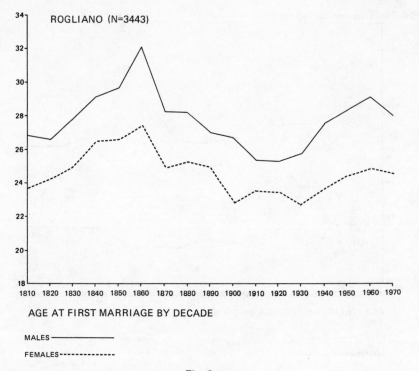

Fig. 9.
Rogliano

fathers' sides. In figure 10, *E* is the fifty-one-year-old bride, and her land, which came through *C* from *A*, would have been divided partially among *I*'s and *J*'s heirs had she not married her fifteen-year-old cousin

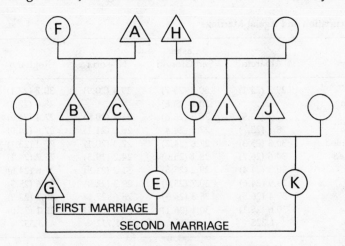

Fig. 10.
Preserving an inheritance

(G). After his first wife's death finally gave him title to all that A had once held, G did remarry, this time to a daughter of J (against whom the first wedding had been directed). The difference is that J's daughter (K) did not stand to gain rights to A's property unless G died without heirs. It turned out that fate denied all these efforts by A, B, and G, since G did die without heirs, causing his property to pass to J's daughter. As this case illustrates, the problem of no heirs was even more serious than that of having too many and, given prevailing mortality rates, hardly less likely.

Delayed nuptials among landowners stemmed not from a desire to limit future offspring but, rather, from difficulty in finding a suitable match. Although propertied men married women from a wider geographic area than did the landless, their pool of potential spouses remained small. Unlike a marriage involving no land, wherein the main considerations were the families' respective *onore*, the propertied also had to calculate an income assessment. Thus it was rigidity of class divisions and a high ratio of landless to landed (see the next chapter) that reduced the marriageable pool of this class and forced its male members to marry later, with greater age differentials between partners and with more volatile variation about mean nuptial age.[17]

In some documents grooms in rural situations listed themselves as distinct from peasants but not as landowners. Many of these designations are clear, as in the case of a miller or a labor gang foreman, but others merely indicate that the husband possessed a mule or a cart available for hire. Undoubtedly some persons who described themselves by the general term *contadino* also owned a cart and were willing to hire out. Nevertheless, it is significant that those individuals who apparently perceived themselves in one way or another to be distinct married at a later age than did men listed as *contadini* or in terms clearly indicating landlessness. Reasons for the delay appear to be similar to factors causing later nuptials among propertied males even though the wealth at stake was less.

Men whose occupations kept them in the town or village center rather than the fields (*cittadini* as opposed to *contadini*)[18] display a marriage age pattern related to the nature of work in each community. In Albareto, where craftsmen produced only for local consumption, the percentage of persons engaged in nonagricultural jobs always was small (333 of 1,225 overall).[19] Space in the village center was limited, and the small absolute number of residences there made turnover of living quarters unpredictable. In a farm situation, on the other hand, scattered houses and surrounding buildings more easily accommodated a flexible number of people. Moreover, a farm couple could plant vegetables, raise fowl, hunt for game, and in a variety of ways provide for their needs as well at the age of twenty-five as at thirty. For *cittadini* the costs of starting a household and maintaining it were greater. Figures in table 8 for Albareto support the conclusion that space limitations and the need for greater savings and cash income caused *cittadini* to marry later than *contadini*. Skilled workers and upper-service employees earned higher wages and therefore married sooner than lower-paid unspecified laborers and secure but poorly remunerated lower-service workers such as postmen, train conductors, and doorkeepers. The cost-of-living squeeze was particularly severe for unskilled men; often their wives also worked for wages, and apparently these men had to choose women closer to their own age who therefore had had more years to acquire savings. Owners of businesses and professionals were among the last to marry in Albareto, presumably because of the efforts they expended on furthering their careers.

In Nissoria also less than one-third of its work force was not directly engaged in agriculture (485 of 1,672 overall), but unlike Albareto, even farm workers clustered into the village center; this made the difficulties of finding a place to live about the same for the poor of Nissoria regardless of specific occupation. The low figure for unskilled laborers (24.2) is technically correct but possibly misleading in the present context. Among 108 such cases, 98 marriages occurred after 1950; at that time formerly underemployed farm laborers in Nissoria, who gained nothing from the supposed land reform of 1951, declared themselves to be unemployed *manovali* (day laborers) in an effort to qualify for recruitment to the factories of Milan and Turin and later to migrate to Australia and Germany. These men did indeed marry at an early age, either choosing a partner before moving to places where familial honor could be scrutinized less easily or else returning even by the age of twenty-four with relatively substantial savings as a result of several years' work at the higher northern wages paid to the unskilled. Service employees and less skilled workers married later than did peasants due, as in Albareto, to higher costs involved in maintaining a family. Skilled men apparently reached this income level a bit sooner. For businessmen and professionals, the Nissoria pattern varies from the other three communities; not only were such men younger than elsewhere (which was true of all Nissorini as well), but more important, these men married rather early relative to other occupational groupings. Professionals, and like every Sicilian town Nissoria produced its lawyers, married early despite extended years necessarily devoted to higher education. One factor promoting marriage at a younger age was that men who went away to school (to Palermo, Catania, or even Naples) circulated among a wide network of elites and met a greater number of potential partners. The other factor is that in Nissoria only the sons of the very wealthiest families had any chance to become professionals (whereas elsewhere this was only usually the case), and these sons hardly had to worry about the expense of starting a household. Entering business and commerce, although less restricted to the upper class, was very uncommon among *contadini*.[20]

In Rogliano, where more than one-third (1,253 of 3,337) of all marriages involved men not engaged directly in agriculture, and in Castel San Giorgio, where the corresponding figure was 2,116 of 3,562, the marriage data are ambiguous. Differentials among various categories are small, especially since skill distribution and the upper/lower–service division are partly a reflection of age. (For example, a twenty-six-year-old "less skilled" bricklayer's helper may become a twenty-eight-year-old bricklayer, or a *carabiniere* may be promoted after a time to *maresciallo*.) This still leaves the unskilled of Castel San Giorgio marrying late, an indication of their inability to begin and maintain a household on low and irregular wages. As in Albareto, business and professional men tended to wed at around the age of thirty.

It is evident that differences in occupation, probable earnings, and likely expenditures necessary to establish and maintain a household caused variations in the ages at which people married. Further detail on how this relationship changed over time may be drawn from the selected groups summarized by decade in table 9. For landholders the table shows a highly volatile pattern, with decennial trends (prior to 1920) toward earlier or later marriages by one sex not matched by the other. For all other groups the marriage-age figures fluctuate congruently, with a relatively constant difference of about three years between husband and wife. The general salience of customarily preferred age differences gave way among landholders to a greater concern for property equality. That is, a spouse of the "wrong" age was likely to be acceptable if his or her family provided a suitable income or settlement. The small absolute number of potential partners of equivalent wealth added to the tendency to match with what was available without too much regard for age. In sum, property holders, although freed from immediate pressures of fluctuations in the economy so severe as to threaten their ability to start a household, delayed or hastened their marriages by as much as five years on average from decade to decade, due in part to the vagaries inevitable in having only a small pool of possible spouses.

Figures for less skilled nonagricultural workers also reveal substantial decennial variations.[21] Here we are dealing with people who indeed struggled merely to survive and for whom the costs of establishing a household, necessitated by pressure upon scarce living quarters in the town's center, loomed large. In Castel San Giorgio these laborers worked either with pick and shovel in the local quarries or at odd jobs generated by local craftsmen and agricultural marketing operations. In bad times they were the first to be underemployed and forced to accept

TABLE 9.   Age at Marriage and Occupation by Decade

| Decade | Rogliano Peasants | Substantial Landowners[a] | CASTEL SAN GEORGIO Town Skilled | Town Less Skilled |
|---|---|---|---|---|
| 1810 | 26.2 (23.6) | 25.2 (23.7) | 25.1 (23.7) | 23.8 (21.7) |
| 1820 | 26.5 (23.9) | 26.0 (23.6) | 26.3 (24.6) | 25.5 (24.0) |
| 1830 | 28.8 (25.8) | 30.6 (23.8) | 29.1 (24.9) | 30.4 (24.8) |
| 1840 | 29.3 (26.9) | 30.3 (22.5) | 28.2 (25.8) | 29.8 (27.3) |
| 1850 | 29.5 (25.7) | 32.0 (27.3) | 27.8 (25.8) | 26.4 (25.0) |
| 1860 | 31.0 (27.4) | 31.5 (23.7) | 29.3 (25.7) | 28.8 (26.4) |
| 1870 | 27.7 (25.0) | 30.7 (26.7) | 28.6 (25.3) | 27.1 (25.7) |
| 1880 | 28.0 (25.3) | 30.4 (24.6) | 28.3 (23.9) | 29.7 (26.7) |
| 1890 | 26.6 (24.8) | 29.9 (23.1) | 27.4 (24.7) | 32.3 (25.8) |
| 1900 | 26.4 (22.8) | 27.5 (23.4) | 26.8 (24.1) | 25.6 (22.6) |
| 1910 | 25.5 (22.5) | 32.3 (25.3) | 28.0 (23.5) | 24.7 (24.8) |
| 1920 | 25.2 (23.6) | 28.0 (27.6) | 27.7 (25.0) | 27.7 (24.2) |
| 1930 | 25.0 (23.6) | 32.8 (30.3) | 25.9 (24.0) | 26.7 (27.3) |
| 1940 | 27.7 (24.0) | 32.6 (26.4) | 28.8 (25.2) | 31.5 (25.2) |
| 1950 | 26.8 (23.6) | 27.8 (21.0) | 27.5 (24.8) | 29.3 (25.8) |
| 1960 | 29.3 (25.0) | 28.7 (21.6) | 27.0 (23.6) | 27.2 (24.9) |
| 1970 | 26.9 (22.5) | 31.2 (26.0) | 27.4 (23.2) | 25.7 (22.0) |
| N cases | 1,701 | 335 | 1,406 | 269 |

NOTE.   Mean male ages followed in parentheses by mean ages of brides according to their husbands' occupations.

[a]The substantial landowners category merges data from all four communities not because propertied elites behave similarly regardless of where they are located (although if this can be said of any class it is most likely true of the rural landed) but in order to amass a sufficient number of cases to establish a statistically significant decennial pattern.

lower real wages. Their vulnerability was reflected in marriage delays that sometimes coincided with those of better paid and more secure workers but were usually much sharper. The advance in the 1890s to a mean nuptial age above thirty-two, a rise unique to this group, was due largely to the closing at this time of mining operations around Castel San Giorgio. Only in the next decade did emigration, whether to nearby Naples or distant New York, allow casual workers sufficient potential savings to marry at an earlier age. But migration possibilities, and the openings available to those who stayed when so many left, decreased in the 1920s, and only after 1950 did the expansion of industry in northern Italy once again offer better opportunities and a corresponding fall in nuptial ages.

With regard to better paid and more secure workers (to use Hobsbawm's term "labor aristocracy" would convey far too much pay and security)[22] table 9 shows a remarkably stable series of oscillations ranging since 1820 from 26 to 29 for men and from 23 to 26 for women. This group shared the general advance in marriage age in the first half of the nineteenth century, but only to a lesser degree the decline apparent among agriculturists after the 1860s and until the 1930s. The most probable explanation for the departure from the *contadini* pattern is that costs of starting a household prevented male nuptial ages among townsmen from falling below a threshold of about twenty-six.[23]

Among Rogliano's *contadini*, it is noteworthy that advances in marriage age occurred primarily in two periods: 1820–60, when increasing population density,abolition of "feudal" rights for gathering and pasturing, and gradual mechanization of agricultural tasks all combined to worsen the peasantry's lot;[24] and 1940–60, when war and then hopelessly inadequate efforts at land reform caused farmers employing traditional methods on poor soil to abandon the effort altogether and leave their fields idle or to the machinery of the Cassa per il Mezzogiorno. Declining marriage ages, on the other hand, occurred when large-scale migration began to reduce chronic underemployment for those who stayed on the land. The nineteenth-century rise and fall in nuptial ages does not correlate precisely with changes in mortality (see chap. 4) or natality (see fig. 12 following), an indication that considerations of family size were neither the cause nor the major consequence of fluctuations in marriage age.

### Political Factors

Another cause of variation in nuptial age may be government intervention through such devices as military conscription, war, and minimum legal ages for marriage with and without parental consent. In the nineteenth century the minimum legal age for marriage was eighteen for males and fifteen for females. Only the king (or his representative) "without violating the principles of puberty and virility" could allow dispensations lowering these minima to fourteen and twelve, respectively.[25] Under the new civil code promulgated by Mussolini, the standard minima became sixteen and fourteen.[26] Another nineteenth-century regulation required consent by both parents in the case of a male under the age of twenty-five; but, "if the parents disagree, the consent of the father is sufficient." The legal justification for allowing under-age marriage with a father's consent over a mother's objection reflects one of the essences of *la famiglia:* "After a formal refusal by the mother, if the refusal were justified, with difficulty the father would have the courage to consent to a marriage that would constitute a lifetime of unhappiness for his son and permanent discord in his family."[27] However, the law allowed a son age twenty-one or more legal redress against paternal opposition to his marriage. Below this age no appeal was possible, and apparently the threat of taking a familial dispute before strangers was sufficient to induce fathers to grant consent at age twenty-one.[28]

These regulations, along with the requirement that fathers personally register their children's births, indicate close congruence between the civil code and a perception of *la famiglia* as an endless process of procreation, primarily from father to son. The law reflected not merely male dominance, although of course this is evident, but also the position of the father as ultimately *responsible* for the family's perpetuation. The portion of marriages by males under twenty-one was small but not trivial: 2.8 percent in Castel San Giorgio, 3.3 percent in Albareto, 6.0 percent in Rogliano, and 8.6 percent in Nissoria. Peaks occurred between 1810 and 1830 and again in Rogliano and Nissoria between 1890–1910 and 1950–70 (see app. C for portions under age twenty by decade).

It is not possible to conclude with certainty how much the law reduced the number of marriages by men under age twenty-one, but the extremely low percentages recorded over several decades, for example in Nissoria between 1840 and 1900, surely leave open the possibility that fathers sometimes withheld their consent when they could and, more probably, avoided situations conducive to their sons' desire to marry at a very early age. If in fact fathers withheld consent, one would expect a sharp increase in marriages at age twenty-one relative to those at twenty, an increase above the normal curve of more marriages at later ages. For all first marriages in three communities between 1840 and 1900, the relevant data are summarized in table 10. Notwithstanding the

TABLE 10   **Male Ages at First Marriage, 1840–1900**

|          | CASTEL SAN GIORGIO | | NISSORIA | | ROGLIANO | |
| AGE | N | % Change | N | % Change | N | % Change |
| --- | --- | --- | --- | --- | --- | --- |
| Under 20 | 16 | ... | 14 | ... | 26 | ... |
| 20 | 18 | 13 | 20 | 43 | 30 | 15 |
| 21 | 42 | 133 | 70 | 250 | 66 | 120 |
| 22 | 76 | 81 | 102 | 46 | 104 | 58 |
| 23 | 104 | 37 | 136 | 33 | 110 | 6 |
| 24 | 166 | 60 | 166 | 22 | 196 | 78 |
| 25 | 114 | –31 | 110 | –33 | 158 | –19 |
| 26 | 122 | 7 | 114 | 4 | 184 | 16 |
| 27 | 140 | 15 | 126 | 11 | 152 | –17 |
| 28 | 148 | 6 | 86 | –32 | 106 | –30 |
| 29 | 172 | 16 | 66 | –23 | 126 | 19 |
| 30 | 126 | –27 | 52 | –21 | 90 | –29 |

caveat against comparing percentage changes where the absolute numbers are different, the age of partial independence from parental consent does appear to have been a critical turning point in male nuptial ages in the last half of the nineteenth century. In all these communities age twenty-one stands out as a time when men married in much greater numbers, an increase without parallels at other ages. Data for females reveal little tendency toward such a uniform exceptional age,[29] lending further support to the hypothesis that the clustering of nuptials by twenty-one-year-old males reflected the impact of parental consent requirements. Especially for the period after 1840, when male nuptial ages declined in these communities (see fig. 9), it seems likely that legislation requiring parental approval for marriages by males under the age of twenty-one worked to prevent overall mean male ages at marriage from decreasing yet further.

The impact of war upon marriage ages is somewhat obscured in figure 9 by the decennial format. During World War I, for example, the absence of males in their twenties obviously altered nuptial patterns. However, the major consequence of this absence was a sharp reduction in the number of marriages rather than a basic shift of long-term consequence in the age at which men wed. From 1915 through 1918 in Nissoria only 30 men married for the first time (compared with 74 and 136 in the preceding and following four years), doing so at a mean age of 28.5. Figures for the other three communities also show that the drop in marriages during the war, while severe, was temporary and caused no consistent alteration in mean nuptial age.[30] Military conscription in nonwar years involved men at an age when marriage was infrequent anyway, and it is not possible to measure statistically the distinct impact of such service upon nuptial ages.

*Social and Cultural Factors*

The curves in figure 9 suggest that modes of choosing a life partner are a particularly significant element in determining marital ages. Choice based either on parental decision alone or that of the marrying couple alone contributed to earlier marriages, whereas during periods of difficult transition from familial to individual choice, nuptial ages increased. Although evidence on these modes cannot be quantified easily and fully, available lore suggests that in the more isolated village of Nissoria parents until recently played a direct and primary role in arranging marriages.

Nearly one in every ten Nissoria weddings involved a girl of fifteen or younger, the husbands of these brides being, on average, eleven years older. Given the Nissorini's rigid chaperoning practices (even today single women of any age avoid being seen in public in the sole company of an unrelated male), it is unlikely that such young girls chose their marriage partners. Villagers tell of former days when husbands returned from the fields to find their fourteen- or fifteen-year-old brides playing children's games in the piazza and forgetting to cook supper. Nor were these child brides pregnant as frequently as females who married at later ages, at least in earlier times. Between 1826 and 1865 there occurred in Nissoria a total of 102 marriages by females under the age of sixteen, but only 14 live births to this age group. There followed 30 births at age sixteen, 25 at seventeen, and 70 at age eighteen, indicating that many child brides may have remained anovulatory for a least two years after marriage. Married women under the age of sixteen gave birth only one-eighth as often as did married women between the ages of sixteen and twenty. Clearly most child brides did not marry in order to legitimize a pregnancy.[31]

But parental involvement in marriage decisions was considerable, no matter what the bride's age. Nissorini did not perceive of children as individuals who grew through stages and adolescence into gradual maturity. Rather, the transition to adulthood and responsibility was swift, sudden, and total; it took place at marriage. Nissorini still refer to unmarried men and women as *giovanotti* and *giavanotte* even when these "youngsters" are in their twenties and thirties, but a married person of any age always is referred to as *l'uomo* or *la donna*. A youth did not prepare for adulthood by learning the ways of his or her parents, by beginning to participate in familial decisions, or even by accumulating savings or a *corredo* (which was the responsibility of parents). Only after a partner had been chosen did courtship formally begin, but more often than not the flirting had started, though not irrevocably, years earlier. Perpetuation of *la famiglia* belonged to the father, and he seldom left this duty to the caprices of romantic love. Instead, a father of *onore* built and maintained a network of reciprocal obligations, favors more readily accepted when linked to calculated *interesse*. Choosing spouses for one's children was a universally understood *interesse*, furthered over years and even generations according to one's means. Even *braccianti*, who literally had only the labor power of their arms, assessed a potential spouse's family for evidence of sexual purity, industriousness, common sense, resourcefulness, and good health. From among families felt to offer a desirable potential match, the father singled out one or two for particular attention: a special courtesy, a helping hand in repairing a cart, an inquiry after a sick brother, a word of praise for the cleverness of their children (always first speaking of a sibling not intended as a marriage prospect). Most mothers participated actively, although without final authority, in the courtship, but professional or "outside" matchmakers were never entrusted with a task deemed so crucial to *la famiglia*. From those in a position to do more, more was expected. Thus began, or perhaps continued from prior generations, the cultivation of mutual *interesse* that, without need for many words or prolonged and formal negotiation, would result years later in an announcement that the two families would be linked through marriage of their children. In an ironic way, the courtship began only when it had ended. The forces of passion and romantic love appeared in Sicilian lore in their traditional form, as threats to the happiness and perpetuation of *la famiglia*, not as a basis for marriage.

As long as romantic love and individualism remained apart from the question of nuptial choice, Nissoria's marriage patterns were stable; men in their late twenties married women younger by nearly a decade or more, the match being arranged by the couple's parents with an eye to extending the *interesse* of *la famiglia* while preserving existing social relationships. But beginning about two generations ago (fig. 9 places the change at 1920), the Nissorini gradually allowed individuals a greater role in choosing their life partners. In part they had to do so; single men who migrated to Chicago or Buenos Aires, despite the many who returned to marry local girls selected by their fathers, inevitably came to act as *uomini*, not *giovanotti*, men who chose their own wives, men who had earned more in one year than their fathers in ten. The independence and individuality of returning emigrants reinforced ideas that were making headway for other reasons. Improving communication and greater integration into a regional, national, and ultimately international economy and society led the Nissorini to adapt traditional values in the light of changing reality. I tried to show in the previous chapter how villagers gradually accepted the universal Catholic practice of celebrating November in honor of the dead while retaining traditional attitudes about the spiritual powers of their ancestors. Analogously, the Nissorini slowly incorporated romantic love into their ways of arranging marriages. At first this meant only that parents sought the acquiescence of their children, even allowing children a "right of refusal" in nuptial choices. This led to an allowance of greater opportunity to meet and judge prospective spouses, although not much greater. In urban areas the evening *passeggiata* provided one such opportunity, but rural folk lacked the time and finery for regular strolling. Young single people in Nissoria generally attended the 10 A.M. Sunday mass and afterward, for about two hours before dinner, lingered in the piazza or at the *caffè*. Here, under the watchful eyes of their fathers (their mothers having returned home to prepare the family meal), they began to choose a possible spouse. But the fathers saw all, and directly in the case of sons or through wives in dealing with daughters, family heads expressed their approval or disapproval, channeling the whims of young love into a desirable union. Late Sunday afternoon was also a time of public assembly, but unlike the after-church social hours, *la famiglia* walked, talked, and ate *arancini* as a unit. This provided the father with a further chance to express his intentions with regard to his children's marital choices by casually spending more and more time inquiring after the health and prospects of a particular family. Other villagers observed these passing conversations, and soon all knew that a wedding would be announced.

Young people in Nissoria today believe that this is still the best way to choose a life partner, although in practice it is giving way to less controlled situations as adolescents travel daily away from the village to school or work in neighboring towns. Generational conflicts tend not to be severe in Nissoria; marriage choice based on the mutual consent of parents and children, *la famiglia* and the individual, works well with relatively little tension. Seduction, elopement, forced marriage, and loss of *onore* are colorful but rare. The basis for harmonious, mutual-consent nuptial choices was expressed well in the previously quoted legal justification for paternal consent to underage marriage. The Nissorini simply do not believe that parents would act against the interests of their children or in ways that would create permanent unhappiness, nor does a child allow a relationship to grow deep if it causes anguish to *la famiglia*. Parents and children make their wishes known quickly and clearly, before the bonds between them can be severely tested by a strong commitment to someone who remains, for the moment at least, an outsider. Figure 9 reflects the successful union of old and new ways in that age curves for Nissoria show only a smooth and gradual shift toward advancing marriage ages for women and the opposite for men. A girl needed the additional years to decide on a husband whom she loved as an individual and whom her family also accepted and honored. Reduction in average age differences, from six or seven years to three or four, appears to be a function both of a greater role for romantic love and of a subtle shift in familial relationships. Although a husband remains the unquestioned head of his household, there has been some tendency in recent decades for spouses to treat each other more nearly as partners (however unequal) than as father figure and helpless child.

In the more integrated towns of Castel San Giorgio and Rogliano, the shift in marital choice from family to individual and from *interesse* to *amore* took place a century earlier and, according to local lore, with a great deal of tension. These towns were larger, containing several churches, squares, and cafes where young people might meet, away from the eyes of their parents. In Rogliano several young men played the guitar or mandolin professionally, and single people regularly gathered to dance. Inevitably, attachments developed of which parents were unaware until long after their children had begun to think of marriage. When parents approved the choice, all was happy, and the marriage took place after a formal engagement lasting only six months or less (to minimize the danger of premarital motherhood). But parents often did not approve. Too many wandering strangers passed through Castel San Giorgio on their way to Naples or through Rogliano along the main southern interior route, people whose families' *onore* could not be known through several generations of close proximity. Both towns had relatively diversified economies, thereby increasing the chance of falling in love with someone of unequal station. When parents in Rogliano did not approve, they consulted a *mago* who, once convinced of the justness of the parents' opposition, prepared two special mixtures to be rubbed by the parents into their child's clothing or, preferably, to be applied directly to the skin. One mixture made the child irritable and unpleasant in the company of a prospective spouse, whereas the other produced charm, grace, and kindness. Then it was only a matter of applying the appropriate ointment, and the child would fall out of love with the unwanted suitor and in love with someone more to the parents' liking. Sometimes this worked but other times not, due not to ineffectiveness of the potions but, according to *mago* and client alike, because parents applied the wrong medicines. Then anything might happen, including an elopment by the couple now under the powers of the *mago*'s herbs and incantations.[32]

Other parents took more practical steps to thwart unacceptable choices by their children. One mother locked her son in a storage room and told his would-be fiancée he had left for America. Only after a week did this mother let the young man out, wrongly assuming that the girl had "gypsy blood" and had by then moved on. Parents with a bit more money in fact sent sons to America to cure them of ill-chosen love and daughters to become domestics under the eye of an aunt who happened to live in some other town.[33] Sending one or both young lovers away was far safer than continued parental opposition which left the children in town. While some children yielded to their parents' wishes, some daughters chose to become pregnant (or merely claimed pregnancy). This immediately transformed all former opponents into insistent supporters of marriage at the earliest moment. However, parents remained hostile to the young couple (with the father of higher station refusing to supply a wedding settlement of land or, in the case of a townsman, money or furniture) until the birth of a first child. Then, in a highly structured ritual of forgiveness, parents came forth with the support denied earlier but now justified because procreation had been assured. The links between in-laws, and in certain cases even between parent and child, were primarily through the grandchild. In essence, a woman who continued to be unacceptable as a daughter-in-law nevertheless found a place in *la famiglia* as a grandchild's mother. And a father deeded land not to his son but to the father of his grandson.[34]

One consequence of tension between *la famiglia* and the individual over the right to make nuptial choices was an increase in mean marital ages, especially among males but also among females. From the data in figure 9 and in appendix C the transition from *interesse* to *amore* may be dated between 1830 and 1860, a time when nuptial ages advanced sharply. Thus in this important sphere of human activity a decline in the force and scope of traditional values appears a half-century earlier than data on mortality alone (from the preceding chapter) would seem to indicate. Note, however, that the earlier transition appears only in the integrated and economically diversified towns of Rogliano and Castel San Giorgio; it is absent from the isolated monocultural village of Nissoria. This diversity by geographic locale and divergence in dates depending upon whether primary focus is on nuptiality or mortality (later I shall add other phenomena) does not mean that the data are hopelessly contradictory or overly ambiguous. Rather, despite the historian's penchant for getting the dates correct, it may be considered more important to employ "traditional" and "modern" as concepts that are related but not opposite. Modern and traditional elements coexist in the same society at any given point, and it is the process of interaction among these elements that is crucial, not an inevitably arbitrary tally of which group is dominant. Thus in the case of nuptiality in Rogliano there is an element of modernity in the transition from familial nuptial choice to individual decision, but much that is traditional remains: use of magic in attempting to break an unwanted liaison; resort to a violation of *onore* in order to assure marriage; ritual celebration of procreation as the means of reconnecting *la famiglia;* renaming and rethinking about disliked in-laws in terms of this new procreativity. Tradition plays a forceful and creative role in times of change.

Clearly related to modes of marital choice is the question of age difference among spouses. In general, age is a significant determinant of status in rural societies, especially among persons of similar occupation or class.[35] Deference to those older than oneself is not reserved only for persons of another generation but extends even to relatively short durations, as that between two brothers or two cousins. The older person is deemed more experienced and therefore wiser. (It is noteworthy that rural rolk who have no need to be precise about their ages in years nonetheless know unfailingly their age rank relative to persons with whom they interact.) To a limited but not insignificant degree the status which accrues to age cuts across sex lines, such that men treat older women differently from those younger than themselves. In the particular case of married partners the husband's domination may be lessened if his wife is of the same age and especially if she is older.

Figure 11 displays data on age differences between spouses in all four communities by decade beginning in 1810. Among the three for which complete data exist, the towns of Rogliano and Castel San Giorgio show similar patterns; these differ substantially from the Sicilian village of Nissoria. Among the Nissorini, who shifted slowly and at a late date to marital choice based on the individual and romantic love and whose economy was undiversified, with an overwhelming number of land-poor peasants, the proportion of nuptials involving older females was small, generally half or less of Rogliano and Castel San Giorgio. Female

villagers (at least those who are not substantially older than their husbands) give two reasons for marriage by a younger man to an older
woman: (1) the nuptial arrangement gave primacy to matters of inheritance; or (2) the older woman was pregnant. Earlier I cited an extreme
case of age differentiation in Rogliano which arose from property considerations. The extreme case, however, points to a general statistical
pattern. Between 1810 and 1869 male property holders appeared in 63 of
979 Rogliano marriages (6.4 percent) overall, but in the 126 nuptials
involving females five years or more older than their spouses, the
landed appeared 17 times (13.5 percent). Among the remainder, 31 percent were townsmen not directly engaged in agriculture, a figure nearly
one-third above their representation in the overall marrying population
for these decades. In sum, landowners and to a lesser degree shopkeepers, artisans, and town officials were far more likely to marry women
older than themselves than were agricultural workers.

A follow-up of this total of 979 marriages reveals that in 87 cases the
couple appeared within 200 days as parents in a birth register entry, but
fully half of these (45 to be precise) involved the 126 couples in which
the wife was at least five years older than her husband. Obviously this

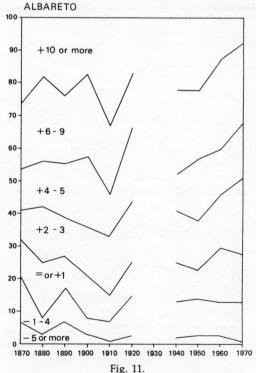

Fig. 11.
Age difference at first marriage, Albareto

measure is imperfect; birth within 200 days after marriage is a certain indication only of a lower-bound estimate of premarital intercourse. Moreover, it is difficult to measure accurately the number of brides who may have suffered a miscarriage or moved to another town, the latter being a strong possibility in the cases of husbands resident elsewhere. Notwithstanding these shortcomings, the figures do yield an estimate of relative magnitude: 36 percent of brides at least five years older than their husbands must have been pregnant when they married; for all other brides the corresponding figure is only 5 percent. Actual levels of premarital conception can only have been higher, but it is probable that the seven to one ratio is about right.

The perception among my interviewees, then, is consonant with statistical findings. Older women marrying younger men tended to be propertied or pregnant. (A most quotable interviewee termed them "piene—o con il denaro o di un bambino.") In either case such a marriage lessened the husband's standing, at home and in the community. At the very least, his wife had the status of greater age. In some cases she also had property, from which la famiglia might profit but which he did not control fully. In other instances she quickly assumed the role of

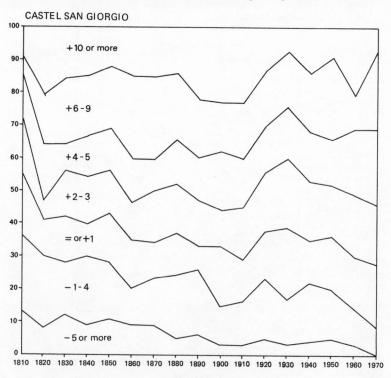

Fig. 11.
Castel San Giorgio

mother and acquired the respect accorded to successful procreation. Her husband's standing, indeed his *onore*, suffered on several counts. Perhaps he was a mere *giovanotto* whose father had arranged the wedding with more concern for property than for his son's wishes. Or perhaps he was an *innocente* in the wily ways of more mature women, one of whom had used her sexual charms to seduce him. With *un uomo* it was supposed to be the other way around. Would his wife be satisfied later on with a boy she had lured so easily? If not, she had demonstrated already what she would do about it. Even after all the gossip had died down the husband tended to find himself in relationships through his wife (for example, to her brothers, brothers-in-law, and cousins) with men who were substantially older than he and to whom he had to act with deference. His wife's interaction with his female relatives tended to be exactly the opposite. In short, marriage to an older woman undermined in a variety of ways the *onore* of the husband and his position as unquestioned head of *la famiglia*.

Nuptials involving husbands substantially older than their wives were more frequent and had an opposite though less sever set of consequences. Rather than counteracting perceived ideals about familial

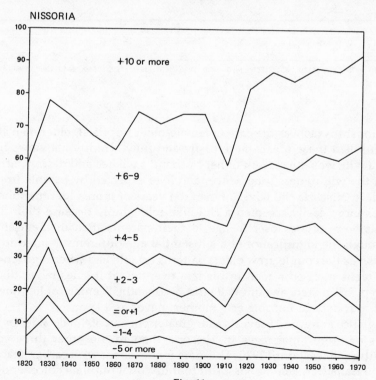

Fig. 11.
Nissoria

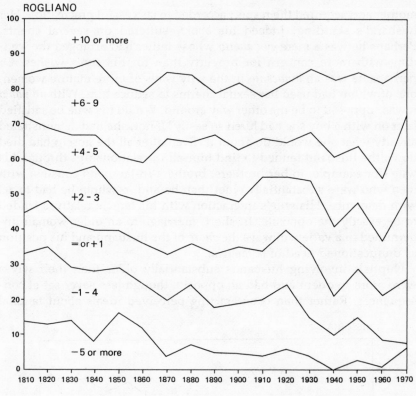

Fig. 11.
Rogliano

relationships (as was the case in female-older nuptials), older men simply fulfilled these ideals more easily and fully. Traditional views held
that a wife was the servant of her husband's wishes and desires, acting
with the willingness, obedience, and love expected by parents from a
child. In Nissoria the wives of men ten years or more older than themselves more easily accepted a childlike role simply because their husbands were often closer in age to their parents than to themselves.
Although the significance of a substantial age difference tended to diminish as the couple grew older, patterns established when a girl in her
mid-teens married a man in his late twenties or thirties never disappeared. Ultimately a young wife did become the "center" of her household, but only in her role as a mother, never as a spouse.

A glance at figure 11 reveals a far greater portion of "male older by ten
years or more" marriages in Nissoria than in the other three communities, at least until 1920. This date is consistent with earlier analysis
of the transition among Nissorini to individual nuptial choice, and the
two phenomena undoubtedly are related. When young men and
women gathered in the piazza on Sunday after mass and began to seek

potential spouses their attentions fell on people relatively close to their own ages. The "peer group" formed in the public square recognized far more fully than their parents the importance of age differentiation, and a woman allowed to participate in choosing her husband was less likely to accept a situation that threatened to reduce her again to a childlike position. She avoided both the immature man younger than herself and the one so old he reminded her of her father. In Castel San Giorgio and Rogliano, where individual marital choice emerged much earlier and was facilitated by the diversity of town life, women not only married later (see fig. 9) but also chose partners closer to themselves in age.

A summary of findings on age differentiation must concede that overlapping and partially countervailing trends make it impossible to "prove" the hypotheses suggested by the data summarized in figure 11. Nevertheless, several tendencies or probabilities do emerge. "Male older by ten years or more" nuptials are more frequent in a village with little economic diversity and in which age is therefore a significant determinant of status for all but a handful of substantial landowners; these male-older nuptials reinforce the husband's role as unrestricted head of the household and father figure even to his wife. Marriages in which the female is older occur more often in towns with complex and diversified economies, where romantic love and individual choice compete with parental decision as the basis of nuptial choice, where mean marriage age for females is higher, and where meeting opportunities among single people are less closely chaperoned. Such marriages result in a threat to the husband's *onore* in the community and to his dominance within *la famiglia*. There is a sharp decline in female-older marriages and a significant reduction in nuptials with the male substantially older where marital choice is individualized and romanticized and where peer groups (which make careful age distinctions) have wide scope. The result is marriages in which husbands and wives begin life together more nearly as partners.

### Demographic Factors

The ages at which females marry may affect the number of children they bear. In societies in which nonmarital births are a small proportion of total births, in which no steps are taken to end fertility prior to menopause, in which fluctuations in mean female nuptial ages fall within the fecund years, and in which fetal wastage does not increase significantly with the lowering of the female's age at conception, it follows that earlier marriage leads to higher birth rates. Whether such increased birth rates result in population growth depends on the mortality rate and on emigration. In the towns of Castel San Giorgio and Rogliano mean female ages at first marriage (see fig. 9) increased by nearly four years between 1810 and midcentury, declined by four years over the next five decades, then rose moderately in the twentieth century. For Nissoria the nineteenth-century fluctuations were much less; if data for the 1830s and 1840s are averaged, the century as a whole to 1920 shows only a slight decrease in female marital ages. The contrast in marriage-age patterns between the village of Nissoria and the towns of Castel San Giorgio and Rogliano is important in judging the implications of the data summarized in fig. 12.

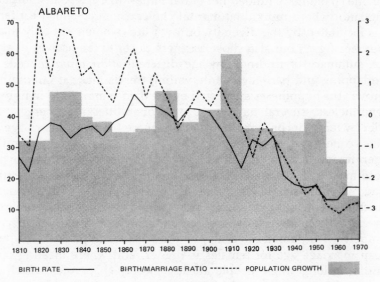

Fig. 12.
Birth rate, birth/marriage ratio, and population growth, Albareto

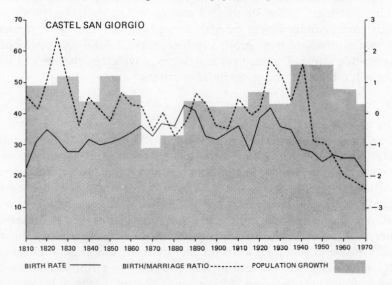

Fig. 12.
Castel San Giorgio

Figure 12 portrays for each of the four communities three distinct but partially related demographic characteristics: (1) the crude birth rate—the number of live births per 1,000 persons per year, shown in five-year averages; (2) the birth-to-marriage ratio (BMR)—the number of live births divided by the number of first marriages, shown in five-year averages at a scale equal to one-tenth of the birth rate; for example,

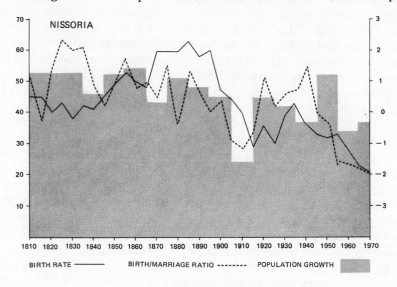

Fig. 12.
Nissoria

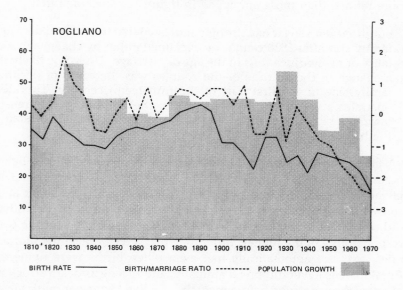

Fig. 12.
Rogliano

the number 50 on the left vertical axis of figure 12 signifies a birth rate of 50 per 1,000 per year and a BMR of 5.0, or five births per marriage; (3) population growth—the annual percentage growth in total population between one census and another, shown as a bar graph with rates in percentages along the right vertical axis.

Birth rates rose, except in Nissoria, from the end of the Napoleonic era for about a decade. There is no clear explanation for this increase, and I suspect that it may be no more than a statistical artifact resulting from improved enforcement of birth registration procedures, since the very earliest figures seem a bit low. In any event, from the late 1820s to the 1850s birth rates increased in Castel San Giorgio and Rogliano; at the same time, it may be recalled, female nuptial ages increased, the opposite of what one should expect. Beginning about midcentury and continuing to 1890 or so, birth rates rose everywhere; but the increase was sharper in Nissoria, where female nuptial ages changed only slightly, than in Castel San Giorgio and Rogliano. Although the direction of change between 1850 and 1890 (nuptial ages going down and birth rate going up) fits the hypothesis that the former allowed or caused the latter, the magnitude involved is too great for the shift to have depended on marital ages alone. The same may be said for the twentieth-century pattern: birth rates declined more precipitously than can be accounted for by the increase in marriage age.

All these negative findings lead to a positive conclusion worth introducing now, even before additional evidence is presented. In his study of general trends in Italian fertility, Livi-Bacci, using techniques far more refined than those employed in figure 12, concluded that

> our discussion so far has strongly indicated that the evident decline of family size after 1820 cannot be explained either by changes in mortality or by modifications in the age of marriage. Thus, it is likely that a change in the attitude of the couples was the cause of declining family size in the first part of the [nineteeth] century. This demonstrates also that the computation of the number of children per marriage radically changes the picture of fertility trends offered by the birth rate series.[36]

"A change in the attitude of the couples" is precisely what I believe occurred as well in Albareto, Castel San Giorgio, Nissoria, and Rogliano. Rural Italians did not shrug helplessly and hopelessly at the consequences of changes in the birth rate; within limits they could and did control family size. Insuring that the family would continue was a responsibility of the highest order, one that, given prevailing mortality rates, was not automatically met even when births were numerous. Rural Italians never did breed annually, and as long as death struck two of every three persons before maturity, six live births per marriage did not constitute a Malthusian menace. In the nineteenth century rising birth rates did not result in rapid population growth until mortality declined, at which point rural Italians turned to emigration as a way to lessen the contest against scarce resources at the local level (to be considered in chap. 8).

The BMR plotted in figure 12 is not a direct measure of family size (which could be calculated only after complete family reconstitution), but it is a very useful index of net fertility in a local community since it includes, quite properly for this purpose, the consequences of mortality and of emigration among married persons. A ratio of five or more births to each marriage is a good yardstick against which to measure fertility in rural societies. E. A. Wrigley's data, for example, show that this level was exceeded only between 1660 and 1710 in Colyton (from a total time span of 1550 to 1830); other findings are quite similar, yielding ratios generally between four and five.[37] By this standard the following periods were times of high fertility: Nissoria, 1821–45, 1856–60, 1876–80, 1886–90, 1921–25, and 1941–45; Albareto, 1821–50, 1861–70, and 1876–80; Rogliano, 1826–30; Castel San Giorgio, 1826–35, 1926–35, and 1941–45. Times of low fertility (BMR below 4) were Nissoria, 1816–20, 1881–85, 1906–19, and 1955–73; Albareto, 1811–20, 1886–90, and 1916–73; Rogliano, 1816–20, 1841–50, 1861–65, 1871–75, 1916–25, 1931–35, and 1941–73; Castel San Giorgio, 1836–40, 1851–55, 1871–90, 1901–10, and 1946–73. Comparison of times of high or low fertility reveals a sharp distinction between the villages of Albareto and Nissoria on the one hand and the towns of Castel San Giorgio and Rogliano on the other. In the more isolated villages, high fertility (BMR above 5) was characteristic of the years until 1880, broken only by the disruptions of war or the cycle of another generation reaching maturity and marrying. But in the integrated and economically more diversified towns of Rogliano and Castel San Giorgio, such high fertility was extremely unusual; indeed, years of low fertility were quite common. Albareto's birth rate for the years 1811–80 was higher (36.3) than Rogliano's (33.9) and Castel San Giorgio's (31.8), despite the fact that its marriage rate was lower (7.07 compared with 8.0 and 7.56, respectively). Albareto's lower nuptial rate resulted from higher rates of emigration by young unmarried adults (see chap. 8); but the fertility of those who remained was high (BMR = 5.13 compared with 4.24 for Rogliano and 4.20 for Castel San Giorgio). In Nissoria, where emigration rates were probably low, birth (47.1) and marriage (8.66) rates were higher than elsewhere (as was its BMR, 5.44 for 1811–80). These findings suggest that fertility was lower in town than in the countryside, especially in towns more fully integrated in regional economic and cultural networks. Wider opportunities for individual fulfillment and alternative avenues for advancement and control over the future may have led town couples to place less primacy on continuation of the familial spiral than did peasants.

Beginning as early as midcentury in Rogliano or the latter decades of the nineteenth century elsewhere, the BMR fell in all four communities. This decline, which continued until the 1920s, was due primarily to the prolonged absence of husbands who had migrated to northern Europe or across the Atlantic in search of work. Marriage rates during these years actually increased (due to improved survival chances among children) but produced no corresponding upsurge in births. Absence of husbands proved to be an effective means of conception control, but one that may have delayed acceptance in these areas of alternative contraceptive techniques. In any event, in the years between the wars, when restrictions by Italian and foreign governments combined to force husbands to stay nearer to home, fertility rose sharply, although not quite to levels of a century earlier. Some rural folk undoubtedly responded positively to Mussolini's promotherhood propaganda during these years. In the three southern Italian communities, the high ratio of births to marriages ended abruptly after World War II as, within a decade, massive emigration by couples (or one spouse alone) during the fecund years and widespread acceptance of conception control devices by those who remained in the village combined to reduce average marital fertility to fewer than three children.[38]

In this and the preceding chapter I have tried to show that changes in a variety of demographic and cultural patterns occurred at varying times over the past two centuries, usually appearing in rural towns before becoming significant in the villages. For example, modes of choosing a spouse shifted from *la famiglia* and *interesse* to the individual and romantic love even before 1850 in Rogliano and Castel San Giorgio. But mortality, especiallly among infants and children, declined most dramatically only half a century later, and if the hypothesis that improved survival chances made fatalism less functional as a basis for the rural folk's world view is correct, it follows that a shift in traditional values centered upon fate occurred only in the twentieth century. High fertility is characteristic of traditional societies, and even if one does not accept all the cultural implications (and rejects the potentially racial implications) of demographic transition theory,[39] it is reasonable to cite a low ratio of births to marriages as evidence of significant change in a much wider range of societal characteristics. Such a low ratio occurred in Albareto after World War I and in the three southern communities a generation later; these dates, it may be recalled, are congruent with the dates given in the previous chapter for the earliest time at which parents might raise their children without the expectation that one-third or much more of them would die. Rural folk acted in the present according to what they had experienced in the past, at least until the future appeared less unknowable and ominous. Only after World War II did experience instruct the *contadini* that three children would be adequate to provide for the continuation of *la famiglia*. But in earlier times no human action could assure that the endless spiral of family would not end. And it was fate that determined who lived, who reproduced, and who died.

## RAMS, ROOSTERS, MEN

Continuation of *la famiglia* was the husband's responsibility. A reading of Italian law related to the family easily yields the conclusion that it merely reflected male dominance; yet a broader perspective, one that includes an analysis of customary ways of flourishing beyond the reach of law, shows that rural folk viewed the groom's future with a mixture of foreboding and promise. He would be the head of a family, a person assured of respectful and even reverential public reference by his wife. But his image was Janus-like to the core, the public "thou" to his face replaced by "the mule" when his wife referred to him among her friends and the formal emphasis on female sexual virtue replaced by jokes directed invariably at suspected *cornuti*. Indeed, marriage revealed the duality of an array of folk images related to procreation: the virgin bride as an insatiable sex goddess; the proud groom, defender of his lineage, as a lowly ass unable to initiate copulation; the powerless daughter as center of *la famiglia*; the family's *onore* at the mercy of the bride's bedsheet. Dominance, yes, but of the most fragile sort. And in the final inversion, only a wife's pregnancy could sustain her husband's masculinity.

The marriage feast was an opportunity not only to gather and celebrate but also to take steps of a practical sort to assist the groom in his procreative responsibilities. Food and prayer provided the way. Rural wisdom drew a close connection between the eating of certain foods and a man's ability to copulate and impregnate his wife. Women, on the other hand, were viewed as perpetually and insatiably fecund and therefore in no need of stimulating nourishment. On the contrary, motherly advice to a bride generally involved an admonition not to "exhaust" or "drain" her husband.

The food/fertility ritual began at *merenda*, the midmorning meal customary in all societies where work starts at dawn. On most days the *contadino* ate only a meager semblance of the festive *merenda*, perhaps a crust of bread during a short break in the fields. But on his wedding day the groom sat before a more lavish table. He and the male members of his family, served in silence by female members who took no further part in the meal, joked loudly, ate tripe, and drank wine. The serving of tripe held a symbolic and nutritional meaning understood by all. The stomach and intestines "are the bowels, the belly, the very life of man" linked both to death and to the generative belly. To continue with the brilliant analysis of Mikhail Bakhtin, "in the image of tripe life and death, birth, excrement, and food are all drawn together and tied in one grotesque knot; this is the center of bodily topography in which the upper and lower stratum penetrate each other."[40] The link to parents was about to be changed, the *onore* of *la famiglia* passing to the son, his father thereby dying. One procreative role ended so that another might begin, thus assuring that the first would not be ended after all. Father and son shared the same plate, eating in communion the finely mixed essence of life and death and joining their separate procreative roles as one. "May you be as fruitful as your father" was the curiously inverted blessing with which the tripe was consumed and cleansed with wine. The meal continued with cheese, a food universally thought to increase male virility. It was the young man's mother who had made the cheese and, although she was now old and her breasts barren, it was to her nourishment that her son returned. All men at the table were offered cheese, thus recalling the boundless fertility of the groom's mother, but only he partook of her nourishment on that day. At the wedding feast itself the choice of foods became more explicit. Reserved for the groom alone and served with a sauce prepared by his mother-in-law with rare and unusual herbs were mountain oysters.[41]

Traditional efforts to stimulate fertility were uniformly directed at males, not only on the wedding day but also in the preparation and consumption of tripe and cheese on other festive occasions. But when such efforts seemed not to work, resort was had to spiritual intervention. One villager in Nissoria told this story about himself, all the while assuring me that similar events had happened to many other people he knew.

> My mother died in 1918 of Spanish influenza, and my father was remarried to a woman from Assoro who had a great reputation for casting spells and finding valuable objects people had lost. I did not believe all this until on the feast of San Giuseppe she transformed herself into Don Paolo [a local priest] and put a curse on me and on her son that we would be unable to consummate our marriages. What she said came true. In desperation I sought my stepmother's advice, whereupon she urged me to pray for relief to San Filippo Neri [who, among other things, grew up with a very kind stepmother]. After a time my prayers were answered, and as you know, I have three fine children and eight grandchildren.

## PARENTS AT CHILDREN'S MARRIAGE

The endless spiral of *la famiglia* was threatened constantly with an abrupt ending, with the reality that what had always continued in the past would not survive in the future. It hardly needs saying, therefore, that marriage not only represented the major event in most individuals' lives but also marked a crucial step in the process of family. A sense of fatalism, well grounded in an intuitive but nonetheless accurate understanding of the realities of prevailing demographic rates, surely gained strength from the fact that until recently only a minority of brides and grooms married before one or more of their parents had died. The issue of how many parents lived to see their children marry and ultimately reproduce has attracted considerable attention from historical demographers. The question (or perhaps the failure to explore it fully) is central to the Laslett/Berkner debate mentioned earlier. As Wrigley pointed out, it makes little sense to calculate how many extended families existed at a given point in time unless one knows how many could have existed. The question of "how many could have existed" is treated by Wrigley as a matter of applying the appropriate mortality tables and doing some simple arithmetic.[42] But as he concedes, the problem is more complex; in addition to selecting appropriate mortality tables (a task that becomes particularly difficult when the question is not life expectancy at birth but life expectancy from the ages at which couples become parents of surviving children), the researcher must assess the impact of parents' mortality upon their children's marriage decisions. For example, if housing space is in such short supply that children delay marriage until at least one parent dies, then more secondary and fewer extended families will exist than one would estimate from the random distribution of mortality tables alone.

Marriage registers for nineteenth-century Castel San Giorgio provide an excellent source from which to assess the issue of how many brides and grooms married while their parents were alive. The Castel San Giorgio documents give this data with a consistency and accuracy lacking in the other three communities, and therefore I shall concentrate on this town and relegate to the endnotes the less reliable figures for other places.[43] There are sixteen possible combinations of parental mortality ranging, obviously, from all four being alive to all four being dead. These are shown in table 11, along with observed frequencies of each type and estimates based on random distribution from life tables. At the risk of oversimplification, it may be said that the "life table estimate" figures show what would have happened if parental death and marriage by children had been unrelated.[44] As a comparison of the columns of numbers reveals, however, the two were in fact related. Observed data show an "excess" of marriages in which all the parents were alive (row 1) and in which all had died (row 16).

Assuming that estimated figures reflect accurately the composition of the whole population, it follows that brides whose parents were alive tended to marry grooms in the same situation, a tendency even more strongly reflected by men and women whose parents all had died. This finding is congruent with a view of *la famiglia* as process and marriage as the crucial step in determining the shape of that process. People married their own kind, not only in the obvious matter of class or occupation but also by matching more subtle variations in familial composition. *La famiglia* was an asset, one of the few that a landless farm laborer had and one that was not inconsequential even among town artisans and small entrepreneurs. Those whose parents had died were often in better short-term economic circumstances as a result, perhaps through the inheritance of a bit of land, takeover of a parent's customary place of work, or acquisition of living quarters. But apparently these "advantages" were not so great as to cause parentless young men and women to seek each other out for marriage. Rather, individuals without live parents were partially cut loose from the ties of *la famiglia*; they lacked an important asset in a society heavily dependent upon *onore* and reciprocity enacted in terms of kinship networks.

TABLE 11   **Parents of Brides and Grooms, Castel San Giorgio, 1810–99**

|      | BRIDE'S | | GROOM'S | | LIFE TABLE | OBSERVED IN |
|------|---------|--------|---------|--------|------------|-------------|
|      | Mother | Father | Mother | Father | ESTIMATE | DOCUMENTS |
| 1.   |   |   |   |   | .186 | .223 |
| 2.   |   |   |   | D | .124 | .134 |
| 3.   |   |   | D |   | .095 | .058 |
| 4.   |   |   | D | D | .064 | .064 |
| 5.   |   | D |   |   | .095 | .084 |
| 6.   |   | D |   | D | .064 | .067 |
| 7.   |   | D | D |   | .049 | .022 |
| 8.   |   | D | D | D | .033 | .043 |
| 9.   | D |   |   |   | .076 | .052 |
| 10.  | D |   |   | D | .051 | .033 |
| 11.  | D |   | D |   | .039 | .019 |
| 12.  | D |   | D | D | .026 | .035 |
| 13.  | D | D |   |   | .039 | .050 |
| 14.  | D | D |   | D | .026 | .037 |
| 15.  | D | D | D |   | .020 | .021 |
| 16.  | D | D | D | D | .013 | .058 |

NOTE.—D = dead; $N$ = 1,291. See text and n. 44 for explanation of figures.

## LIVING TOGETHER

One of the major reasons for interest in the question of parents' survival to their children's marriage centers on living arrangements. Once upon a time, every schoolchild learned that in some bygone day multigenerational extended families lived together, presumably in great harmony, under one roof. The Industrial Revolution changed all that, it was asserted, as highly mobile nuclear families went their separate ways and avoided coresiding with grandparents, brothers, and especially mothers-in-law. Demographers, beginning nearly two decades ago, undertook to examine closely census returns and similar documents from preindustrial western Europe and colonial America. They found that rather few extended families ever lived under one roof, thereby exploding both the historical basis and the causal reasoning for asserting that industrialization destroyed the extended family and established in its place nuclear living arrangements. In the process of casting aside one myth, however, some of these historical demographers drew a new picture that proved to be somewhat misleading. While there is little doubt that at any given point a majority of households were not extended, scholars disagree about what this "fact" means and about why it is so.[45] The Castel San Giorgio data allow some comment on the issues of extended families and living arrangements.

In the nineteenth century for this Neapolitan town the observed frequency with which various familial structures existed at the point of marriage is as follows:[46]

extended (both parents alive) with the bride's parents:     48 percent
extended with the groom's parents:                          41 percent
secondary with the bride's remaing parent:                  36 percent
secondary with the groom's remaining parent:                39 percent

In terms of actual living arrangements, these figures must be reduced by as much as one-third, since married couples, on average, had two siblings each who would also marry and form a household potentially shared by parents.[47] In brief, the maximum percentage of *castelsan-giorgesi* couples who could have lived in a multigenerational extended household was 27–32 percent, while the maximum for secondary households was 24–29 percent.[48]

*La famiglia* is a flexible process that facilitates joint living arrangements whenever these appear useful. In the scattered outlying houses of Rogliano as late as 1951[49] and in the village of Albareto especially when emigration rates fluctuated greatly, more than one married couple and their children often shared the same house. It was functional to do so. The home that once belonged to Andrea Berzolla (no. 43) in Albareto, a typical example, provided living quarters according to need and, as figure 13 shows, needs changed frequently.[50]

Andrea was born in house 43 in 1860, and as the youngest son, he stayed there upon his marriage in 1884 to Colomba Orsi. His mother lived with them until she died eight years later. A year earlier, however, Andrea left for America to work for five years, leaving the house and a few cows to his ailing mother, his wife, and their five children. Their daughter, Angela, was severely deformed from birth and remained at home until her death in 1940. The oldest boy, Luigi, married in 1910 and thereupon emigrated to London, where he operated an ice cream parlor bought with part of his father's New York City savings. The second son, while still unmarried, left in 1917 to become a copartner in his brother's ice cream business (and at the same time to avoid serving in the war. There he married Anne Webb, who was less a stranger than her name might indicate, since her mother and Colomba Orsi were second cousins. Andrea's youngest son married in 1930 and moved his wife into the family house, of which he became the legal head only ten years later when his father died. In the interim Alfonso's wife gave birth three times. For three years (1931–34) the household also included Alfonso's older brother's daughter, a sickly child sent "home" from London in the hope that the good mountain air of Albareto would make her well (which it did not). At the outset of the Second World War the wife and two daughters of Alfonso's eldest brother and the wife and four offspring of his elder brother all returned to live in house 43. This safety measure proved disastrous in 1943 when the bitter partisan struggle erupted in Albareto, but these women and children survived and returned to London. Although the figure does not show it, since 1945 the children and now grandchildren of Alfonso's older brothers returned frequently to Albareto and lived with him at number 43 for two months in the summer. Alfonso's three daughters married in the 1950s; one of these resides four houses away, another settled in Parma, while the youngest lives at number 43 with her husband and two children. When she married in 1927, Alfonso's youngest sister moved a mere two houses away, where she still lives, joined there since 1958 by her daughter, son-in-law, and their two children.

Two points emerge from the Berzolla case. One is the significance of Hammel's warning against a static and "snapshot" approach to a process. It is easy enough to calculate that for thirty-four years house 43 contained only Andrea and his wife and children, and that for thirteen years Alfonso lived in a similar arrangement (from 1945 when his sisters-in-law, nieces, and nephews left until 1958 when a son-in-law moved in), but this hardly tells us that the nuclear family is dominant. Rather, the Berzollas' experience reveals that living space was an asset shared in varying degrees according to need and circumstance by the process of la famiglia. Aged parents remained until they died, a niece returned for reasons of health and sisters-in-law for safety. Alfonso ultimately received title to house 43, but with this title went the obligation to provide space as needed for la famiglia, just as Severino joined Luigi's ice cream business in London, and both would have made room for Alfonso had the need existed.

After a brief survey of data on seventeenth-century English villages, Peter Laslett concluded that, "unless all these communities happen to have been very exceptional indeed, living with in-laws can only have been occasional in the world we have lost."[51] Laslett is correct in a technical sense if "occasional" is read loosely to imply 25 percent or less, but the interpretation he and others have given to this finding (in short, that nuclear families were the norm in the preindustrial world and therefore that industrialization is not a necessary and sufficient explanation for the modern nuclear family) is static and misleading. Andrea lived in house 43 with in-laws for only ten of his eighty years; his daughter-in-law, on the other hand, has done so for thirty-two of her sixty-five years. But both figures are trivial because they fail to convey the relation of house 43 to the people who at one time or another slept there.

The second point that emerges from the Berzolla example is related to the first: living space is only one among many life situations that rural Italians confront within the context of *la famiglia*.[52] Two doors away from Alfonso live his sister Agata, her children, and her children's children. The family—Agata and Alfonso, Alfonso and Attilio, his children and hers—share activities: gathering mushrooms and chestnuts, reading a letter from their brothers in London, playing cards in the late afternoon, feasting and praying, celebrating and mourning. For a variety of reasons the range of activities in which *la famiglia* is a primary consideration is narrower in Albareto than in the southern communities of Castel San Giorgio, Rogliano, and Nissoria.[53] But even in Albareto, family as process always has meant much more than housing arrangements alone.

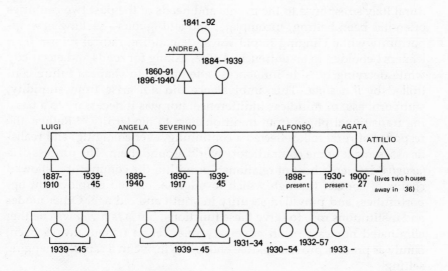

Fig. 13.
House no. 43. Dates refer to periods when these persons lived in house 43.

## GENERATIONS

The ideal of a full complement of four parents watching their children wed and carry forward the spiral of *la famiglia* has been realized regularly only in the last two decades. Although mortality rates decreased sharply beginning in the 1890s, the multigenerational impact of this demographic change is only now being fully felt. In earlier times it was uncommon for a bride's and groom's parents to be alive; in fact, until after the Great War this occurred in fewer than one of every three weddings. And prior to 1860 the ratio was fewer than one in five. There was, then, during the nineteenth century a substantial improvement in the life expectancy of those who reached adulthood. This created an increasing number of extended families, whether or not such families lived under the same roof, and ultimately an increase as well in potential secondary units as one or the other parent survived. Thus the demographic consequences of improved longevity allowed an expanded role to *la famiglia* over a longer time even as other forces worked simultaneously to reduce the significance of familial ties. Emigration, geographic mobility, centralizing political administration, wage work and division of labor, romantic love, formal education, population pressure on local resources, and integration into wider economic networks all tended to undermine and counteract the primacy of *la famiglia*. But at the same time improved survival rates, first for adults and then among children, meant more family members and therefore more extended, living, and vital links in a network of kin-based *onore* and reciprocity. Rural Italy's response to the events and needs of the past two centuries often has been halting, incomplete, and ambiguous—seeking new opportunity while clinging to old ways, demanding radical reform from leaders beholden to an entrenched elite, asking for roads and electricity while decrying outside influences, attempting to shape a future controlled by *il destino*. This ambivalence did not arise from stupidity, stubbornness, or mindless indifference; nor was it necessary to a passing transitional phase from traditionalism to modernity.[54] Rather, the response of rural folk reflected a continuing, ever changing, and realistic assessment of the contradictory world around them. The process of *la famiglia* defined a host of relationships within the community, allowed chains of contact through which to migrate, offered employment opportunities, and provided security in youth and old age. Other modes and institutions rose to serve these functions, but *la famiglia* was neither eliminated nor cast in an adversary role, for as it had always been, family as process proved flexible enough to thrive in a rapidly changing setting.

# 6
# Work

Poveri

Non hanno più una meta
ma solo freddo e fame
nel corpo lacero e nell' anima stanca
Entrano nella casa del SIGNORE
Ma come cani puzzolenti sono evitati
Camminano senza scopo
e affidano la vita al tempo:
—ora all' angolo di un palazzo
Ora sui gradini di una chiesa (quando è festa)
I poveri son disprezzati
I poveri sono umiliati

Rosa Runco

Among the many villagers whose insights have shaped my thinking about processes of change and continuity in rural Italy, none has had a more profound impact than Rosa.[1] She grew up in a cluster of humble houses near Rogliano, sharing fully the joy and anguish of *i contadini del sud*. Although poverty is hardly unique to the mountains of Calabria, it is here that the psychosis of *la miseria* takes its most complete form. Of course *la miseria* means being underemployed, having no suit or dress to wear for your child's wedding, suffering hunger most of the time, and welcoming death. But for Rosa and the Calabresi it means more: houses with cracked and crumbled walls, unborn children you know will be malnourished, abandoned lands, hostile lands, faces and hands burned by the sun. *La miseria* is a disease, a vapor arising from the earth, enveloping and destroying the soul of all that it touches. Its symptoms are wrinkles, distended bellies, anomic individualism, hatred of the soil, and the cursing of God. Optimists proclaim that the wonders of American aid after the Second World War, the Common Market, and the Cassa per il Mezzogiorno have wiped out the disease.[2] Rosa is less sanguine. True enough, *la miseria* does not appear regularly on television, nor can it be seen while cruising down the Autostrada del Sole. But it is there all the same—in country hamlets and urban shanties,

among educated but unemployed youths and inflation-racked pensioners, in untended vines and regimented Fiat plants, in absent fathers and
lonely wives.[3]

In earlier times *la miseria* may have been more widespread than it is
today but it never was universal. Richard Gambino captures well the
spirit that could overcome harsh material conditions:

> Despite its hardness, life was sensuous, bright, throbbing with the
> joys of everyday life, pleasures made sweeter by their constant jux-
> taposition with life's hard and lethal side. The contadino mirrored his
> land. He reflected the brilliant, unnaturally lucid Mediterranean light
> that makes life so much more clear and sharply defined; the scorching
> sun and the refreshing shade . . . . universal contrasts made everything
> more alive, infinitely more visible and valuable in the Mezzogiorno.[4]

Anton Blok raises a related question when he asks whether peasants in
a western Sicilian town loved the land. He concludes that they did not,
adding a cautionary note that this finding may be unusual or even
exceptional.[5] To ask whether Italian peasants loved the land (I refer to
the period prior to the Second World War) is in essence to ask of their
world view[6]—whether they were victims of *la miseria*, for if they did not
cherish the soil, *contadini* turned to violent hatred of the land, never to
indifference, as the source of their affliction.

Agricultural workers in Rogliano and Castel San Giorgio did not love
the land. They resented its stones, its treacherous ravines, its constant
thirst, its incessant demand for labor, its cunning ability to provide
precisely enough to leave its dependents forever hungry and malnourished without causing outright starvation. Those who lived and
worked in town had only contempt for the crude ways of folk who
resided in isolated hamlets or who left town before dawn for fourteen
hours of labor in the dirt. With their own eyes *contadini* could see an
idle town life that appeared to thrive only on their work under the hot
sun—bureaucrats, traders, refiners, packagers, moneylenders, and
prostitutes. The *contadini* did not understand, or understood all to well,
their helplessness to remedy the injustice. Their envy of the town folk's
better life often blinded these agricultural workers to any realistic collective steps to ameliorate their condition.[7] Instead, they cursed *fortuna*
for assigning them such a hard station in life. And in their anger the
images of fate, God, nature, and earth became blurred and fused, until
they came to hate the soil itself as the source of their *miseria*.

In Nissoria and Albareto seemingly different material conditions
nevertheless provided milieux for a similar and positive attitude toward
the land. Agricultural laborers in Nissoria were poorer than in Castel
San Giorgio and Rogliano, suffered higher mortality, and supported an
even more exploitative leisure class. Albaretesi, on the other hand, were

better nourished and housed than peasants in Castel San Giorgio and Rogliano; they enjoyed greater geographic mobility and a somewhat lower mortality rate. They shared and vigorously defended their right as citizens of the community to gather firewood, mushrooms, and chestnuts freely. Both the Nissorini and the Albaretesi loved the soil, because it seemed to yield them all that it could; they did not see and interact daily with a complex town economy that appeared to rob them of their just earnings. When an apparently exploitative class did emerge in Nissoria, the poorer folk turned against its leading family rather than the land.[8] But the greatest exploiters lived invisibly in palaces at Palermo and Messina. They were too remote, socially and geographically, to be fit objects of envy, and so the peasantry could hate them. Albareto's economic interaction was with Genoa and the large towns of the Ligurian coast; villagers believed that, since their labors could not possibly be the means of supporting such a giant city, it was they who were sharper in trade than the coastal folk. (In fact this was not the case at all. Albareto's higher standard of living relative to the other three communities was due to its low population density.)

In short, I suggest that it was not the absolute level of poverty and exploitation that determined the peasantry's world view but, rather, the mode of that impoverishment and exploitation. Agricultural laborers who lived hard by a substantial segment of *cittadini* just enough above them to be objects of envy rather than fear or hatred tended to despise their land (Castel San Giorgio and Rogliano). They suffered *la miseria*; their rage and their hunger turned them against each other. On the other hand, peasants who lived mostly among their own kind and whose exploiters were remote, physically or through rigid class barriers, developed and maintained a flourishing and rich, derivative yet autonomous cultural life, one marked by doubled and inverted images, grotesque humor, sensuous gestures, and folk carnivals (Albareto and Nissoria). They laughed when they cursed the soil; they were proud of their tough hands; they walked with straight shoulders and committed adultery with their eyes. Their rage and their hunger brought them together.

Obviously an examination of only four communities cannot do more than suggest possible ways for explaining varying peasant attitudes toward the land and toward each other; proof is not possible. The fullest recent treatment of whether peasants loved the soil, in Mediterranean areas generally and in Calabria explicitly, comes from anthropologist Joseph Lopreato. He concludes that peasants hated the land and that Robert Redfield's original assertion to the contrary (in a classic study of a Mexican village) arose from his romantic nostalgia and misguided idealism. Other researchers, including one who worked in the same village where Redfield had found that peasants loved the land, saw little evidence of particularly strong attachment to the soil.[9] But stating the problem as a hard, either/or dichotomy seems to me to be somewhat misleading, because such an approach does not capture the basic ambivalence and doubled imagery of peasant culture. La miseria reflects the failure of agrarian folk to respond effectively to life's realities. It cripples meaningful collective action by undermining the basis for social cohesion. Hatred of the land is one aspect of la miseria. However, peasants also know la gioia, moments of abundance, celebration, feasting, defiance of fate, love making, communal protest. These moments, precisely because they are rare, weigh far more heavily in the formation of peasant culture than a purely numerical count would suggest. Whether times    joy, however infrequent, overcome la miseria, for which there is likely to be an ample material base in most peasant societies, depends on the pattern of conjunctures between rural/peasant economy/culture and urban/capitalist economy/culture.

Redfield himself referred to part of this equation when he suggested that hatred of the soil among peasants in the Mediterranean basin might be due to the major role of towns and cities throughout the region and to the ancient and continued preference for urban life among its peoples.[10] For peasants in Italy after 1800, I believe it is essential to consider not only the role of urbanism but also the degree and type of agricultural capitalism prevalent in a particular region. Where capitalism and urbanism flourished, so also did la miseria, at least until the total proletarianization of those agricultural workers who did not emigrate. Where urban centers were remote and where feudal vestiges remained strong, a self-sustaining peasant culture provided ritual channels for coping with misery and ample ways to celebrate la gioia.

So much has been written on the transition in western Europe from feudalism to capitalism, some of it very intelligent, that a very brief historiographical digression is in order. In the detailed analysis that follows, I shall accept as a given that rural Italy by 1800 was a semiperipheral sector within a capitalist world system. The semiperiphery, following Immanuel Wallerstein, included "former core areas [of Europe] turning in the direction of peripheral structures" where labor was neither forced, as in the periphery, nor free, as at the core. Sharecropping (or other forms of risk sharing) dominated semiperipheral zones such as Italy. Wallerstein's main focus is on the sixteenth century, but his analysis has been applied with considerable success to nineteenth- and twentiety-century western Sicily by Jane and Peter Schneider. They use the concept of "broker capitalism" to understand Sicily's wheat economy and the role of local powerholders. In so doing, they treat agricultural capitalism as a developmental process rather than a fixed configuration, thereby superseding the confines of the Dobb/Sweezy controversy over whether some intermediate mix of feudalism and

capitalism constituted a distinct economic system.[11] Capitalism as process provides the framework for both Emilio Sereni's outstanding
studies of agriculture in Italy and the more technical research of Giorgio
Giorgetti on rural labor contracts. They both proceed from the assumption, as I shall, that the economy of rural Italy was part of a dynamic
capitalist system but that particular configurations of production at the
local level varied widely. I suggest that these variations were sufficient
to give rise to a bifurcated rural culture, characterized by love of the soil
and hatred of the soil, by social cohesion and distrust, by *la miseria* and
*la gioia*. Paired opposites existed in the same places and even in the
same persons, though in different mixes.[12]

Examination of the interaction of economy and culture may begin
with a fairly simple index of economic diversity: the percentage of adult
males engaged directly in agriculture (see fig. 14). The percentages refer
to all agriculturists, from day laborers to substantial holders (further
along I shall separate various categories among agriculturists), but in all
cases 90 percent or more were peasants who held little or no land.[13]

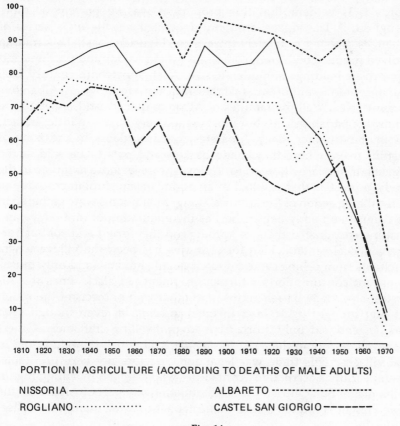

PORTION IN AGRICULTURE (ACCORDING TO DEATHS OF MALE ADULTS)

NISSORIA ——————            ALBARETO ---------------------

ROGLIANO ················           CASTEL SAN GIORGIO — — — — —

Fig. 14.

Until after the Great War a majority of adult males in each community were engaged directly in agriculture. Between the wars in the towns and villages of the Mezzogiorno the graph shows sharp increases in the proportion of *cittadini*, especially in Nissoria, where formerly there had been few such persons. The 1940s saw some return to farming among residents of Castel San Giorgio and Rogliano (as industrial recovery became concentrated in the north). The dramatic decline of agriculturists in the past fifteen years, although overstated due to the nature of the source employed,[14] has been substantial. But before drawing further comparisons and generalizations it may be appropriate to present some detail on each community's economy beyond that provided earlier in chapter 2.

## ALBARETO

Throughout the nineteenth century, and indeed until the 1950s, at least nine of every ten Albaretesi engaged primarily in farming. Figure 14 does not provide data prior to 1870, but from military conscription records it is evident that this proportion was 90 percent or more throughout.[15] The village economy depended heavily on a series of exchanges directed ultimately toward the Ligurian coast. This trading involved produce both from communally held woods and pastures and from private holdings of moderate size. A late nineteenth-century local history provides important insights into the workings of Albareto's economy. Nearly all the families of Albareto owned land, asserted the author (the parish priest), but most owned very little—so little, in fact, that in the summer many Albaretesi lived outdoors in the zone of chestnut trees, where they made baskets and pots to be sold at the August fair in nearby Borgotaro. Animals were let loose to forage in the woods, a practice that resulted in an abundant mushroom crop due to the fertilizing action of the animals' dung. Mushrooms were gathered in late August and early September, as the alternation of rainy days and sunshine encouraged them to sprout, and then dried and sold at Tarsogno, a local center which for centuries has been the village where merchants from Genoa came to purchase mushrooms (and only mushrooms) for consumption or further shipment. At slack times the Albaretesi also made barrels, cribs, and other wood objects of the rough sort that brought pride (and income) to *contadini* even though such work engendered only scorn from town-dwelling craftsmen. Others journeyed on foot to the coast to buy olive oil which they then sold in local villages. This trade was legal and therefore not very profitable. Greater earnings accrued to "contadini" who engaged in smuggling. In the hamlet of San Quirico (itself administratively part of Albareto), the noble Fieschi centuries earlier had established a toll station for collection of the *gabella* or *dazio*. This the Duchy of Parma revived in 1815 to collect taxes on such items as salt, tobacco, and gunpowder. But less than twenty kilometers from Albareto was the Tuscan town of Pontremoli, where, due to tax differentials, prices of these items were less than half of prevailing levels in Parma. Risk of confiscation of goods and a few days in prison at Borgotaro did not deter the Albaretesi from engaging in this lucrative trade. They knew their mountains far too well to be caught by city-bred tax collectors from Parma, and despite the absence of a tradition of *omertà* in the northern Apennines, local villagers were not about to report on illegal doings by their fellows. The Albaretesi also profited from their involvement in transhumance. In May, when the last snows melted and the upper valleys became lush once again, villagers went to the coast west and south from Genoa to arrange contracts for pasturage of goat herds. Until late October the goats remained in the mountains, their *albaretesi* tenders returning to the coastal owners a quantity of cheese fixed to allow an ample profit for the villagers. A similar exchange, although on a smaller scale, existed for turkeys, which were set loose in the woods in the spring to be hunted in the fall. To all these activities must be added the gathering of chestnuts (consumed locally in place of grain), fishing for trout, and raising and hunting of game and fowl.

In sum, Albareto's economy involved villagers in frequent exchanges, use of cash or informal credit, and a great variety of tasks. That formal documents listed nearly everyone as a *contadino* reflected a style of life that was neither undifferentiated nor backward. Rather, the radix of Albareto's economy was its communal land, and although villagers sustained themselves in varying ways from that land, their mutual dependence upon it cast them in a shared position. They were at one and the same time thoroughly dependent upon communal holdings and ruggedly independent about how and where they bartered and exchanged the land's produce.

Provisions for regulation of use rights in the common and defense against outsiders appear in local government deliberations. In addition to provincial and even national forest guards, the municipality of Albareto hired its own full-time sheriff to protect the commons. The task was eased because only one road led into and out of the village and because the most desirable forest product, the mushroom, foiled the greedy. No mechanical devices existed to locate or pick mushrooms, and violating the woods by bringing in a gang of workers would surely have been found out. The sheriff assured me that very few outsiders passed his notice for more than a few hours. On any good day for finding mushrooms dozens of village women were in the forest, and they always used a special call to report any intruder. Today, summer renters from Milan and Genoa are allowed in the woods only as long as they remain fairly inept at finding the mushrooms and bring home no more than a basketful. By law posted on numerous trees, they may not pick anything, but the sheriff is a moderate fellow. Chestnuts were abundant, and their gathering was not controlled except when crop failure or war sharply reduced the grain supply. In such years rules prohibiting nonresidents from entering communal woods were enforced strictly. The town council also allocates to this day how much wood each family may cut annually. The wood is to be used only for heating or for making utensils and furniture, nor for sale to outsiders.

Although Albareto's communal land is a major factor in the village's economy, the Albaretesi never engaged solely in gathering and in community celebration. Tables 12 and 13 provide data on the regional and local economy in a format that facilitates comparisons with other

TABLE 12   **Economic Structure of the Region around Albareto (%)**

|  | 1871[a] | | 1881[b] | | |
|  | Male | Female | Male | Female | 1936[c] |
|---|---|---|---|---|---|
| Smallholders | ... | ... | 28 | 13 | ... |
| Sharecroppers | ... | ... | 13 | 7 | ... |
| Tenants | ... | ... | +[d] | +[d] | ... |
| Long-term contracts | ... | ... | 14 | 31 | ... |
| Daily wage laborers | ... | ... | 8 | 4 | ... |
| Pastoralists | ... | ... | 1 | 1 | ... |
| Substantial holders | 6 | 11 | 10 | 12 | ... |
| All agriculturists | 81 | 73 | 74 | 68 | 75 |
| Textiles | 3 | 12 | 2 | 3 | ... |
| Food | 3 | 1 | 2 | 1 | ... |
| Building | 2 | ... | 3 | ... | ... |
| Other industry | 1 | +[d] | 1 | +[d] | ... |
| All industry | 9 | 13 | 8 | 4 | 13 |
| Commerce/credit | +[d] | +[d] | 1 | +[d] | 5 |
| Transport/communications | 1 | ... | 1 | ... | 2 |
| Domestic economy | 1 | 2 | 1 | 4 | 2 |
| National defense | 1 | ... | +[d] | ... | ... |
| Public administration | 1 | +[d] | 1 | +[d] | 2 |
| Religious | 2 | ... | 1 | ... | ... |
| Liberal professions | 1 | +[d] | 1 | +[d] | 1 |
| Others | 1 | 1 | 1 | +[d] | ... |
| Housewives | ... | ... | + | 21 | ... |
| Unemployed/student | 2 | 11 | 11 | 3 | ... |
| N persons | 9,668 | 11,035 | 7,782 | 9,646 | 7,215 |

[a]Figures are for the district of Borgotaro for persons age 15 and over.
[b]Figures are for the district of Borgotaro excluding the municipality of Borgotaro for persons age 9 and over.
[c]Figures are for the municipality of Borgotaro including Albareto and excluding all persons (51.2 %) not in the work force.
[d]More than 0 but less than 0.5%.

areas (see tables 14–19).[16] The columns in table 12 for the 1881 census provide a particularly useful breakdown on agricultural labor. In Albareto and the surrounding region smallholders dominated the male working population, and more than eight of every nine agriculturists had some claim to land or to long-term employment. According to Sereni and Giorgetti, capitalist penetration of Italian agriculture resulted in cash tenancy (risk assumed by the tenant) rather than sharecropping (shared risk) and short-term wage labor (*braccianti* in the 1881 census) rather than long-term contracts (*contadini—lavoro fisso*). At least according to these rather sensible criteria, agriculture in Albareto had not reached a mature capitalist level.

Economic activity among women also merits attention, if for no other reason than to highlight distortions caused by changing classification schemes. In 1871, when the Italian census did not include "housewife" as a category, only 11 percent of females over age fourteen appeared as unemployed. Women outnumbered men by better than two to one (1,245 versus 582 in the region) among substantial holders. Most other women were listed as peasant (*contadina*) or spinner (*filatrice*). It would be all too facile to assume that these designations merely reflected the whims of census takers who classified all rural women as peasants and village-center dwellers as spinners. My sense that the designations *contadina* and *filatrice* reflected work that women did rather than their husbands' or fathers' labor is borne out by the 1881 census. Note in particular the variation between male and female percentages in different categories of agricultural labor. In this census, for which the category "housewife" did exist, the reported figures show that most women were classified independently of their male relatives. The high percentage holding a long-term contract or some other form of steady employment confirms more scattered evidence from other sources indicating that females, married or not, made individual transhumance contracts, hired by the season as cheese makers, and sharecropped. The substantial portion of the resident population counted as being in the work force in the 1936 census suggests that women in Albareto continued to play a highly visible role in the local economy even in the fascist era. As will be seen shortly, women held diverse economic roles elsewhere in rural Italy as well, although in different numbers.[17]

Table 13 refers to the municipality of Albareto in the twentieth century and provides some measure of the process of industrialization in the village. Above all, one may note the low ratio of workers to firms in all three census years and the absence of substantial machine power even after World War II. Utilities, transport and communications, and health and safety were part of the national economic sector determined largely by Rome. While this sector clearly had an impact on the village's

TABLE 13 **Industrial and Commercial Activity in Albareto**

| | 1927 | | 1951 | | | 1971 | |
| --- | --- | --- | --- | --- | --- | --- | --- |
| | | | | | Horse- | | |
| | Firms | Workers | Firms | Workers | power | Firms | Workers |
| Wood | 10 | 14 | 2 | 2 | 3 | 6 | 6 |
| Food | 21 | 27 | 14 | 21 | 46 | 5 | 12 |
| Mechanical | 1 | 1 | 2 | 2 | 15 | 7 | 18 |
| Textile | 10 | 19 | 8 | 9 | ... | 1 | 1 |
| Transport/ | | | | | | | |
| communications | 7 | 15 | 5 | 14 | ... | 19 | 26 |
| Agriculture | 11 | 20 | ...[a] | ...[a] | ... | 2 | 8 |
| Construction | 1 | 1 | ... | ... | ... | 10 | 36 |
| Health/safety | 1 | 2 | 1 | 2 | ... | 3 | 3 |
| Chemical | 1 | 9 | 2 | 8 | ... | 2 | 16 |
| Utilities | 2 | 3 | 4 | 9 | 51 | ... | ... |
| All industry | 65 | 111 | 38 | 67 | 115 | 55 | 126 |
| Banking | 1 | 1 | 2 | 2 | ... | 1 | 2 |
| Wholesalers | 7 | 22 | 9 | 11 | ... | 1 | 1 |
| Retail food | 22 | 44 | 16[b] | 46 | 2 | 23[b] | 47 |
| Other retailers | 1 | 1 | ... | ... | ... | ... | ... |
| Restaurants/hotels | 3 | 4 | 8 | 16 | ... | 12 | 22 |
| Other | 1 | 2 | 1 | 1 | ... | 15 | 19 |
| All commerce | 35 | 74 | 36 | 76 | 2 | 52 | 91 |

[a]Not included.
[b]Combines food and all other retailers.

economy, its size and shape were not determined locally. Among other categories, food dominated. The food industry was composed of millers and cheese makers, none of whom employed more than one or two people. Commerce was also on a small scale, especially with the decline of wholesalers who in earlier times had bought and sold animals as part of transhumance arrangements. The chemical industry consisted of bottling mineral water and used no mechanical energy. By 1971, with the transformation of Albareto into a summer retreat for well-to-do city dwellers (including a good number of emigrant Albaretesi), the number of construction enterprises and restaurants grew substantially. At the same time, however, textile and agricultural activities declined, with the net result that over the past fifty years industry advanced only slightly and commerce, although growing according to the census, shrank to a summertime oasis. All in all, neither fascist orderliness nor the postwar economic miracle brought about fundamental alterations in Albareto's economy. In the nineteenth century Genoa sent goats, whereas now it sends people. According to Sheriff Varacchi, the results are about the same, except that the people are more trouble ("danno più fastidio").

## NISSORIA

Work patterns in the Sicilian village of Nissoria differed strikingly from the communal orientation of Albareto. Largely dependent upon wheat, the local economy gave rise to a small but powerful group of "notables" and a chronically impoverished peasantry. Scholars who locate the fundamental sources of Sicily's plight in international shifts in the production, transportation, and consumption of grains and in the political exigencies of capitalist core regions are undoubtedly correct.[18] But agricultural laborers in Nissoria saw their situation in more personal terms. Their lot appeared to them to result from the avarice of local dons—the Nascellis, owners of a salt mine; the Buscemis, controllers of milling operations; the Olivieris and Ferlantos, *gabellotti;* and especially the Squillacis, holders of spiritual and temporal power. It is this local configuration that I wish to explore.

Chapter 2 described Nissoria's economy as monocultural (wheat), with fractionalized holdings and a high percentage of smallholders among all agriculturists. The cadastral survey of 1929 provided details on precisely how small many holdings were and confirmed the pessimistic appraisal of the peasantry's condition offered forty years earlier by the Jacini inquiry. Pessimism was in order. Tables 14 and 15, constructed in the same fashion as tables 12 and 13 for Albareto, provide some of the relevant data. The Jacini inquiry's finding that four-fifths of all agriculturists in the Nicosia district owned some land is probably true, but so are the 1881 census figures showing that less than one in seven owned enough land to be classified as even a smallholder. A tiny fraction of substantial owners (female dominated) aside, farming in the Nissoria region involved *contadini* in very tenuous circumstances. Tenants were twice as numerous as sharecroppers, and among males, *braccianti* outnumbered laborers with longer-term arrangements. Both ratios indicate, as does the concentration of large holdings, substantial capitalist maturation and concomitant proletarianization of the workforce.

Nearly one-third of all agricultural laborers were women; this in a district where a 1910 inquiry reported that

a moral woman ought not to work for wages in the countryside. This work is meant only for the most miserable; for those abandoned by their husbands or for widows or for girls who are disgraced . . . . Women work at home, and not too hard, which is one of the principal reasons that even in times of cruelest misery the Sicilian race saved itself from degeneration, and the children, despite the saddest hygienic conditions of house and village, generally grow robust and healthy.[19]

The attitude against women's work and the reality that women worked combined to exacerbate elite disdain for the peasantry. And a majority

TABLE 14 **Economic Structure of the Region around Nissoria** (%)

|  | 1871[a] | | 1881[b] | | |
|---|---|---|---|---|---|
|  | Male | Female | Male | Female | 1936[c] |
| Smallholders | ... | ... | 9 | 2 | ... |
| Sharecroppers | ... | ... | 4 | 1 | ... |
| Tenants | ... | ... | 8 | 2 | ... |
| Long-term contracts | ... | ... | 20 | 15 | ... |
| Daily wage laborers | ... | ... | 23 | 5 | ... |
| Pastoralists | ... | ... | 3 | +[d] | ... |
| Substantial holders | 4 | 8 | 3 | 7 | ... |
| All agriculturists | 78 | 29 | 70 | 32 | 77 |
| Mines | 3 | ... | 6 | +[d] | ... |
| Textiles | 3 | 7 | 3 | 41 | ... |
| Food | 2 | +[d] | 2 | 1 | ... |
| Building | 4 | ... | 7 | +[d] | ... |
| Other industry | 2 | ... | 2 | 3 | ... |
| All industry | 14 | 7 | 20 | 45 | 14 |
| Commerce/credit | 1 | +[d] | 1 | +[d] | 3 |
| Transport/communications | 1 | ... | 1 | +[d] | 1 |
| Domestic economy | +[d] | 2 | 1 | 4 | 1 |
| National defense | +[d] | ... | +[d] | ... | ... |
| Public administration | 1 | +[d] | 1 | +[d] | 3 |
| Religious | 1 | 1 | 1 | +[d] | ... |
| Liberal professions | 1 | +[d] | 1 | +[d] | 1 |
| Others | 2 | 16 | 1 | 1 | ... |
| Housewives | ... | ... | ... | 16 | ... |
| Unemployed/student | 1 | 45 | 3 | 2 | ... |
| N persons | 28,409 | 28,923 | 27,605 | 27,198 | 949 |

[a]Figures are for the district of Nicosia for persons age 15 and over.
[b]Figures are for the district of Nicosia excluding the municipality of Nicosia for persons age 9 and over.
[c]Figures are for the municipality of Nissoria excluding all persons (65.7%) not in the work force.
[d]More than 0 but less than 0.5%.

of peasant children died before adulthood. Cultural opposition to women's work nevertheless kept many females out of the labor force, as reflected in the high percentages of unemployed in 1871 and spinners in 1881 and the low percentages of persons active according to the 1936 census.

When they were not working their own land, which was most of the time, peasants hired out to operators of large estates. Latifundism may have reached its greatest proportions in western Sicily, but it was by no means absent from Nissoria. According to the 1910 inquiry cited above, Nissoria contained five *latifondi* with a total of 2,038 hectares, or 33.2 percent of the communal total. By comparison, the *comune* of Blok's estimable study reported 50.6 percent in *latifondi*, the Palermo district as a whole 37.7 percent, Caltanissetta 44.1 percent, and Catania 34.5 percent. All other Sicilian provinces reported lower average figures than Nissoria's, although individual communities recorded much higher figures. In sum, the prevalence of latifundism in Nissoria was fairly typical for Sicily as a whole, less than in some western agrotowns but clearly sufficient to have a major impact on the local economy.[20]

Agricultural production on Nissoria's *latifondi*, as almost everywhere in Sicily, yielded lower returns than did smaller holdings (in Nissoria 33.2 percent of the land but only 21.1 percent of revenue). Parliamentary experts gave five reasons for low cereal production on big estates: (1) absentee owners who lacked industrial spirit and were ignorant of peasant needs; (2) *gabellotti* who did not plough fallow properly or aid in threshing efficiently from the small plots they sublet; (3) short-term leases; (4) lack of housing in the fields; and (5) lack of technical skills, animals, and equipment among peasant workers.[21] Questionnaires returned from forty-nine *latifondi* in the region around Nissoria reported only 10 percent with any irrigation, 36 percent with malarial water, and 78 percent with no technological improvements or plans to make any.

TABLE 15   **Industrial and Commercial Activity in Nissoria**

|  | 1927 | | 1951 | | | 1971 | |
|---|---|---|---|---|---|---|---|
|  | Firms | Workers | Firms | Workers | Horse-power | Firms | Workers |
| Wood | 5 | 5 | 4 | 4 | ... | 5 | 5 |
| Food | 9 | 14 | 19 | 39 | 75 | 4 | 7 |
| Mechanical | 2 | 4 | 5 | 9 | ... | 3 | 4 |
| Textiles | 9 | 12 | 10 | 13 | ... | 10 | 10 |
| Transport/ communications | 3 | 6 | 7 | 16 | ... | 10 | 13 |
| Agriculture | ... | ... | ...a | ...a | ... | 1 | 4 |
| Construction | ... | ... | 7 | 16 | ... | ... | ... |
| Health/safety | 4 | 5 | 8 | 13 | ... | 3 | 3 |
| Mines | 2 | 4 | 3 | 3 | ... | ... | ... |
| Utilities | ... | ... | 1 | 1 | ... | ... | ... |
| Other | 1 | 1 | ... | ... | ... | ... | ... |
| All industry | 35 | 51 | 64 | 114 | 75 | 36 | 46 |
| Banking | 1 | 8 | 5 | 6 | ... | 1 | 1 |
| Wholesalers | ... | ... | 2 | 2 | ... | 1 | 1 |
| Retail food | 15 | 24 | 19b | 24 | ... | 44b | 49 |
| Retail clothing | 7 | 10 | ... | ... | ... | ... | ... |
| Retail chemicals | 1 | 2 | ... | ... | ... | ... | ... |
| Restaurants/hotels | ... | ... | 6 | 8 | 4 | 6 | 8 |
| Other | 4 | 8 | 5 | 8 | 1 | ... | ... |
| All commerce | 28 | 52 | 37 | 48 | 5 | 52 | 59 |

aNot included.
bCombines food and all other retailers.

Many were confronting the labor shortage caused by emigration by shifting from wheat to pasture.[22]

Two forms of labor contract prevailed on Nissoria's *latifondi*. Although both constituted steps in what was essentially a capitalist system producing for a well-formed national market, the one based on subletting contained important feudal vestiges and irrational (from a capitalist perspective) features aimed at spreading risk rather than at maximizing profit. The sublease practiced in Nissoria was generally a rent-in-kind rather than a sharecropping contract. In the abstract, rent arrangements shifted risk to the peasant. In addition, the cultivator had to agree to any or all of a series of obligatory additional payments such as *la camperia* for care of the estate, *la cuccia* or gift to the armed guard, *la messa* to pay for a priest to come and say mass, *la questue* to aid mendicant friars, and *i carnaggi* or gifts of fruit and meat to the owner. The *gabellotto* generally advanced the necessary seed, at 25 percent interest, and a *soccorso* so that the peasant's family might eat between December and August. When emigration rates advanced sharply after 1900, some peasants ate the *soccorso* and then left before the harvest, causing *gabellotti* to refuse such advances, but it appears that in earlier times the *soccorso* worked both to shift the risk of a bad harvest back to the intermediary and simultaneously to enmesh the peasant with debts that would never be repaid.[23] Indebtedness also resulted from another form of contract, one by which the peasant received all the fava beans from a plot in a given year with the obligation to remand to the owner two-thirds (instead of the normal one-half) of the wheat crop in the next. There were many variations of this arrangement, at least until emigration-induced labor shortages caused owners to grant what may have seemed fair to peasants all along; the *contadino* got all the fava beans, plus a thank-you from the *padrone* for having restored the soil somewhat, with no obligations on anyone's part for the next year.[24]

The other form of employment common on Nissoria's *latifondi* involved wage labor hired daily or by the season. At the head of an estate of 200 hectares or more was a factor who earned 569 lire plus perquisites annually (in 1906, when cereal land sold for an average of 1,000 lire per hectare). Below him were one or more armed guards at 269 lire annually, plus what they extorted from the peasantry. Then came the chief ploughman and herdsman at 269 lire, the head cheese maker at 244 lire, and monthly employees at 45 lire. The cost of renting a pair of mules for a day of ploughing was 9 lire, or five times the pay of the peasant who guided them. Reaping of grain commanded a higher daily wage than any other task, up to 2.50 lire, with other jobs descending in pay to 1.50 lire for picking beans. Women, children, and worn-out men earned less, about 1 lire per day. Even at these wages few peasants labored more than 150–200 days annually, most of these in the summer when work began at five in the morning and continued until eight in the evening. Parliamentary inquiries include numerous calculations of the cost of living among Sicilian peasants, and all conclude that, on average, most became a little more indebted each year.[25]

A 1910 survey of work conditions captures well both the physical difficulty of wage labor on a *latifondo* and the possibilities it offered for camaraderie and cultural solidarity. The *zappatura* common in Sicily was a form of hoeing rather than ploughing, done with an ancient and crude instrument. The sharp oblique angle of the blade to the handle forced the *contadino* to stoop over constantly, with heavy stress on the back muscles. Peasants worked in rows of eight or ten, one acting as leader and urging on the others by words and by example. At resting times, three in the winter and perhaps five in the summer, each worker broke off a piece of his own bread but flavored it with garlic and oil passed around by the leader. Sometimes a wine flask also appeared. The midday break might last two or even three hours, but the others were much shorter. Reaping also meant long hours of intense work in groups of up to a dozen, while women, either wives and daughters or else very poor widows and orphans, gleaned. The men ate more abundantly on these hard, hot days: bread and salad in the morning, bean soup at midday, bread and cheese at midafternoon, and macaroni at night. (The cost of the communally served food was deducted from wages.) Then, before going to sleep,

> someone sings a song or plays a tune on the pipe and the younger peasants, as if to defy their weariness and loosen joints knotted by reaping all day, dance furiously, men with men (rarely do the few women present join in), until tiredness overwhelms them and they fall helter-skelter to sleep. The more fortunate ones bed down in the stables, storerooms, or haystacks, but most must make do with the bare ground and the open sky.

As soon as reaping was completed, peasants began the task of threshing, hours on end of walking in narrow circles behind two blindfolded mules, whipping them on and choking out the grain dust that filled the air. Women and older children often did this job. There followed in August and September the time of slack, of celebration, and of death, until the fall rains and the first *zappatura* for the next year.[26]

Capitalist latifundism depended upon a pliant and ample labor force. Already in the 1890s, as highlighted by the Fasci movement, Sicilian agricultural workers were by no means pliant, if they ever had been. But the sporadic and ultimately ineffective protests of rural laborers contributed less to the decline of great estates than did labor shortages. These began about 1900 and reached alarming proportions (to the owners) by 1906, at least for the Nissoria region. As previously noted, sub-

stantial holders decided against mechanization and instead shifted
their land to pasture. But animal husbandry on a large scale did not
succeed, and even before the First World War, *latifondisti* began to sell
their holdings in small parcels to repatriates. This process will be
explored more fully in chapter 8. For the moment, it suffices to note that
by 1929 all the 2,038 hectares in Nissoria classified in 1910 as *latifondi*
had been divided and sold. Peasant control and ownership of land thus
increased at the very time, 1910–40, that the viability of peasant farming
throughout western Europe withered under devastating technological
and political challenges. Mussolini's call for Italian self-sufficiency in
wheat proved to be a cruel hoax for Nissoria's peasants, who worked for
a generation barely to survive and who, when the economic miracle
came after 1950, had neither the skills nor the capital accumulations of
which such miracles are made. Table 15 provides the raw figures indicating that in Nissoria, to a greater extent even than in Albareto, the
twentieth century was one of economic retrogression. Local crafts, milling operations, and road construction were replaced by nothing. The
business of Nissoria today is exportation—of Nissorini.

Despite all their internal differences, nineteenth-century Nissoria
and Albareto shared a fundamental similarity. In both villages the *contadini* lived in a self-contained world which, although it allowed contact
with outside forces, was not permeated by them. In the case of Albareto
the keys were geographic isolation from the Ligurian coast and mutual
dependence upon communal lands. In Nissoria, on the other hand, the
outside world actually had its intermediaries resident in the village.
But the *gabellotti* became a culture apart; they lived in the village but in
a curious sense were not part of it.[27] Beyond the notables' barricades of
class distinction, use of cash, and connections to Palermo/Messina there
flourished a peasant culture which knew only itself and the land. Not
until the twentieth century did improvements in communication and
transportation, local overpopulation, new efforts by urban and industrial elites to penetrate potential rural markets, and improved survival
chances combine to foster an examination and partial breakdown of
traditional peasant culture. With this examination ultimately came acceptance of the *cittadino*'s disdain for the *contadino*, abandonment of the
soil, envy of the town worker's apparent amenities, and even hatred of
the land.

## ROGLIANO

The percentage of Roglianesi engaged in agriculture was only margin-
ally lower than percentages for Albareto and Nissoria (compare table
16 with tables 12 and 14). Nevertheless, the Calabrian community developed a far more active, aggressive, and domineering town economy.

TABLE 16   Economic Structure of the Region around Rogliano (%)

|  | 1871[a] | | 1881[b] | | |
|---|---|---|---|---|---|
|  | Male | Female | Male | Female | 1936[c] |
| Smallholders | ... | ... | 5 | 1 | ... |
| Sharecroppers | ... | ... | •5 | 1 | ... |
| Tenants | ... | ... | 3 | +[d] | ... |
| Long-term contracts | ... | ... | 19 | 18 | ... |
| Daily wage laborers | ... | ... | 26 | 9 | ... |
| Pastoralists | ... | ... | 7 | +[d] | ... |
| Substantial holders | 6 | 1 | 6 | 5 | ... |
| All agriculturists | 71 | 15 | 71 | 34 | 68 |
| Mines | ... | ... | +[d] | ... | ... |
| Textiles | 6 | 29 | 5 | 41 | ... |
| Food | 2 | 1 | 2 | 1 | ... |
| Building | 4 | +[d] | 6 | 2 | ... |
| Other industry | 3 | ... | 3 | +[d] | ... |
| All industry | 15 | 30 | 16 | 44 | 17 |
| Commerce/credit | 1 | +[d] | 1 | +[d] | 5 |
| Transport/communications | 2 | +[d] | 2 | +[d] | 4 |
| Domestic economy | 1 | 3 | 2 | 2 | 2 |
| National defense | 2 | ... | +[d] | ... | ... |
| Public administration | 1 | +[d] | 1 | +[d] | 3 |
| Religious | 2 | +[d] | 1 | +[d] | ... |
| Liberal professions | 1 | +[d] | 1 | +[d] | 1 |
| Others | 2 | 1 | 1 | +[d] | ... |
| Housewives | ... | ... | ... | 18 | ... |
| Unemployed/student | 2 | 51 | 4 | 2 | ... |
| N persons | 50,198 | 61,397 | 51,940 | 64,282 | 2,941 |

[a]Figures are for the district of Cosenza for persons age 15 and over.
[b]Figures are for the district of Cosenza excluding the municipality of Cosenza for persons age 9 and over.
[c]Figures are for the municipality of Rogliano excluding all persons (66.2%) not in the work force.
[d]More than 0 but less than 0.5%.

One useful source of evidence for recapturing the extent and variety of Rogliano's town economy is its death register. Pre-1860 entries reveal over seventy different occupations (compared with less than thirty in Albareto and Nissoria for the entire nineteenth century). Deaths of judges, lawyers, legal aides, notaries, security guards, a judicial secretary, and a tribune reflected Rogliano's bureaucratic functions. Its peacekeeping needs required mounted police, regular police, street patrollers, a brigadier, and several marshalls. Its religious life included priests at three parishes, monks, nuns, members of mendicant orders, sacristans, and two hermits. Other spiritual needs were met by resident sorcerers and fortune tellers. The town (and it is worth recalling that in 1860 its population was under 5,000) also counted among its members a variety of marginal persons: beggars, a prostitute, a brigand, gypsies, and traveling comics, singers, musicians, and storytellers. And then there were the fifty-three construction workers, twenty-six metalworkers, thirty-four tailors, thirty-eight cabinetmakers, and forty-one shoemakers who died between 1811 and 1859. All these people cannot have served the needs solely of the local population.

Rogliano was a center, albeit a subsidiary one, into and through which people and goods flowed.[28] Unlike ancient olive trees and stubborn soil, which year after year threatened to yield less and never more, town life offered a frenzied pace: street dances and processions, a market every Sunday, fairs three times a year, and the possibility that good fortune would strike or talent and cunning be rewarded. Except for a few residents of outlying *case sparse,* agricultural workers in Rogliano lived just around the crowded center, close by all the activity but never fully participating. Theirs was to envy what they saw before them, a false existence stolen from the *contadini*'s soiled hands. Also before their eyes stood the palace of Baron Ricciulli, in all its earthquake-defying splendor, and the elegantly attired sons and daughters of the Clausi and Morelli families.

The arrogance of town folk may well have been hardened by the fact that Rogliano's commercial, bureaucratic, and industrial activities declined in the nineteenth century, a decline confirmed by a comparison of occupational listings in marriage and death registers. Death certificates refer to a much older age group and provide a portrait of the economy as it had existed in earlier years, whereas marriage entries indicate the economy's future direction (since individual occupational mobility between marriage and death was not great).[29] Contraction of the town's economy is most evident in figures for nonagriculturists, which were nearly 33 percent smaller in the replacement (marrying) generation. This contraction, which lasted through the years of Risorgimento and unification and until the Great War, resulted from Rogliano's unsuccessful competition against neighboring Cosenza. In the course of the nineteenth century Cosenza's population nearly tripled (from under 8,000 to over 21,500), whereas Rogliano's increased by only 40 percent. Although both were growing in absolute terms, Cosenza's course led to its becoming the region's only city, the place to which most agricultural produce destined for nonlocal markets ultimately gravitated. Moreover, industrial production and a distribution system made possible by improved transportation rapidly replaced the artisanal work and regional fairs that had been crucial to Rogliano's economy. Finally, overthrow of the Kindgom of Naples and the replacement of its de facto policy of local autonomy with increasing centralization of political authority left the town with the apparatus but not the substance of power over the surrounding plateau. As a result of these pressures Rogliano declined from a preindustrial *collegio* in 1815 to a once grand but now moribund rural town a century later. At the same time that the town economy stagnated and even contracted, thereby offering little outlet for agriculturists who dreamed of escaping *la miseria,* the peasantry's lot grew worse.[30]

Land came to be concentrated in fewer hands (percentages of *possidenti* and *civili* dropping by more than half from the early to the late nineteenth century), and more hectares than ever before were diverted to non-labor-intensive olive and fig tree plantings.[31] Persons who formerly had designated themselves as agriculturists or cultivators after 1860 used the term *bracciante* to describe their condition. The shift was not due simply to new guidelines issued by Rome or to a town clerk's whim.[32] Rather, it reflected accurately the early conversion of Rogliano's rural labor force into proletarians, wage workers detached completely from the informal benefits of more traditional agricultural modes.[33] In earlier times wealthy magnates had allowed cultivators the "privilege" of maintaining a few vines, rows of vegetables, and perhaps a stand of wheat along particularly inaccessible steep slopes or among olive groves. In return peasants hoed and earthed the owner's olive trees twice a year without remuneration and assembled willingly when the magnate's agent issued calls for pruning and harvesting (for which pay was at daily rates in oil). But after 1860, perhaps in response to fears of peasant unrest that were no less real for having made no significant appearance locally, owners forced "squatters" off the land, largely dispensed with hoeing and earthing, and paid in cash at piece rates for picking and pruning. Former cultivators, now reduced to wage laborers, had to look beyond Rogliano to compensate for their chronic underemployment. But elsewhere in Calabria they found only more misery. In general, the pre-1860 pattern (and more probably the pre-1830 pattern) had been far from idyllic; it provided cultivators, whose numbers had been reduced periodically by epidemics and constantly kept low by high mortality even in good years, with subsistence but not much more. *La miseria* flourished where peasants developed little cultural unity or distinctiveness apart from their collective envy of townspeople. After 1860 (and perhaps beginning a generation earlier), with the rapid proletarianization of landless peasants who nevertheless formerly had exercised traditional rights to use of small parcels, *la miseria* became total. Self-abasement and dignified pity among peasants, which outsiders confused with legendary *calabrese* stubbornness, guaranteed the success of landowner efforts to impose the worst features of capitalist agricultural modes while abolishing the saving graces of older ways.

The years following the Great War saw only a modest improvement in the position of Rogliano's agriculturists. Wage laborers decreased substantially in absolute and proportional numbers, their places taken largely by *contadini.* These *contadini* were, of course, the same persons (or their sons) who earlier had called themselves *braccianti*, but the shift in terminology points to something real. Faced with potential labor shortages arising from considerable emigration (whether to Cosenza or to Pittsburgh) by farm laborers, owners began to sell small portions of their holdings to returnees. (The reader may recall a similar phenomenon for Nissoria; it occurred as well throughout the Mezzogiorno.) These repatriates and their relatives, lacking sufficient wealth and grandeur to perceive themselves as *possidenti*, were content merely to claim the status of *contadino*. Simultaneously, big owners attempted to retain an adequate labor force by granting informal access to small plots to loyal *braccianti*, who thereupon declared themselves to be *contadini* as well. Thus, during a period when everywhere in Italy the term *contadino* implied degradation, it was for Rogliano's victims of *la miseria* a deceptive improvement.

That changes in the economy in the twentieth century were far from satisfying is evident from the data summarized in table 17. Industry and commerce in Rogliano existed on a greater scale than in Albareto or

TABLE 17   **Industrial and Commercial Activity in Rogliano**

|  | 1927 | | 1951 | | | 1971 | |
|  | Firms | Workers | Firms | Workers | Horse-power | Firms | Workers |
|---|---|---|---|---|---|---|---|
| Wood | 3 | 10 | 15 | 49 | 71 | 8 | 10 |
| Food | 5 | 15 | 15 | 21 | 126 | 3 | 6 |
| Mechanical | 6 | 11 | 7 | 7 | . . . | 9 | 14 |
| Textiles | 23 | 44 | 37 | 49 | 12 | 40 | 41 |
| Transport/ communications | 19 | 37 | 14 | 50 | . . . | 4 | 37 |
| Agriculture | 1 | 1 | . . .[a] | . . .[a] | . . . | . . . | . . . |
| Construction | 9 | 19 | 2 | 35 | 44 | 12 | 118 |
| Health/safety | 3 | 4 | 14 | 19 | . . . | . . . | . . . |
| Mines | . . . | . . . | 2 | 22 | . . . | 1 | 4 |
| Utilities | 2 | 6 | 2 | 2 | . . . | 1 | 6 |
| Other | 3 | 4 | 5 | 7 | . . . | 4 | 6 |
| All Industry | 74 | 151 | 113 | 261 | 253 | 82 | 242 |
| Banking | 3 | 10 | 3 | 5 | . . . | 4 | 12 |
| Wholesalers | 2 | 12 | . . . | . . . | . . . | 2 | 10 |
| Retail food | 37 | 50 | 67[b] | 79 | . . . | 111[b] | 141 |
| Retail clothing | 23 | 26 | . . . | . . . | . . . | . . . | . . . |
| Retail furniture | 7 | 17 | . . . | . . . | . . . | . . . | . . . |
| Retail chemicals | 4 | 11 | . . . | . . . | . . . | . . . | . . . |
| Restaurants/hotels | 19 | 28 | 8 | 10 | . . . | 13 | 22 |
| Other | 10 | 11 | . . . | . . . | . . . | 12 | 15 |
| All commerce | 105 | 165 | 78 | 94 | . . . | 142 | 200 |

[a]Not included.
[b]Combines food and all other retailers.

Nissoria (see tables 13 and 15) and with a higher ratio of workers to firms, but growth between 1927 and 1971 was totally inadequate to absorb the many *contadini* who abandoned the land to join the ranks of unskilled industrial laborers. Figure 14 shows a decline of more than 60 percent in the percentage of Rogliano's men who worked in agriculture, or about 600 people. Three-fourths of these cannot have found steady work in town; they were forced to emigrate, perhaps to Turin or, more probably, to Germany, Switzerland, or Belgium.

## CASTEL SAN GIORGIO

Castel San Giorgio, like Rogliano, was a place where peasants did not love the land, where *contadini* dominated by *cittadini* failed to sustain a culture of their own. As in Rogliano, Castel San Giorgio's economy involved a wide range of occupational designations, a reflection of its intensive division of labor even before industrialization. Pre-1860 marriage registers indicate the presence of such specialists as hat makers, coach makers, leather workers, wine-barrel scrapers, cloth cutters, coffee grinders, dyers, stokers, sawyers, hemp dressers, weavers, seed-bed tenders, ax and cleaver makers, soap makers, table makers, undertakers, colliers, jewelers, and hoop makers among more than eighty distinct occupations noted. All of these are among the usual range of positions found in a preindustrial town. They are characteristic of an economy in which agriculture, even if it was the pursuit of a majority of residents, did not dominate.[34] Whereas the Albaretesi and Nissorini made their own soap, scraped their own wine barrels, and buried their dead in homemade coffins (or exchanged these services on an informal basis with payments in kind), the Castelsangiorgesi paid "professionals" in cash for such services. However, a town of Castel San Giorgio's size (4,963 in 1861) did not provide ample demand to occupy all these specialists. Rather, the local economy depended heavily on supplying the needs of travelers moving between southeastern interior regions and the metropolis of Naples. The town was less successful in this role than its neighbor to the northeast, Mercato San Severino, which straddled the junction between the roads to Salerno and Naples. Nevertheless, enough trade seeped throughout Naples's densely populated and geographically mobile hinterland to allow a substantial degree of complexity in Castel San Giorgio's economy.[35]

Because so many opportunities of various sorts appeared to exist, because a hungry laborer should have been able to walk to Naples and join the throng there, because the absolute number of persons in the area was so great that everyone knew of local success stories, because ready access to the Mediterranean seemingly meant unlimited possibilities, the peasantry for centuries had blamed only itself for its sorry

condition. A vine tender or nut gatherer in the mountain hamlet of
Aiello might pride himself on his *onore*, but this he lost when he
traveled to Castel San Giorgio's center. He might grow up with a certain
affection for the soil, but this too gave way before the cold glances of
*cittadini* who passed by. He might wish to work and live out his life
involved in no more than simple exchanges of his labor for items
needed to support *la famiglia*, but Castel San Giorgio's economy did not
work that way.

Tables 18 and 19 provide data, in the same format used for tables
12–17, on this Neapolitan town's economy. Alone among the four com-

TABLE 18   **Economic Structure of the Region around Castel San Giorgio (%)**

|  | 1871[a] | | 1881[b] | | |
|  | Male | Female | Male | Female | 1936[c] |
| --- | --- | --- | --- | --- | --- |
| Smallholders | ... | ... | 3 | 1 | ... |
| Sharecroppers | ... | ... | 4 | +[d] | ... |
| Tenants | ... | ... | 6 | 1 | ... |
| Long-term contracts | ... | ... | 7 | 6 | ... |
| Daily wage laborers | ... | ... | 20 | 11 | ... |
| Pastoralists | ... | ... | 3 | +[d] | ... |
| Substantial holders | 7 | 8 | 6 | 5 | ... |
| All agriculturists | 54 | 37 | 49 | 24 | 49 |
| Mines | ... | ... | 1 | ... | ... |
| Textiles | 8 | 24 | 9 | 32 | ... |
| Food | 5 | 1 | 6 | 1 | ... |
| Building | 5 | +[d] | 9 | +[d] | ... |
| Other industry | 5 | +[d] | 4 | 1 | ... |
| All industry | 23 | 25 | 29 | 34 | 36 |
| Commerce/credit | 4 | +[d] | 3 | +[d] | 5 |
| Transport/communications | 4 | +[d] | 4 | +[d] | 3 |
| Domestic economy | 1 | 2 | 2 | 2 | 2 |
| National defense | 2 | ... | 1 | ... | ... |
| Public administration | 1 | +[d] | 1 | +[d] | 3 |
| Religious | 2 | 1 | 1 | +[d] | ... |
| Liberal professions | 2 | +[d] | 1 | 1 | 2 |
| Others | 4 | 4 | 3 | 1 | ... |
| Housewives | ... | ... | +[d] | 35 | ... |
| Unemployed/student | 3 | 31 | 6 | 3 | ... |
| N persons | 86,732 | 89,006 | 85,530 | 90,458 | 2,209 |

[a]Figures are for the district of Salerno for persons age 15 and over.
[b]Figures are for the district of Salerno excluding the municipality of Salerno for persons
age 9 and over.
[c]Figures are for the municipality of Castel San Giorgio excluding all persons (65.4%) not
in the work force.
[d]More than 0 but less than 0.5%

TABLE 19   Industrial and Commercial Activity in Castel San Giorgio

| | 1927 | | 1951 | | | 1971 | |
|---|---|---|---|---|---|---|---|
| | Firms | Workers | Firms | Workers | Horse-power | Firms | Workers |
| Wood | 2 | 3 | 22 | 50 | 78 | 13 | 83 |
| Food | 2 | 2 | 16 | 96 | 327 | 18 | 420 |
| Mechanical | 2 | 2 | 11 | 13 | ... | 12 | 108 |
| Textiles | 5 | 5 | 43 | 45 | ... | 7 | 7 |
| Transport/ communications | 6 | 44 | 25 | 62 | ... | 4 | 41 |
| Agriculture | ... | ... | ... | ... | ... | 1 | 1 |
| Construction | ... | ... | 15 | 26 | ... | 28 | 267 |
| Health/safety | ... | ... | 18 | 19 | ... | 5 | 5 |
| Mines | 2 | 15 | 8 | 127 | 149 | ... | ... |
| Utilities | ... | ... | 1 | 2 | ... | 3 | 3 |
| Other | 1 | 11 | 1 | 1 | ... | 4 | 58 |
| All industry | 20 | 82 | 160 | 441 | 554 | 95 | 993 |
| Banking | ... | ... | 3 | 7 | ... | 4 | 14 |
| Wholesalers | 3 | 4 | 10 | 12 | ... | 3 | 6 |
| Retail food | 51 | 53 | 87[a] | 126 | 3 | 115[a] | 148 |
| Retail clothing | 6 | 6 | ... | ... | ... | ... | ... |
| Retail furniture | 1 | 1 | ... | ... | ... | ... | ... |
| Retail chemicals | 5 | 5 | ... | ... | ... | ... | ... |
| Restaurants/hotels | 3 | 3 | 7 | 9 | ... | 20 | 31 |
| Other | 18 | 84 | 8 | 9 | ... | 19 | 24 |
| All commerce | 87 | 156 | 115 | 163 | 3 | 161 | 223 |

[a]Combines food and all other retailers.

munities under intensive study, Castel San Giorgio witnessed both overwhelming proletarianization of its agricultural labor force in the nineteenth century and substantial industrial expansion in the twentieth. Unlike Rogliano, where proletarianization made major inroads only after 1860, *braccianti* appear in Castel San Giorgio's pre-1860 marriage and death registers three times as frequently as the next most common designation (*colono*) and more often than all other agricultural worker designations combined. As discussed in chapter 2, holdings in Castel San Giorgio were highly fractionalized. Most peasants owned no land at all, and a majority of those who held something owned so little that they regularly had to seek additional employment. Early use of a cash wage system and short-term employment, often one day at a time, reflected not only the requisites of an integrated town economy but also conscious profit maximization on the part of landowners great and small. Whereas in Nissoria and Rogliano the legal abolition of the last vestiges of feudalism between 1812 and 1838 spurred big holders to adopt labor contracts that in one way or another continued to share production risks, in Castel San Giorgio the end of feudalism meant the end of emphyteusis. Copyholders, according to the 1882 Jacini inquiry volume for the Campania region, had been at the forefront of agricultural progress. When they lost their long-term tenancies and became daily wage laborers, they also lost interest in scientific crop rotation, permanent irrigation, and progress. Nevertheless, concluded the Jacini inquiry, even though "there is always a collision of interests between the owner and the worker/renter," the fault for agricultural stagnation is "with the owner not the cultivator." Owners assumed the risks of ploughing and reaped the profits of harvesting. Their success in keeping labor costs to a minimum apparently was nothing short of triumphal; according to one observer, a *bracciante* in Campania "lives like an ass and dies like a dog."[36]

Beginning about 1860, as expanding local mining operations and the lure of work in distant places made more accessible by the railroad combined to reduce significantly the percentage of laborers remaining in agriculture, owners switched to a tenant system. A man who took this position became known as a *colono;* he paid a cash rent for use of land during a growing season but gained no legal or customary right to a particular plot. Rentals may have been low (according to fragmentary records for the 1880s approximately the price of two quintals of prime tomatoes for one hectare), but most parcels were divided into tiny square *passi* (1/30 of a hectare), an indication that former *braccianti* had very little cash with which to attempt tenant farming. On one-thirtieth of a hectare the remuneration had to be small no matter what the rental involved. Most *coloni* rented multiple *passi*, but these may well have included inferior and widely scattered parcels. All in all the system did nothing to encourage soil conservation, labor or mechanical efficiency, wise crop rotation, or a meaningful change in status for the *colono* or his children. Between the Great War and the end of World War II, the bulk of Castel San Giorgio's landless agriculturists began to refer to themselves as *contadini*, but this involved no change in their relation to the land and its owners. The only real solution was to abandon the soil, and this the *contadini* have done in massive numbers in the past thirty years.

Table 19 on commercial and industrial activity indicates why some Castelsangiorgesi today are optimistic that they have found an alternative both to massive emigration and to impoverishment on the land. The industrial work force has expanded more than tenfold in the past fifty years, and Castel San Giorgio participates in Italy's economic miracle: larger, more efficient, and more heavily capitalized firms employ more workers than ever before. When the superhighway bypassing Naples is complete, some men will be out of work, but they may find jobs if the big tomato canning plant and the new furniture factory expand. The commercial sector, which many Castelsangiorgesi characterize as "parasitic," has not grown unduly, and jobs are available for women, especially in the canning plants. In sum, Castel San Giorgio made progress of a sort: impoverished *braccianti* in the nineteenth century gave way to poorly paid but secure (trapped?), unskilled *manovali* in the twentieth.

## CLASS AND DEATH

That peasants toiled merely to survive and seemingly to support an idle town life led them to envy those who were visibly better off or to hate unseen and unknown oppressors. Rural folk culture claimed only two characteristics in common with town elites and big landowners: the smell of their excrement and death. But as to the latter, significant mortality differentials by class existed through most of the nineteenth century and in some ways actually increased over time. Examination of these differentials may begin with the data summarized in table 20. The parity level against which to assess these numbers is 100, the point at which no difference in mortality exists between one class and another. The degree to which members of a class suffered more than their random share of deaths at various ages is measured by numbers above 100. (For example, the 117 figure for peasants to 1860 dying under age forty in Rogliano means 17 percent more deaths occurred in this group than their total numbers in the population would justify.) Numbers under 100, of course, reflect a relative paucity of deaths among members of the age group and class shown.

Prior to 1860, deaths among adult males who never reached their fortieth birthday consistently involved peasants more frequently than their proportion in the total population justified. This excess ranged from 5 percent in Castel San Giorgio to 17 percent in Rogliano and usually meant a paucity of men who survived to age seventy or more—10 and 14 percent fewer in Castel San Giorgio and Nissoria, respectively. For substantial landowners the situation was dramatically the reverse; anywhere from 17 to 60 percent too few deaths under age forty and 7–20 percent too many survivors to age seventy or more. Patterns among townsmen were more varied. In Nissoria they clearly enjoyed superior health, but in Castel San Giorgio this did not hold true beyond the age of forty, and in Rogliano it is clear that *cittadini* died in excessive numbers at early ages. Nonetheless, their experience everywhere was superior to that of peasants.

Adult male death at early ages was a function of two related factors, chronic malnutrition and contagious disease.[37] The food intake of agricultural workers in rural Italy, especially those in monocultural districts, lacked vitamins, protein, and balance. Dietary deficiencies took a high toll in the prenatal and infant stages of life but thereafter abated as

TABLE 20    Deaths of Adult Males by Age and Class: Ratios of Observed to Expected
Frequencies

|  |  | AGE GROUP | | | |
|  | CASES | 20–39 | 40–59 | 60–69 | Over 69 |
|---|---|---|---|---|---|
| Rogliano: | | | | | |
| Peasants to 1860 | 297 | 117 | 104 | 88 | 90 |
| Landowners to 1860 | 166 | 67 | 85 | 133 | 119 |
| Townsmen to 1860 | 158 | 104 | 108 | 88 | 100 |
| N cases | ... | 153 | 167 | 90 | 211 |
| Peasants 1860–1909 | 494 | 102 | 98 | 95 | 103 |
| Landowners 1860–1909 | 100 | 83 | 133 | 83 | 108 |
| Townsmen 1860–1909 | 212 | 104 | 89 | 119 | 89 |
| N cases | ... | 169 | 178 | 144 | 315 |
| Peasants 1910–45 | 284 | 93 | 77 | 89 | 113 |
| Landowners 1910–45 | 34 | 57 | 0 | 86 | 157 |
| Townsmen 1910–45 | 146 | 122 | 166 | 125 | 63 |
| N cases | ... | 56 | 72 | 96 | 240 |
| Castel San Giorgio: | | | | | |
| Peasants to 1860 | 132 | 105 | 90 | 97 | 107 |
| Landowners to 1860 | 27 | 83 | 100 | 75 | 125 |
| Townsmen to 1860 | 60 | 96 | 121 | 118 | 75 |
| N cases | ... | 52 | 56 | 33 | 78 |
| Peasants 1860–1909 | 125 | 80 | 93 | 111 | 102 |
| Landowners 1860–1909 | 42 | 80 | 120 | 80 | 107 |
| Townsmen 1860–1909 | 112 | 130 | 100 | 95 | 95 |
| N cases | ... | 33 | 57 | 56 | 133 |
| Peasants 1910–45 | 147 | 86 | 95 | 119 | 100 |
| Landowners 1910–45 | 27 | 100 | 100 | 38 | 125 |
| Townsmen 1910–45 | 170 | 112 | 104 | 94 | 96 |
| N cases | ... | 63 | 74 | 69 | 138 |
| Nissoria: | | | | | |
| Peasants to 1860 | 156 | 112 | 103 | 96 | 86 |
| Landowners to 1860 | 20 | 40 | 100 | 150 | 120 |
| Townsmen to 1860 | 24 | 75 | 83 | 83 | 175 |
| N cases | ... | 47 | 70 | 40 | 43 |
| Peasants 1860–1909 | 337 | 100 | 99 | 103 | 99 |
| Landowners 1860–1909 | 37 | 50 | 163 | 75 | 100 |
| Townsmen 1860–1909 | 65 | 127 | 73 | 100 | 107 |
| N cases | ... | 96 | 138 | 81 | 124 |
| Peasants 1910–45 | 182 | 104 | 87 | 106 | 99 |
| Landowners 1910–45 | 12 | 0 | 220 | 80 | 120 |
| Townsmen 1910–45 | 42 | 111 | 122 | 78 | 100 |
| N cases | ... | 35 | 45 | 47 | 109 |
| Albareto:[a] | | | | | |
| Peasants 1870–1909 | 128 | 103 | 94 | 99 | 102 |
| Landowners 1870–1909 | 9 | 133 | 67 | 67 | 117 |
| Townsmen 1870–1909 | 10 | 29 | 200 | 143 | 57 |
| N cases | ... | 38 | 28 | 35 | 46 |
| Peasants 1910–26 | 73 | 98 | 74 | 101 | 107 |

NOTE.    Ratio = [[observed in cell/(row total × column total)]/N] × 100.
[a]There are too few cases for meaningful results in years after 1909 for landowners
and townsmen.

a direct cause of death until the age of forty or so. At this point the cumulative impact of malnutrition gave rise to diseases such as scurvy and pellagra. The latter, although closely associated with excessive consumption of maize, is a niacin deficiency disease spurred by inadequate intake of high quality protein. It was widely believed, for the most part correctly, that pellagra stopped at the city gates. Even more consequential was the debilitating effect of years of poor nourishment as a factor contributing to death from endemic diseases such as tuberculosis, pulmonitis, bronchitis, and malaria.[38]

After 1860 the experience of *cittadini* grew rapidly worse in Castel San Giorgio and Nissoria (and after 1910 in Rogliano as well), due partially to more frequent outbreaks of cholera, a disease that struck especially hard in densely populated town centers where procedures for disposal of human waste were inadequate. More generally, the increasing significance of contagion relative to nutrition as a cause of death, highlighted by pandemic influenza in 1918, worked to the relative disadvantage of *cittadini*. Throughout the period 1810–1945 a decrease in the proportion of adult male deaths occurring under the age of forty (from nearly 25 percent prior to 1860 to less than 10 percent after 1909 except during the influenza epidemic) was accompanied by a greater relative improvement for peasants than townsmen.[39] This trend did provide a factual base for the claim, of recent origin, by peasants that their environment was purer, cleaner, and healthier, but this claim hardly succeeded as a counterweight to the *cittadini*'s growing disdain of rural folk. Nor were mortality trends uniformly in the peasantry's favor.

Agricultural workers were more likely than landowning and town fathers to suffer deaths among their children. Evidence to support this conclusion is suggestive but imperfect (due to lack of a fully reliable control to test the possibility that greater mortality among peasant children was the result of greater natality for this class). Castel San Giorgio's and Nissoria's death registers consistently listed fathers' occupations for entries involving children but did not list them for fathers in birth registers; for Rogliano precisely the opposite information is available. Therefore the test of differential fertility must rest on data from Rogliano, whereas the mortality data are from Castel San Giorgio and Nissoria. The absolute level and decennial fluctuations in Rogliano's birth rate were similar to those of Castel San Giorgio. Although this does not guarantee that class differentiation was the same in both places, there is no reason to suspect great differences for these two towns. Figure 15 portrays differential natality and mortality among peasants in terms of the ratio of these events to marriages by peasants.[40] The calculation and interpretation of scores is similar to that employed in table 20, except that "expected" frequencies are derived from marriage registers.[41]

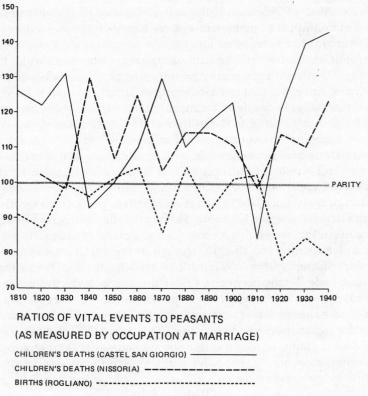

RATIOS OF VITAL EVENTS TO PEASANTS
(AS MEASURED BY OCCUPATION AT MARRIAGE)

CHILDREN'S DEATHS (CASTEL SAN GIORGIO) ———————
CHILDREN'S DEATHS (NISSORIA) ——————————————
BIRTHS (ROGLIANO) ------------------------------------

Fig. 15.

The natality trend, especially after about 1830 (before that date under-registration by peasants is a distinct possibility, since the communal registry system had been in effect for less than a generation), was oscillatory around parity. That is, peasants did not register consistently more or consistently fewer births than townsmen relative to their respective numbers in the marrying population. Only after the Great War, when improved health left too many competitors for scarce land and induced peasants to migrate (either in terms of occupation or geography) did birth registers show a consistent paucity of *contadini* (due not to their lesser fecundity but to their removal from the population). In sum, any tendency among peasants toward a higher fertility level than townspeople generally was offset by the combined impact of greater mortality, morbidity, and migration among the former. Differential natality, then, does not appear to be an adequate explanation of differential mortality.

Before examining detailed fluctuations in mortality ratios, it should first be noted that generally they are above parity (the opposite of natality trends), sometimes substantially so. Although it is impossible to prove that the bitter resentment and envy so often expressed by *contadini* toward *cittadini* reflected an accurate perception of these mortality differentials, their magnitude should not be dismissed too lightly. A score of 120, which appears frequently in figure 15, assuming an average family of eight children of whom three survived (until the 1880s the proportion was no higher), meant just two survivors for the peasant father but four for the townsman. Given the variation masked by this sort of statistical averaging, peasants inevitably faced the reality of burying their only surviving son or daughter far more often than did *cittadini*, perhaps twenty-five times as frequently.[42] Only in years of epidemics—cholera in the 1840s in Castel San Giorgio and deadly influenza, war, and occasional starvation in the 1910s everywhere—did the peasantry's relative lot become no worse than the townsmen's. But except for these decades (and possibly underreported figures for Nissoria's peasants in the first generation of its communal record keeping), the pattern throughout was greater mortality among the children of rural folk. Some decades were worse than others; none was good. And when health did improve substantially after 1890 and especially after 1920, it was the *contadino* who gained least. Increases in absolute levels of child survival were great indeed, but they may not have hidden from the peasant the reality that his family's survival chances improved much more slowly.

## BORN A PEASANT, DIED A PEASANT

Clerks registering a birth, death, or marriage asked respondents to state their "condizione, professione, o mestiere." The use of these particular words is significant.[43] A person with a *mestiere* had a trade, one involving a recognized skill such as carpentry, shoemaking, or plastering. Nonetheless, through most of the nineteenth century death registers consistently recorded day- or month-old infants with *mestieri* such as shoemaker or carpenter. In the case of children of professionals (doctors, pharmacists, lawyers, and so forth) a different pattern held; dead children of professionals had "infant" as their *professione*. Apparently one could be born a bricklayer but not a notary. But the majority of rural Italians had neither a profession nor a trade; rather, they occupied a certain *condizione*. The word may be translated properly into English as rank, position, station, circumstance, or status. It referred to something less rigid than caste and less internally coherent than class but more permanent than occupation and of wider cultural significance than job. The incongruity of a day-old female shoemaker was lessened to the extent that her father's trade did indeed shape his daughter's future. The status of *la famiglia* in this case was *calzolaio*, and that alone allowed accurate prediction of where its members lived, what they ate, whom they married, and how they died. Although born into an explicit *condizione*, an individual might through luck, hard work, or calculated deception (education being deemed a mixture of all three) ascend to a higher status. Conversely, poor fortune, laziness, or honesty bordering upon innocence might lead to a loss of rank.

Previous tables in this chapter outlined the absolute percentages of persons occupying various *condizioni* in Albareto, Castel San Giorgio, Nissoria, and Rogliano. The data summarized in table 21 allow an initial assessment of intergenerational movement from one status to another. At the outset a major caveat is in order; figures reflect the experiences only of those who remained to marry or die in the local community. (For mobility involving migration, see chaps. 7 and 8.) That is, the data provide a statistical indicator of change within the community but not of the total experience of all who were born there. Individuals chose, however circumscribed that choice, either to remain or to migrate; the analysis that follows deals only with the former.

TABLE 21  **Status Mobility among Sons and Fathers at Adult Sons' Deaths (%)**

| FATHERS | ALBARETO (1870–1926) SONS | | |
| | Peasant (564) | Landowner (20) | Town (22) |
| --- | --- | --- | --- |
| Peasant (551) | 94 | 35 | 55 |
| Landowner (35) | 3 | 60 | 27 |
| Town (20) | 3 | 5 | 18 |
| | CASTEL SAN GIORGIO (1810–1970) SONS | | |
| | Peasant (78) | Landowner (25) | Town (98) |
| Peasant (94) | 91 | 8 | 22 |
| Landowner (35) | 1 | 80 | 14 |
| Town (72) | 8 | 12 | 64 |

NOTE.  *N* cases in parentheses.

In both Castel San Giorgio and Albareto more than nine of every ten men who died as peasants had been born into that status; landed and town sons, on the other hand, arose from peasant origins far more often in Albareto than in Castel San Giorgio.[44] This finding takes on added significance in light of the larger absolute number of townsmen in Castel San Giorgio, where a growing town sector offered at least a possibility for substantial mobility by peasants. Intergenerational persistence by townsmen, however, closed off peasant opportunity in Castel San Giorgio, where among seventy-two town fathers only three had sons who died as landholders and six as peasants; the other sixty-three remained in their fathers' *condizioni*, occupying nearly two-thirds of all *cittadini* places. Mobility was far greater on a percentage basis in

Albareto, but here the small size of landed and town sectors precluded substantial status changes among those who remained in the village.

Data summarized in table 22 provide confirmation and amplification of findings derived from death registers. These data, calculated from marriage registers, involve sons in their late twenties (on average) and fathers in their late fifties (on average). Generally, all fathers along with town and business/professional sons had by these ages reached their

TABLE 22 **Status Mobility among Grooms and Their Fathers (%)**

| | ALBARETO GROOMS (1870–1909) | | | |
| | Peasant | Landowner | | Business/ Professional |
| FATHERS | (279) | (37) | Town (16) | (10) |
|---|---|---|---|---|
| Peasant (283) | 98 | 0 | 50 | 10 |
| Landowner (41) | + | 97 | 6 | 30 |
| Town (12) | 2 | 3 | 44 | 10 |
| Business/professional (6) | + | 0 | 0 | 50 |

| | CASTEL SAN GIORGIO GROOMS (1810–1909) | | | |
| | Peasant | Landowner | | Business/ Professional |
| | (191) | (30) | Town (162) | (20) |
|---|---|---|---|---|
| Peasant (215) | 93 | 3 | 20 | 20 |
| Landowner (34) | 1 | 87 | 2 | 15 |
| Town (135) | 6 | 3 | 74 | 10 |
| Business/professional (19) | 0 | 7 | 4 | 55 |

| | NISSORIA GROOMS (1820–1909) | | | |
| | Peasant | Landowner | | Business/ Professional |
| | (133) | (29) | Town (20) | (17) |
|---|---|---|---|---|
| Peasant (124) | 89 | 7 | 10 | 5 |
| Landowner (25) | 2 | 69 | 0 | 18 |
| Town (38) | 9 | 21 | 85 | 18 |
| Business/professional (12) | 0 | 3 | 5 | 59 |

| | ROGLIANO GROOMS (1810–1909) | | | |
| | Peasant | Landowner | | Business/ Professional |
| | (417) | (12) | Town (97) | (19) |
|---|---|---|---|---|
| Peasant (424) | 99 | 0 | 11 | 5 |
| Landowner (14) | + | 83 | 2 | 5 |
| Town (90) | 1 | 0 | 86 | 16 |
| Business/professional (17) | 0 | 17 | 1 | 74 |

NOTE. *N* cases in parentheses. More than 0 but less than 0.5% shown as +.

highest rank (among the four used in this table), but the figures may underestimate the number of peasant sons who eventually acquired land. If so, the underestimate cannot be very great, judging from ratios obtained from death certificates. Several rows and columns in the table clearly involve too few cases upon which to base a reliable statistic, and they are included only so that readers may judge the full range of available data. (As a general guide, rows or columns based on fewer than twenty cases, although they may be important, are not statistically significant.)[45]

In all four communities throughout the nineteenth century high clusters appear along the upper left to lower right diagonal, the one that measures the tendency of a groom to have been of the same status as his father. That landed men in their late twenties came overwhelmingly from landed families is hardly surprising and merely confirms school-boy wisdom about property holding in a traditional society. But that same wisdom claims opportunity to have existed for an especially enterprising or talented peasant. If so, such persons usually had to leave their village, since available places in the local community apparently were reserved for young men whose fathers held similar positions. Rural businessmen and professionals formed a small and inbred elite drawn largely from themselves, from landowners, or from particularly successful town artisans. Even townsmen, and here are included such unwelcome positions as tufa miner in Castel San Giorgio and street cleaner in Rogliano, drew young additions largely from town families rather than from among the peasantry.

The sharply limited degree of status mobility shown in tables 21 and 22 stands in distinct contrast to figures in table 23, which measure status differences between grooms and their fathers-in-law. Levels of mobility need not be overstated; clearly the majority of young couples came from similar socioeconomic backgrounds. Nevertheless, considering the absence of substantial shifts in overall ratios of agriculturists (refer to fig. 14) and the relative paucity of status differences among fathers and sons, levels of cross-status marriage are significantly (statistically and historically) high. The major avenue of status mobility for nineteenth-century rural Italians who remained in their villages was marriage. Thus, an event central to the process of *la famiglia* and to its perpetuation operated also as a primary vehicle for mobility. The power of *fortuna*, which rural folk saw generally as an evil force condemning them to present vicissitudes and boding even worse for the future, working under the guise of individualism and romantic love, produced change rather than continuity. Such changes were seldom an unmixed blessing, however, since cross-status marriage simultaneously involved upward and downward movement of some sort. To emphasize either the rising peasant son or the declining landed daughter would miss the

TABLE 23   Status Mobility among Grooms and Their Fathers-in-Law (%)

| FATHERS-IN-LAW | ALBARETO GROOMS (1870–1909) | | | |
| | Peasant (364) | Landowner (69) | Town (15) | Business/ Professional (14) |
| --- | --- | --- | --- | --- |
| Peasant (376) | 97 | 11 | 40 | 50 |
| Landowner (63) | 1 | 78 | 13 | 29 |
| Town (16) | 2 | 6 | 47 | 0 |
| Business/professional (7) | + | 5 | 0 | 21 |
| | CASTEL SAN GIORGIO GROOMS (1810–1909) | | | |
| | (522) | (41) | (508) | (44) |
| Peasant (469) | 64 | 4 | 25 | 14 |
| Landowner (76) | 2 | 66 | 5 | 32 |
| Town (541) | 33 | 10 | 69 | 36 |
| Business/professional (29) | 1 | 20 | 1 | 18 |
| | NISSORIA GROOMS (1820–1909) | | | |
| | (457) | (35) | (47) | (24) |
| Peasant (463) | 92 | 12 | 62 | 33 |
| Landowner (42) | 3 | 74 | 1 | 13 |
| Town (27) | 3 | 0 | 28 | 4 |
| Business/professional (31) | 2 | 14 | 9 | 50 |
| | ROGLIANO GROOMS (1810–1909) | | | |
| | (473) | (11) | (116) | (18) |
| Peasant (497) | 95 | 0 | 28 | 17 |
| Landowner (17) | + | 55 | 13 | 33 |
| Town (95) | 5 | 36 | 57 | 17 |
| Business/professional (9) | 0 | 9 | 2 | 33 |

NOTE.  N cases in parentheses. More than 0 but less than 0.5% shown as +.

essential ambiguity, suspicion, and hostility with which both families regarded such matches. A person who married above his or her station necessarily rejected the cultural and economic ways of *la famiglia*, thereby questioning its values and threatening its perpetuation. To be *sistemato bene* meant a marriage consistent with and earned by a family's *onore*; a secure situation could not rest long on *fortuna* which, whatever its temporary gifts, had to be repaid thrice over.

In the villages of Nissoria and Albareto more than one in every ten landed grooms married a peasant girl, about the same portion that wed daughters of nonagriculturists. In Castel San Giorgio and Rogliano, on the other hand, 30–45 percent of landed grooms married town girls, whereas fewer than one in twenty wed a peasant. Such proportions are predictable mathematically simply in terms of relative numbers of "available" spouses in each category. Landed grooms married townsmen's daughters more often where there were more townsmen's daughters. But rural folk did not make such availability calculations, at least not to two decimal places. Notwithstanding mathematical probabilities, many familial networks among Albareto's and Nissoria's peasants included a landed member, whereas in Castel San Giorgio and Rogliano such links were to town life. Herein is part of the demographic basis for the absence of *la miseria* in Albareto and Nissoria. Their peasantries, less involved through marriage in town life, were more thoroughly joined in kin networks with families of property. The building of *onore* through maintenance of reciprocal favors in accordance with ability to provide enriched yet further the significance of peasant ties to landowners, at least to those of the lesser variety who lived locally. In Castel San Giorgio and Rogliano, where avenues out of the peasantry led to town, nonpeasant members of *la famiglia* were often not in a position to exchange favors. They shared less fully the tiller's concern for sun, rain, and wind; their homes contained no space for a needy relative; their cash earnings were steadier yet less flexible than the agriculturist's income. In the peasants' view, landowners were superior, whereas townsmen were merely different; they had not earned the right to look with disdain upon the *contadino's* station in life.

Nonpeasants viewed cross-status marriage differently. For landowners, town artisans, businessmen, and professionals, marriage offered a possibility of expanding the family's economic base in new directions. Again, significant distinctions emerge between the towns of Castel San Giorgio and Rogliano on the one hand and the villages of Albareto and Nissoria on the other. In the towns, business and professional grooms wed landed daughters twice as often as they wed peasants, precisely the reverse of what happened in the villages. Whereas a clear majority of Castel San Giorgio's and Rogliano's townsmen married women of the same status, only a minority did so in Albareto and Nissoria. In sum, village figures reflect either lack of status mobility (as in Nissoria for businessmen and professionals) or openness to the peasantry (as in both town columns and among business/professional persons in Albareto), while town figures (Rogliano and Castel San Giorgio) show cross-status nuptials for all combinations except those involving the peasantry. Town/countryside interpenetration was actually least where potential opportunity for such interaction was greatest. This suggests that where town life was of sufficient size and vitality to exist at least semiautonomously from agriculture, townspeople reduced occasions of intermarriage with peasants. Where town life remained an adjunct of agriculture devoted primarily to serving local needs, rural folk retained access through marriage to town opportunities, limited though these were, and a substantial number of town grooms wed peasant brides.[46]

## CONTADINO AND PADRONE

At the outset of this chapter I suggested that the viability of a sustaining peasant culture, one that offered an alternative to *la miseria*, depended at least in part upon mode of agricultural production and upon the quality of town/countryside interaction. It appeared that where feudal vestiges remained consequential at the local level, even within a capitalist macrosystem serving an integrated national market, peasants less easily and fully fell victim to self-abnegation and pity. When pro-letarianization of rural labor occurred, especially if this happened in a setting dominated by town economy, *la miseria* flourished.

Albareto, with its communal lands, provided a particularly clear in-stance of the impact of a feudal remnant even into the twentieth cen-tury. Nissoria, at least until massive emigration beginning in 1900, offered a more ambiguous case, but one of great importance because of its "typicality" for important areas of the Mezzogiorno. That the objec-tive quality of life in Nissoria was miserable there can be no doubt. The *latifondisti* deserve no historical exculpation and would be too facile a target for condemnation. But the system of latifundism and its relation to peasant culture merit close inquiry and understanding. A similar need for analysis exists with regard to the contest between *cittadini* and *contadini* in places such as Castel San Giorgio and Rogliano.

Evidence from registers of births, marriages, and deaths showed that mobility into and out of the peasantry was minimal. Some peasants acquired land, more often through marriage than through a lifetime of labor, but very few entered the ranks of substantial holders. It may well be, as Anton Blok suggests, that many Sicilian *gabellotti* were "peasant entrepreneurs," but this was not the case in Nissoria, where lease-holding intermediaries came from the landed class. Even where *gabel-lotti* were of peasant origin, the ratio of one to the other and the rapidity with which these *nouveaux riches* attempted to obliterate their former cultural ties meant that this avenue of escape from *la miseria* was narrow indeed. Movement into town economy also was rare, at least until after World War II when the failure of agrarian reform hastened abandon-ment of the countryside. Throughout the nineteenth century, the bar-riers blocking entry to town life were strongest precisely where town economy seemed most vigorous, where more places potentially were available. As with the acquisition of land, a peasant's major chance for becoming a *cittadino* was through marriage, but townspeople's disdain for *contadini* kept such possibilities at a minimum. In short, status mo-bility was not a meaningful alternative to *la miseria*. Anyone born a peasant was most likely to die a peasant, and at an earlier age than a substantial landowner or a townsperson. Work did not offer a means of advancement or even of change. "People have to work in order not to die," commented one Sicilian. That goal, too, was unattainable.[47]

There is no surprise ending to this tale; the reader hardly needs to be told that for many Italian peasants the ultimate escape from their plight was emigration, an option to be evaluated shortly. Before doing so, however, I wish to explore a bit further the nature of relations between peasants and their "betters" in the nineteenth century, when each depended on the other.

Emilio Sereni presents in compassionate, militant, incisive fashion an orthodox (insofar as any Italian thinker is orthodox) Marxist analysis of relations between *contadini* and *padroni*. He demonstrates with considerable subtlety that Italian agriculture was capitalist throughout the nineteenth century, even though the process of capitalism took several strange turns due to the regional concentration of feudal vestiges. In particular, the dominance of sharecropping in central Italy (and especially in Tuscany) and the presence of latifundism in much of the south combined to thwart an agrarian revolutionary potential during the Risorgimento. Sereni, following Gramsci, was too sensitive to suggest a narrow reading of Engels and a consequent judgment that Italy's problem was a deficiency of capitalist development. The past could not be undone, and to quote Sereni, an effective understanding of Italy's economy therefore required full recognition that in half of the country capitalism was "grafted onto an ancient feudal trunk," and that the economy remained "profoundly infected with feudal vestiges." These feudal vestiges, according to Sereni, resulted in particularly fierce oppression of poor peasants and in *la miseria*.[48] At one level, this conclusion appears to be directly opposite to what I have maintained in the present chapter—that is, proletarianization heightened *la miseria*, whereas feudal vestiges offered a shelter behind which *la gioia* might flourish. The contradiction is resolved, however, by a careful distinction between material conditions and cultural solidarity. When Sereni's main focus was on material conditions, he used the phrase "la miseria" to describe economic circumstances. These were so deplorable throughout the south that it would be trivial to quibble about whether they were even worse in the rice belts of the Po Valley or on the Venetian plains.[49] But *la miseria* also refers to culture, to the response pattern of peasants to disease, hunger, underemployment, and exploitation.

Sereni recognized this usage of "la miseria" in his analysis of differences between Sicily and the continental south. On the island (through the nineteenth century) the dominance of landed magnates of feudal origin was far more complete than on the continent, where small and medium holders constituted a politically important rural bourgeoisie. On the island intermediate *gabellotti*, although they were capitalists, used "semifeudal" means such as usury in kind and a *soccorso* to achieve profits and to plunge workers into dependency. Exploitation on the island took the form of "robust barbarism," whereas on the continent more "refined" methods developed.

In Sicily, the semifeudal structure of the *entire* society continues to assure a certain solidarity; in the dominant class, as among the peasant masses, associative tendencies are profoundly effective; solidarity is widespread and ardent, class struggles assume a particularly fierce aspect and, in their way, an organization. In the continental south, instead, all social strata, from the landed magnates to the peasants, appear about to disintegrate and decompose.

The apex of the grand feudal edifice, that which acted as the keystone, here fell apart centuries ago: the landed magnates, variable and compound in their origin, lack organization and cohesive autonomy.... Life and [its] social contrasts—though full of vitality—in the [continental] south are squandered, often in a thousand rivulets; the significant common needs of classes and of interest groups are diluted into municipal, local, and individual concerns; [class interests] succeed in being expressed in coherent collective thought and action, capable of achieving meaningful organizational form, only with difficulty.

Sereni's analysis of broad regional differences thus reaches conclusions congruent with the present findings from local levels.[50]

In Castel San Giorgio and Rogliano agricultural laborers hated the land; they did not organize effectively to improve their lot; they cursed their fate and pitied themselves. A 1910 parliamentary inquiry into the principal causes of *la miseria* began with a statement that the peasant of the Mezzogiorno was "inferior" and proceeded to propose steps for elevating the southern agrarian class to the level found in the north, "which is not better by nature, merely more fortunate." The futile steps recommended to counteract bad fortune need not concern us, since there is little evidence that the original premise of inferiority was useful or correct. The "southern question" and *la miseria* are as severe today as they were decades ago, perhaps more so.[51] In the Rogliano region, according to the same 1910 government source, peasants respected the "better" classes, acting with reverence, especially toward the great landowners (who were described as ignorant, afraid of the risks involved in new methods, and absentee). Relations between *cittadini* and *contadini* were limited; peasants living in the countryside came to town only on special feast days, while those residing in town were constantly and corrosively reminded of the townspeople's less severe situation. An 1882 report on the Campania region concluded without emotion that, although many peasants were of good faith, they had been stripped of the "dignity of a man." For the few peasants who remain today, dignity is still a goal.[52]

In Nissoria, as in the surrounding region of central Sicily, material conditions were even worse than on the mainland. Yet there is evidence, not a massive array but a few scattered suggestions, that peasant solidarity, nurtured on festival days, during long walks back to the village, in collective hostility to semifeudal magnates and capitalist

gabellotti alike, and in group work patterns, overcame la miseria. When
labor contracts with latifondisti included provision for half pay for
walking time between home and field above half an hour, estate man-
agers offered instead a free plate of vegetable soup and some straw for
those who remained overnight. But the contadini walked two hours or
more anyway, after 14–16 hours work. According to government observers, throughout the region priests were viewed by the peasantry as
tools of the elite, as dissolute and avaricious intriguers. State officials
were also agents of the powerful, and to them peasants responded with
lies and with silence. Extreme poverty led to frequent "thefts" in the
countryside, lack of respect for the law, and a belief that honesty in
caring for the owner's property was a defect and a sign of stupidity.
Owners treated peasants as slaves, as pariahs, as beasts; owners were
ambitious and fanatical; more than capitalists they should be called
usurers, "an accursed race of vampires who sucked human blood." Any
respect shown by the contadino toward the padrone was totally superfi-
cial; the peasant always held the owner to be his cruel enemy and his
oppressor.[53] Only occasionally did such hatred, focused not on the land
but on its owners and the political apparatus they dominated, become
manifest in open violence.[54] On other days, of work and of celebration,
of famine and of feast, of la miseria and of la gioia, the peasants of
Nissoria endured.

# 7
# Space

E te veco 'n'ata vota
casa mia paese amato!
Te lassaje, so' turnato
pe' nun te lassà maje chiù,
pecchè dint' 'a chistu core
'nce staje sulamente tu!
Peppino De Filippo[1]

Space was the Italian peasant's enemy. When it came to land for cultivation, the *contadino* never had enough; what he had demanded back-
breaking labor for only meager returns. When it came to exchanging
goods and services, the costs of traversing lengthy distances condemned the peasant to reliance on exploitative local intermediaries and
distant patrons.[2] The need to control space, to understand and to create
order out of the seeming infinity of space, gave rise to *campanilismo*, a
melodious world which literally refers to the sound of the church bell.
In a curious symbiosis of space and person, Italian peasants (and to a
lesser extent the rural elite as well) perceived a fundamental distinction
between their *paesani*, born within the bell's ring, and *stranieri*, outsiders. To some observers the quantitative difference between the amount
of space contained within a village, generally no more than 10,000 hectares, and the rest of the world is so great as to make comparison
absurd. But the peasant, viewing the village, as it were, through a
high-powered microscope while seeing the world in telescopic fashion,
readily came to equate the space in each. The world was divided into
two parts, even two halves: we and they. The *contadino*'s labor efforts,
his land, his family, his past, and his future all lay within the village.
And this was true of his neighbors as well. Their unity seemed essential
in the endless contest against the vastness of space in the world outside.
(The reader who is willing to substitute the earth and earthlings for the
village and villagers, the universe for the outside world, and man made
in God's image for *paesani*, will share the author's understanding of
space and *campanilismo*.)

Campanilismo involves pride in the village and an intimate knowledge
of all it contains. Nissorini who knew I had interviewed the parish

priest at some length warned me, with no more than a trace of disre-
spect and mistrust, that the cleric's information might be faulty, since
he was a stranger to the village; he has been in the parish nearly thirty
years and was born less than fifty kilometers away. Conversely, when I
presented villagers with viewpoints and recollections of former Nissorini who had emigrated to Chicago before the Great War, the possibility
that these "memories" might be tainted by a half-century of living in
America never came up until I specifically suggested that this might
well be the case. Even then, most villagers defended the accuracy of
their *paesani*'s memories, struggling to account for out-of-order events,
impossibly large landholdings, and names without people. In Albareto
and Castel San Giorgio villagers identify less with the legal *comune* as a
whole than with the particular hamlet in which they were born. Vital
registers reflect the persistence of this identification: place of birth entries with hamlet names scratched out and replaced by the legally required town name.[3]

Walking about the village with several *paesani* soon reveals the
depths of knowledge and pride that make *campanilismo* (or what I am
trying to convey by the word) more than a cultural code, more than
parochial village chauvinism. Even where land is divided into tiny and
seemingly unmarked plots, as in parts of Castel San Giorgio and Rogliano, villagers know the precise boundaries not only of their own
holdings but of everyone else's as well. In one village each plot has its
own name, a name that may now be obscure but that once reflected
some characteristic of the land, its owner, or the means by which it was
acquired.[4] Whether named or not, boundaries are seldom fenced or
marked by human contraptions; rather, villagers recognize the peculiar
twist of a particular olive tree, the faint trace of what was once a path,
the course of richer soil where centuries ago a river flowed. Other de-
marcations are clearer—giant boulders, ridges, ravines—although these
can be a source of great contestation, as in Albareto when the swelling
of tiny streams changes land boundaries.

Villagers' knowledge of the human history of their birthplace is
equally rich and subtle: who lived and died in each house, where the
May dance took place and who attended and which couples slipped
away, the spot where San Biagio performed a miracle or where the
Squillacis were put to death, how a plot came to its present owner.
Knowledge of land transfer is particularly interesting; dates are usually
missing or approximate, but the sequence and circumstances of exchanges, inheritances, and sales are remembered with surprising accuracy and a persistent concern to reconstruct all links leading to the
present. This reflects something beyond legal wrangling. Indeed, two
families look on their children's marriage with particular favor if it
brings together holdings that once were united, no matter how meager

the plots involved. *Campanilismo*, then, is a conserving and preserving force, defined by birth (and therefore by fate), immutable and immune to human intervention, circumscribing the present by the past.

But *campanilismo* coexists with its opposite. Space may be an enemy and attachment to the village a futile defensive reaction, but space and the outside world simultaneously entice and repel the peasant. The attractions of the stranger and especially of the city have been noted by anthropologists studying a wide spectrum of peasant societies. George M. Foster summarizes the point well:

> The emotional dependence of the peasant on the city presents an especially poignant case. Peasants throughout history have admired the city, and have copied many of the elements they have observed there. The city, with its glitter and opportunity, holds a fascination, like a candle for a moth. . . . Peasants know they need the city, as an outlet for their surplus production and as the source of many material and nonmaterial items they cannot themselves produce.[5]

This particular anthropologist includes in the very definition of a peasant society (as opposed to a primitive tribal one) this borrowing from the wider society. His view that "cultural elements seem to flow principally outward and downward from city to peasant village" is, in my judgment, incomplete as a summary of cultural exchanges in Italy, but certainly Foster is correct in calling attention to this phenomenon.[6] The flow of customs, behavior patterns, ideas, inventions, and goods and services from city to countryside, from town to village, from hamlet to hamlet takes place in a variety of ways. These are amply demonstrated in Castel San Giorgio, Nissoria, Albareto, and Rogliano over the past two centuries.[7]

Castel San Giorgio is an excellent example of a crossroads town in the hinterland of a giant city, Naples. It has a weekly market at which local goods are exchanged, and sellers on their way to or from Naples and Salerno stop there to trade. In fact, travelers on all sorts of errands had passed through Castel San Giorgio regularly and for so long that their arrival became routine and caused no special stir or communal gathering. Castelsangiorgesi, including older women who always lived in one of the more isolated hamlets to the east, without exception had been to Naples, as had their parents. First-hand knowledge of the city—its smells, its streets, its noises, its people—diminished the awe with which rural folk in different circumstances tended to regard city dwellers. Moreover, the region around Castel San Giorgio was so densely populated, even in the early nineteenth century, that one town spilled into another, at least along the plain connecting Naples with Salerno. Thus, whether on foot or by mule there was little sense of going from Castel San Giorgio to a distinct and separate place with clear boundaries and kilometers of uninhabited land between. The absence of sharp physical barriers between Castel San Giorgio and its immedate neighbors (even the town centers are not walled in this region) and the nearness of a giant city certainly did not make the Castelsangiorgesi cosmopolitan, but it did undermine their sense of *campanilismo*, of attachment to a unique and identifiable space.

At the opposite extreme from Castel San Giorgio is the situation of Nissoria. The Sicilian village, its houses crowded within invisible walls, is circumscribed on every side by at least seven kilometers of wheat fields in which there are no permanent inhabitants. Surrounding towns, walled and perched on hills, are visible in the distance as distinct entities. The daily lives of most Nissorini did not afford opportunities to "pass by" Leonforte, Assoro, Agira, or other neighboring settlements. Going to another town was a planned and purposeful event, one that occurred only infrequently, one for which special arrangements had to be made, one that other villagers learned about in advance and thereupon came by to ask that a message be delivered to this or that relative. Nearly three of every four older women we interviewed in Nissoria had never been to Palermo, and over half had not seen Catania, either. Most never had traveled outside of Sicily, and only four in ten had touched saltwater.[8] For men the isolation was far less, due in large part to military conscription. But for both sexes it was normal for peasant villagers, at least until the last two decades, to venture to another town no more than two or three times in a year, to go to the provincial center of Enna only if required to do so by some government regulation, and to travel to Palermo or Catania rarely if at all in a lifetime. Information coming into Nissoria was absorbed with eager fascination. Returning villagers were "debriefed" in the evening in the piazza, and by the next morning even women and children knew all the latest news about Leonforte or perhaps even Palermo. This communal curiosity and communication network remains intact to the present day. Whereas in Castel San Giorgio even after several weeks we were able to walk about and meet townspeople who had not previously known anything of our presence, at Nissoria after the first night everyone knew our name and purpose, knew that our daughter was a whiz at jumping rope "American" style, and "had heard" about whom we had interviewed. On the night of June 3, 1860, news of the effort to wipe out the Squillaci family must have spread with equal rapidity. The contrast between poor outside communication and total knowledge within the village reinforces Nissoria's geographic isolation and provides a fertile soil for *campanilismo*. Villagers prefer to act within the sphere they know so well.

Although the hamlets of Albareto are also geographically isolated, the Albaretesi traditionally have ranged over a great amount of space.

"Their" mountains and woods extend over a vast triangle that starts from the Ligurian coast and continues along the Cisa Valley nearly to Parma. Throughout this space the Albaretesi, along with neighboring villagers, were masters of every stream, meadow, and wood. Women went about unaccompanied to gather chestnuts or mushrooms, and there was little concern even if they did not return immediately at dusk. With resonant echoes of individually recognizable calls and responses, the Albaretesi signaled their location and safety from one mountaintop to another. Whenever the village was threatened, whether by the French in 1799 or the Germans in 1944, villagers en masse took to the woods where, maintaining all the while their cows and chickens, they lived by gathering chestnuts and catching fish and small game. Intimate knowledge of the land was a primary means by which for over fourteen months local *partigiani* withstood, neutralized, and ultimately assisted in the triumph over vastly superior nazi firepower. Yet these same Albaretesi, when they emigrated to New York, São Paulo, and Buenos Aires, clustered together in apartments situated in a radius of only a few blocks, worked for the same handful of restaurants, and generally married other Parmigiani.[9]

In a curious way, the boundaries within which *campanilismo* flourished, although much wider than those of the Nissorini, were equally rigid for the Albaretesi. In earlier chapters I sought to demonstrate that Albareto's economy involved trade with cities along the Ligurian littoral from La Spezia to Genoa but that this interaction did not produce high levels of cultural and social penetration by coastal centers into mountain regions. The cautious, fearful, sometimes hostile way in which Albaretesi carried on their trade facilitated simultaneous economic integration and sociocultural isolation. Villagers only rarely and reluctantly journeyed to the "city" itself. Rather, a string of collection and distribution centers, small towns relative to the cities they served, emerged inland from the Ligurian littoral at the base of the first ridge of mountains parallel to the coast.[10] It was to these towns, and not to the cities, that the Albaretesi brought their mushrooms; here they gathered flocks for summer grazing on the high pastures and purchased salt and tobacco. They came to and returned from these towns by winding mountain paths unknown to city dwellers and camped in the woods when overnight stays were necessary. The city merchants with whom they dealt (the Albaretesi drove too hard a bargain to leave margin for expensive intermediaries) also journeyed to these midway towns, but by the main road; they slept at the local inn. Albareto, then, represents a case that does not conform well with anthropologist Foster's generalization quoted earlier. Whatever fascination the city held for these villagers was not sufficient to draw them directly within its environs even for a brief chance to see for themselves this strange world. Rigid separation of the two spheres persisted despite seven centuries of relatively continuous economic integration.

The fourth case, Rogliano, involves yet another configuration. As a mountain gathering point that dominated the Sila Plateau and surrounding countryside, Rogliano's economy, although declining, remained lively nearly to the end of the nineteenth century even against the competition of the nearby and considerably larger provincial capital of Cosenza. Only with the extension and perfection of railway transport and the effective imposition of national and formal regional government did Rogliano's sphere of influence diminish greatly. Before that time the town's weekly Sunday market and especially its three annual fairs were major events in the region extending south and east deep into interior Calabria. At Rogliano there were lawyers who had studied at Naples, bureaucrats from Reggio Calabria, merchants from Paola and even Palermo, and priests who actually had seen the pope. The well-to-do in Rogliano affected city manners and chose spouses from distant places; it was this version of cultural "donation" that the surrounding region received.[11] To the markets and fairs there came also gypsies, wandering entertainers, and traders who in the course of a year traveled throughout the southern provinces exchanging their wares. It was among these folk that the less thoroughly studied but equally important communication network among villages was maintained. In Calabria, perhaps to a greater degree than elsewhere in Italy, even nearby villages, isolated from one another by poor roads and treacherous ravines, tended to develop distinctive cultural traditions. These are most easily recovered by historians who look to matters of dress, food preparation, dialect, and nuances of labor arrangements, but the range of distinction undoubtedly was yet wider in many cases.[12] Transmission of these distinct and sometimes "new" ways that had emerged in a particular village took place in towns such as Rogliano. In sum, Rogliano served not only as a transmitter of ideas and ways from city to countryside but also as a locus for the exchange from village to village of both tradition and innovation.

The space and communication networks of these four communities, then, may be summarized as follows: Castel San Giorgio—fluid boundaries, limited space, direct contact with cities, conductor of outside communication, weak internal communication; Nissoria—rigid boundaries, limited space, remote contact with cities, receiver of outside communication, highly developed internal communication; Albareto—rigid boundaries, extended space, indirect contact with cities, receiver of outside communication, moderately developed internal communication; Rogliano—rigid boundaries, extended space, indirect contact with cities except for the upper class, gatherer and transmitter of outside communication, moderately developed internal communication.

Notwithstanding these differences, there are a number of communication modes common to all four places, and to rural Italy generally, that despite their obviousness deserve mention. First among these is the church. Apart from matters of popular belief (the treatment of which must await another volume), the church established and remained central to notice and celebration of major turning points for both the individual and the village as a whole. Each of life's stages—birth, puberty, marriage, reproduction, death—was marked by an appropriate ceremony, one that communicated a universal state of being. The language of these ceremonies was unintelligible, but their physical and visual symbols invoked for rural folk a sense of community that extended both horizontally to all other "Christians" and vertically to their ancestors. (In Castel San Giorgio it was widely believed that if during the baptismal ceremony the celebrant left out a word the baby would be plagued for life by misfortune. Since very few can have known whether a word had been skipped, the belief flourished without possible contradiction, until the recent imposition of liturgical reforms opposed by the Castelsangiorgesi for this very reason.) For the village as a whole, and indeed for vast regions, the church also organized and marked seasonal changes, times for feasting or fasting, and such longer-term occasions as jubilees and centennials. All these offered not only modes for transmitting tradition but also ways to present, and if necessary to impose, innovation. In addition to his role in these regular and official functions, the local priest served as a principle vehicle for communication into and out of the village. Peasants seeking an emigration permit, news of a relative, or delivery of a message often turned to their priest.[13]

Another major avenue of communication for rural Italy was military conscription. Everywhere by the 1870s and in large areas as early as the Napoleonic wars, all males by age eighteen or twenty had to appear before conscription boards. Many were exempted from service for a variety of physical, familial, or vocational circumstances, and even among the remainder not everyone served. But from every *comune* some males were chosen. Within six to thirty-six months these young men returned to share ultimately with the entire village their knowledge of strange places and their contact with people of different ways. The ambiguous consequences of military service are reported in some detail in the Jacini inquiry's section on the province of Catania (including Nissoria). In earlier days, according to one report, wailing, crying, and desperation accompanied a soldier's departure, whereas now (1885) he goes "with the thought of returning quickly, educated and having seen so many beautiful cities." Another town submitted that "the peasant leaves as a boor, violent and uncultured; he returns educated, civilized, respectful, and obedient, and he knows how to read and write." In Leonforte, directly adjacent to Nissoria, on the other hand, a year or so in the army proved unable to overcome the peasantry's "innate spirit of mafia and brigandage." And in nearby Giarre officials lamented the profligate tendencies of soldiers who had been corrupted at city brothels. Several towns which were less explicit in their reservations about military service nevertheless noted that familiarity with the vices of great cities and the consequent development of artificial needs rendered *contadini* dissatisfied and even rebellious over their inability to satisfy their new desires.[14] Obviously their military experience gave these men an incomplete and distorted picture of the world outside, and as individuals they were hardly neutral conduits of information, but this did not reduce their significance in the overall network by which a village learned.

In addition to such personal conveyors of knowledge as priests and soldiers, villagers came into contact with a range of physical artifacts that communicated information. Coins, postal stamps, legal seals, paper currency, and posters legal or otherwise generally circulated at a slower pace than orally and personally conveyed news, but what they lacked in speed was more than counterbalanced by their authoritativeness. In the stormy years immediately following the formal proclamation of Italy's existence as a national state, even in parts of the Mezzogiorno with relatively good communication links, such as Rogliano, only the appearance and circulation of currency with King Vittorio Emmanuele's profile finally assured townsmen of what had occurred. From coins and stamps, signatures and seals isolated folk may learn their history, their "high" cultural heritage, or, as Il Duce knew well, a dramatic new turn of events. Conversely, only the quick disappearance of Mussolini's formerly ubiquitous posters finally convinced the Nissorini that the Allies had liberated more than Sicily.[15]

The spread of literacy, as shown in tables 24 and 25, ultimately greatly enhanced the success with which urban Italy, its culture and its economy, penetrated the countryside.[16] Universal public instruction, however, is a phenomenon of the twentieth century, and in some areas of the rural south as late as 1950 a majority of the adult population was unable to read or write. Moreover, recent imposition of a national Italian language and consequent decay of local dialect,[17] combined with geometric increases in the quantity of information available and necessary for effective decision making, render a substantial percentage of rural folk functionally illiterate even today. Add to the many villagers who need aid in filling out routine bureaucratic forms or postal money orders the hundreds or thousands from every southern community who have spent years in Germany, Switzerland, or Turin (all places where

TABLE 24  **Literacy Percentages over Time**

| YEAR AND AGES | PARMA M F | PRINCIPATO CITERIORE M F | CALABRIA CITERIORE M F | CATANIA M F |
|---|---|---|---|---|
| 1861:[a] | | | | |
| 5–12 | 10  5 | 8  2 | 13  1 | 4  1 |
| 13–19 | 19  10 | 16  5 | 20  3 | 9  2 |
| Over 19 | 21  8 | 20  5 | 24  3 | 12  2 |

| | BORGOTARO M F | SALERNO M F | COSENZA M F | NICOSIA M F |
|---|---|---|---|---|
| 1871: | | | | |
| Over 6 | 23  10 | 22  11 | 19  3 | 14  4 |
| 1901: | | | | |
| 7–9 | 36  36 | 31  23 | 23  15 | 25  17 |
| 10–15 | 66  62 | 48  39 | 36  25 | 26  25 |
| 16–21 | 65  63 | 48  40 | 35  23 | 22  22 |
| 22–30 | 64  55 | 50  35 | 39  18 | 26  18 |
| Over 30 | 46  25 | 35  17 | 34  8 | 23  8 |

| | ALBARETO M F | CASTEL SAN GIORGIO M F | ROGLIANO M F | NISSORIA M F |
|---|---|---|---|---|
| 1911: | | | | |
| Over 6 | 60  49 | 57  42 | 45  29 | 36  30 |
| 1921: | | | | |
| Over 6 | 77  73 | 71  63 | 46  45 | 38  34 |
| 1931: | | | | |
| Over 6 | 85  81 | 76  65 | 61  42 | 48  49 |

[a]Centers under 6,000 population.

"their" language is not understood), and it becomes evident that illiteracy is still a problem.

For the nineteenth century, census figures paint a truly dismal portrait. Historian John Briggs recently warned against exclusive emphasis on such data; he concedes the approximate accuracy of the official returns but argues vigorously that they measure "past opportunity" rather than "future response to schooling." Briggs finds that peasants were victims of elite power holders who feared the social unrest that an end of ignorance might bring and who flagrantly ignored or violated national legislation on schooling. When *contadini* finally received an opportunity to learn, whether in their villages or as emigrants in America, they seized it avidly. Briggs's case is persuasive to a point, especially on the role of elites in perpetuating illiteracy among the masses and on the inappropriateness of using illiteracy levels to

TABLE 25    Literacy by Age Group, 1881 (%)

| | BORGOTARO | | SALERNO | | COSENZA | | NICOSIA | | ITALY | |
| AGE | M | F | M | F | M | F | M | F | M | F |
|---|---|---|---|---|---|---|---|---|---|---|
| 6 | 10 | 3 | 11 | 7 | 8 | 3 | 8 | 4 | 17 | 16 |
| 7 | 16 | 13 | 20 | 14 | 14 | 5 | 13 | 8 | 31 | 27 |
| 8 | 27 | 19 | 27 | 20 | 15 | 6 | 18 | 8 | 40 | 35 |
| 9 | 39 | 27 | 35 | 25 | 23 | 14 | 15 | 11 | 47 | 41 |
| 10–11 | 40 | 35 | 36 | 26 | 24 | 8 | 15 | 11 | 49 | 43 |
| 12–14 | 46 | 40 | 36 | 25 | 21 | 8 | 14 | 11 | 49 | 43 |
| 15–19 | 43 | 37 | 34 | 24 | 23 | 9 | 13 | 9 | 49 | 42 |
| 20–24 | 49 | 30 | 40 | 21 | 26 | 8 | 19 | 7 | 53 | 38 |
| 25–29 | 51 | 25 | 36 | 18 | 33 | 6 | 22 | 7 | 53 | 35 |
| 30–34 | 47 | 19 | 30 | 14 | 29 | 5 | 21 | 5 | 48 | 30 |
| 35–39 | 48 | 18 | 33 | 14 | 33 | 6 | 24 | 7 | 48 | 29 |
| 40–44 | 40 | 14 | 27 | 11 | 27 | 4 | 15 | 4 | 43 | 24 |
| 45–49 | 29 | 10 | 30 | 12 | 29 | 5 | 20 | 7 | 44 | 24 |
| 50–54 | 30 | 10 | 25 | 9 | 26 | 3 | 15 | 4 | 39 | 20 |
| 55–59 | 29 | 10 | 30 | 11 | 31 | 5 | 22 | 6 | 42 | 20 |
| 60–64 | 28 | 6 | 23 | 9 | 26 | 4 | 14 | 4 | 38 | 17 |
| 65–69 | 29 | 6 | 33 | 13 | 34 | 5 | 22 | 7 | 43 | 19 |
| 70 and over | 24 | 4 | 26 | 9 | 27 | 4 | 18 | 4 | 38 | 16 |

"prove" that peasants were content with their lack of education.[18] But the facts remain that most *contadini* could not read or write; that educational opportunities spread far more rapidly in urban areas and in the north, thereby exacerbating the dualism of Italy's economy; and that rural women suffered particular disadvantage.[19]

Parliamentary inquiries noted, only occasionally with dismay, that southern peasants were uniformly illiterate, an observation validated in the census figures through at least 1881. In that year in Nissoria forty-seven children attended school; actually there was no school proper but, rather, four teachers, one female for the twenty-two girls and three males for the twenty-five boys. Although the legal minimum annual salary for teachers was 770 lire, Nissoria's educators each received only 605 lire; pupils and teachers had no permanent building and instead used abandoned rural structures described as "malsani" (unhealthy, dilapidated). Results were termed mediocre. No children of the peasantry appear to have been in attendance, nor could they have frequented private, evening, or holiday schools, since none existed.[20] In the more integrated town of Rogliano as late as 1906 more than one-third of the residents required by law to attend school in that year had never done so.[21] Even the impact of military conscription (note the 3–6 percent increase in male literacy after age twenty in the 1881 census figures in table 25) left most rural Italian males illiterate.

The absolute infrequency of literacy among peasants promoted the influence of intermediary power brokers who, for a fee or a favor, would read a letter, explain a contract, or witness a document. The need to communicate over vast distances, and therefore in written form, increased enormously when overseas migration reached massive levels in the later 1890s. The gap between peasant illiteracy and the need to write created a special role for intermediaries on both sides of the Atlantic and gave great impetus to the *padrone* system that has attracted so much attention from scholars of immigration.[22] The *padrone* in 1900, like the priest half a century earlier, intercepted messages sent by the dominant culture and passed them on, often in self-serving and ambiguous ways, to the peasantry.

Not until after the Great War, however, did modes of communication penetrate directly and consistently into the Italian home and thereby to *la famiglia*. But the advent of radio (and later of television) in an ironic way actually served to isolate rural folk further, at least in some respects. These electronic devices communicated only in one direction; they carried vast amounts of information, generally with greater levels of accuracy than had prevailed earlier, to the peasant; but they allowed no return message. The ever growing sophistication of one-way electronic communication hastened the atrophy of earlier modes that, for all their slowness and uncertainty, were bifunctional. The priest, the vagabond, the soldier, and the *padrone* not only brought news in but carried messages and customary ways out. These persons or their functional equivalents still exist, but their role as two-way conveyors is enormously reduced. Rural folk today need make little effort to keep abreast of the latest world crisis, but they have lost the means to communicate news of their own.[23]

All indications are that attachment to the local village has diminished over the past two centuries in rural Italy. Geographic mobility is an obvious and important aspect of this change, a by-product of technological breakthroughs in transportation. The effort and cost in real wages of going from Nissoria to Chicago in 1910 were no greater than they had been a century earlier for a trip from the village to Rome. That is, even without increasing the human effort (whether calculated in wages or horsepower) expended in physical movement, villagers came suddenly (for steamship and railroad development occurred within a generation) to have much greater access to distant places. Statistical measures all reflect increased levels of individual migration over time; these will be examined shortly in some detail. First, however, a caution may be entered against interpreting these figures as a simple index of the decline of *campanilismo*. Throughout this study I have tried to show how demographic realities supported and made functional a rural world view dominated by fatalism, honor, family, and village. In the analysis of marriage records that follows it will be obvious that over time, more and more villagers chose to marry "outsiders" and therefore that families so formed cannot have been wed solely to a single village. But this phenomenon led less to a diminution in the force of *campanilismo* than to an extension of its scope over more space and new space.[24] Village attachments gave way to regionalism and, in the hands of ambitious totalitarians of the right and left in the present century, to national racism. Rampant nationalism contains all the elements of *campanilismo*, the major difference between them being the amount of space they claim. Mussolini's call for national greatness and the recovery of "Our Sea" appealed to rural folk precisely because they now identified, after half a century of extensive migration, with a wider Italian community flung over vast and discontinuous space.[25] It is more than ironic that fascist nationalism, which superficially represented the antithesis of peasant traditionalism, contained within it so many parallel appeals: the grandeur of Rome with the village's mythical golden past; *Mare Nostrum* with our mountains; 100 million Italians with continuation of the familial spiral; trains running on time with individuals of honor who kept their word; *il destino* with fate.[26] In short, the maps and tables that follow indicate not the decline of *campanilismo* but its persistence over grander spaces made small by technological sophistication.

The primary documents to be used to assess attachment to the village are the marriage registers. These uniformly contain the place of birth of the bride and groom, thereby allowing a straightforward and consistent measure of precisely how many families had connections to more than one place. The importance of such connections, which formed the networks through which flowed reciprocal obligations based on honor, extended in diminished form to the entire village.[27] Unlike episodic fairs, or the sweep of military forces, or even the decision to seek temporary work in a foreign country, all of which tended to place peasants in environments they did not command, marriage forged a potentially permanent link across space. Prevailing over the geographic error of Nissorini who believe that Chicago is closer than Rome is the reality that the village indeed is linked to "its" cousins who have married the Poles, the Irish, and even the Americans of Chicago. But full treatment of transatlantic migration must await the next chapter; my concern at present is with villagers who stayed and who married locally.

Table 26 displays percentages of marriages in all four communities over time according to the spouses' place of birth. A fully endogamous marriage is one in which both bride and groom were born in the very village or town where two decades or so later they married. A double exogamous marriage, and note how few of these there are even in recent years, refers to one in which neither spouse was born in the place where

Space

163

TABLE 26   Endogamous and Exogamous Marriage in Four Communities over Time (%)

| PLACE AND DATE | FULLY ENDOGAMOUS | EXOGAMOUS Groom | EXOGAMOUS Bride | DOUBLE EXOGAMOUS | N CASES |
|---|---|---|---|---|---|
| Nissoria: | | | | | |
| 1811–59 | 68 | 21 | 7 | 4 | 319 |
| 1860–1909 | 66 | 21 | 8 | 5 | 594 |
| 1910–45 | 50 | 27 | 15 | 8 | 428 |
| 1946–73 | 34 | 35 | 22 | 9 | 464 |
| Albareto: | | | | | |
| 1870–1909 | 84 | 7 | 7 | 2 | 482 |
| 1910–26 | 62 | 19 | 15 | 4 | 294 |
| 1946–73 | 51 | 25 | 16 | 8 | 521 |
| Castel San Giorgio: | | | | | |
| 1811–59 | 61 | 33 | 4 | 2 | 693 |
| 1860–1909 | 51 | 36 | 8 | 5 | 887 |
| 1910–45 | 41 | 40 | 7 | 12 | 777 |
| 1946–73 | 29 | 38 | 21 | 12 | 1,294 |
| Rogliano: | | | | | |
| 1811–59 | 73 | 18 | 5 | 4 | 858 |
| 1860–1909 | 72 | 16 | 7 | 5 | 854 |
| 1910–45 | 60 | 17 | 11 | 12 | 800 |
| 1946–73 | 42 | 28 | 19 | 11 | 934 |

they married. The middle two columns refer to cases in which one but not the other spouse was born locally.

Among 1,870 marriages celebrated before 1860 only 68, or less than 3 percent, involved partners both of whom were born outside the place in which the nuptial was recorded. This proportion grew only very slightly over the next decades until the eve of the Great War. Even in the twentieth century, percentages of nuptials involving couples having no immediate link by birth to the place where they married are low: 8 or 9 percent in the villages of Nissoria and Albareto, 11 or 12 percent in the towns of Castel San Giorgio and Rogliano. The true numbers of "outsiders" to the place of marriage is yet lower than these estimates, since some spouses with distant birthplaces happened to have been born while parents were temporarily elsewhere in search of work. For example, entries in Albareto's registers showing a man born in London marrying a woman born at Marseilles reflect not internationalism but an attachment to the village so strong that it persisted despite decades of migration. To restate, even during recent years in about nine of every ten marriages in these rural communities either the bride or groom or both were born there. This 90 percent figure is down from 97 percent a century earlier, but such a moderate trend, especially in the face of two major wars and rapid economic dislocation, indicates an essential stability in this dimension of *campanilismo*. Outsiders, new people with new ways, are not entering rural Italian villages and towns, at least not in a permanent, familial way.

More striking changes have occurred in rates of fully endogamous marriage. For the nineteenth century roughly two-thirds of brides and grooms had both been born in the place in which they subsequently married.[28] Figures for the isolated mountain village of Albareto are even higher, while those for integrated Castel San Giorgio, with its fluid boundaries and densely populated surroundings, are lower. It is interesting to note that, although over time the proportion of fully endogamous marriages dropped everywhere, the rank order of endogamy percentages for the four communities remained unchanged. The persistence of this order, from Albareto to Rogliano to Nissoria to Castel San Giorgio, reflects their varying space and communication patterns as noted earlier in this chapter. A trend away from marrying a local man or woman appeared first in Castel San Giorgio and only after World War I in the other communities. But everywhere the trend continued, until now only about one-third of all nuptials are fully endogamous. This is clearly a long way down from the two-thirds who married locally as recently as fifty years ago. Nevertheless, it is not a trivial figure, especially since these communities range in total population from only 3,000 to 9,000, which makes the pool of potential partners small indeed, to be counted in tens.

Nor has marriage to an outsider usually involved someone from a great distance. Let us for the moment ignore not only Fiats and trains but even mules and assume that prospective brides and grooms must have walked to meet each other and yet returned home by nightfall. That it was their fathers who in many cases arranged the match, changes who did the walking but not much else, since peasants of any age and sex normally did not sleep under a stranger's roof. Such a "round trip on foot in a day" world cannot have extended to a radius much beyond 15 kilometers. It involved an area beyond the church bell but well within the space a peasant might know at the microlevel, feeling in control of himself and his environment, able to sense a wind shift, take a familiar shortcut, meet an old acquaintance, or pass a field he had toiled upon in earlier years.[29]

Among 5,234 spouses who wed in a place other than that of their birth, more than half married within the day's-walk world of 15 kilometers.[30] Table 27 provides a more detailed breakdown of these partially or fully exogamous marriages. The figures accord well with what was stated earlier about these communities. Albaretesi who did not marry someone born in the village nevertheless in a majority of cases chose a spouse from one of the adjacent mountain settlements. Interestingly, however, the percentage of Albaretesi marrying someone

TABLE 27    Distances Involved in Exogamous Marriages (%)

| | KILOMETER DISTANCE BETWEEN PLACE OF MARRIAGE AND BIRTH | | | | | |
| | Under 16 | 16–45 | 46–95 | 96–195 | Over 195 | N CASES |
|---|---|---|---|---|---|---|
| Albareto | 56 | 12 | 18 | 7 | 7 | 612 |
| Castel San Giorgio | 57 | 28 | 7 | 4 | 4 | 2,284 |
| Nissoria | 59 | 20 | 10 | 8 | 3 | 845 |
| Rogliano | 34 | 41 | 7 | 7 | 11 | 1,493 |

born far away, for argument's sake say more than 45 kilometers (a distance that surely could not be covered round trip in a day), is greater than in the other three communities. Albareto's space was extensive, reaching nearly to the Ligurian coast for economic exchanges, and the 18 percent figure shown for nuptials in the 46–95-kilometer range reflects the demographic consequences of the village's economy. The reverse is also true; Albaretesi sometimes initiated new exchange patterns or confirmed precarious ones through marriage alliances. The relatively high proportion of nuptials in the category "over 195 kilometers" results from the high rates of repatriation among emigrants from the village (see the following chapter). In sum, nuptial distance patterns provide statistical confirmation that, although absolute distances were greater than elsewhere, the Albaretesi nevertheless married within the space they knew well.

Marriage distances in the other three communities also follow closely overall space and communication configurations. Nearly 80 percent of the Nissorini who married outsiders chose a spouse from one of the five immediately adjacent towns. Castelsangiorgesi wed predominantly persons born nearby in the densely populated belt between Naples and Salerno. Only in Rogliano did a majority of exogamous marriages involve spouses born in places beyond a day's walk. The cluster of nuptials in the 16–45-kilometer range reflects the town's role as a marketing and bureaucratic center for the surrounding region. People who came to Rogliano's Sunday markets and especially to its three annual fairs stayed overnight, participated in festive dancing, and with some frequency chose a spouse.

Further information on the kinds of marriage links formed by rural Italians may be obtained by combining place of birth entries from marriage registers with census data. In order not to burden the analysis with too many numbers, I have included population figures only for 1871, generally a reliable census year and one that divides the total period under consideration reasonably well.[31] Tables 28 and 29 summarize the percentages of exogamous spouses born in places of varying

TABLE 28   Density Levels, in 1871, and Exogamous Marriages (%)

|  | DENSITY LEVELS (PERSONS/KM²) OF PLACES OF BIRTH | | | | |
|---|---|---|---|---|---|
|  | Under 50 | 50–99 | 100–199 | Over 199 | |
|  |  | (Fully |  | (High | N |
|  | (Sparse) | Settled) | (Congested) | Density) | CASES |
| Albareto | 12 | 42 | 33 | 13 | 379 |
| Castel San Giorgio | 1 | 5 | 4 | 90 | 2,263 |
| Nissoria | 22 | 37 | 33 | 8 | 842 |
| Rogliano | 8 | 38 | 34 | 20 | 1,485 |

density and population levels. How many persons a square kilometer of land can support depends, of course, on the quality of land if the economy is purely agricultural or, in the case of commercial and industrial development, the ability of the area to draw supplies. Approximate population density "ceilings," given the agricultural technology of nineteenth-century rural Italy, were fifty persons per square kilometer in pastoral economies and 100 persons where good land was intensively farmed. Ceilings for commercial and industrial areas undoubtedly exist but are extremely difficult to estimate and increased rapidly during the nineteenth century. For present purposes it is sufficient to note that densities above 200 generally indicate extensive nonagricultural activity. The 100–199/km² category includes the vast areas of rural Italy that had temporarily exceeded the "ceiling" which the land could support, areas where peasants suffered chronic malnutrition and were ready to consider emigration when the opportunity arose.[32]

As to the four communities in this study, their densities in 1871 were as follows: Albareto, 40; Nissoria, 55; Castel San Giorgio, 350; and Rogliano, 120. Relating these figures back to table 28, it is evident that, except for Albareto, marriage to outsiders was not a primary vehicle for solving problems of overpopulation or, more precisely, of population

TABLE 29   Absolute Population, in 1871, and Exogamous Marriages (%)

|  | POPULATION OF PLACES OF BIRTH | | | | |
|---|---|---|---|---|---|
|  |  | 3,500– | 7,501– |  | Over |
|  | Under | 7,500 | 12,500 | 12,501– | 100,000 |
|  | 3,500 | (Small | (Large | 100,000 | (Big | N |
|  | (Village) | Town) | Town) | (City) | City) | CASES |
| Albareto | 24 | 40 | 18 | 14 | 4 | 387 |
| Castel San Giorgio | 15 | 24 | 26 | 31 | 4 | 2,272 |
| Nissoria | 20 | 11 | 51 | 16 | 2 | 842 |
| Rogliano | 71 | 11 | 5 | 11 | 2 | 1,503 |

distribution. Density levels in the birthplaces of exogamous spouses ranged widely or were about the same as those in the place where the nuptials occurred. The exceptional case, Albareto, involves a distinct tendency to marry folk from more densely populated areas; that is, marriage served to facilitate movement of people between a pastoral/ gathering economy and ones based on more intensive agriculture in the lower valleys and commerce near the coast. These figures confirm other evidence (see chap. 8) indicating high levels of migration among the Albaretesi.

Although marriages to outsiders generally may not have been aimed at correcting maldistribution of population, it does not follow that such choices were purely random. Marriage to an outsider meant communication between two places, probably prior to the nuptial ceremony and often afterward as well. Hard evidence on social and economic interaction among villagers and between villages and cities too easily disappears from the historian's grasp even for relatively recent periods. In this regard marriage links offer a clue. The fact that between 1870 and 1890 seven Albaretesi married people born in the mushroom-gathering town of Tarsogno, near the Ligurian coast, whereas only two wed persons born in the city of Parma, is hardly a precise index of total interaction, but surely it reflects an important dimension of the village's collective experience. It is in this way that figures 16–19, maps which display marriage links for the four communities, should be viewed.[33]

Compare, for example, the links of Nissoria with those of Albareto. The Sicilian village's isolation was severe: no marriage links at all between 1820 and 1972 with ten of Italy's twenty regions and fewer than a dozen with the entire area north from Naples. Only occasionally, on average once every seven years, did a wedding in Nissoria involve someone born on the mainland. For good reason do some villagers consider themselves Sicilians by birth, Americans by kinship network, and Italians not at all. In Albareto, on the other hand, weddings involving people born in distant places occurred much more often. Only two regions (Val d'Aosta and Sicily) contributed no marriage partners, and considering the village's size and isolation, interaction with northern industrial and coastal regions was substantial. Note in particular the flow into Albareto from Liguria rather than from the intensive agricultural zone of the Po Valley.

Marriage links to the towns of Castel San Giorgio and Rogliano, as might be expected, were even more extensive. The Calabrian town's economy and its bureaucratic functions brought its people into extensive contact not only with Calabresi further south but also with residents of Puglia, Campania, and Sicily. Nor were ties to the north absent, although most of these are from the twentieth century. Castel San Giorgio's marriage network was somewhat more restricted than Rogliano's, concentrated in Campania and secondarily in Lazio, with fewer ties to the north even in recent years. Such a configuration confirms its continuing role as a way station between interior Campania and Naples.[34]

To this point I have treated *campanilismo* as an attachment by the village or town as a whole to its space and to the culture contained therein and known so well. But obviously the force of *campanilismo* is not equal for all residents, and there is good reason to suspect that levels of attachment to place of birth varied with age, familial structure, and class. Analysis of data contained in marriage registers allows some comment on each of these factors.

The chances that men and women would marry outsiders varied only slightly with their ages. Data on the tendency of grooms of various ages to wed in the *comune* where they were born are summarized in table 30.

TABLE 30   **Endogamous Marriage by Grooms' Age Cohort (%)**

| PLACE AND DATE | GROOMS' AGES | | | | | | |
|---|---|---|---|---|---|---|---|
| | Under 23 | 23–27 | 28–32 | 33–37 | 38–42 | Over 42 | N CASES |
| Albareto: | | | | | | | |
| 1870–1909 | 96 | 95 | 93 | 65 | 94 | 97 | 482 |
| 1910–26 | 83 | 86 | 83 | 85 | 69 | 85 | 296 |
| 1946–73 | 73 | 82 | 79 | 74 | 81 | 81 | 522 |
| Rogliano: | | | | | | | |
| 1811–59 | 81 | 80 | 75 | 77 | 79 | 73 | 858 |
| 1860–1909 | 77 | 82 | 76 | 65 | 91 | 84 | 853 |
| 1910–45 | 75 | 77 | 69 | 50 | 57 | 57 | 800 |
| 1946–73 | 68 | 65 | 55 | 56 | 56 | 69 | 932 |
| Nissoria: | | | | | | | |
| 1811–59 | 84 | 77 | 65 | 87 | 80 | 56 | 317 |
| 1860–1909 | 78 | 78 | 76 | 53 | 70 | 60 | 590 |
| 1910–45 | 65 | 67 | 64 | 69 | 71 | 62 | 428 |
| 1946–73 | 50 | 62 | 54 | 48 | 73 | 46 | 463 |
| Castel San Giorgio: | | | | | | | |
| 1811–59 | 68 | 69 | 63 | 68 | 54 | 51 | 696 |
| 1860–1909 | 68 | 63 | 54 | 59 | 61 | 48 | 893 |
| 1910–45 | 56 | 45 | 57 | 48 | 26 | 39 | 779 |
| 1946–73 | 50 | 52 | 49 | 53 | 53 | 18 | 1,296 |

Except for men in their early thirties who wed during the decades between Italy's unification and the First World War, there appears to have been little correlation between age at marriage and tendency to wed an outsider. Or, to state the matter positively, in any given period and place the likelihood that a man would marry locally was about the same no matter what his age. This finding contradicts an "exposure to risk" model (such as that used in standard actuarial procedures) for explaining nuptials to outsiders and the migration necessarily involved

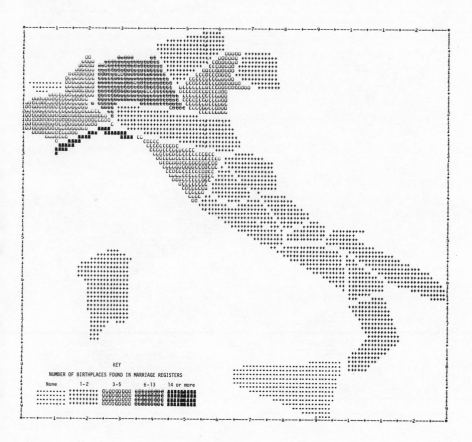

Fig. 16.
Place of birth of persons married in Albareto, 1870–1972.

in such marriages. An exposure to risk approach would predict that as a man had more years to travel about, whether in search of work or to attend fairs and dances, his opportunities to know and therefore possibly to wed an outsider should increase. But for rural Italy, at least, such a predictive and cumulative model is inapplicable. The force of *campanilismo* was there, undiminished over the course of a lifetime, and marriage to an outsider was not a function of opportunity (exposure to risk) but of unpredictable and unknowable fate. The exception outlined in table 30, that during the late nineteenth century men in their early and mid thirties were considerably more likely to marry an outsider than men of any other age, probably reflects the impact of high levels of migration during these years. The present data, of course, refer only to those who remain in or returned to the village, but even among these persons the consequences of emigration are evident. It is noteworthy,

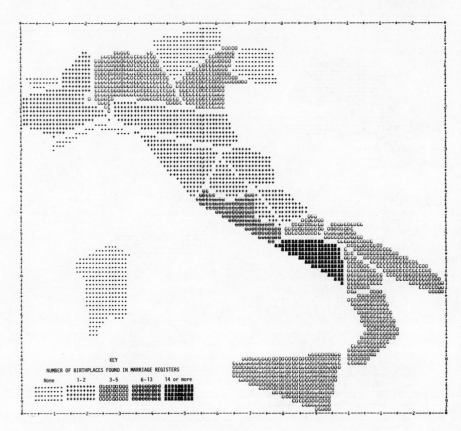

Fig. 17.
Place of birth of persons married in Castel San Giorgio, 1811–1972.

however, that after several decades of dislocation and sharp decreases in endogamous marriage by men in their thirties, there was a return to the earlier pattern. The proportion of men who wed locally indeed decreased everywhere, but once again after World War I, the likelihood that a man would not marry someone he had known from earliest childhood remained about the same as he grew older. Although figures for four communities on the relationship between endogamy and grooms' ages hardly constitute a sufficient base from which to criticize modernization and demographic transition models, which implicitly or explicitly rely heavily on an exposure to risk approach, it is noteworthy that here again such a linear perspective may be misleading. There is a clear trend away from local marriage, but at the same time there persists an unpredictable and fatalistic aspect to marriage choices. The young man who has not had time to see the world and who therefore marries

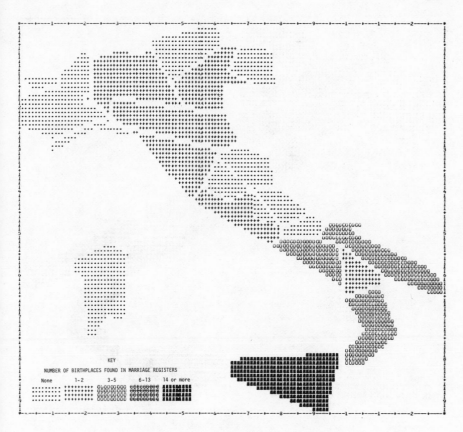

Fig. 18.
Place of birth of persons married in Nissoria, 1811–1972.

locally is balanced by the mature man who returns home to choose a
wife.

A predictive exposure to risk approach is even more inappropriate for
female nuptial choices. (Table 31 provides a summary of the relevant
data.) For some places and times older brides (say past the age of
thirty-two) were considerably more likely than younger females to
marry an outsider, but in many instances the opposite held true. The
figures also reveal a distinct tendency for very young brides not to wed
locally, especially in the towns of Rogliano in this century and in Castel
San Giorgio after 1860. The absence of this phenomenon from the villages of Albareto and Nissoria confirms findings discussed at length in
chapter 5 on familial/*interesse* versus individual/*amore* modes of choosing a spouse. Where parental involvement in nuptial choice was great,
very young brides married locally, to a family whose *onore* was known

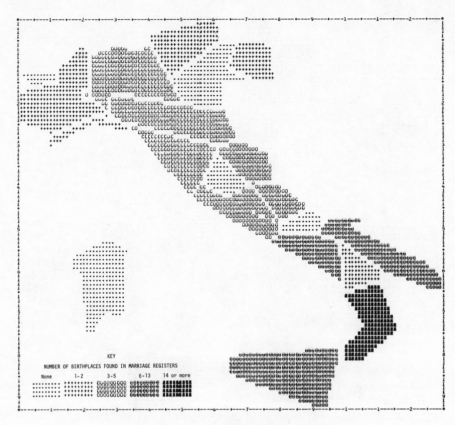

Fig. 19.
Place of birth of persons married in Rogliano, 1811–1972.

intimately over generations and whose proximity would facilitate reciprocal exchanges of favors within the safe sphere defined by *campanilismo*. In sum, attachment to place of birth, at least as reflected in
marriage links, remained about the same as people grew older.

The force of *campanilismo* depends heavily on familial networks, on
the unbroken spiral from then until now that ties villagers to the cultural space they know and are part of. Because family and place are so
thoroughly intertwined—indeed, for many of the villagers we spoke
with the two are fused completely—it follows that rupture of the familial spiral when parents died should have affected tendencies to marry
locally. Some measure of the impact of parental death upon spouses'
nuptial choices is provided in table 32. The most reliable and consistent
data come from Castel San Giorgio, where rates of endogamous marriage were always lower than elsewhere. In this town in the first half of

TABLE 31 **Endogamous Marriage by Brides' Age Cohort (%)**

| | BRIDES'AGES | | | | | | |
|---|---|---|---|---|---|---|---|
| PLACE AND DATE | Under 18 | 18–22 | 23–27 | 28–32 | 33–37 | Over 37 | N CASES |
| Albareto: | | | | | | | |
| 1870–1909 | 91 | 96 | 92 | 92 | 93 | 88 | 482 |
| 1910–26 | 86 | 86 | 88 | 91 | 92 | 80 | 296 |
| 1946–73 | 78 | 83 | 89 | 88 | 81 | 81 | 522 |
| Rogliano: | | | | | | | |
| 1811–59 | 85 | 91 | 92 | 91 | 82 | 88 | 859 |
| 1860–1909 | 91 | 92 | 89 | 89 | 77 | 76 | 854 |
| 1910–45 | 67 | 77 | 83 | 74 | 81 | 70 | 800 |
| 1946–73 | 57 | 69 | 69 | 76 | 76 | 83 | 932 |
| Nissoria: | | | | | | | |
| 1811–59 | 89 | 92 | 87 | 87 | 75 | 77 | 316 |
| 1860–1909 | 90 | 89 | 88 | 76 | 94 | 67 | 595 |
| 1910–45 | 74 | 78 | 75 | 83 | 80 | 79 | 428 |
| 1946–73 | 74 | 70 | 71 | 65 | 44 | 46 | 464 |
| Castel San Giorgio: | | | | | | | |
| 1811–59 | 85 | 93 | 96 | 92 | 95 | 86 | 697 |
| 1860–1909 | 63 | 86 | 91 | 87 | 85 | 77 | 893 |
| 1910–45 | 56 | 78 | 84 | 88 | 76 | 64 | 779 |
| 1946–73 | 72 | 56 | 76 | 66 | 64 | 65 | 1,296 |

the nineteenth century the figures reveal that men whose parents had
both died were considerably more likely to marry an outsider than were

TABLE 32 **Endogamous Marriage by Mortality of Spouses' Parents (%)**

| | ENDOGAMOUS GROOM | | | | ENDOGAMOUS BRIDE | | | | |
|---|---|---|---|---|---|---|---|---|---|
| PLACE AND DATE | Father Dead | Mother Dead | Both Dead | Both Alive | Father Dead | Mother Dead | Both Dead | Both Alive | N CASES |
| Albareto: | | | | | | | | | |
| 1870–1909 | 98 | 91 | 96 | 95 | 97 | 98 | 96 | 96 | 470 |
| 1910–26 | 83 | 82 | 90 | 84 | 89 | 93 | 85 | 88 | 285 |
| 1946–73 | 83 | 79 | 79 | 78 | 85 | 97 | 75 | 85 | 467 |
| Rogliano: | | | | | | | | | |
| 1860–1909 | 80 | 73 | 81 | 85 | 86 | 86 | 84 | 91 | 694 |
| 1910–45 | 73 | 78 | 60 | 73 | 76 | 76 | 64 | 79 | 756 |
| 1946–73 | 66 | 50 | 71 | 62 | 79 | 80 | 82 | 67 | 798 |
| Nissoria: | | | | | | | | | |
| 1811–59 | 77 | 81 | 68 | 79 | 89 | 84 | 82 | 92 | 287 |
| Castel San Giorgio: | | | | | | | | | |
| 1811–59 | 69 | 71 | 56 | 65 | 92 | 92 | 92 | 96 | 664 |
| 1860–1909 | 58 | 60 | 55 | 62 | 89 | 94 | 73 | 90 | 854 |
| 1910–45 | 52 | 51 | 51 | 47 | 82 | 87 | 71 | 84 | 735 |
| 1946–73 | 54 | 53 | 58 | 49 | 70 | 76 | 68 | 67 | 1,168 |

men with living parents. Sons with only one parent alive were especially likely to wed locally. For women the same pattern emerged only after 1860 and continued until the Second World War. Overall, the data indicate that the shift from family-centered marital choice to individual decisions based on romantic love occurred earlier for men than for women, or at least that men were earlier free to range over more space in choosing a spouse. With the triumph of individualism in nuptial choice, the significance of parental mortality declined as a factor binding sons and daughters to their places of birth. Throughout the twentieth century for men and since 1945 for women, there is no evidence that the presence or absence of parents affected the likelihood of marrying an outsider.

There remains, then, the question of endogamous marriage and occupational category or, to state the relationship in terms of its larger implications, the interaction of *campanilismo* and class consciousness. Table 33 provides the figures. Above all, and in sharp contrast to the small differences and occasionally ambiguous results of the previous two tables, striking variations appear between peasants and landowners.[35] Moreover, these differences exist consistently over time for the towns of Castel San Giorgio and Rogliano, while they are just as con-

TABLE 33  **Endogamous Marriage by Grooms' Occupations (%)**

| Place and Date | Peasants | Landowners | Professional/ Business | Town Workers | N Cases |
|---|---|---|---|---|---|
| Albareto: | | | | | |
| 1870–1909 | 93 | 83 | 50 | 83 | 466 |
| 1910–26 | 74 | 76 | 71 | 55 | 296 |
| 1946–73 | 82 | ...[a] | 36 | 48 | 456 |
| Rogliano: | | | | | |
| 1811–59 | 76 | 48 | 38 | 62 | 858 |
| 1860–1909 | 78 | 25 | 48 | 59 | 794 |
| 1910–45 | 70 | 31 | 32 | 50 | 798 |
| 1946–73 | 54 | ...[a] | 23 | 47 | 910 |
| Nissoria: | | | | | |
| 1811–59 | 75 | 76 | 44 | 32 | 351 |
| 1860–1909 | 74 | 44 | 35 | 50 | 589 |
| 1910–45 | 58 | 66 | 8 | 27 | 423 |
| 1946–73 | 44 | ...[a] | 34 | 28 | 444 |
| Castel San Giorgio: | | | | | |
| 1811–59 | 67 | 41 | 40 | 59 | 690 |
| 1860–1909 | 47 | 29 | 22 | 58 | 871 |
| 1910–45 | 37 | 23 | 26 | 46 | 768 |
| 1946–73 | 26 | ...[a] | 20 | 32 | 1,260 |

[a]Too few cases for meaningful results.

sistently absent for the village of Albareto and for Nissoria prior to
1860 and again after the Great War. It may be recalled that the great
landholders in Nissoria were absentee and therefore turn up only infrequently in local marriage registers. Thus the "landowner" category
includes mostly *gabellotti*, exploitative and capitalist agricultural intermediaries; among these, the more talented or favored during the crisis
decades after unification sought to expand their power through marriage alliances with substantial holders or with other rising entrepreneurs. The sharp drop in endogamous marriage by Nissoria's landowners (mostly *gabellotti*) between 1860 and 1910 reflects their expansive efforts in these years. For other decades in Nissoria, and throughout for Albareto, landowners married locally with about the same frequency as did peasants. This shared tendency, in conjunction with the
existence of familial networks in these villages that included both
landed and landless (discussed in the previous chapter), supported and
maintained a local, peasant-dominated, village culture. *Campanilismo,*
especially where it cut across class lines, served as an antidote to *la
miseria*. Precisely in the places where prevailing attitudes toward the
soil were positive, rural folk of all classes married locally. Given the
small absolute number of landholders in these villages, the result was a
highly inbred landed class, but one whose spatial boundaries were
about the same as those of the peasantry.[36]

How different the situation in the towns of Rogliano and Castel San
Giorgio, where in the past two centuries a majority of landowners always
have wed outsiders. Such choices undoubtedly were based on
property-matching considerations rather than an explicit desire to get
away from their places of birth. Nevertheless, the result of marriage
links to outsiders was the creation and maintenance among the landed
class of a cultural space vastly different from that of the peasantry. In
Rogliano until 1945 about three of every four peasants wed locally,
whereas for landed persons the corresponding figures were under two
in five. Extended familial networks connected Rogliano's landless only
to each other, indeed locked them within a world of hatred for the soil,
self-pity, and *la miseria*. The landed, whose space extended through
marriage alliances deep into interior Calabria and, somewhat more
tenuously, from Reggio to Naples, created a distinct and conscious
world apart from and closed to the peasantry. Landless agriculturists
slowly developed a consciousness of themselves as a class apart, but
unfortunately that consciousness was in essence imposed from without
and laced with negative definition and deprecation. The confluence of
*campanilismo* and self-abnegation provided a milieu throughout the
Aspromonte conducive to anarchy, banditry, and similarly colorful but
defective forms of social protest.[37] But on most days, characterized by

gnawing hunger rather than hopeless protest, Rogliano's peasants blindly cursed the soil where they were born, and where they would die.

Professional and business persons, for obvious reasons connected with their educational and employment experience, frequently married outsiders. The tendency holds in both villages and towns and in all time periods. For other townspeople the pattern is more complex. In Albareto, Nissoria, and Rogliano, *cittadini* clearly wed locally less often than did *contadini*. Such a result follows logically from the much greater contact with outsiders that town dwellers must have enjoyed. Similarly, movement into a town or village was easier for a town worker than for a peasant having no prior familial link through which to locate and to find a place to remain permanently. But for Castel San Giorgio, where a majority of the population did not engage directly in agriculture, the pattern was reversed after 1860; *cittadini* wed locally more often than did *contadini*. This would suggest that as town life grew and flourished relative to agriculture, the locus of *campanilismo* shifted from the soil to the densely populated town center. Opportunity, both in terms of a growing pool of potential spouses and in the wider but less tangible factor of pride and hope for the town, encouraged residents to marry locally.

Narrowly defined, *campanilismo* refers to the particularly strong attachment felt by rural Italians to their villages of birth. If one goes no further, it is easy to conclude from the foregoing analyses that over the past two centuries *campanilismo* (1) declined considerably everywhere; (2) was replaced by regional, national, and even multinational attachments; (3) gave way to consciousness along class lines; and (4) existed partially independent of age and familial network considerations. Although such conclusions rest in the present case primarily upon marriage register data, there is little reason to suspect that other kinds of evidence would yield substantially different results. Marriage registers offer the advantage of statistical exactness, precise dating of changes, and reference to events or decisions that surely were central to people's lives. Consistently in different times and places, configurations of marriage links were highly congruent with patterns of economic activity and lines of political power. In sum, among rural Italians the village is less and less a reference point, a factor in making decisions, a way of viewing the world.

To say no more, however, would be to ignore the larger human need of which *campanilismo* is but one variant, a variant linked to demographic experience. The need to identify, to forge orderly categories, to distinguish us from them, may take many forms: racial, religious, ethnic divisions; civic pride; nationalism; class consciousness. Seen from this perspective, *campanilismo* has persisted, although in modified form,

according closely with changing spatial and communication configurations. After twenty-five years of work in northern Fiat plants Nissorini
remain just that, and not Torinesi. They return "home" for the August
festival to see their *paesani* and to celebrate with them. Without exception, those who are away say they would return if work were available.
In Castel San Giorgio, the hamlet in which a local candidate lives remains today a major factor in political contests, long after so few engage
in agriculture that diversion of irrigated water from one place to another
is not a serious problem. Very few Albaretesi of the older generations
have any interest in traveling to Genoa or Parma; rather, they willingly
pay higher prices for a much narrower range of goods available in
nearby mountain towns. Rogliano's town council expends money to
maintain and repair the ancient and now useless town walls while
rejecting proposals to pave outlying roads.

And when they must deal with greater spaces, rural Italians often
understand and act in a *campanilismo* way. The PCI's local festivals of
unity appeal brilliantly to the peasantry's traditional anticipation of a
harvesttime celebration involving everyone in the community. The fascination of rural folk with news of America is related less to its super-
power status than to the presence there of *paesani*. Peasants who
habitually dissect local space nevertheless transcend and collapse im-
mense distant space. The same Nissorini who distrust a priest born two
towns away found it sensible to ask American soldiers (white and black
alike) during World War II about the welfare of their relatives in
Chicago.

# 8
# Migration

When I was in Italy, a boy, I was a republican, so I always thinking republican has more chance to manage education, develop, to build some day his family, to raise the child and education, if you could. But that was my opinion; so when I came to this country I saw there was not what I was thinking before, but there was all the difference, because I been working in Italy not so hard as I been work in this country. I could live free there just as well. Work in the same condition, but not so hard, about seven or eight hours a day, better food. I mean genuine. Of course, over here is good food, because it is bigger country, to any those who got money to spend, not for the working and laboring class, and in Italy is more opportunity to laborer to eat vetetable, more fresh, and I came in this country. When I been started work here very hard and been work thirteen years, hard worker, I could not been afford much a family the way I did have the idea before. I could not put any money in the bank. I could no push my boy some to go to school and other things.

Nicola Sacco

Among many strategies employed by rural Italians in responding to the dramatic changes of the past two centuries, emigration, above all others, has drawn the attention of the outside world: politicians, businessmen, speculators, and scholars. Until recently, however, this attention was aimed primarily at understanding or profiting from emigrants in their new setting. The complex phenomena involved in the original decision to move became obscured in metaphoric description, usually studded with allusions to water; migration occurred in trickles, streams, tides, crests, floods, waves, flows, currents, or torrents. Early efforts to portray the Old World backgrounds of migrants to America met with only limited success.[1] Even when this work was accurate at a descriptive level, it failed to explain why some peasants emigrated while others did not. The sheer enormity of numbers with six zeroes, millions of Italians leaving their homeland, often obscured the fact that a majority chose not to emigrate. Legislation, economy, and shipping rates may have opened a "floodgate," but most Italians chose not to go through.

In the past decade, a host of useful studies have begun to inquire seriously into the specific institutions and cultural ways of Old World Italians in order better to understand their transatlantic lives.[2] Overall, these efforts reach the conclusion that traditional values shaped the immigrants' initial movement and settlement patterns, prepared them effectively for dealing with their new economic situations, and lasted in meaningful though modified fashion into the present generation.[3] The same may be said, I suggest, about the course of traditional values among Italian villagers who stayed.

To decide to emigrate seemingly involved a clear rejection of *fortuna*, for it necessitated seizing the moment and seeking opportunity. Yet to the extent that apparently uncontrollable population pressures on available economic resources made emigration "inevitable," even this choice was less a matter of free will than of an honorable response to destiny. Similarly, the older value of *onore*, dignity before any fate, gave way at least partially to the emigrants' quest for status through wealth. But *onore* remained forceful in migration chains, sponsorship of relatives, self-help and no-welfare attitudes, tidy homes and gardens, beliefs about sexual practices, political opinions, indeed in every aspect of the emigrants' lives. So also with *la famiglia*. Often migration resulted in years of separation from the nuclear family. Even when mother, father, and children moved together, the older "father-headed, mother-centered" family underwent change. But to label this change deterioration rather than adaptation is a value judgment based perhaps on an overly static view of *la famiglia*. Family was not a fixed thing but a process, one that underwent modification in both the Old and New Worlds. Lastly, although leaving the village obviously meant a weakening of *campanilismo*, both emigrants and those who stayed behind retained in a variety of ways an attachment to sharply defined and deeply known spaces.

Precisely how many rural Italians left their native villages and towns cannot be known with certainty. For every person who emigrated permanently, two, three, four, or more others may have spent months or years in urban Italy or in a foreign land and then returned home. Some good work has been done on repatriation of Italians who migrated to the United States, but the official figures, upon which estimates necessarily are based, vastly understate actual levels of human movement.[4] For the most part, local records are equally deficient in recording temporary migration. Two estimates of total migration, one from Albareto in the nineteenth century for young men and the other from Nissoria between

1934 and 1973, indicate between three and five temporary migrants for every permanent departure.[5] But this is one area in which I definitely would not assert that findings are applicable to rural Italy generally. As soon as one moves beyond vague and incorrect statements about waves of *contadini* flowing from everywhere in southern Italy, it becomes evident that all too little is known about patterns of migration in particular locales and among various classes. Until much more work is done on total migration levels, I believe it may be more useful to concentrate, at least initially, on net migration, a statistic that can be calculated with a good degree of accuracy and that allows comparative evaluations. If during the period between two censuses no one moves in or out of a given area, the entire change in population must be due to natural growth (intervening births minus deaths). It follows that the difference between "natural population growth" and the change between two censuses must be due to migration (assuming the enumerations are accurate). It is this difference that I refer to as net emigration.[6] Figure 20 portrays rates of natural population growth and net emigration beginning in 1810 for Albareto and Rogliano and in 1860 for Nissoria and Castel San Giorgio.[7]

The fluctuations in net emigration shown in figure 20 represent a central factor in the demographic, cultural, and economic histories of these four communities, histories that cannot be understood fully within the framework of a "push-pull" model. It is true that rural Italians were pushed by poverty, population pressure, and oppressive landlords and that they were pulled by higher wages, familial opportunities, and chances for self-fulfillment. But the *contadini* were more than inanimate objects shoved here or there, more than droplets flowing into streams and floods. Rather, rural Italians estimated as accurately as possible, given their limited access to reliable information and within perimeters ranging from legal barriers to exorbitant transportation costs, the possible outcomes of each alternative that seemed open to them. Stay in the village, move to the nearest city, seek work in Milan or Turin, emigrate to Germany or France, cross the Atlantic to Argentina or the United States, go alone, travel with spouse and children, help finance a brother's passage—these were choices, strategies of survival or calculations of gain. A history of the people of Albareto, Castel San Giorgio, Nissoria, and Rogliano must include their role in deciding where they went and how long they stayed. This is not to deny the importance of changes in objective factors clearly beyond local control but simply to suggest that the total impact of such factors left rural Italians with meaningful decisions to be made. In this chapter I shall begin with an analysis of the "objective" factors, first those that were essentially oscillatory and then a group that produced seemingly irreversible changes. Then I shall consider how migration decisions were made and evaluate the overall consequences of emigration for rural Italy.

## RAIN AND SUN, MEAT AND CEREAL

In his classic study of Italian emigration, Robert Foerster correctly pointed out that Mediterranean climate was far from idyllic and that the

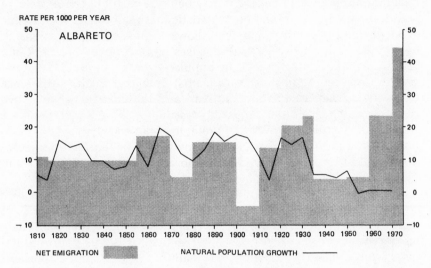

Fig. 20.
Net emigration and natural population growth, Albareto

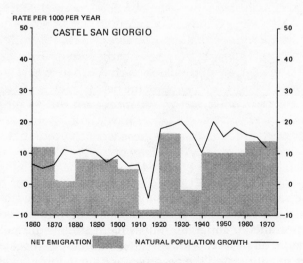

Fig. 20.
Castel San Giorgio

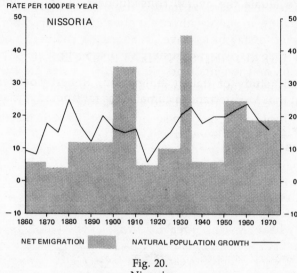

Fig. 20.
Nissoria

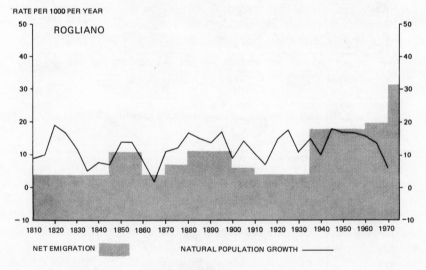

Fig. 20.
Rogliano

absence of rainfall in the spring and summer promoted latifundism, poor crop yields, and low utilization of labor. Nature, then, pushed southern peasants to emigrate.[8] Subsequent studies did not deal with the weather at all or else, with only slight variation, repeated the idea that nature too oppressed the peasantry. Without doubt, overall rainfall patterns limited the number of people that the land could support and therefore acted to push rural Italians from the countryside. But it was annual variation in the weather that affected the harvest and encouraged *contadini* to stay or to leave. In an earlier chapter I noted reports from Sicily that in years when harvest prospects seemed poor, some sharecroppers and tenants working on large estates ate their *soccorso* and left the village for the season. Owners of small plots also might emigrate in a year that looked bad, leaving their spouses to take care of the plot (or hire someone to do so since poor harvests meant an abundant labor supply and lowered wages).

Ironically, whereas absence of precipitation acted overall as a push factor, it was when the rains came that the *contadino* left. In general for the Mediterranean, a wet year is also a cool year and one during which rain falls in concentrated and plant-damaging torrential fashion. Precipitation from April on nearly always did more harm than good for Nissoria's wheat growers, threatened vegetable seedlings in Castel San Giorgio, and stripped away blossoms on olive and fig trees in Rogliano. Consecutive cool and wet years were particularly ominous.[9] Sicilian proverbial wisdom welcomed the warm high-pressure systems originating in Africa that forced back cool and wet low-pressure flows from the north: "Suli càuru cu assai ventu / Vaju a casa e su' cuntentu[10]" (When there is a hot sun and a strong wind / I go home contented); or, "Sicca annata 'un è affamata" (In a dry year there will not be hunger); or "Un sittembri càudu e asciuttu / Maturari fa ogni fruttu" (A hot and dry September / Matures every kind of fruit).

In order to attempt to assess in a more systematic way the impact of weather on migration, I gathered precipitation and temperature data for Catania monthly from 1811 to 1972.[11] These are correlated with net emigration rates to produce the statistics shown in table 34. Given the soil conditions, crop mixes, and agricultural techniques of southern Italy (along with the Mediterranean pattern that hot and dry growing seasons were often preceded or followed by abundant precipitation during the rainy months of late fall and winter), heavy rainfall between April–May and October should be positively correlated with increased emigration, whereas the opposite should be true from November to March–April. All the statistically significant figures in table 34 are consistent with this suggestion (as are thirty-eight out of forty-eight signs of coefficients). When it rained hard in late spring, a significant number of *contadini* judged that the harvest would be poor and decided to leave.

Data on temperature provide even stronger confirmation that rural Italians responded to the weather by doing more than cursing and praying. If a warm dry growing season led to a good harvest which in turn persuaded agricultural workers not to emigrate, there would be a negative correlation between temperature increases and net emigration rates. Since sunny skies in the winter are useless ("Chiaranzana di

TABLE 34    Correlations between Temperature and Precipitation, and Net Emigration
            Rate, 1811–1972

| | ALBARETO | | CASTEL SAN GIORGIO | | NISSORIA | | ROGLIANO | |
|---|---|---|---|---|---|---|---|---|
| | Temp. | Rain | Temp. | Rain | Temp. | Rain | Temp. | Rain |
| January | – | – | – | – | + | + | –.20 | + |
| February | – | – | – | – | – | + | –.19 | –.17 |
| March | – | + | – | .18 | – | – | –.20 | – |
| April | –.21 | – | –.18 | – | –.25 | – | –.21 | + |
| May | + | + | + | + | –.35 | .18 | – | .23 |
| June | –.20 | + | –.26 | + | –.35 | + | –.37 | .16 |
| July | –.25 | + | –.23 | + | –.39 | – | –.33 | + |
| August | –.31 | + | –.27 | – | –.22 | – | –.36 | + |
| September | –.18 | – | – | + | –.30 | .27 | –.33 | + |
| October | –.21 | + | – | + | – | + | – | .16 |
| November | – | –.23 | + | –.27 | – | – | –.15 | – |
| December | – | – | –.17 | – | + | – | –.21 | – |

NOTE.—All correlations not significant at the .05 level have been deleted from the
table, although the signs of deleted coefficients are shown.

'nvernu, diàvulu di 'nferno''), the temparature/net emigration relationship should not hold as strongly outside the growing season. The figures for Nissoria (see table 34) fit virtually perfectly with the
hypothesis. When a warm spring boded well for the winter wheat crop
to be harvested in June, the Nissorini stayed in their village. Fast
growth even allowed a second cereal sowing in late June to be reaped
before the November rains. Hot dry days also meant fuller grapes,
pressed and fermented to produce a wine of unusually high *gradi*
(which for the poor allowed greater dilution with water rather than
better quality). In Albareto, with its longer and cooler growing season,
the correlation held at a significant level through October, whereas the
relationship in Castel San Giorgio, although less strong, reflects its
year-round growing season. For Rogliano the situation is a bit more
complex; strongest correlations between high temperatures and low net
emigration rates occurred during the summer growing season, but a
significant relationship emerged as well in the winter months. At nearly
700 meters above sea level, low temperatures in Calabria threatened
Rogliano's extensive olive and fig tree plantings with frost damage.
Even when the trees survived, damage to branches and to new blossoms was sufficient to make an abundant harvest unlikely.

In four widely separated Italian communities, then, there appears
over the past 160 years a consistent relationship between temperature
levels, especially during the growing season, and net emigration. The
relationship is more than casual; indeed, a quite sensible link appears
in harvest levels and their impact on local underemployment. On aver-

age, about 10 percent of overall fluctuations in net emigration rates occurred in congruence with temperature changes. The 10 percent figure is not trivial; to get beyond water-related metaphors about tides of emigration means developing more complex, multifaceted explanations, some of which may be expressed mathematically. With grain already sown, a cool, wet growing season meant a poor crop; nothing could be done about it except, of course, to emigrate in an effort to avoid the consequences of underemployment. And some of those who left "temporarily" chose not to return.[12]

The same historical consensus which asserts that arid climate forced peasants to leave home claims an analogous but far more powerful role for poverty. Again, there can be no doubt that, overall, poverty (which resulted from highly inequitable distribution of a total product that was too small to begin with) pushed *contadini* to emigrate. But the truth of that generalization should not obscure the particular decisions that peasants made in fighting against hunger and misery. Some emigrated permanently, others returned, and quite a few never left their villages at all. A large number of "temporary" emigrants, people who left intending to return, acted in response to their estimations of relative opportunities created by oscillatory fluctuations in economic conditions locally and in far away places.[13] Roglianesi who received word in the 1880s that coal miners in a place called Pennsylvania were getting two dollars per day did a bit of arithmetic and estimated that in two years they could save enough to return and buy sufficient land to support a family. After a few years, when a majority of those who had left did not return or came back crippled or habitually drunk (not to mention the dozen for whom only a death certificate came back), the Roglianesi recalculated; the local situation seemed to be improving. Most rural Italians who emigrated found employment as manual laborers in the personal service sector or in heavy industry. Their life-styles required low maintenance expenditures (housing, food, and clothing) and allowed high rates of saving. This was especially true when heavy demand and inflation in advanced capitalist economies sent wages higher while causing only marginal increases in maintenance costs for emigrant workers. For example, women from Castel San Giorgio who worked as servants in England and France around 1900, when it was fashionable in such places to hire a seemingly dumb but constantly smiling girl, received room, board, and a uniform (the cost of which did not matter much to either party) plus wages that, although small, went entirely to savings. Or consider the men from Albareto who went to New York and obtained jobs as waiters (graceful servility being easily acquired) in any of the numerous restaurants that provided a cot in the storeroom, leftovers for meals, no wages, and only half the tips to be kicked back to the owner. Weighed against available options, both jobs made sense.

Such examples, although they may merit more extensive analysis, cannot yield a long-term estimate of the ways in which rural Italians responded to two economies. In one economy were the meat eaters, the consumers of high-cost-per-calorie foods who lived in heated rooms, hired servants, and commanded labor. In the other economy were the cereal eaters, peasants for whom survival was an accomplishment, for whom a job was a gift, for whom life was a contest against death. The two economies interacted, gained from each other, fed upon one another in ways both found beneficial. From the *contadino*'s perspective, prosperity in the elite sector meant a job and a chance to save. In the world of the elite, good times meant an opportunity to extend a helping hand, to do mankind a favor by hoisting a bright but uneducated peasant to the first rung of the ladder of success. An initial way of assessing overall levels of interaction between the two economies, which following Fernand Braudel's perception may be labeled material life and capital life, is by a measurement of the interaction between them.[14] Table 35 summarizes a series of relevant correlations; these can do no more than hint at, but not quite define the limits of, the relationships among peasants and foreign elites.

TABLE 35   **Correlations between Wages and Prices, and Net Emigration Rate**

|  | Albareto | Castel San Giorgio | Nissoria | Rogliano |
|---|---|---|---|---|
| Real wages, 1871–1900 | .92 | .91 | .90 | .91 |
| Real wages, 1901–59 | .61 | .40 | .24 | .15 |
| Wheat wages, 1905–60 | .50 | .19 | .18 | .11 |
| Polish wheat prices, 1818–80 | .04 | −.14 | −.20 | .31 |
| Prussian rye prices, 1816–82 | .06 | .12 | .08 | .26 |
| Cheese prices, 1812–99 | .31 | .08 | .05 | .42 |
| Meat prices, 1811–1914 | .24 | .48 | .05 | .50 |
| Wheat prices in England, 1811–93 | −.20 | −.21 | −.26 | −.21 |
| Wheat prices in France, 1811–93 | −.53 | −.61 | −.65 | −.41 |

No claim is made that rural Italians in the nineteenth century had access to indexed price series on European grains, meat, and cheese. What I am testing is the way in which net emigration rates correlated with such price fluctuations. The commodities measured in table 35 fall into three categories based on cost per calorie (in land and labor) and relation to rural Italy's economy: (1) northern European grains, with a low cost per calorie (Polish wheat and Prussian rye);[15] (2) high-cost-per-calorie items (cheese and meat);[16] and (3) low-cost-per-calorie items with prices reflecting Mediterranean harvest results (wheat prices in England and France).[17] Except possibly in Rogliano, price fluctuations in northern European grains show no particular relationship with net emigration rates, indicating that north central Europe in the nineteenth century remained outside the orbit of migration decisions for most rural Italians.

Within the Mediterranean a very different pattern emerges: consistent negative correlations, quite strong in the case of French prices and significant for England as well.[18] The negative sign means that net emigration increased when wheat prices declined and decreased when prices rose. To the degree that rural Italians in the nineteenth century were market oriented and sold crops for cash, it would follow that poverty and hard times caused by low prices forced them to emigrate, thereby confirming one element of the traditional push-pull explanation of migration. On the contrary, however, I suggest that the correlation figures (which are necessarily silent on causal direction) reflect precisely the reverse. In a word, peasants emigrated during "good times," which were years of low cereal prices. Consider the many agricultural laborers who worked for wages. Their income depended in part on wage levels, which rose in years of abundant harvest as demands for labor increased, and in part on total days employed, which rose in the same years for the same reason. Abundance indeed forced prices down, thereby lowering the per unit profit of substantial landowners and agricultural middlemen who had paid higher wages over more hours to bring in the crop, but such decreases had a favorable impact on proletarianized agricultural laborers. Not only did their purchasing power increase, but they might also save enough to finance the initial costs of migration. Consider next the many peasants who worked on their own small plots or as sharecroppers and controlled the disposition of what they produced. High yields, even though the consequence was a lower unit price, also benefited them. When yields were low, they had nothing at all to sell and, indeed, often had to go into debt to feed their families. They probably derived no satisfaction from knowing that the meager supplies in their storerooms might command a high price if sold, since selling meant starving. High yields, for peasants whose primary aim was subsistence, meant a full stomach and a bit left over to sell, albeit at a low price. The cash could be used to buy needed items, to repay debts, or to finance migration costs. In sum, increased supplies, which drove down the prices of what they produced, were beneficial to subsistence-oriented agriculturists and both allowed and induced them to migrate in search of yet better opportunities.

They found such opportunities by filling labor needs within the elite economy. Its performance, reflected in table 35 by meat and cheese prices, fluctuated greatly by year and by locale, so that the present analysis can do no more than suggest the broader trends. The pattern for Mediterranean grains (negative correlations) is uniformly reversed in the case of elite consumption items. Increases in the price of cheese (which the Albaretesi sold) and meat (which most rural Italians only rarely consumed, thereby remaining immune to its price) resulted in greater opportunity for emigrants. Good times for the elite economic life meant greater demand for protein-rich foods and consequent price increases. Villagers then emigrated to seek employment in the capital life sector and returned home with ample savings, since high prices in that sector did not affect material life consumption very much.[19] However, conversion from cereal to pasture in order to meet rising demands for high-protein foods (and in Sicily the speculations of grain buyers) ultimately forced increases in cereal prices and reduced the savings potential of emigrant workers. The Roglianesi, living in a town itself engaged in agricultural marketing operations, apparently were best able to discern and respond to these cyclical fluctuations, followed closely by the Albaretesi. The Nissorini, who made emigration decisions more slowly and collectively and whose deep impoverishment left most of them unable to finance the initial costs of temporary migration, at least in the nineteenth century, responded too late to take advantage of price fluctuations in the elite sector.

Closer to home, *contadini* learned about wage levels in Italy and sometimes responded by migrating. Wage data before 1870 are too irregular to construct a reliable national index;[20] but figures for 1871–1900 (see table 35), which average the salaries of all male workers and express wages in relationship to the price of wheat, show a close association between real wages and net emigration (correlations of .90 or more).[21] The source of such high correlations is that in the 1870s, a decade of low net emigration, real wages were extremely low (mean hours work necessary to purchase a quintal of wheat was 168). In the next two decades the mean work hours figure dropped to under 100 (due primarily to a decrease in the price of wheat); at the same time net emigration rates rose everywhere. The relationship between the two phenomena is not direct and causal, but neither is it purely casual or spurious. Relative to the 1870s, the next two decades actually may have witnessed some improvement in the economic situation of rural Italian workers.[22] Only after 1900 did high rates of net emigration reduce local underemployment enough to force a rising wage level. But before this occurred, people had to choose to leave. They did so when real wages rose enough to cover transportation and relocation costs, a situation which apparently existed between 1880 and 1900. That people act decisively in times of rising expectations is hardly new to students of protest movements. (Emigration and protest are similar in that both may require individuals to seize the moment in an attempt to determine *fortuna*.) The figures lend support to the view that rural Italians left their towns and villages after making realistic calculations of economic opportunity.

They neither sought a monetary panacea, nor were they pushed solely by the poverty of the countryside.

The situation in the twentieth century is less clear, although in all cases the direct association between wage levels and emigration is reduced. The real wage figures, based on nominal wages as a fraction of Italy's cost-of-living index, consistently show stronger associations than the wheat wage data,[23] which express the hard wheat purchasing power of farm laborers in Sicily.[24] While the differences are not great, they do indicate that the push of changes in rural wages was less strongly associated with net emigration than the pull of general economic conditions. Once again, all correlations are positive, lending further support to the hypothesis that people left in good times. Substantially higher correlations for Albareto indicate that these northern villagers were better able to respond quickly and precisely to wage fluctuations. Their response, facilitated by geographic proximity to northern Europe and therefore better knowledge of prevailing wages, owed its felxibility to the Albaretesi's more individualistic pattern of decision making.

## BRIDGES AND BARRICADES

In addition to evaluating such oscillatory variables as weather, local and distant wages, and prices, rural Italians considering emigration had to cope with factors of a more rigid sort. Perhaps the most immediate of these was transportation, the impact of which is evident in figure 20. Sharp increases in net emigration began around 1850 in Rogliano and within the next decade in Castel San Giorgio and Albareto. This 1850–70 movement developed in response to the coming of the railroad.[25] Clearing of new roadbeds and laying of tracks provided jobs, while fourth-class stand-up space on existing lines offered an inexpensive and rapid way to get to work. The value of migrant labor was meager, whether measured in terms of wages paid by employers or, more meaningfully, by the savings remaining to laborers after a term of work. The long duration, uncertainty, and cost of water transportation in the Mediterranean before 1880 exceeded the value of migrant labor. Thus the railroad served as a bridge factor in two ways, whereas previously transportation cost and time had been a barrier to migration. Railway connections from Sicily to the mainland did not exist until 1881, precisely when, as figure 20 shows, net emigration from the Sicilian village of Nissoria began to increase.[26]

The decade following the railroad boom saw a drop in net emigration rates in all four communities, a hiatus between reliance on land routes and the emergence of low-priced transatlantic voyages. But by 1880, for

$15 (or $28 in 1900)[27] one could buy steerage space on a ship going from Naples to New York. Let Rosa describe the passage:

> All us poor people had to go down through a hole to the bottom of the ship. There was a big dark room down there with rows of wooden shelves all around where we were going to sleep.... The girls and women and the men had to sleep all together in the same room. When the dinner bell rang we were all standing in line holding the tin plates we had to buy in Havre, waiting for soup and bread.... [During a storm] we had no light and no air, and everyone got sick where we were. We were like rats trapped in a hole, holding onto the posts and onto the iron frames to keep from rolling around. Why had I worried about Santino? We were never going to come to America after all! We were going to the bottom of the sea![28]

There is no evidence that Italians ever thought America's streets were paved with gold, nor did they easily overcome their fear of dying in a faraway land where no one might know them or care enough to arrange a "Christian" burial.[29] The general attracting force was not a dream but a closely calculated balance sheet. Assuming work was available, a sober and industrious male might expect to earn $35 monthly and save perhaps $25. Subtracting passage costs still left about $100 after six months' work.[30] Thus began the annual migration: an Atlantic crossing in the early spring, followed by a long summer of hot and hard work in mining or heavy industry, then in late fall return home for the more leisurely pace of winter. Some found year-round work and did not return, some called for their families, and a few achieved their savings goal, acquired a piece of land or a shop, and left migration to others. But in the aggregate, increased net emigration between 1880 and 1914 reflected a twisted and inverted form of transhumance. Instead of sending sheep from the plains to the mountains to feed on the rich high grasses of summer, Italian villages and towns sent their men and women across an ocean to acquire cash, the nutrient for survival in a modern economy. And just as transhumance became institutionalized, protected by safeguards, rules, and privileges, so also did the transatlantic passage develop the *padrone* system, chains of emigration, and the Mafia.[31]

A closer analysis of figure 20 reveals that this transatlantic emigration phase in three of the communities peaked before 1900. In Albareto, where a net rate of 16/1,000/year kept the village's absolute population stable between 1880 and 1900, the first decade of this century saw return levels in excess of emigration. Less dramatic but nonetheless statistically significant reversals occurred as well in Castel San Giorgio and Rogliano. In Nissoria, on the other hand, net emigration rates reached 35/1,000/year (double the rate of natural population growth), a level three times as high as the national average for the years 1901–10.[32] Thus none of the four communities seems to be "typical" or "representative" of broad patterns of Italian emigration. Three peaked too soon, during the pre-1900 pioneer period, and the other had a zenith so high that, had the rate continued for another two decades or so, no one would have remained. Combine all four rates for 1901–1910, however, and they approximate the national average fairly closely. More than a statistical conundrum is involved here; the figures illustrate well the limits of aggregate data, certainly at the national level and for many purposes at the regional level as well. In particular, large aggregate numbers lead to metaphors about migration streams and obscure the role of individual decision. Many Nissorini, like many Sicilians, faced an array of factors between 1900 and 1910 that induced them to emigrate, but most Nissorini in the same decade, like most Sicilians, chose not to leave. In the same years more Albaretesi returned than left, a situation that merits understanding and that could not be explained by large aggregate data even if such data went in the same direction. This is not to call for detailed studies of every village and every migrant (although more are to be welcomed); rather, it is to suggest that general explanations be built from particular cases rather than the reverse. Inexpensive transatlantic transportation facilitated certain migration strategies beginning about 1880, but other factors influenced precisely when, if at all, rural Italians chose to leave. Until the late 1950s steamships remained the primary means of transoceanic migration, although governmental efforts to eliminate some of the more squalid aspects of overcrowding in steerage caused shipping companies to raise prices to a level that lengthened to two years or more the minimum time necessary for most temporary migrants to cover expenses and return with savings. In the last two decades an increasing number of rural Italians have migrated by airplane to Toronto, New York, Sydney, or Buenos Aires. In two to six weeks they expect to be able to save the price of the ticket, so that transport costs in real wages are now once again about what they were in 1900.

As with transport facilities, governmental policies variously forbade, discouraged, or induced migration but left individuals and families with meaningful decisions to make. A full history of national legislation directly or indirectly affecting migration is beyond the scope of the present study. Nevertheless, a brief summary of major developments should allow a fuller understanding of some parameters of rural Italian emigration. As early as 1865 the national state warned against the abuses of emigration agencies and forbade the departure of young men subject to military service. Neither measure had much effect, except to increase clandestine movement, but only in 1888, under Crispi's urging, did parliament approve a comprehensive national policy. It offered some protection against shipping company abuses and attempted to count more accurately numbers of migrants, but little more. Not until after 1913, the peak year of exodus, did the Italian government use its power to refuse permission to emigrate, a policy strengthened by the closing of borders once Italy went to war. Thus the well-known fascist response to internal disorders in 1926—withdrawal of passports— reflected a "liberal" government policy initiated more than a decade earlier. In short, after centuries during which peasants did not have the right to move freely, a fifty-year period of unrestricted movement ended in 1914. Because Italy's industrial capitalist development was not sufficiently labor intensive to absorb population growth, the state since that time often approved rather freely requests to emigrate, but the right to refuse was always present and was often exercised. Under fascism, for example, only passport applications from party members in good standing had much chance of approval.[33]

Among receiving nations, the right to decide who might enter always remained with the state, even when, for example, the quota policy was no quota. Medical examinations and health certificate requirements, seemingly an obvious and minimal regulation, greatly affected migration decisions in malaria-ridden areas of southern Italy. Literacy tests, such as that of Australia in 1901 and especially that of the United States in 1917, have been linked to increased interest in adult education in rural Italy, surely an indication of careful and prolonged planning by peasants considering migration. Requirements that immigrants possess monetary sums affected persons going to Canada in the 1920s (although not always in the way the government anticipated) as, in an opposite way, Brazil's subsidized transport after its abolition of slavery tended to attract some rural Italians more than others. European nations in both the nineteenth and twentieth centuries made extensive use of Italian laborers in times of industrial expansion and acted with equal vigor in restricting and even expelling "foreigners" during periods of stagnation.[34]

In addition to direct legislation, government policy on a wide range of matters affected migration decisions. After nearly two decades of relatively free trade, during which northern Italian industry gained a modest but crucial advantage over the south, where craftsmen and small firms proved unable to compete with imports, Italy switched in 1878 to a mildly protectionist policy. Twenty years of rising duties, culminating in the Franco-Italian tariff war of 1888–98, may have been necessary for Italy's economic development (a matter of some controversy), but there is no doubt that drastic reductions in agricultural exports led to underemployment in the south. At about the same time, 1880–1900, real wages rose for those who found work, a classic depression situation and one that simultaneously fostered savings for the fortunate few and growing impoverishment for the many.[35]

If migration was one response to savings, debts, and depression, political protest was another. Historian J. S. MacDonald suggests that militant working-class organization kept agricultural laborers at home, that where the government smashed worker efforts to change the status quo, emigration increased. Whatever doubts there may be about the universality of MacDonald's hypothesis, it points to an important factor in understanding emigration decisions in a village such as Nissoria.[36] In the early 1890s, faced with depressed agricultural conditions and reduced sulfur output, *contadini* organized throughout the Nicosia district to seek higher wages and lower rents. Their actions, part of the Fasci movement that swept into interior Sicily in 1893 from the coastal centers of Catania and Palermo, were not without effect. In Nissoria peasants successfully pressured normally absentee *latifondisti* to trim the power of leaseholding intermediaries by renting some smaller parcels directly to cultivators. Wage workers, although unable to secure a pay increase directly, won a reduction in deductions for meals provided during the day. But the ultimate price for such small gains proved high indeed. In January 1894, Crispi imposed martial law throughout Sicily and brutally suppressed all working-class *fasci*. Six months later he introduced a very moderate land reform measure, but it quickly died in parliament. By the harvest of 1894, then, Nissorini had all the evidence they needed to recognize that collective action would not alleviate their distress in the near future. The alternative of migration was considered in the light of such realities.[37]

Transcending all other factors—weather, wage fluctuations, transportation, and government regulation—was demographic experience, the needs and abilities of members of *la famiglia*. Data on the overall relationship between population pressure (natural population growth) and net emigration, shown earlier in figure 20, allow some comment on migration decisions at the communal level.

In Albareto between 1810 and 1955 the two rates remained in close balance, indicating that this mountain village could support a maximum density of 45/km² or about 4,500 persons. Density hovered most often around 40/km², a level at which woods and valleys were intensively utilized. Because it was isolated and developed little industry, Albareto could not support a population above this level. A highly fractionalized land-tenure pattern, jealous protection of communal rights, and high land prices all reflected the pressure of population.[38] The cyclical character of Albareto's emigration before 1955 suggests that as soon as economic space became available villagers chose to remain. The situation since 1955 is altogether different; despite a natural growth rate only barely above replacement levels, net emigration continues to soar. Density dropped to 33/km² in 1961 and 25/km² a decade later.[39] The Albaretesi, especially the young, are no longer constrained by demographic pressures; rather, they are lured by the apparent elegance of urban life in Parma, Milan, or New York.

In Castel San Giorgio there is a rather different relationship between net emigration and natural growth, one that remains unchanged. Located on a plain and integrated with the coastal cities of Naples and Salerno, in the nineteenth century the town supported a density of about 350/km², a figure that rose to 635/km² by 1971. Before World War I crafts and extractive industry provided work, and since that time many townspeople have commuted to jobs in neighboring cities. The plain soil is devoted heavily to labor-intensive vegetable crops, and in the past a substantial number of resident *braccianti* sought work throughout Campania. Although life is by no means abundant in Castel San Giorgio, its residents never were pushed out by population pressure alone.

The curves for Rogliano show a situation that combines elements present in Albareto and Castel San Giorgio. Rogliano's mountainous terrain, devoted primarily to crops that were not labor intensive, provided little room for population growth. In the last two centuries emigration by outlying residents kept constant the density of this sector at about 25/km².[40] But in the compact town center lived 4,000 people (in 1861), a figure that grew to over 7,000 by 1961, thus yielding an overall density level that rose from 110/km² to 171/km². A majority of these townspeople were chronically underemployed, first as *braccianti* and later as *manovali*. However, their underemployment was seasonal, with labor shortages occurring during harvest time and in peak building construction months; idle days numbered from 200 to as many as 300 per year.[41] Alternation of labor shortages with idle time kept lower-class families at the edge of malnutrition and in dangerously unsanitary and overcrowded living arrangements. But paradoxically, population growth made the situation only a little worse, and emigration did not enhance greatly the position of those who chose to remain. Rogliano's economy condemned a substantial segment of its residents to poverty and yet provided room for population growth. As in the case of Castel San Giorgio, the pressure of numbers did not in itself push the Roglianesi to emigrate, at least until the 1930s. Before that decade, for most of the preceding 120 years, an essentially stagnant economy supported a growing population.

Nissoria's wheat lands have never supported more than about 3,400 people (a density of 55/km²), and each major period of emigration reduced this to 45/km², a level at which residents apparently no longer felt constrained to leave. Historically, any population above this level found no work at all in Nissoria and either starved, went to the sulfur mines, or emigrated.[42] The last choice was impossible without credit facilities to finance initial costs and the establishment of an emigration chain (perceived by most to be a necessity). These developed only slowly and inadequately, contributing to the retardation, suddenness, and massiveness of movement from Nissoria. The Nissorini, like the Albaretesi, responded to demographic experience by emigrating, but unlike the Albaretesi, they did so in short bursts, at least until 1950. In the last two decades some Nissorini have been lured by higher wage levels in the North and in Germany; others have migrated to a new land of opportunity, Australia.

Taken together, the curves in figure 20 suggest the need for caution in drawing too direct a correlation between a low standard of living and a desire to emigrate. In a variety of ways, most treatments of Italian emigration paint a dismal picture of the *contadini*'s economic circumstances and move easily to the seemingly obvious conclusion that poverty was ample reason for leaving.[43] The portrait is indeed accurate, but the causal link is more complex. The majority of *contadini* did not leave. Moreover, as the cases of Castel San Giorgio and Rogliano illustrate, an economy that condemns the majority to a brutally low standard of living may sustain demographic growth for many decades. Poverty induced people to migrate primarily if population pressure threatened to erode the existing standard of living. This might be dreadfully low, as in Nissoria, or relatively high, as in Albareto. The Albaretesi, even the poorest among them, had a substantially higher standard of living (measured by diet and housing conditions) than the lower class of Castel San Giorgio and Rogliano. Emigration by Albaretesi served to maintain the economic level of those who remained. But in Rogliano emigration gave too little economic advantage to townspeople who stayed, and absolute population increased steadily. In Castel San Giorgio proximity to Naples offered alternatives to moving out. The consequences of population growth, then, vary greatly with the local geophysical and economic situation. And it is the threat of lowered living standards, not the absolute level of those standards, that induces emigration.

## THE DECISION

A peasant's decision on whether to migrate involved the following queries. What future is there for me if I stay here and continue with what I am doing now? What else can I do here? Where shall I go? When shall I go? What are the opportunities and risks there? What are the requirements or restrictions for going there? How shall I get there and pay for the trip? When, if at all, do I intend to return? With whom shall I go? A social scientist with a penchant for such things easily might draw a flowchart of decision boxes with yes and no arrows to describe migration. Although that would be an improvement over water metaphors, it would tend to miss the interactive quality of the peasant's decision-making process. I suspect that the subtlety of this process can be captured fully only by the methods of historical biography, an approach that must await another volume. Moreover, the analysis that follows rests on limited data. In Castel San Giorgio and Rogliano I was unable to locate more than a scattering of emigration permits, and these did not yield sufficient information to document so difficult a question as why one peasant left whereas another did not. Extensive interviews among the Albaretesi and briefer but very informative fieldwork in Nissoria, combined with good written evidence at least for some years, justify concentrating on migration in these two villages. In short, I shall attempt to illutrate a decision-making process with two extended examples. No claim is made that all rural Italians came to the same conclusions, although I do believe that most evaluated a similar set of queries.

Beginning in 1807, young men in Albareto were subject to military conscription once they reached their twentieth birthday.[44] On the appointed day they appeared for a physical examination and presented any reasons for being excused from service. But quite a few did not appear. Instead, a member of the family testified that the young man was "oltre il confine," off in a foreign land. The conscription board drew up a list of all such absentees and posted it with law enforcement officials who were ordered to arrest anyone who returned. Table 36 summarizes percentages of such "emigrants" by decade through 1899. The figures are approximate; they may include some draft evaders who had not emigrated, and they exclude men who neither appeared nor sent anyone to explain their absence.[45] Caveats aside, the figures show that nearly one of every six males by age twenty left his family behind and established himself in a foreign land for an extended stay. Avoiding military service undoubtedly was a factor, but it was only one among several that villagers had to evaluate.

Dependent upon common pastures and woodlands and with private holdings generally large enough to support only one family, Albaretesi responded to population growth by emigrating. Figure 20 documents this relationship at the communal level, but actual decisions were made in the context of land and family. Notwithstanding laws requiring equal inheritance, the Albaretesi avoided subdivision of holdings. A male in his late teens who had a younger brother and whose parents owned

TABLE 36   **Twenty-Year-Old Males Certified as Away from Home (%) (N cases = 2,078)**

| Year | Away from Home | Year | Away from Home |
|------|----------------|------|----------------|
| Pre-1820 | 14 | 1860–69 | 18 |
| 1820–29 | 16 | 1870–79 | 12 |
| 1830–39 | 37 | 1880–89 | 13 |
| 1840–49 | 15 | 1890–99 | 16 |
| 1850–59 | 17 | Overall | 16 |

land was expected to emigrate or to become a priest. Draft records for the nineteenth century indicate that among every 100 twenty-year-old males, fifty had one or more brothers; of these fifty perhaps forty came from families holding at least some land; among the forty about five became priests, ten stayed even though they were expected to leave, and twenty-five emigrated.[46] The eldest brother left first, and it was the youngest who stayed on the family plot and, in exchange for caring for aging parents, inherited his father's holdings. If the youngest male predeceased his parents, became a priest, migrated, or died before his own children reached maturity, an elder brother returned to become *capo famiglia*.[47]

The mores of inheritance and emigration among the Albaretesi remained unchanged well into the twentieth century. The family provided each of its children with something, but only one with land, and support obligations extended to sons but not to grandsons. Fathers paid the initial costs of emigration, and sons relinquished claims to the land. Thus disinherited, the emigrant worked for his own account, sharing nothing with his kin who remained in the village. There is a savings bank in Albareto, and emigrants did send money back home, but it was to their personal accounts and not for support of family.[48] Men who returned to wed left again with their wives. Among married Albaretesi even temporary migration without one's spouse was rare; instead, both sought employment, thereby doubling their rate of saving. These customary ways both reflected and shaped the role of *la famiglia* in this mountain village. When all went well, those who stayed and those who left worked on their own to achieve individual and "nuclear" family goals. Kin ties were relegated to fireside stories, weddings and funerals, and feast days. But when the need arose—a retarded sister, a dead brother, safety in time of war, a good business venture—family as process responded swiftly and vigorously. Requests were granted, as long as they were both rare and justified.

For a brief but important period, 1890–1910, good records remain on emigration among 125 families resident in the center of Albareto. Altogether in twenty years, 272 moves occurred, an average of more than two per family. Table 37 provides data on the economic status of each family and the intended destinations of their emigrating members.

The pressure of land, the need to prevent further partition of holdings by encouraging all but the youngest son to leave, appears most forcefully in the row of table 37 that deals with families from which no one emigrated. Only fourteen of 125 families had no emigrating sons, a statistic to be kept in mind as an indicator of the emormous impact of migration on the village. Moreover, the figures reveal that land pressure was greatest precisely among smallholders (no families without emigrants) and, to a lesser degree, among substantial owners (67 percent less

TABLE 37  Emigration by Males from Albareto Centro Families, 1890–1910: % over or under Expected Frequency for Occupation and Place

| Destination | Large Holders | Small Holders | Sharecroppers and Tenants | Agricultural Wage Workers | Town Workers | Uncertain | N Cases |
|---|---|---|---|---|---|---|---|
| North America | −11 | +5 | +85 | −233 | −185 | −18 | 55 |
| South America | −100 | +17 | +133 | +50 | ...ᵃ | ...ᵃ | 17 |
| British Isles | +30 | +39 | −21 | −669 | −10 | −35 | 61 |
| France | +29 | −70 | +6 | 0 | −55 | +88 | 47 |
| Germany/Belgium | −133 | −175 | −251 | +71 | +300 | +14 | 20 |
| Switzerland | −233 | +40 | ...ᵃ | +130 | +10 | 0 | 26 |
| Italy | +50 | 0 | −72 | +50 | −9 | −50 | 32 |
| None emigrated | −67 | ...ᵃ | 0 | +140 | +120 | +60 | 14 |
| N cases | 39 | 73 | 58 | 34 | 28 | 40 | ... |

ᵃNo emigrants in this category.

than the expected number of families with no emigrants). At the opposite pole, farm wage laborers and town workers, who had no land to protect from excessive subdivision, showed a distinct tendency not to emigrate (140 percent and 120 percent, respectively, above random distribution). Although the evidence is fragmentary, it does point to a need to investigate closely standard assumptions about masses of landless agricultural laborers who, forced out by desperate poverty, migrated to the New World and elsewhere at the turn of this century. There were in rural Italy many more laborers than owners, and therefore any absolute count of emigrants must turn up an overwhelming number of landless *contadini.* But from the perspective of the local village and the family, at least in Albareto, a more complex picture emerges. To be sure, the poor migrated. However, they were less likely to do so than were the children of landowners,[49] small and large, whose departure arose not from abject poverty but from their families' effort to maintain their standards of living. At the very least, emigration was a significant safety valve not only for the rural proletariat but also for its petty bourgeoisie.

Important differences by economic status also characterized decisions about where to go. Persons with skills useful in an urban or industrial setting tended to move to northern Europe, particularly Germany and Belgium (+300 percent); they clearly failed to take advantage of any opportunities in North and South America. The choice reflected a realistic assessment of savings possibilities; emigration to northern Europe meant less time lost in travel, lower transportation costs, higher wages due to greater recognition of skills,[50] and an easier return home.

For agricultural wage laborers the choice was much narrower. Often they lacked savings to pay for transportation to very far places and found it difficult to obtain credit. The families of *braccianti* were less stable than other Albaretesi, and they had fewer kin in the village.[51] When they could afford to move at all, it was to nearby Switzerland, where they worked as domestics or as unskilled factory operatives, a position also open in Germany. In general they could not afford the fare to North America, and the remuneration in England for servants or unskilled laborers was too low to cover the costs involved in getting there. Those who went to Brazil did so under work contracts that included passage; they have not returned, and their grandchildren now work as skilled operatives in São Paulo.[52]

Tenants and sharecroppers sometimes shared the poverty of agricultural wage laborers but differed from *braccianti* in their ability to obtain credit or benefit from familial assistance. For most of them credit was neither new nor strange. A tenant or sharecropper could expect to borrow from his landlord a sum sufficient to pay for his son's emigration. Indeed, the very inability of the landlord to provide a place for the son made the loan a matter of *onore* (but one bearing interest!), part of a network of unwritten obligations between two villagers of unequal station.[53] Other tenants in Albareto were relatives, often siblings, of landowners, and customary practices usually assured that initial migration costs would be paid, or at least that each child would receive something. Although the time goes somewhat beyond the dates in table 37, one villager's story illustrates one outcome of this obligation:

> My parents, who owned good lands, set aside 3,600 lire for each of us. Two used the money in studying for the priesthood, one bought a shoe store, another went to America, and another established a business buying and selling cows. As for me, inflation had set in, and my 3,600 lire bought only two lambs; these we ate at the wedding dinner.

Sharecroppers and tenants chose overwhelmingly to emigrate to the New World. For siblings not destined to inherit land, there was little future in Albareto. Temporary employment elsewhere in Europe, even if savings were likely, offered no meaningful solution, since without land the savings would soon dissipate. Purchase of a tract in Albareto was infrequent; prices were artificially high, measured against reasonable return estimates, due not only to land scarcity but also to the traditional obligation to keep one's holdings intact to be passed on to the chosen youngest son. In short, elder sons knew from an early age that they must leave the mountains of Albareto for many years. Those who went to South America did so not as *braccianti* under passage-for-labor contracts but with a bit of cash and the intention to save for a few years and then open a small business. These families still write occasionally to their *cugini* in Albareto, but with few exceptions, they do not return even for a visit. A substantial proportion are successful, but they measure that success by investments in their New World businesses and by full integration into their adopted cultures.

Albaretesi in the United States followed a different pattern. They came to work for wages, nearly always in New York City, in jobs marked by long hours and piece work. Whether as waiters, nonunion small independent construction workers, garment workers, hairdressers, or cooks, their occupational choices even to the third generation reflected a desire neither for security nor for status. Above all, Albaretesi in North America valued a job's savings potential; they sought positions that allowed speedups, sixteen-hour days, and pay based on output. All this they did (and still do) with a single goal in mind, never abandoned and often attained: return to Albareto. Because the village's economy was so limited, the return often involved buying apartments or shops in the nearby town of Borgotaro, the city of Parma, or along the Ligurian coast. Nevertheless, the goal was residence in Albareto. It was this goal, not lack of savings, that caused them to shun American business investments that would have required close supervision. Similarly, they placed little value on education; professional positions were not readily transferable to Italy, and monetary rewards were too delayed and uncertain. Albaretesi in the United States are proud to recall that none of them has ever been unwillingly unemployed; they are indifferent to the fact that few of their children and grandchildren complete a college education.[54]

The pattern among smallholders is closer than any other to random distribution, indicating that they exercised a wide range of migration strategies. When a cold and damp spring threatened a poor harvest, some sought domestic work in nearby Switzerland. When sons became old enough to do men's work, one or more (or even the father) journeyed to England for several years of employment, perhaps as a butcher, a waiter, or a cook. A few sold their holdings and moved more permanently to the New World.

Substantial landowners emigrated primarily to England, France, and other parts of Italy. The most common pattern was that a father, intent on avoiding land partition and ultimate reduction to the status of *contadino*, used a portion of his capital to start his elder sons in business. In London the children of well-to-do Albaretesi established ice cream parlors; in Paris they opened beauty salons; along the Ligurian coast they purchased apartments for rental to tourists. All these investments involved substantial initial capital but relatively little risk thereafter. Geographic proximity allowed frequent returns to Albareto, and especially until the Second World War, many of these families allowed their children to be raised by siblings in Albareto while mother and father ran businesses elsewhere in Europe.[55] The rural elite, able to pay the high initial cost of instant success in the advanced economies of England and France, apparently saw little reason to move to more distant opportunities in the New World.

\* \* \*

The second case study on migration decisions concerns the Nissorini in the years 1934–1973. During this period the *comune* kept individual file cards and a register on everyone who moved into or out of the village. Table 38 contains a summary in five-year intervals of the migration register.[56] Even during the fascist era, when movement was severely curtailed, one-fifth of Nissoria's people moved in or out every five years. Once every week, on average, an individual or a family established a new residence and abandoned an old one in Nissoria. About 90 percent of this movement, however, was within Sicily, and much of it occurred in the context of marriage, as discussed in the previous chapter. Two families returned after twenty years in Argentina, apparently intending to settle permanently in the village, but within six months they left again for South America. Fewer than a dozen Nissorini went to the United States, less because of quota restrictions than because they had heard that jobs were difficult to find in Chicago. The economic outlook was not very promising in Sicily either, however, and no "Americani" returned home. Depression, restrictive legislation, and war meant that for at least ten years most Nissorini decided not to migrate.

During the next decade, 1944–53, which included years of peace, prosperity, and relatively freer movement, Nissorini at home and away also chose to stay where they were. So much for linear push-pull explanations and waves of migration. According to people I spoke with, including many who ultimately did emigrate, in the late 1940s and until the clear failure of agrarian reform after 1952, villagers optimistically calculated that the land would be divided into viable wheat farms, the government would aid in converting pastures to high-profit animal husbandry, and industry would come to interior Sicily. *Contadini* cast free ballots for the first time in their lives and, proverbial Sicilian cynicism aside, believed their votes counted. They formed an association of direct cultivators and initiated steps to organize cooperative harvesting, milling, and marketing. In short, the present was bearable, and the future seemed worth fighting for. Some men and women left for industrial cities in the north, about eighty altogether in the decade; but even their departure was intended to be temporary, a year or two to earn money and gain skills in order to participate more fully in the local economy when the promised factories came to Nissoria.[57]

Beginning in 1955, villagers much more frequently decided to leave, often traveling great distances. Between that year and 1958 over 200 Nissorini (one of every fifteen) left, usually with their families, for Australia. In so doing, they took advantage of bureaucratic provisions actually intended to encourage northern Italians while discouraging

TABLE 38   Immigration and Emigration in Nissoria, 1934–73

| | 1934–38 | 1939–43 | 1944–48 | 1949–53 | 1954–58 | 1959–63 | 1964–68 | 1969–73 |
|---|---|---|---|---|---|---|---|---|
| Number of immigrants | 336 | 351 | 366 | 414 | 299 | 428 | 382 | 562 |
| Number of emigrants | 284 | 311 | 410 | 562 | 694 | 714 | 637 | 824 |
| Net migration | + 52 | + 40 | − 44 | −148 | −395 | −286 | −255 | −262 |
| Number of moves in | 140 | 123 | 158 | 178 | 159 | 211 | 191 | 249 |
| Number of moves out | 123 | 129 | 167 | 205 | 359 | 300 | 291 | 349 |
| Immigrant family size (% in each category): | | | | | | | | |
|     Male | | | | | 21 | 18 | 17 | 14 |
| Single | 19 | 14 | 23 | 24 | | | | |
|     Female | | | | | 13 | 14 | 15 | 10 |
| 2 | 13 | 9 | 11 | 10 | 13 | 11 | 11 | 9 |
| 3–4 | 35 | 35 | 34 | 24 | 29 | 28 | 25 | 36 |
| 5 or more | 33 | 42 | 32 | 42 | 24 | 29 | 32 | 31 |
| Emigrant family size (% in each category): | | | | | | | | |
|     Male | | | | | 21 | 13 | 12 | 13 |
| Single | 26 | 21 | 23 | 20 | | | | |
|     Female | | | | | 12 | 13 | 16 | 11 |
| 2 | 8 | 12 | 7 | 9 | 12 | 10 | 7 | 10 |
| 3–4 | 26 | 27 | 31 | 24 | 25 | 22 | 31 | 33 |
| 5 or more | 40 | 40 | 39 | 47 | 30 | 42 | 34 | 33 |
| Immigrant prior residences (% in each category): | | | | | | | | |
| Sicily | 92 | 98 | 92 | 97 | 76 | 80 | 69 | 56 |
| Southern Italy | 1 | 1 | 4 | 1 | 4 | 4 | 2 | 6 |
| Northern Italy | 3 | 0 | 3 | 2 | 5 | 6 | 17 | 14 |
| Europe | 1 | 0 | 1 | 0 | 1 | 1 | 4 | 18 |
| South America | 3 | 1 | 0 | 0 | 3 | 2 | 1 | 1 |
| North America | 0 | 0 | 0 | 0 | 6 | 1 | 1 | 2 |
| Australia | 0 | 0 | 0 | 0 | 5 | 6 | 6 | 3 |
| Emigrant intended destinations (% in each category): | | | | | | | | |
| Sicily | 86 | 87 | 83 | 89 | 44 | 60 | 51 | 40 |
| Southern Italy | 4 | 7 | 4 | 4 | 3 | 5 | 4 | 5 |
| Northern Italy | 4 | 6 | 13 | 6 | 8 | 19 | 24 | 21 |
| Europe | 0 | 0 | 0 | 0 | 4 | 2 | 1 | 19 |
| South America | 3 | 0 | 0 | 1 | 6 | 1 | 1 | 0 |
| North America | 3 | 0 | 0 | 0 | 6 | 1 | 2 | 4 |
| Australia | 0 | 0 | 0 | 0 | 29 | 12 | 17 | 11 |

Sicilians. Their success in overcoming legal obstacles was due to the rapid formation of family-based chains and a patronage system similar in structure to those developed fifty years earlier when the destination was Chicago. Years of greatest movement corresponded closely to times of prosperity in Australia, an indication of effective communication and decision making. Nevertheless, nearly one of every six emigrants to Australia returned, usually within two years. All those I interviewed said that they had intended to stay permanently but had not found jobs or housing to their liking. Those who returned to Nissoria found little opportunity in the village and soon migrated again, this time to the industrial north.[58]

Also starting in the mid 1950s, villagers calculated the advantages of temporary migration to northern Italy or Europe and many decided to go: to England in 1956, to France in 1960, to Belgium and Germany in 1968 and heavily in 1971 (nearly 200 persons), to the Turin-Milan-Genoa triangle (about 400 persons since 1958). These moves were intended from the outset to be temporary relocations. For Nissorini, the goals were savings and return home, but to what? For the receiving sector, migration meant supplying advanced industries with a reservoir of low-skilled workers from among the ranks of southern Italy's unemployed. The Common Market facilitated not only the exchange of goods but also a multinational distribution of labor. The 200 Nissorini in Germany in 1971, and the tens of thousands of southern Italians who went with them, relieved somewhat the financial and political pressures arising from the failures of Italy's programs for the Mezzogiorno. At the same time, the importation of these workers reduced Germany's labor shortage, thereby ameliorating the perceived threat of wage inflation in its booming industrial sector.[59] Overall, the abruptness of shifts in migration to Europe, northern Italy, and even Australia since 1955 suggest that the Nissorini were on the lookout for opportunities and quickly seized what was available, even though the volume of their emigration and return was determined in some measure by forces beyond their control.

In the face of these external pressures, the Nissorini nonetheless showed a remarkable ability to defend the integrity of la famiglia. Inspection of table 38 reveals that a substantial majority of all persons coming into or leaving Nissoria moved with their families. The fact that there is little correspondence between shifts in destination and fluctuations in size groupings indicates that family units dominated not only local movement but also international and overseas migration. Moreover, since 1945 the proportion of emigrants moving alone has been less than the proportion of immigrants listed singly, a statistic indicating, on balance, an effort at restoration and renewal of familial groups. Because net migration is outward, this effort in absolute terms is unsuccessful; but noting that since 1954 the emigrant to immigrant ratio for males moving singly is 1.52 to 1, whereas for women it is 1.76 to 1, it seems likely that women were joining their husbands in northern Italy while other men returned to join their wives in Nissoria. The statistics are consistent with such a hypothesis, and villagers believe that this has been happening. That is, the relative prosperity of the postwar years offered the possibility of reuniting the family or of emigrating with spouse and children in tow. Nissorini consciously chose this possibility even when it entailed some economic sacrifice, as in the substantially higher living costs of maintaining a family in Milan rather than leaving them behind in the village. In sum, the Nissorini responded to the potential for economic advancement through migration within the framework of the values of *la famiglia*.

Despite a certain lack of meaningful choice about migration strategies, the Nissorini do not end up randomly in one country or another. It may be recalled that in the case of Albareto at the turn of the century, various economic divisions corresponded closely to particular patterns of migration. Table 39, which deals with declared permanent international migration by adult Nissorini after World War II, also reveals differentials worthy of attention.[60] Nearly one-fourth of these emigrants were illiterate, and another 8 percent had substantially less schooling than the law required. Perhaps no more telling fact need be set forth to indicate the tragic limits of Rome's efforts, during and after Mussolini's regime, to provide the southern peasantry with even the minimal requisites for success in bureaucracy-laden postwar Italy: one of every four could not fill out the forms needed to break away. Only the more literate were able to cope with restrictions upon emigration to North America; the others signed on, indeed they were recruited, for places in Argentina and northern Europe.

The sex ratio figures are interesting primarily because they reveal a substantially higher proportion of females than appears in statistics for

TABLE 39  **International Emigration from Nissoria, 1952–71: % over or under Expected Frequency (N cases = 260)**

|  | Australia | South America | North America | Europe | Overall |
|---|---|---|---|---|---|
| Schooling: |  |  |  |  |  |
| Illiterate | −4 | +26 | −26 | +26 | 24 |
| 5 years or less | +4 | +2 | −20 | −9 | 8 |
| Over 5 years | −18 | ...ª | +259 | +1 | 68 |
| Sex: |  |  |  |  |  |
| Male | +2 | −8 | −12 | +15 | 52 |
| Female | −2 | +8 | +12 | −15 | 48 |
| Occupation: |  |  |  |  |  |
| Smallholder | +18 | +186 | ...ª | ...ª | 11 |
| Sharecropper or tenant | +25 | +96 | ...ª | ...ª | 7 |
| Agricultural wage laborer | +9 | +37 | −20 | −45 | 42 |
| Town skilled | −46 | ...ª | +166 | +130 | 17 |
| Town low-skilled | −1 | ...ª | −3 | +68 | 23 |
| % married | +16 | −20 | −27 | −42 | 45 |
| Age married (mean) | 23.4 | 22.6 | 20.7 | 24.0 | 23.1 |
| Age Emigrated (mean) | 27.1 | 22.0 | 24.2 | 27.1 | 26.0 |

ªNo emigrants in this category.

Italy as a whole. Migration to the northern industrial zone was heavily male, and from the table it is evident that this imbalance applied as well to relocation in northern Europe, which, although categorized as permanent in official documents, was temporary in the minds of the persons who went.[61] A majority of those who left for Australia were married couples, so that the relatively even number of males and females there is not unexpected. The New World pattern is more complex. Monticelli believes that "female emigration has been an emigration of women leaving Italy to join their families" and that "the largest number is comprised of young women aged 14–30."[62] The data on mean age for Nissorini confirm the dominance of the 14–30 age group but, as table 39 shows, most emigrants to the New World were not married. They cannot have been joining parents who left years earlier, since virtually no Nissorini emigrated overseas between 1935 and 1955 (see table 38). Nor do the village's annual data reveal a time lag in the postwar period, whereby males left first and related females followed them a few years later. In short, young women in Nissoria did not leave in order to join their spouses or parents. On the contrary, they left their parents, and in a number of cases their husbands, to seek cash employment, most often as factory operatives. Several interviewees, in Italy and in America, describe this new migration as follows:

> In the village, a girl realizes at about age fifteen that marital prospects are few. Looking around her, she sees the likelihood that in the years ahead she will be torn between the absence of a husband working in distant Milan or Germany and joining him for a crowded, marginal life among the urban poor. She is glad to work, or will be when she completes school, but there are no jobs. She has relatives in America or Argentina, aunts and uncles sympathetic to her innocent prettiness and dismal future. Hints are dropped, and a kindly *zio* and *zia* agree to sponsor the girl and advance the airfare. Surely she will find work, and in the interim she can help her aunt clean house, cook, or care for the children. The girl's parents will miss her, but there never was much chance that she would have settled in the village anyway. And, most important, she will continue under the watchful eye of *la famiglia*.

Differentiation in destination also appears to be related to occupation. Agriculturists, whether the owners of small plots, tenants, or wage laborers, dominated the ranks of migrants to Australia, who generally left without intending to return. Farmers also chose to go to South America in substantial numbers, whereas nonagriculturists headed more often for North America and northern Europe. In the case of skilled workers, this choice was required by American and Canadian legislation favoring immigration by persons with skills deemed to be in short supply. Emigration agreements with Common Market countries

arranged for selection from lists of the unemployed and therefore dis-
criminated against farm laborers, who were chronically underemployed
but not technically unemployed. With regard to occupation, then, destination patterns were imposed upon the Nissorini rather than generated by their own economic circumstances.

A booklet issued as part of Nissoria's celebration of the fiftieth an-
niversary of Italy's victory in World War I accurately summarizes the
village's view on recent emigration:

> The land, still cultivated with inadequate methods, has not been able
> to satisfy the increasing needs of its people, who have found in emi-
> gration the possibility of survival. Nissoria today has many of its chil-
> dren, and not the worst ones, spread throughout the world, but they
> are ready to come back and place their youthful energy at the service
> of the village as soon as they shall be given the possibility of a good
> life.[63]

The Nissorini, and rural Italians in general, display a variety of feelings
when they speak of emigration: sadness over familial separations, frus-
tration over the land's inability to support its people, pride in the ac-
complishments of their sons and daughters, thankfulness for the abundance of the New World, anger at their own government's ineptitude
and obstructionism. But above all, those who remain sense that, of all
the responses by the village to the changes of the last two centuries,
none so deeply threatens its very existence as emigration.

## THE CONSEQUENCES

Scholars, politicians, and more important, rural Italians differ sharply
over the consequences of emigration. Optimists generally see the migrant as a thinking individual pulled by economic opportunities found
in the cities and in foreign lands. Pessimists, on the other hand, tend to
emphasize the grinding poverty of the countryside and to see the migrant as a wandering soul pushed out, condemned to exile among
strange exploiters. But just as the push-pull dichotomy fails to capture
fully the process of making decisions among rural Italians, so also does
it allow only limited understanding of the consequences of emigration.
In a better world, there would be no ever widening chasm between
north and south, there would be jobs for all right in the local community, people would be treated by macroeconomists as assets, not
liabilities, everyone would earn at least a "mean" income. In the real
world, however, the Mezzogiorno remains impoverished, the unemployment rate rises, population growth is a menace, and "the rich
are truly rich and the poor truly poor." Emigrants responded to the real

world and, in so doing, served in an ironic way as a force that contributed to the stagnation and even retrogression of rural Italy.

I should emphasize here that I am not referring to the vast contributions made by rural Italian emigrants to the economy and culture of many nations throughout the world. Rather, I am concerned with the impact of emigration on the communities of exodus. Earlier in this chapter I tried to show how the Albaretesi maintained a pastoral economy and communal use rights by encouraging all sons but one to leave the land. Apart from the particulars of its situation and such specifics as migration by elder sons, the case of Albareto illustrates well one of the conserving and preserving aspects of emigration, which acted as a "safety valve" throughout the nineteenth century and perhaps through the Second World War. And what was the outcome? Cyberneticized scholars such as myself may find it difficult to understand why young Albaretesi today uniformly abandon the soil, forgoing the gathering of mushrooms and chestnuts to work in a factory. But the Albaretesi are not foolish romantics; they prefer white bread to chestnut mush and clean gas heating to free firewood. They do not intend to be trapped, as their ancestors were, in a feudal vestige.

The Nissorini represent a more typical case. Their migration at the turn of the century resulted in a substantial infusion of cash into the local economy and the purchased transfer of great estates to smallholders. And what was the outcome? *Latifondisti* unloaded an asset of dubious value and acquired the means to invest in heavy industry along Sicily's coasts and in the north; nineteenth-century *baroni* became twentieth-century *capitalisti*. The *contadini*, meanwhile, remained *contadini*, told by Mussolini to plant wheat and make babies. In much of the Mezzogiorno the great prewar migration did little more than perpetuate an obsolete economy for another two generations, thereby contributing mightily to the "new" postwar exodus of several million southerners.

These new migrants, according to Rome's center for emigration study, use their remittances for the following: purchase of land, house repairs, building a new house, furnishings, food, clothing, education for their children, nondurable consumer goods, automobiles, and in a few cases investment in a small business. The same list might be drawn for rural Italians who find work locally. Indeed, the new migration, although "temporary" according to the migrants' expectations, seems to be a structural component of Italy's economic miracle. Some experts suggest that work abroad be institutionalized as a three-year term of service, analogous to a volunteer army, as if the problem involved no more than a shortcoming in the economy of fixed and measurable proportion. But the consequences are fare more severe: loneliness, familial

separation, xenophobia, criminality, alienation, ignorance, consumerism, exploitation. Emigrant workers vote overwhelmingly
against the party in power, against the miracle that left them in
Wolfsburg, Berne, or Lyon.[64]
Whatever disagreements there may be about other consequences of
emigration, all concur that it has had a profound impact on rural demography. Population is declining in the countryside, and in a most
distorted way. On the streets of most rural villages and in the main
plaza, on weekdays and holidays, at midday and in the evening, one
sees many old people, a fair number of children, and a few mothers. But
the fathers are absent, as are unmarried and childless adults of both
sexes. Figure 21, which portrays the age and sex compositions of the
populations of Albareto and Nissoria in 1971, gives ample evidence of
what is happening. Births are declining, due to both increased use of
conception control devices and the absence of one spouse or the other
for years at a time. A lower birth rate may be a good thing, but what
future is there for Albareto if people over age sixty-nine continue to
outnumber the entire school-age population? In both villages there are
sharp indentations, shortages of people, for the age groups born during
the world wars, but this "natural" shortage in each case is exacerbated

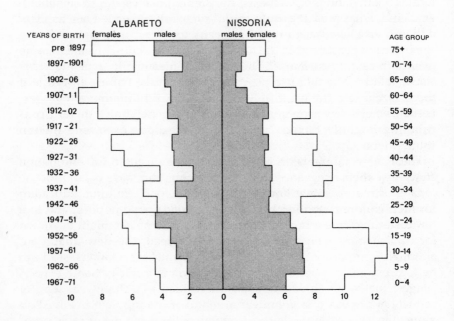

Fig. 21.
Age pyramids for Albareto and Nissoria, 1971

by emigration-caused shortages that extend from about age twenty to age fifty-five.

More specifically, Nissorini are absent in their late twenties, when many males have not yet married and when couples who have married do not yet have children, so that they may emigrate together to work and save joint earnings. They return in their early thirties to raise their children, often supplementing a meager local income with the savings of their earlier years. Within a decade these savings tend to run out, and at the same time the family reaches a point in its life cycle when expenses are greatest (all children have been born and none is old enough to work). Therefore, a second emigration is necessary, often by the husband alone (note the drop in the sex ratio), which lasts until he has earned a pension. The substantial increase in the sex ratio (from ninety-seven to 115 at age fifty) confirms that, once beyond their childbearing years and when their youngest children are of school age, women emigrate in significant numbers.

The trends evident in Nissoria appear with even greater force in Albareto, which due to emigration is fast becoming a charming but economically moribund retreat for pensioners and summer visitors. The Albaretesi are absent most heavily from the ages of twenty-five to forty, after which those who have been most successful begin to return and live on their savings, along with earnings from whatever local work is available. The sex ratio during these years indicates that both husband and wife emigrate; only at age fifty-five do women begin to outnumber men consistently in Albareto's resident population. The sex ratio among the elderly is due less to sex-differentiated mortality rates than to the tendency of widows to return to the village, whereas widowers more frequently remain in the country to which they emigrated. But these patterns are matters of detail; the major conclusion to be drawn from figure 21 is portrayed in the outward slope of almost the entire pyramid for Albareto. Retirees outnumber children, and both are more numerous than the working-age population. Of 1,140 residential houses in Albareto in 1971, 336 were unoccupied.[65]

One of the Albaretesi aptly described the current situation: "Non siamo più un paese ma soltanto un punto sulla carta geografica" (We are no longer a village but a point on the map).

# 9
# Epilogue: Future

Avengers, partisans, schoolteachers:
Three stories, two sides, one sting.
Rudolph M. Bell

## AVENGERS

The Squillacis were killed by a squad of paid goons from Leonforte
who had sold out to the Bourbons. The family had been in the forefront of the movement for Italian unification.

The Priest

The Squillacis opposed unification and had turned against
Garibaldi. They were killed by poor peasants from Leonforte.

A University Student

Sad indeed were the events of June 3, 1860, when during a single
night thirteen illustrious persons were killed, of whom six were
members of the Squillaci family. There followed two years of crude
brigandage, tragic deaths, and unbelievable repression. But generally
the Nissorini have always been good-natured and religious folk.

The Mimeographed Text Used in Nissoria's Elementary School

The Squillacis were tyrants. They controlled the economy, the politics, and the church. We Nissorini decided we had had enough and to
do away with them. We got all but one of them; he escaped by hiding
under a woman's skirts. We prayed to San Giuseppe to be able to kill
him too.

A Peasant

1860 was a fateful year for the Nissorini. The Squillaci family for
decades had dominated life in the village. With the exception of only a
few years between 1800 and 1860, the parish priest had been a Squillaci.
Lest anyone forget, each successive incumbent had had his portrait
painted and hung on the church walls. Members of the family had been
top village administrators on twelve separate occasions, alternating
with only four other families, into each of which at least one of their
female members had married. The medical doctor, the pharmacist, the
biggest miller, and the animal trader were all named Squillaci. They
owned substantial tracts of land in their own right and held leases for

further sublet not only in Nissoria but also in Leonforte and Assoro. As with so many local dons in the Sicilian summer of 1860, the Squillacis were less concerned with unification or Bourbons than with retention of their power in the village.

The band that killed them, although surely influenced by Garibaldi's march across Sicily, acted primarily to avenge local grievances. There is every likelihood that the band included men from both Nissoria and Leonforte, and it is reasonable to assume that among the latter were peasants employed on Squillaci holdings. Whether any of the participants were paid cannot be determined. The killings displayed considerable organization and planning, mostly short range. Judging from the timing of attacks, as listed in the death registers, and the locations of death, the band must have subdivided into at least three groups which acted more or less simultaneously. If the recorded times of attack are approximately correct, each separate group cannot even have been certain that the others had carried out their assigned missions. That the survivors uniformly stated that the attacks occurred without any forewarning, several within a few hundred meters of each other, also suggests a coordinated strategy rather than a rampage. In all cases knives were the only weapons used: no clubs, stones, or other more brutal but less lethal instruments. None of the victims' bodies was stabbed repeatedly, mutilated, or desecrated, and reports make no mention of looting or rape. Every victim was male; wives, daughters, and mothers sleeping in the same room were not harmed. Only two males named Squillaci survived. One was the parish priest, against whom no efforts were made; the other was a child of two, for whom the band searched unsuccessfully as he remained asleep hidden under his grandmother's nightshirt. The next day all known local *contadini* were at their accustomed tasks and appropriate fields. No legal proceedings were instituted, nor are there any records listing suspected perpetrators by name.

Perhaps "generally the Nissorini have always been good-natured and religious folk," especially if the "religious folk" include those who prayed to Saint Joseph that the remaining Squillaci youth would be killed. The "night of the knives" is not typical of day-to-day life in the village, but its occurrence highlights tensions existent in various forms throughout Sicily and among peasants everywhere. Its continuing significance in the collective memory of the Nissorini is undeniable. The conflicting "evidence" on the event cited at the outset of this chapter is hardly a major historical problem; indeed, it is not a problem at all but striking confirmation of the rigidity of class barriers and the convergence of past, present, and future.

Nissoria's peasantry, deeply imbued with a twisted understanding of the transmission of power along dynastic lines—they knew only hereditary monarchy—view the "night of the knives" as an event that aimed to change the future by avenging the past. Grievances against the priest were greater perhaps than against any other member of the Squillaci family, and the band that killed three boys and vigorously sought a fourth cannot have spared the cleric because they feared heavenly retribution. Rather, and here the evidence comes from modern-day peasant perceptions, the importance of which transcends the fact that we cannot recover what actually went through the minds of the unknown perpetrators of 1860, the band intended to wipe out the family, to exterminate its seed, to attack its only vulnerable point—the future. The priest, prevented by holy vows from legitimately propagating the Squillaci clan, was no danger and went unharmed. The women, who could not transmit the name, did not count. Yes, they could and did maintain all the family holdings or sell them in large blocs to equally oppressive members of the same class. But the Squillaci name would die with them, and as Nissorini not only knew but acted upon, everyone must die.

Denying the Squillacis a future evened the score for the family's past and present domination and exploitation. The peasantry in 1860 made no successful effort to improve their immediate lot, to expropriate, to educate, to organize, to resist; but they tried to make certain, absolutely certain, that their children's children would never tip their caps to a Squillaci. Fate, making its appearance in the ample folds of an old woman's nightshirt, intervened to preserve the family's name, and so the "night of the knives" ultimately failed. In 1902 the surviving Squillaci, who married early and by then had fathered three living sons, became mayor of Nissoria.[1]


PARTISANS

1943 was a bad year for the Albaretesi. The war was lost, or so it seemed, and back to the village came disoriented and maimed young men who knew not why they had been fighting. When it turned out, quite inexplicably, that Mussolini and his fascists were not defeated after all and that the Germans would be around in massive numbers, former soldiers such as Guido Varacchi decided to stay home in Albareto, prepared to live for a while in the nearby woods, and awaited developments. Fascist officials quickly reentrenched themselves at Parma and along the Ligurian coast, especially at Chiavari, but met with indifference and even hostility among the mountain folk. Many times in the past Albareto's links to the coast and to Parma had been threatened or cut completely, and villagers knew well how to cope with the situation. During the winter of 1943–44 they lived mostly on chestnuts.

In February 1944, an informal group of about two dozen, all ex-soldiers and mostly the sons of modest *contadini*, labeled themselves the Gruppo Centocroci, a name that harkened to the major pass over which many wars had been fought and which linked the Taro Valley (including Albareto) to the coast. These men, who had retained their weapons, met in the mountains while hunting rabbits or fishing for trout with which to supplement their families' diet of chestnuts. Word circulated about *partigiani* organized in Piedmont to fight against nazi-fascism, but at the local level there was ample stimulus of a different sort for concerted resistance: German soldiers occasionally intercepted returning hunters and at gunpoint took their freshly caught rabbits; fascists from Parma tried to force "ex-comrades" to rejoin the war effort. Gradually members of the Gruppo Centocroci decided for self-protection to move about only in twos or threes; to avoid harm to their families they no longer returned home at night but camped in the woods. When in early March one of their number was picked up by the Germans and locked away at Borgotaro, several of his friends surprised and captured a nazi soldier. An exchange was quietly arranged, and from that moment on an organized partisan force existed in the Taro Valley, so defined by nazi-fascist officials well before local hunters articulated a politically conscious program.

Spring is not an easy time to live in the mountains. Fish and game are available, but supplies are uncertain and the staple of any peasant diet, bread or grain in some form, is hard to come by. Partisans overcame the shortage by borrowing food and money from neutral local families and by requisitioning (stealing?) from hostile or profascist households. Ammunition became a more severe problem. The government effectively denied all access to bullets, guns, and powder for explosives from usual local sources. Primarily because of their need for ammunition and weapons, the *Centocrocisti* made contact with better organized partisans from the Piedmont region. These supplied not only war materiel but key advisers and comrades in fighting. What had begun as a highly local, unfocused, and essentially responsive and defensive effort became fused with a coherent, patriotic, class-conscious movement.

Partisan strategy began as and remained one of hit-and-run, always avoiding a direct battle against German troops. The mountains between Parma and the coast became less a battlefield than a scene retaining for hours and days its tranquil pastoral life, only to be interrupted suddenly and briefly by the staccato of gunfire. In order to protect their military vehicles from daytime ambush along isolated mountain roads, the Germans strapped randomly selected local women and children to the fenders. Partisans threw their grenades anyway. At night, when nazi forces retreated to their camps, the *Centocrocisti* carried the war to the villages and hamlets of the Taro Valley. Then it was civil war: lean young men against paunched veterans of the Great War; hungry men against owners of storerooms filled with grain, cheese, and sausages; mountain men against city folk; men fighting for a better future against those committed to the past. There were no winners. By April 1944, the Gruppo Centocroci approved a written set of rules stating their twofold objective: to disrupt by guerrilla action the enemy's occupation and to stop in every possible way the reemergence of fascism.

By July the German occupying force initiated peace negotiations with *Centocrocisti* representatives through a clerical intermediary. The Germans asked that their traffic be left alone and that bridges and roads be kept open. Their war was against the Anglo-American invaders. They offered in exchange to allow the partisans to continue their civil war against local fascists. The partisan position called for suspension of all acts of repression against the local population, freedom for partisans to circulate with arms, and nazi assistance in forcing all fascist troops to leave the area. Captured German soldiers were exchanged for partisans, and it was agreed to convert Albareto's municipal building into a temporary hospital open to soldiers and civilians on all sides; but mutual distrust proved too great. The hospital became a battleground, and negotiations gave way to higher levels of fighting.

Gradually increased control of the air by Anglo-American forces allowed regular ammunition drops and rapidly multiplied partisan firepower. The earlier strategy of nighttime civil war and concentration of efforts against local fascists gave way under Allied suggestion and pressure to tactics aimed solely at liberation from the Germans. Along with Allied gunpowder, partisans accepted that for now they must blow up roads, rail tracks, and bridges. Class warfare could wait. The Gruppo Centocroci agreed to reorganize along the latest lines of military organization and, *all' italiana,* elected officers for a hierarchy of command. Nazis, realizing that terrorism directed against the local population did more to discredit their fascist satellites than to weaken the partisans, began to employ methods more closely aimed at keeping transport open. Freed at least temporarily from nazi repression, villagers fell under partisan control. The grain harvest in 1944 went to the antifascists.

Hopes raised high by news in late summer of the invasion of Normandy and the fall of the Gotica line soon were dashed. By October it was clear that the allied advance had halted at Florence. General Alexander's message of November 12 over open radio waves confirmed the *Centocrocisti*'s worst fears—there would be no liberation before the following spring. Moreover, local nazi commanders, assured by Alexander himself that they had nothing to fear over the winter, now turned their full might against the troublesome partisans who under Allied prodding had shifted their efforts from civil war against fascists to a war of liberation fought by impeding German transport. The *Centocrocisti* now had to pay for a double error: their harsh methods had alienated much of the local population, which now was protected by deep and track-revealing snow, while their liberators had not kept their "promises." German strategy was simple—at all cost and by whatever means necessary, wipe out partisan resistance before spring.

The strategy failed. On April 23, 1945, remaining *Centocrocisti* joined with partisans from throughout Emilia-Romagna to trap 16,000 nazi troops at Fornovo. Two days later the Germans surrendered to the advancing Allies, insurrection broke out at Milan, and Italy was liberated. The *Centocrocisti* returned to their woods to carry on the fight against profascist remnants, especially those who had denied them aid during the harsh days of January and February.

But in May the Allies called all the mountain partisans to Parma for three days of free celebration. When the feasting ended, the Americans made the *Centocrocisti* pass through a corridor and surrender their arms. Guido Varacchi recalls the scene as drunken sheep bleating contentedly at the slaughter house. He remembers vividly his own dirty face and ragged uniform when he first saw a contingent of black soldiers with shiny boots and clean shirts. For him the war had begun ten years earlier in Ethiopia when he had signed on as a flute player; he believed that he had been had, double-crossed. Still wearing his "fighters for liberty" pin and with money in his pocket given by his Allied hosts as a reward for services, he went to a leading merchant to purchase a sack of "real" flour. The businessman, a Mussolini sympathizer to the end, accused Guido and his gang of being thieves and refused to sell him anything. The fascists preferred doing business with the Americans.[2]


## SCHOOLTEACHERS

1974 was an ambiguous year for rural Italy. Major defects in the nation's economy, highlighted by the consequences of an international oil crisis, were evident. Young men in Rogliano who intended to go to Turin to seek assembly-line work learned that jobs were not available and that people were actually being laid off. In Switzerland a combination of antiforeign prejudice, technical efficiency, and softness in heavy production sectors meant less work for Italians. Immigrant workers bore the brunt of increased unemployment in West Germany, Sweden, Belgium, and France. More than a dozen of the men and women who returned to Nissoria for the August festival decided that there was no point in going away again just yet. Not that any jobs were available locally, but they had some savings, enough to carry them through the following spring, and by then the situation might improve. In Castel San Giorgio a nearby large furniture factory had eliminated overtime and declared several half-pay no-work days; on the other hand, business was excellent at the tomato canning plants, where calls for temporary workers went unfilled. At Albareto guest rooms were available even during the height of the summer season, but construction was booming, and skilled bricklayers, plasterers, and woodworkers had months of backlogged orders, more than they could complete before the snows.

Rosa Runco of Rogliano and Rita Pantò of Nissoria were still seeking their first jobs, the latter since 1972. Both had completed *Magistero* and were fully qualified to teach at the intermediate school level. They had entered the necessary regional examinations and done very well, but no places were available. In fact some new people were hired, people who were not on the examination list at all or who were lower down than Rosa and Rita, for which there was always some excuse; those hired were transfers, returnees, temporaries, friends of someone or other. Under a regional effort to ameliorate the plight of would-be teachers in the province of Enna, the list on which Rita's name appeared third was passed along to the post office. Rita was offered a position, as a clerk, on a three-month trial basis and without any of the benefits that accrue to permanent employees, at a postal office three towns away. The only way for her to appear on the job at 8 A.M. was by a series of four buses beginning from Nissoria at 4:30 A.M. She would return home at 7 P.M., having worked for five and one-half hours and commuted for nine. Because of the long travel with strangers and because they knew no one in the new town, Rita's mother insisted that her younger brother, age twenty-two, accompany her, at least for the three-month provisional period. After two weeks Rita quit the job, and her name was therefore deleted from the list of qualified teachers seeking employment. Rosa writes poetry.

Before the war neither girl would have attended university at all. One is the daughter of a low-skilled factory worker who has been in Germany for the last nine years; the other's father died of a heart attack fifteen years ago, leaving his wife and three small children with two hectares of good wheat land, which they lease, and a small house, where the widow Pantò cooks simple fare for workers temporarily in town. Both note with deep resentment that by the time Italy had changed enough to allow them to attend the university, a diploma had become a passport to unemployment or misemployment. Nevertheless, they do not look backward; they do not decry the changes that brought them to their present plight; even when they curse their fate they do not wish for the forced ignorance that in earlier days might have made them content with less.[3]

## ONE STING

Over the past two centuries rural folk have been shrewd, patient, and flexible in responding to the world about them. The way they understand, their world view, has been highly functional and directly related to their experience. When they had no hope to control or change the future, they lived for the past. When death occurred randomly, inexplicably, unpredictably, and at all ages, they made little effort to plan ahead. When summer heat brought uncontrollable tragedy, they instituted defiant counterfestivals of joy and abundance. When the birth of eight or ten children meant only that three would survive, they gave birth to eight or ten children. When the world of contracts, union rights, and legal agreements was closed to them, they acted through a network of reciprocal obligation based on mutual *interesse* and on *onore* built with past deeds. When survival required individuals to submerge themselves within *la famiglia*, they formed marriage alliances that sacrificed love to need. When the space they could know had to be covered on foot, they wed locally. When better opportunities beckoned them across the Atlantic, they went.

Now that death occurs mostly to old people who die of diagnosed diseases, they set aside money for future investment. Now that infants are born as infants and not as shoemakers or sharecroppers, they go to the university. Now that Italy is a democracy, they vote. Now that day laborers are unionized, they file grievance appeals against unfair employers. Now that the births of three children mean that three will grow to adulthood, they give birth to only three children. Now that they may leave Palermo in the morning and be in New York by evening, they follow eagerly reports on the weather 5,000 miles away. Now that they marry for love, they support the law that allows divorce.[4] Now that they must blame or praise only themselves for their present circumstances, they are greedy, haughty, abject, self-abasing, angry.

But anomalies persist and earlier values return. Why should Rita and Rosa not curse fate for allowing them to graduate precisely when there are no jobs? Why should Rosa's father have to be self-exiled in a German factory when he so loves the harsh mountains of Calabria? Why should Guido Varacchi bother to vote when the PCI program includes government concern for shopkeepers? Why should some rich industrialist (academic translation of Angelo's phrase, "quello stronzo") from Milan drive by in a Mercedes when Angelo's home in Castel San Giorgio has no running water? Why should Luigi not prefer to work for people he trusts when, on the one occasion that he went to the union office to complain, they told him the employer was right? Why should a group of *contadini* in Nissoria not laugh with resigned irony when *un professore americano*, his wife, and daughter suddenly appear in the village, ask a lot of questions and, when Giuseppe defends "modernity" despite all its defects, remark that according to some newfangled theory the world is now postmodern?

# Note on Demographic Sources

The basic documents used in this study are the registers of individual births, marriages, and deaths maintained by every *comune* in Italy. As indicated by my acknowledgments, these are not usually open to public inspection. A person who needs a birth certificate or similar document must ask the communal clerk to check these registers to locate the original document. The record is handwritten on multipage forms, and for obvious reasons there are some problems with lost, illegible, incomplete, or incorrect entries. Especially in the years before 1870, when entries were sometimes made on individual folios rather than in bound volumes, the record may be incomplete. Nonetheless, these documents provide far more information than is available from any of the annual and census demographic reports which the *comune* also files and which I have used to control against missing sections in the vital registers.

The registers, sampled where indicated below, were microfilmed or copied by hand during 1972 and the summer of 1974. The data specified below were transferred to machine-readable punch cards to facilitate mathematical analyses performed with an electronic calculator.

## ALBARETO

### Birth Registers

1780–May 2, 1806, from *Liber baptizzatorum ecclesie partis S$^{te}$ Marie ville Albareti:* date of birth, date of registration of birth, sex (as determined by name), parents' names.

1808–13, from *Commune de Valdena registre des actes del état civil:* same information as above.

1814–17, from *Comune d'Albareto* untitled yearly volumes: same information as above.

1818–31, from *Comune d'Albareto* summary sheets only with names in alphabetical order and page references to registers now lost.

1832–78, from *Comune d'Albareto* untitled yearly volumes: same information as for pre-1818.

1879–1910, above information plus the age of the mother and the child's legitimacy.

1911–24, above information except for mother's age.

1925–27, above information plus mother's age.

1928–45, *comune* of Albareto suppressed and records kept at Borgotaro, where permission to consult registers was denied.

March 20, 1946–1973, information as for 1879–1910, with mother's year of birth rather than age after 1961.

## Marriage Registers

1780–April 30, 1806, from *Liber matrimoniorum ecclesie partis S^te Marie ville Albareti:* date of marriage, spouses' names.

1808–74, from *Commune de Valdena* through 1813, the *Comune d'Albareto:* summary sheets only with spouses' names and date of marriage. The sheets for 1820 are incomplete.

1875–1927, from *Comune d'Albareto* untitled yearly volumes: date of marriage, spouses' names, ages, places of birth (hamlet identified through 1920), whether parents were alive and if so, their occupations, whether married previously (consistent only after 1881).

1928–45, as for births.

May 5, 1946–1973, information as for 1875–1927, with spouses' years of birth rather than age after 1961.

## Death Registers

1808–74, from *Commune de Valdena* through 1813, then *Comune d'Albareto:* summary sheets only with deceased's name and date of registration of death.

1875–1927, from *Comune d'Albareto* untitled yearly volumes: date of death, date of registration of death, deceased's sex (as determined by name), age, occupation, place of birth (hamlet identified through 1920), whether parents were alive and their occupations whether alive or not.

1928–45, as for births.

March 11, 1946–1973, information as for 1875–1927 with deceased's date of birth rather than age after 1961.

## CASTEL SAN GIORGIO

### Birth Registers

1810–1973, in untitled yearly volumes except for 1866–1903 and 1909–27, when there were two yearly volumes, one for Lanzara and the hamlets on the plain, the other for Castel San Giorgio center and the mountain *frazioni:* date of birth, date of registration of birth, sex (as determined by name), parents' names, mother's age (year of birth after 1961). The 1856 volume is severely damaged.

## Marriage Registers

1810–1973, in untitled yearly volumes (1 in 2 sample beginning with the first entry in even-numbered years and the second in odd-numbered years): date of marriage, spouses' names, ages (year of birth after 1961), places of birth, whether parents were alive and if so, their occupations, whether married previously, groom's occupation.

## Death Registers

1810–1973, as for birth registers (1 in 2 sample as for marriages): date of death, date of registration of death, deceased's sex (as determined by name), age (year of birth after 1961), occupation, occupation of the father in the case of a child, whether the father was alive (after 1874). The 1853 volume is incomplete.

# NISSORIA

## Birth Registers

1761–1820, from *Liber baptizatorum* at the parish: date of baptism, sex (as determined by name), parents' names.

1821–1973, in untitled yearly volumes: date of birth, date of registration of birth, sex, parents' names, mother's age (year of birth after 1961). Registers for 1827, 1828, and 1837 are missing. From 1852 through 1922 entries include the father's age.

## Marriage Registers

1761–1820, from *Liber matrimoniorum* at the parish: date of marriage, spouses' names.

1821–65, in untitled yearly volumes (1 in 2 sample as for Castel San Giorgio): date of marriage, spouses' names, ages, places of birth, whether parents were alive and if so, their ages and occupations (fathers only), whether previously married, groom's occupation. The 1827 register is missing.

1866–1973, same as above except that no information is provided on spouses' mothers and spouses' fathers' occupations are given whether or not they were alive.

## Death Registers

1761–1820, from *Liber defunctorum* at the parish: date of burial, age and sex of deceased; many names torn and illegible.

1821–1973, in untitled yearly volumes (1 in 2 sample as for Castel San Giorgio): date of death, date of registration of death, sex (as determined by name), age (year of birth after 1861), occupation, occupation of the father in the case of a child. The 1829 register is missing.

## ROGLIANO

### Birth Registers

1809–1973, in untitled yearly volumes: date of birth, date of registration of birth, sex, parents' names and ages (year of birth after 1961), father's occupation, child's legitimacy (by implication from father's occupation).

### Marriage Registers

1810–1973, in untitled yearly volumes (1 in 2 sample as for Castel San Giorgio): date of marriage, spouses' names, ages (year of birth after 1961), places of birth, groom's occupation. After 1832 additional entries on whether spouses' fathers were alive and if so, their occupations. After 1875, additional entries on whether either spouse had been married previously and whether spouses' mothers were alive.

### Death Registers

1810–1973, in untitled yearly volumes (1 in 2 sample as for Castel San Giorgio): date of death, date of registration of death, sex (as determined by name), deceased's age (year of birth after 1961) and occupation.

## ADDITIONAL MANUSCRIPT DEMOGRAPHIC SOURCES

"Cartella di casa" or "Folio di famiglia" for all four communities—these were begun in 1931 and are "maintained" at the various municipal offices. They are extremely useful for providing a dynamic portrait over time of each household. The major difficulty in their use is the uneven way in which they are maintained. According to the rules, whenever a birth, marriage, or death is recorded, an entry must be made in the appropriate household folder. Similarly, an entry must be made whenever a family member emigrates or returns. New folders are begun when a new household with a legal capo famiglia establishes itself. When the last remaining member of a household dies or emigrates, the folder is moved to an inactive file. Unfortunately such entries are not made with much consistency. Birth and death entries are fairly accurate, but the same may not be said for emigration, return, and shifts in "head of household" status. In short, the documents are not sufficiently accurate on the question of familial or household structure to justify extensive statistical analysis. Nevertheless, reading over the several thousand family folders for the four communities cannot but leave the researcher with a profound sense of the flexibility and continuing importance of familial ties and attachment to household.

Military conscription lists for Albareto: "Lista dei coscritti di comune di Valdena" from 1807 through 1813; 'L'inscription des conscrits (Commune *d'Albareto)" for 1814 and 1815; "Leva dell'anno (Comune di Albareto)" for 1817 through 1899*—information provided: name, occupation, place of birth, current residence, whether parents were alive, height, reason (if any) for exemption, result of physical examination for those not exempted by reason of familial status or occupation, and whether called to serve.

*Immigration and emigration registers in untitled volumes for Nissoria from 1934 through 1973 plus card file*—information provided: name or names of persons migrating as a group, place to or from which migrating, number and sex of persons migrating as a group, migrants' years of birth, marriage, and migration, occupations, and levels of schooling.

*Voting results by electoral section within each "comune" for the national elections of 1953, 1958, 1963, 1968, 1972, and the 1974 referendum to repeal the divorce law*—information provided: number of registered voters by sex, number of actual voters, results by party for house and senate or response to referendum.

*Emigration permits at the "comuni" of Albareto, Rogliano, and Nissoria*—these are retained only in haphazard fashion (actually scattered in drawers) and contain information for individuals as follows: name, place of birth, year of birth and emigration, intended destination, skills, and health (always *buono*).

## PRINTED DEMOGRAPHIC SOURCES

This list includes only works used extensively in calculations or as a control against manuscript sources for the four communities. For more general demographic work, see the notes to various chapters.

*Annali di statistica: fascicolo XII* (Rome, 1888) on Castel San Giorgo.

*Annuario statistico dell' emigrazione dal 1876 al 1925* (Rome, 1926).

*Catasto del 1929* (Rome, 1936) for landholding in Castel San Giorgio, Nissoria, and Rogliano.

*Censimenti di Lombardia, di Parma e di Modena (1857–58)* (Turin, 1862).

*Censimento generale dell' agricoltura* for 1970.

*Censimento generale della popolazione* for 1861, 1871, 1881, 1901; 1911, 1921, 1936, 1951, 1961, and 1971.

*Censimento industriale e commerciale* for 1927, 1951, and 1971.

*Comuni e loro popolazione ai censimenti dal 1861 al 1951* (Rome, 1960).

Giunta per l'Inchiesta Agraria e sulle Condizioni della Classe Agricola. *Atti*, II, VII, IX, and XIII (Rome, 1881–86).

*Inchiesta parlamentare sulle condizioni dei contadini nelle province meridionali e nella Sicilia*, V and VI (Rome, 1910).

Izzo, Luigi. *La popolazione calabrese nel secolo XIX: demografia ed economia* (Naples, 1965).

Livi-Bacci, Massimo. *A History of Italian Fertility during the Last Two Centuries* (Princeton, N.J., 1977).

*Risultati dell' inchiesta sulle condizioni igieniche e sanitarie nei comuni del regno* (Rome, 1886).

*Statistica del Regno d'Italia—industria: industrie manuali della Provincia di Parma, anno 1861* (Florence, 1866).

# Note on Participatory Interviews

Some of the conclusions and "facts" set forth in this book are drawn from interviews. Indeed, at several points the best that may be said for accompanying statistical data is that they do not contradict an interpretation that obviously rests upon interviews. More important, I think, is that the nature of the questions I have asked—the subjects that seemed central to a demographic study of this type, the way things are organized, the linkages between birth, marriage, death, and life—are shaped by what people said. It seems appropriate, therefore, to say something about how these interviews, which I have termed "participatory" in the sense in which Francis Ianni (*A Family Business*) uses the term, were conducted.

Interviews in the villages were conducted in 1972, during a second stay in 1974, and intermittently in 1976–77. In all four communities the first persons interviewed were those who assisted in securing access to the municipal registers, in part to answer their questions about what we were really up to. Beyond these, we talked with anyone who was willing to speak with us. In such a method there is obviously no claim to a random or representative sample; interviewees range from a waiter to a shopkeeper to a lawyer to several of my daughter's schoolmates. Whenever people were willing, I used a questionnaire, which gave more structure to the interview but may have reduced spontaneity. Questions other than those of a biographical nature quickly became open-ended, even when that was not my intention, and did not elicit quantifiable responses.

No pseudonyms are used, and direct quotations are always from interviewees who were told that their words (rendered into English) might be quoted. No one hesitated about allowing his name to be used, but in the final writing I have sometimes thought it best not to footnote a particular name, since the original consent to quote may have been given out of friendship that obscured at least temporarily some of the implications of such a formal and public citation.

Interviews in the United States with emigrants from the four communities now residing in New York, New Jersey, Chicago, and San Francisco were conducted between 1972 and 1977. Again, there is no claim to a scientific sample. Especially in the case of the Albaretesi, one of whom is married to my wife's brother, even the term "interview" is inappropriate. An important aspect of responses from emigrants about life in their place of birth is that they reflect an arrested view. Whereas village residents tend to telescope and merge the events of their lives and to reinterpret the past in terms of the present, emigrants (especially those who left in their teens or twenties between 1900 and 1924) retain a perception of their village as unchanged. Despite fifty or more years in America, their memories successfully isolate and keep purified of New World experiences numerous details from the prewar period.

The interview schedule was as follows:

1. *Biographical data*—name, age, occupation, family status, residence, places visited or lived in.

2. *The supernatural*—tell us about saints, relics, sites, etc., that are particularly important to you or in the village generally. Do you (or others you know) consult fortune tellers, spiritual healers? How do you explain evil?

3. *Power*—who in the village has good connections to Palermo; Parma, Naples, etc., depending upon the place? If you needed to borrow money, to whom would you turn? If you needed a job recommendation, to whom would you go? (Of less literate persons) who helps you when you need to fill out government forms? Why do things get done/ not get done around here?

4. *Customs at vital events*—Birth: How are godparents chosen? What continuing relationship do they have with the family? What is their responsibility if the parents die? Why are sons preferred? Describe for us a baptismal day. Marriage: When are boys/girls too young/old to marry? How are spouses chosen? What if parents oppose or if the girl is pregnant? Who brings what as a dowry? Where does the couple go to live? Must older siblings marry first? Describe for us a wedding day. Death: Do people make a will? Do sons inherit more? What do people think when widows/widowers remarry? Describe for us a funeral and mourning customs.

5. *Land*—how rich is the richest family in the village? What portion of the villagers are poor? What does it mean to be poor? How does someone become rich and stay that way? How is land divided? What is grown, where, when? How is labor employed? Describe for us the rental arrangements used in this area.

6. *Emigration*—what sort of people emigrate? Describe how they decide to go. Why are they successful/unsuccessful? Are they happy? Do they maintain family ties? (Of villagers who praised emigrants as more dynamic and successful, which most did) then why are you still here?

7. *Terminology*—I began by explaining that I would be using terms commonly employed by social scientists (professors) but that I was very interested in what these words or ideas meant to my interviewees: *modernità, la miseria, campanilismo* (most did not understand this term

but were more than willing to expound on village attachment), *fortuna,*
*onore, famiglia, tradizione.*

8. *Family*—how are things decided in your family? Do brothers and
sisters quarrel a lot? When they do, what are the reasons? Describe for
us the significance of a series of kin relationships (I shifted to this form
after trying an ordinal ranked questionnaire, such as the one below for
job prestige, which made too many interviewees uncomfortable and
which several dismissed as stupid and trivial).

9. *Job prestige*—rate from 1 to 10 how happy you would be if your
son/daughter entered or acquired the following kind of work: farm laborer, priest, small shop owner, landowner, construction worker,
typist, domestic servant, lawyer, teacher, butcher, waiter, nun, skilled
factory worker, draftsman, engineer, police officer, mechanic, cook,
miner, truck driver, train conductor, shoemaker, doctor, office clerk.
Why did you rate the occupations this way—salary? status? security?
job satisfaction? education?

For every question or subject I asked specifically as necessary about
the time period interviewees were referring to and whether things were
different earlier/later.

# Appendix A
# "What Is a Peasant?"

Scholars have set forth literally hundreds of different answers to this question; many are illuminating, none is universally accepted. For the present study the major problem is less a theoretical one than an empirical need to collate the maze of terminology used in various regions of Italy over the past two centuries. What follows is a glossary of relevant terms encountered in the primary sources and a classification scheme indicating the English phrases used to convey them.

## SUBSTANTIAL LANDOWNERS

In the text the phrase "landowners" always refers to substantial holders who did not do manual labor on their holdings.

| | |
|---|---|
| *benestante* | well-to-do |
| *civile* | civilized; used in the south, mostly between 1860 and 1930, for non-noble large holders who left even the supervision of their estates to others |
| *gentildonna* | gentlewoman; used intermittently for daughters of substantial landowners in marriage registers |
| *nobile* | noble |
| *possidente* | landowner; generally owned more (or was more pretentious) than a *proprietario* and less than a *civile* |
| *proprietario* | landowner |

## AGRICULTURAL CAPITALISTS OR MIDDLEMEN

| | |
|---|---|
| *agronomo* or *agronaio* | agricultural specialist who was educated |
| *amministratore* | administrator; large estates in Sicily and Calabria |
| *arbitriante* | arbitrator; a leaseholder who in turn subleased; cited in the Jacini inquiry as particularly parasitic |

227

| | |
|---|---|
| *campese* | armed guard; more often extorted from peasants than protected them |
| *fattore* | factor; landowner's agent to supervise an estate |
| *gabellotto* | leaseholder who in turn hired sharecroppers |
| *intraprenditore agricolo* | agricultural contractor; generally a labor boss who received a fixed sum for ploughing or harvesting and in turn paid (as little as possible) a gang of workers to do the actual labor |
| *massaro* | estate supervisor, usually on a Sicilian *latifondo* |

AGRICULTURAL MANUAL WORKERS

*Assumed to Be Smallholders*

| | |
|---|---|
| *borgese (borgise)* | smallholder, often very small |
| *borgese colono* | smallholder; certainly owned so little that he also worked for others |
| *colono proprietario* | owner of a small plot; copyholder |
| *coltivatore diretto* | smallholder; the term is used only after the Second World War |

*Assumed to Be Landless*

| | |
|---|---|
| *aratore* | ploughman |
| *borgese mezzadro* | small sharecropper |
| *bracciante* | agricultural wage laborer; generic term |
| *bracciante annaluoio, iarzura,* or *picuraro* | annual contract wage laborer |
| *bracciante curatolo* | monthly contract wage laborer |
| *bracciante zapugliaturo* | weekly contract wage laborer |
| *carrettiere* | carter |
| *colono fittuario* | renter of a small plot |
| *curatolo* | chief herdsman, cheese maker |
| *(a) fittaiuolo* | tenant farmer |
| *garzone fisso* | errand boy or youthful helper, especially with animals |
| *giardiniere* | gardener |
| *giornaliero* | wage laborer hired by the day |
| *metatiere* | sharecropper |
| *mezzadro* | sharecropper |
| *nomade* | nomad; had fixed residence but traveled widely in search of work; a pejorative term |
| *pastore* | shepherd; other terms note distinctions |

| | among swineherders, goatherders, cow-herders, etc. |
| *vagabondo* | vagabond; had neither fixed residence nor work |
| *villico* | rural laborer; pejorative |
| *zappatore* | tiller employing no animals |

*Ambiguous as to Whether Any Land Is Owned*

| | |
| *agricoltore* | farmer |
| *campagnuolo* | countryman; disdainful emphasis on rusticity |
| *colono* | farmer; generic term never used for even a modestly well-to-do agriculturist |
| *coltivatore* | husbandman |
| *contadino* | peasant |
| *villano* | rustic; more pejorative than *contadino* except possibly in Sicily, where it was generic |

Many other phrases appear in the general literature to describe specific tasks, modes of payment, stability of employment, and cultural appraisals but the above terms are the ones used in registering births, marriages, and deaths in four communities over two centuries. I use the term "peasant" or *contadino* throughout the text to refer to *all* agricultural manual worker categories noted above (smallholders, landless, and ambiguous) and specifically to exclude substantial landowners and agricultural capitalists or middlemen. I use the term "agriculturists" to include these classes and the terms "rural folk" or "rural Italians" to include all residents of the four communities regardless of whether they were directly engaged in agriculture.

Such an empirical definition of what a peasant is obviously has theoretical implications. It is more restrictive than Raymond Firth allowed when he included Malay fishermen as peasants but more expansive than the confines of Robert Redfield's insistence that peasants "*control* and cultivate *their* land." The definition makes no comment on Alfred Kroeber's classic characterization of peasants as "part-societies with part-cultures" nor does it address George Foster's emphasis on structural relationships between village and state. These and other issues will be raised in the text.

# Appendix B

**Monthly Distribution of Deaths by Age Group (Calculated as for Fig. 2)**

| AGE GROUP | JAN | FEB | MAR | APR | MAY | JUN | JUL | AUG | SEP | OCT | NOV | DEC |
|---|---|---|---|---|---|---|---|---|---|---|---|---|
| | | | | | | Albareto, 1870–1973 ($N = 5,252$) | | | | | | |
| 0–60 days | 186 | 136 | 173 | 161 | 74 | 86 | 12 | 74 | 25 | 112 | 74 | 86 |
| 2–11 months | 50 | 100 | 100 | 100 | 150 | 25 | 100 | 187 | 175 | 88 | 50 | 76 |
| 1 year | 53 | 106 | 119 | 132 | 119 | 53 | 92 | 211 | 211 | 13 | 40 | 53 |
| 2–5 years | 98 | 64 | 85 | 106 | 91 | 78 | 78 | 120 | 169 | 106 | 91 | 113 |
| 6–19 years | 64 | 142 | 110 | 79 | 31 | 79 | 79 | 158 | 142 | 110 | 126 | 79 |
| 20–29 years | 169 | 113 | 127 | 85 | 155 | 184 | 71 | 56 | 71 | 98 | 14 | 56 |
| 30–39 years | 140 | 60 | 140 | 160 | 80 | 40 | 40 | 160 | 100 | 60 | 160 | 60 |
| 40–49 years | 40 | 180 | 140 | 200 | 100 | 40 | 20 | 20 | 80 | 100 | 160 | 120 |
| 50–59 years | 122 | 82 | 143 | 122 | 122 | 122 | 102 | 163 | 20 | 61 | 61 | 82 |
| 60–69 years | 110 | 176 | 110 | 77 | 77 | 100 | 110 | 88 | 88 | 77 | 77 | 110 |
| 70–79 years | 182 | 120 | 131 | 79 | 102 | 52 | 56 | 108 | 102 | 97 | 102 | 68 |
| 80 and over | 143 | 130 | 124 | 124 | 74 | 92 | 98 | 62 | 92 | 49 | 106 | 106 |
| Overall | 121 | 116 | 122 | 113 | 96 | 78 | 74 | 112 | 110 | 82 | 88 | 88 |
| | | | | | | Castel San Giorgio, 1811–1973 ($N = 16,476$) | | | | | | |
| 0–60 days | 128 | 112 | 116 | 92 | 95 | 84 | 111 | 101 | 67 | 84 | 72 | 130 |
| 2–5 months | 44 | 80 | 101 | 88 | 73 | 124 | 182 | 191 | 101 | 90 | 50 | 80 |
| 6–11 months | 43 | 50 | 44 | 31 | 88 | 131 | 180 | 240 | 105 | 118 | 84 | 63 |
| 1 year | 57 | 57 | 80 | 67 | 67 | 148 | 212 | 168 | 113 | 76 | 75 | 76 |
| 2 years | 117 | 95 | 126 | 59 | 119 | 127 | 110 | 102 | 109 | 41 | 117 | 75 |
| 3–5 years | 95 | 78 | 91 | 96 | 84 | 101 | 116 | 115 | 142 | 103 | 89 | 78 |
| 6–10 years | 87 | 97 | 116 | 108 | 131 | 78 | 90 | 72 | 117 | 139 | 44 | 116 |
| 11–19 years | 143 | 104 | 87 | 77 | 76 | 96 | 127 | 49 | 103 | 123 | 97 | 97 |
| 20–29 years | 98 | 58 | 83 | 118 | 111 | 58 | 104 | 144 | 115 | 114 | 56 | 116 |
| 30–39 years | 124 | 102 | 97 | 71 | 115 | 94 | 127 | 112 | 58 | 122 | 102 | 80 |
| 40–49 years | 97 | 66 | 126 | 90 | 69 | 65 | 108 | 117 | 98 | 64 | 124 | 162 |
| 50–59 years | 86 | 123 | 121 | 79 | 85 | 67 | 118 | 71 | 83 | 128 | 102 | 128 |
| 60–69 years | 125 | 117 | 133 | 86 | 68 | 71 | 100 | 86 | 89 | 88 | 94 | 126 |
| 70–79 years | 162 | 103 | 136 | 114 | 74 | 68 | 105 | 66 | 71 | 53 | 108 | 129 |
| 80 and over | 186 | 135 | 126 | 94 | 62 | 63 | 90 | 72 | 76 | 86 | 88 | 116 |
| Overall | 112 | 95 | 109 | 86 | 83 | 91 | 122 | 112 | 91 | 89 | 89 | 110 |

**Monthly Distribution of Deaths by Age Group (Calculated as for Fig. 2) (cont.)**

| AGE GROUP | JAN | FEB | MAR | APR | MAY | JUN | JUL | AUG | SEP | OCT | NOV | DEC |
|---|---|---|---|---|---|---|---|---|---|---|---|---|
| | | | | Rogliano, 1810–1973 (N = 16,332) | | | | | | | | |
| 0–60 days | 137 | 101 | 130 | 142 | 109 | 71 | 65 | 95 | 67 | 97 | 89 | 98 |
| 2–5 months | 96 | 104 | 118 | 86 | 73 | 77 | 86 | 140 | 155 | 73 | 77 | 114 |
| 6–11 months | 70 | 66 | 80 | 55 | 66 | 62 | 108 | 236 | 136 | 97 | 146 | 77 |
| 1 year | 76 | 94 | 48 | 73 | 59 | 77 | 113 | 181 | 172 | 158 | 85 | 65 |
| 2 years | 70 | 47 | 89 | 38 | 58 | 35 | 61 | 216 | 190 | 200 | 108 | 89 |
| 3–5 years | 132 | 64 | 74 | 92 | 71 | 95 | 77 | 114 | 134 | 130 | 114 | 106 |
| 6–10 years | 140 | 77 | 77 | 68 | 112 | 47 | 72 | 150 | 120 | 98 | 124 | 115 |
| 11–19 years | 71 | 102 | 91 | 61 | 74 | 108 | 149 | 115 | 108 | 119 | 104 | 98 |
| 20–29 years | 95 | 114 | 82 | 98 | 84 | 71 | 76 | 128 | 133 | 114 | 101 | 103 |
| 30–39 years | 89 | 64 | 83 | 106 | 73 | 89 | 108 | 154 | 96 | 137 | 77 | 125 |
| 40–49 years | 89 | 79 | 95 | 109 | 109 | 113 | 67 | 115 | 113 | 85 | 83 | 143 |
| 50–59 years | 114 | 66 | 116 | 110 | 92 | 72 | 86 | 84 | 131 | 102 | 86 | 139 |
| 60–69 years | 127 | 113 | 98 | 106 | 88 | 61 | 78 | 77 | 101 | 116 | 110 | 127 |
| 70–79 years | 122 | 130 | 103 | 103 | 96 | 65 | 68 | 94 | 92 | 97 | 90 | 140 |
| 80 and over | 156 | 118 | 103 | 110 | 83 | 54 | 78 | 101 | 112 | 100 | 86 | 100 |
| Overall | 113 | 97 | 96 | 98 | 86 | 71 | 83 | 120 | 115 | 113 | 96 | 113 |

# Appendix C

**Age at First Marriage by Decade (%)**

| | FEMALE AGE COHORT | | | | | | MALE AGE COHORT | | | | | |
| Decade | 12–19 | 20–24 | 25–29 | 30–34 | 35–39 | 40+ | 12–19 | 20–24 | 25–29 | 30–34 | 35–39 | 40+ |
|---|---|---|---|---|---|---|---|---|---|---|---|---|
| | | | | | | Albareto | | | | | | |
| 1870 | 14 | 33 | 36 | 10 | 3 | 4 | 0 | 23 | 38 | 9 | 10 | 20 |
| 1880 | 21 | 49 | 20 | 8 | 1 | 1 | 0 | 35 | 47 | 13 | 1 | 4 |
| 1890 | 25 | 49 | 17 | 4 | 1 | 4 | 4 | 35 | 37 | 11 | 6 | 7 |
| 1900 | 34 | 50 | 12 | 3 | 1 | 0 | 1 | 42 | 36 | 16 | 3 | 2 |
| 1910 | 20 | 47 | 20 | 8 | 1 | 4 | 2 | 27 | 36 | 18 | 9 | 8 |
| 1920 | 26 | 45 | 21 | 7 | 1 | 0 | 2 | 41 | 32 | 14 | 7 | 4 |
| 1940 | 13 | 44 | 23 | 11 | 5 | 4 | 0 | 23 | 36 | 21 | 16 | 4 |
| 1950 | 12 | 40 | 28 | 12 | 3 | 5 | 0 | 20 | 35 | 23 | 17 | 5 |
| 1960 | 11 | 46 | 28 | 7 | 5 | 3 | 0 | 21 | 42 | 21 | 8 | 8 |
| 1970 | 13 | 56 | 18 | 6 | 2 | 5 | 2 | 31 | 42 | 16 | 3 | 6 |
| Overall | 19 | 46 | 22 | 8 | 2 | 3 | 1 | 30 | 38 | 17 | 8 | 6 |
| | | | | | | Castel San Giorgio | | | | | | |
| 1810 | 12 | 52 | 23 | 8 | 4 | 1 | 8 | 53 | 28 | 6 | 3 | 2 |
| 1820 | 12 | 36 | 31 | 14 | 5 | 2 | 7 | 30 | 32 | 22 | 5 | 4 |
| 1830 | 12 | 30 | 31 | 12 | 9 | 6 | 1 | 18 | 46 | 13 | 13 | 9 |
| 1840 | 4 | 38 | 27 | 18 | 5 | 8 | 1 | 22 | 33 | 18 | 11 | 15 |
| 1850 | 4 | 31 | 37 | 14 | 7 | 7 | 1 | 19 | 37 | 24 | 7 | 12 |
| 1860 | 5 | 44 | 21 | 18 | 6 | 6 | 0 | 13 | 36 | 32 | 8 | 11 |
| 1870 | 5 | 39 | 35 | 14 | 3 | 4 | 2 | 26 | 33 | 22 | 15 | 2 |
| 1880 | 8 | 37 | 41 | 7 | 4 | 3 | 1 | 26 | 38 | 23 | 8 | 4 |
| 1890 | 9 | 46 | 30 | 8 | 5 | 2 | 2 | 26 | 44 | 17 | 5 | 6 |
| 1900 | 12 | 53 | 28 | 6 | 0 | 1 | 1 | 32 | 44 | 15 | 4 | 4 |
| 1910 | 12 | 52 | 29 | 4 | 2 | 1 | 2 | 27 | 48 | 17 | 4 | 2 |
| 1920 | 8 | 46 | 36 | 7 | 1 | 2 | 2 | 31 | 42 | 16 | 6 | 3 |
| 1930 | 9 | 54 | 30 | 5 | 0 | 2 | 1 | 32 | 48 | 13 | 4 | 2 |
| 1940 | 8 | 42 | 30 | 13 | 4 | 3 | 0 | 22 | 40 | 23 | 9 | 6 |
| 1950 | 7 | 36 | 42 | 7 | 6 | 2 | 1 | 23 | 43 | 21 | 6 | 6 |
| 1960 | 12 | 48 | 27 | 7 | 3 | 3 | 1 | 24 | 46 | 22 | 5 | 2 |
| 1970 | 14 | 48 | 30 | 4 | 0 | 4 | 0 | 24 | 44 | 25 | 4 | 3 |
| Overall | 9 | 44 | 32 | 9 | 3 | 3 | 1 | 26 | 42 | 20 | 6 | 5 |

**Age at First Marriage by Decade (%) (cont.)**

| | | | | | | | | | | | | |
|---|---|---|---|---|---|---|---|---|---|---|---|---|
| | | | | | Nissoria | | | | | | | |
| 1820 | 54 | 25 | 10 | 3 | 3 | 5 | 5 | 36 | 31 | 12 | 2 | 14 |
| 1830 | 44 | 35 | 9 | 3 | 2 | 7 | 4 | 39 | 30 | 11 | 4 | 12 |
| 1840 | 58 | 29 | 7 | 6 | 0 | 0 | 1 | 48 | 28 | 11 | 2 | 10 |
| 1850 | 47 | 34 | 10 | 5 | 0 | 4 | 0 | 36 | 44 | 11 | 4 | 5 |
| 1860 | 46 | 37 | 11 | 3 | 2 | 1 | 1 | 25 | 46 | 21 | 6 | 1 |
| 1870 | 51 | 35 | 11 | 2 | 1 | 0 | 1 | 39 | 49 | 6 | 3 | 2 |
| 1880 | 48 | 32 | 15 | 3 | 1 | 1 | 0 | 41 | 38 | 13 | 6 | 2 |
| 1890 | 49 | 32 | 12 | 4 | 2 | 1 | 3 | 43 | 33 | 13 | 6 | 2 |
| 1900 | 50 | 36 | 9 | 2 | 2 | 1 | 1 | 44 | 39 | 7 | 5 | 4 |
| 1910 | 56 | 30 | 10 | 2 | 2 | 0 | 6 | 32 | 30 | 19 | 3 | 10 |
| 1920 | 47 | 38 | 10 | 5 | 0 | 0 | 18 | 40 | 27 | 9 | 2 | 4 |
| 1930 | 53 | 25 | 14 | 3 | 2 | 3 | 12 | 46 | 24 | 13 | 3 | 2 |
| 1940 | 41 | 38 | 13 | 6 | 2 | 0 | 10 | 32 | 34 | 15 | 5 | 4 |
| 1950 | 45 | 41 | 8 | 1 | 1 | 4 | 11 | 41 | 31 | 8 | 3 | 6 |
| 1960 | 42 | 31 | 19 | 2 | 3 | 3 | 9 | 31 | 36 | 17 | 5 | 2 |
| 1970 | 44 | 35 | 8 | 6 | 2 | 5 | 5 | 47 | 28 | 10 | 3 | 7 |
| Overall | 47 | 34 | 12 | 3 | 2 | 2 | 6 | 39 | 35 | 12 | 4 | 4 |
| | | | | | Rogliano | | | | | | | |
| 1810 | 17 | 47 | 21 | 11 | 3 | 1 | 8 | 41 | 26 | 15 | 3 | 7 |
| 1820 | 25 | 40 | 18 | 11 | 1 | 5 | 10 | 38 | 24 | 16 | 4 | 8 |
| 1830 | 15 | 35 | 33 | 11 | 4 | 2 | 3 | 30 | 36 | 18 | 7 | 6 |
| 1840 | 10 | 42 | 22 | 14 | 7 | 5 | 2 | 26 | 39 | 15 | 9 | 9 |
| 1850 | 12 | 32 | 32 | 12 | 7 | 5 | 4 | 20 | 35 | 22 | 9 | 10 |
| 1860 | 8 | 35 | 24 | 16 | 10 | 7 | 3 | 14 | 28 | 27 | 12 | 16 |
| 1870 | 7 | 50 | 26 | 11 | 5 | 1 | 0 | 18 | 52 | 21 | 7 | 2 |
| 1880 | 9 | 45 | 28 | 11 | 2 | 5 | 1 | 30 | 42 | 15 | 5 | 7 |
| 1890 | 18 | 42 | 26 | 4 | 6 | 4 | 4 | 39 | 31 | 15 | 5 | 6 |
| 1900 | 20 | 54 | 17 | 8 | 0 | 1 | 5 | 33 | 39 | 17 | 1 | 5 |
| 1910 | 24 | 41 | 19 | 10 | 4 | 2 | 8 | 33 | 36 | 20 | 0 | 3 |
| 1920 | 23 | 47 | 17 | 9 | 1 | 3 | 9 | 42 | 36 | 6 | 5 | 2 |
| 1930 | 25 | 48 | 17 | 4 | 5 | 1 | 5 | 42 | 36 | 11 | 4 | 2 |
| 1940 | 24 | 42 | 20 | 9 | 3 | 2 | 3 | 29 | 39 | 17 | 8 | 4 |
| 1950 | 18 | 41 | 27 | 8 | 4 | 2 | 3 | 26 | 38 | 19 | 8 | 6 |
| 1960 | 17 | 50 | 15 | 9 | 4 | 5 | 1 | 17 | 43 | 24 | 10 | 5 |
| 1970 | 16 | 40 | 23 | 15 | 3 | 3 | 0 | 23 | 50 | 20 | 1 | 6 |
| Overall | 18 | 43 | 22 | 10 | 4 | 3 | 4 | 30 | 37 | 17 | 6 | 6 |

# Appendix D
# Classification of Occupations

AGRICULTURAL

For agricultural occupations and classification, see appendix A. Occupations listed there as "Agricultural capitalists or middlemen" are included in chapter 6 with "Landowners."

TOWN

## Marginal Persons

| | | |
|---|---|---|
| band player | grape squeezer | porter |
| beggar | guitar player | prostitute |
| boat hand | gypsy | rag picker |
| brigand | hermit | servant |
| car waxer | indigent | sorcerer |
| comedian | laborer | stevedore |
| day laborer | meal monger | street cleaner |
| digger | mendicant | street sweeper |
| domestic | messenger boy | traveling bard |
| drifter | mountaineer | traveling singer |
| errand boy | oarsman | washer |
| fisherman | palm reader | whitewasher |

## Less Skilled

| | | |
|---|---|---|
| apprentice | driver | road repairman |
| axeman | hair comber | road worker |
| barkeeper | handyman | rope maker |
| barrel scraper | lumberman | sailor |
| basket weaver | miner | saloon worker |
| cabman | needleworker | sawyer |
| cabriolet driver | pickman | seamstress |
| carriage driver | pile driver | stone breaker |
| charioteer | postillion | sulfur miner |
| coachman | presser | truck driver |
| coffee grinder | procession bearer | tufa miner |
| collier | quarry worker | wagon hauler |
| construction helper | quilt maker | waiter |

## Skilled

arms maker
artisan
assistant master
  builder
athlete
auto-ignition repairer
axe and cleaver maker
baker
barber

barrel maker
binder
blacksmith
bread maker
brick maker
bulldozer operator
cabinetmaker
candlemaker
candy maker
carpenter
carver
cashier
cement worker
ceramic worker
chair maker
clog maker
cloth cutter
coach maker
construction worker
cook
cooper
coppersmith
cotton worker
craftsman
cream maker

decorative painter
door maker
dough cutter

dough maker
dyer
electrical mechanic
electrician
electronic technician

factory worker
foreman
foundryman
glass maker
glove maker
grinder
gunpowder maker
hairdresser
harness maker
hat maker
hoop maker
jockey
joiner
lathe operator
leather worker
machinist
marble polisher
marble worker
measurer
mechanic
metal worker
milkman
miller
milling-machiner
molder
painter

paper hanger
pastry maker
patternmaker

pavement layer
perforator
photographer
plasterer
plaster-figurine
  maker
plumber
pot maker
printer
quill maker
saddle maker
sandal maker
sausage maker
shoemaker
slaughterer
soap maker
soda distributor
stoker
stonecutter
strainer maker
table maker
tailor
tanner
technical assistant
tinker
tinter
varnisher
vase maker
weaver
welder
wheelwright
wool carder

## Lower Service

arsenal guard
assistant agent
bailiff
bank teller

guard
jailer
letter carrier
lottery ticket seller

salaried office worker
sales clerk
scribe
security guard

| | | |
|---|---|---|
| bookkeeper | mounted police officer | signalman |
| cashier | police officer | soldier |
| cemetery custodian | postal worker | street patroller |
| clerk | prison guard | sub-official |
| custodian | railway agent | tax agent |
| firefighter | railway employee | ticket collector |
| forest guard | railway timekeeper | town crier |
| | sacristan | water distributor |

### Upper Service

| | | |
|---|---|---|
| agent | lance corporal | police squad leader |
| brigadier | lieutenant | postmaster |
| colonel | marshall | sergeant |
| dental assistant | mortgage procurer | sergeant major |
| judicial secretary | nurse | telegrapher |
| | official | vice-brigadier |

### Business

| | | |
|---|---|---|
| arbiter | gold dealer | restaurant owner |
| builder | grocer | seller |
| businessman | hotel owner | shopkeeper |
| butcher (owner) | innkeeper | store owner |
| cafe owner | insurance agent | tavern owner |
| contractor | jeweler | trader |
| delicatessen owner | manufacturer | traveling salesman |
| entrepreneur | master builder | undertaker |
| factor | merchant | used goods salesman |
| fish seller | middleman | wholesaler |
| fruit seller | pawnbroker | wool manufacturer |

### Professional

| | | |
|---|---|---|
| accountant | head curate | professor |
| agronomist | interior decorator | prosecutor |
| architect | judge | rector |
| barrister | lawyer | sculptor |
| bleeder | lay monk | ship captain |
| canon | legal aide | soccer coach |
| chancellor | magistrate | substitute magistrate |
| cleric | map maker | substitute teacher |
| dentist | medical doctor | surgeon |
| denture maker | midwife | surveyor |
| doctor of law | musician | tax attorney |
| doctor of philosophy | music teacher | tax collector |
| draftsman | notary | teacher |

elementary school
  teacher
engineer
friar

nun
orchestra conductor
pharmacist
priest

town manager
town vice-manager
tribune
university student
veterinary

# Notes

## Chapter 2

1. This arrangement began in 1814 when the duchess of Parma recognized Albareto as a separate *comune*. The component clusters and their populations in 1871 are Albareto, 750; Buzzo, 144; Cacciarasca, 329; Campi, 287; Codogno, 243; Folta, 149; Gotra, 363; Groppo, 170; Monte Groppo, 541; Pieve di Campi, 320; San Quirico, 226; and Tombeto/Boschetto, 211.

2. The foregoing account is based on personal observation, interviews, and the following published sources: Gian Battista Poletti, *Brevi cenni storici di Buzzo* (Borgotaro, 1934); Pompeo Squeri, *Memorie storiche delle alte valli del Taro e del Ceno* (Piacenza, 1959); Tommaso Grilli, *Manipolo di cognizioni con cenni storici di Albareto di Borgotaro* (Borgotaro, 1893).

3. The hamlets and their 1871 populations are Castelluccio, 496; Fimiani, 432; Lanzara, 832; Santa Croce, 280; and Trivio, 165.

4. The hamlets and their 1871 populations are Aiello, 436; Campomanfoli, 517; Cortedomini, 172; Santa Maria a Favore, 239; and Torello, 470.

5. Giunta per l'Inchiesta Agraria e sulle Condizioni della Classe Agricola, *Atti*, VII (Rome, 1882), pp. 59–61, 101, 114 (hereafter cited as Giunta per l'Inchiesta Agraria).

6. Istituto Centrale di Statistica (ISTAT), *Catasto del 1929* (Rome, 1936), Province of Salerno, p. 183.

7. From a survey of wine barrel capacity located in the Municipio, Castel San Giorgio. Twenty percent produced four quintals or less, an amount sufficient for little more than home consumption.

8. The foregoing account is based on personal observation, interviews, and the following: Vito Grimaldi, "Elargizioni nei secoli del popolo di Castel S. Giorgio alla Badia di Materdomini," *Eco di Materdomini* (October–December 1969), n.p.; Grimaldi, "Note sugli alberi di Lanzara" (mimeograph, n.d.); Grimaldi, "L'antica Castel San Giorgio sceglie la strada dell'industrializzazione" (mimeograph, n.d.); "Castel San Giorgio . . . ieri e oggi" (mimeograph, 1974, of selected work of children at the elementary school in Lanzara).

9. Throughout this study the additions to Rogliano in the administrative reforms of 1928 (of Mangone, Manzi, Parenti, and San Stefano di Rogliano) are excluded from all calculations.

10. ISTAT, *Catasto del 1929,* Province of Cosenza, p. 80.

11. Giunta per l'Inchiesta Agraria, IX (Rome, 1883), p. 118.

12. Ibid., pp. 102–6, 110–12.

13. The foregoing account is based on personal observation, interviews, and the work of Antonio Guarasci, *Politica e società in Calabria dal risorgimento alla repubblica: il collegio di Rogliano* (Cosenza, 1974), pp. 71–114, and Gustavo Valente, *Dizionario dei luoghi della Calabria* (Cosenza, 1973), pp. 824–27.

14. ISTAT, *Catasto del 1929,* Province of Enna, p. 43.

15. Giunta per l'Inchiesta Agraria, XIII (Rome, 1885), fasc. 3, pp. 96–126. Readers familiar with Giovanni Verga's haunting short story of the same name may find it ironic that the thick volumes of the Jacini inquiry for Sicily duly report statistical evidence on incest.

16. Eric R. Wolf, *Peasants* (Englewood Cliffs, N.J., 1966), pp. 17, 32–33.
17. Giunta per l'Inchiesta Agraria, XIII, fasc. 1, p. 61.
18. Ibid., pp. 63–77.
19. The foregoing account is based on personal observation, interviews, and the work of Salvatore Gioco, *Nicosia Diocesi: erezione, comuni, monumenti* (Catania, 1972), pp. 500–504.

## Chapter 3

1. Eric J. Hobsbawn, *Primitive Rebels: Studies in Archaic Forms of Social Movement in the 19th and 20th Centuries* (New York, 1959), is clearly sympathetic. Also see Eric R. Wolf, *Peasants* (Englewood Cliffs, N.J., 1966), pp. 91–95 and 106–9, and the same author's *Peasant Wars of the Twentieth Century* (New York, 1969). An excellent review of the literature on rural movements is Henry A. Landsberger, "Peasant Unrest: Themes and Variations," in *Rural Protest: Peasant Movements and Social Change*, ed. Landsberger (London, 1974), pp. 1–64. Also very useful is Jeffery M. Paige, *Agrarian Revolution: Social Movements and Export Agriculture in the Underdeveloped World* (New York, 1975), esp. pp. 18–45.
2. Herbert Butterfield, *The Whig Interpretation of History* (London, 1931).
3. Hobsbawm, *Primitive Rebels*, p. 10. In *Bandits* (London, 1969), p. 21, however, Hobsbawm apparently reformulates his view of rural protests: "A social revolution is no less revolutionary because it takes place in the name of what the outside world considers 'reaction' against what it considers 'progress.' "
4. A comparison between the official life of Saint Gregory of Armenia (*Acta sanctorum* for March) and recollections of his life among Nissorini is revealing. Villagers knew of his healing powers and his connections with the nobility, but they knew nothing of his extreme asceticism.
5. For a brilliant analysis of Sicilian attitudes toward their patron saints, see Charlotte G. Chapman, *Milocca: A Sicilian Village* (Cambridge, Mass., 1971), pp. 159–95; and for comparative purposes Jeremy Boissevain, *Saints and Fireworks: Religion and Politics in Rural Malta* (London, 1965).
6. See, e.g., Edward Shils, "Tradition," *Comparative Studies in Society and History* 9 (1971): 122–59.
7. Lloyd I. Rudolph and Susanne H. Rudolph, *The Modernity of Tradition: Political Development in India* (Chicago, 1967), p.3.
8. Ibid., pp. 4–28; Wolf, *Peasants*, pp. viii and 18–37.
9. See the insightful discussion by Abdelkader Zghal, "The Reactivation of Tradition in a Post-traditional Society," *Daedalus* (Winter 1973), pp. 225–37.
10. Cited in Livy, *The War with Hannibal*, ed. Betty Radice, Penguin Classics (Baltimore, 1965), p. 15.
11. Vito Grimaldi, "Appunti e spunti storici su Santa Maria a Castello," (newspaper clipping, undated). For assistance in locating the factual basis (or lack thereof) for this "history" and for events as told in Nissoria, I am indebted to my colleague, John Lenaghan.
12. Salvatore Gioco, *Nicosia Diocesi: erezione, comuni, monumenti* (Catania, 1972), p. 501.
13. Antonio Guarasci, *Politica e società in Calabria dal risorgimento alla repubblica: il collegio di Rogliano* (Cosenza, 1974), pp. 20–33.
14. On the early history of Albareto, see Tommaso Grilli, *Manipolo di cognizioni con cenni storici di Albareto di Borgotaro* (Borgotaro, 1893), pp. 16–25. For the history of the area in general and the forces in conflict, see Jacques Heers, *Gênes au XVᵉ siècle: activité économique et problems sociaux* (Paris, 1961), pp. 11–46, 511–611; and Brian Pullan, *A History of Early Renaissance Italy: From the Mid-thirteenth to the Mid-fifteenth Century* (London, 1973), pp. 83–162, 203–301. On French influence, see Angus Heriot, *The French in Italy, 1796–99* (London, 1957), pp. 230–61; and R. John Rath, *The Fall of the Napoleonic*

*Kingdom of Italy (1814)* (New York, 1941). On the *partigiani*, see Luigi Canessa, *La strada era tortuosa: sedici mesi di guerriglia sugli Appennini Liguri-Emiliani* (Rapallo, 1947).

15. Feliks Gross, *Il Paese: Values and Social Change in an Italian Village* (New York, 1973), p. 140.

16. Ibid., p. 190.

17. For a moving account of the lower-class response to Gramsci, see Gino's autobiography in Danilo Dolci, *Racconti siciliani* (Turin, 1964), esp. pp. 108–9. The relationship between the PCI and the peasantry is a very complex and controversial subject that cannot be treated fully in the context of the present study. Most of my work deals with the relationship as viewed by peasants, but several sources that shed light on the PCI side may be noted. For Antonio Gramsci, see esp. his *Scritti giovanili, 1914–1918* (Turin, 1958), pp. 246–50; *L'ordine nuovo, 1919–1920* (Turin, 1954), pp. 22–27; *Socialismo e fascismo: l'ordine nuovo, 1921–1922* (Turin, 1966), pp. 311–13; and all of *Il Risorgimento* (Turin, 1949). A good introduction in English is John M. Cammett, *Antonio Gramsci and the Origins of Italian Communism* (Stanford, 1967), pp. 213–22. On the more recent period, see Sidney G. Tarrow, *Peasant Communism in Southern Italy* (New Haven, 1967); and Enrico Berlinguer, *La proposta comunista* (Turin, 1975), esp. pp. 113–14.

## Chapter 4

1. Among several formulations of this point, the one that comes closest to my own is Pierre Bourdieu, "The Attitude of the Algerian Peasant toward Time," in *Mediterranean Countrymen*, ed. Julian Pitt-Rivers (Paris, 1963), pp. 55–72.

2. Thomas J. Cottle and Stephen L. Klineberg, *The Present of Things Future: Explorations of Time in Human Experience* (New York, 1974), pp. 163–69.

3. Stephen Toulmin and June Goodfield, *The Discovery of Time* (New York, 1965), pp. 232–35, shapes my thinking on this point.

4. Lewis Mumford, *Technics and Civilization* (New York, 1934), p. 197.

5. For a trenchant analysis of class-differentiated perceptions of time, see Georges Gurvich, *The Spectrum of Social Time* (Dordrecht, 1964), esp. pp. 89–102. Indispensable on time in a modern setting is Sebastian DeGrazia, *Time, Work, and Leisure* (Garden City, N.Y., 1964). Also see J. D. Mabbott, "Our Direct Experience of Time," in *The Philosophy of Time*, ed. Richard M. Gale (London, 1968), pp. 304–21.

6. Clifford Geertz, *Person, Time and Conduct in Bali: An Essay in Cultural Analysis* (New Haven, 1966).

7. The accuracy of reported ages at death varies, but not too greatly for present purposes. Ages recorded in days surely were accurate, as were those noted in months or years and months. Since few deaths are recorded at age eleven months, these were probably rounded to one year, and reports such as one-and-one-half probably often mean only more than one and less than two. Reports of ages between two and eighteen show no clustered or short years and seem to be highly reliable. From age twenty on there is definite clustering at decennia and an apparent excess of even numbered ages. In Rogliano, for example, the clustering at decennia resulted in reporting three to four times as many deaths as in adjacent ages. Reports of persons dying at ages beyond eighty are subject to considerable overstatement.

8. The demographic data in this chapter are drawn from the material discussed in the Note on Sources, and therefore individual records and files will not be cited here.

9. In other words, graph plot points = (observed cell frequency/observed row frequency)/8.33.

10. Instructions for recording deaths specified a rigid and lengthy prose form for the *Atto di morte* with distinct wording for celibate persons, wives, widows, widowers, husbands, persons without recorded birth certificates, deaths outside the home, involving

the police, of unknown persons, in a prison, as a punishment, at sea, of unknown parentage, from abroad, in military service, without recovery of a body, and reported more than twenty-four hours after death. These are summarized in *Istruzioni sull' uso dei modelli e delle formole per la compilazione degli atti dello stato civile* (Rome, 1874), pp. 123–28, and *Formulario dello stato civile* (n.p., n.d., but apparently Rome, 1865), pp. 252–58. At a minimum these forms required a statement of the hour and place of death; this in turn led to use of blank lines at the bottom of the form for "explanations" concerning uncertainty in answering standard questions.

11. Based on 2,308 cases for Castel San Giorgio and 3,587 for Nissoria in which the father was not listed as dead or, due to the age of the deceased, presumed to be dead. Illegitimacy rates from marriage registers were 1.3 and 1.7 percent for brides and grooms in Castel San Giorgio and 2.4 and 2.2, respectively, in Nissoria. Birth reports include two types of unknown parentage; the *trovato* or foundling, usually reported as found at the church steps, may or may not have been born locally. The more frequent report was by the *levatrice* (midwife) who, in strict accordance with Italian law, stated only that a birth occurred to a woman "che non consente d'essere nominata," which meant that neither parent was legally responsible for the child or, in cases where the mother chose to care for the child, as a result of "la sua unione naturale con un uomo non parenti, non affini nei gradi che ostano al riconoscimento." In Albareto a majority of reports in which one parent recognized the infant were made by the father rather than the mother, the purpose being to protect the legal dignity of the woman involved. Even taking all these reports, they total only 2.3 percent of births in Castel San Giorgio and Nissoria.

12. Ministero di Agricoltura, Industria e Commercio, *Statistica delle cause delle morti: anno 1881* (Rome, 1882), pp. 123–27. In this case "urban" refers to the 284 largest cities and all district capitals.

13. Ibid., *Anno 1886*, pp. 93–133.

14. For comparative data on illegitimacy, see Peter Laslett, *Family Life and Illicit Love in Earlier Generations* (New York, 1977), pp. 102–73.

15. Giunta per l'Inchiesta Agraria, XIII, tomo 2, p. 394.

16. Lloyd deMause, "The Evolution of Childhood," in *The History of Childhood*, ed. deMause (New York, 1974), pp. 26–31, and the material cited in his n. 110.

17. See Richard C. Trexler, "Infanticide in Florence: New Sources and First Results," *History of Childhood Quarterly* (Summer 1973), pp. 98–116; William L. Langer, "Infanticide: A Historical Survey," *History of Childhood Quarterly* (Winter 1974), p. 354; and Barbara A. Kellum, "Infanticide in England in the Later Middle Ages," *History of Childhood Quarterly* (Winter 1974), pp. 360–69.

18. Giunta per l'Inchiesta Agraria, XIII, tomo 1, p. 641; tomo 2, p. 94.

19. For an excellent account of feeding and swaddling dangers, see David Hunt, *Parents and Children in History: The Psychology of Family Life in Early Modern France* (New York, 1970), esp. pp. 115–17 and 127–29.

20. J. W. Schereschewsky, "Heat and Infant Mortality," *Proceedings of the American Association for Study and Prevention of Infant Mortality*, Fourth Annual Meeting (1913), pp. 99–132.

21. M. W. Beaver, "Population, Infant Mortality and Milk," *Population Studies* (July 1973), pp. 243–54.

22. Obviously the reconstruction of causes of mortality from only scattered notes that were never intended to be careful listings of symptoms must be tentative. The timing and frequency of death, however, provide additional clues, as do seasonal variation in age structure and differentiation by social class. In the above and following efforts at "diagnosis" I have relied primarily on Isaac Abt, ed., *Pediatrics* (London, 1923), esp. vol. 2; and Louis Fischer, *Diseases of Infancy and Childhood* (Philadelphia, 1907), for earlier terminology and understanding. Useful for other reasons were Henry Barnett and Arnold Einhorn,

eds., *Pediatrics*, 15th ed. (New York, 1972); and D. B. Jelliffe, *Diseases of Children in the Subtropics and Tropics*, 2d ed. (London, 1970). I am indebted to Dr. Sheldon Guss for his insights on the data summarized in fig. 2 and in app. B.

23. Vicenzo Bruno, *"Evoluzione della mortalità per cause di morte nella prima metà del secolo XX in base alle tavole di mortalità del 1899–1902 e 1950–1953,"* (Pisa, 1960), table 1.

24. The findings discussed in detail for Nissoria are confirmed by available data for Italy generally. As an example, I have summarized below data for 1881 in percentages by categories of causes of death. The data are for the 284 largest cities and district capitals as reported for legitimate children to age five and all persons above that age in the reports cited in n. 12 above.

| CAUSE OF DEATH | 0–1 MONTH M | F | 1–12 MONTHS M | F | 1–5 YEARS M | F | 6–20 YEARS M | F | 21–60 YEARS M | F | OVER AGE 60 M | F |
|---|---|---|---|---|---|---|---|---|---|---|---|---|
| Cg | 21 | 22 | 1 | 1 | ... | ... | ... | ... | ... | ... | ... | ... |
| Ct | 4 | 4 | 22 | 23 | 39 | 40 | 35 | 33 | 12 | 9 | 5 | 4 |
| Cs | 30 | 31 | 11 | 12 | 15 | 14 | 24 | 35 | 30 | 38 | 19 | 22 |
| N | 16 | 15 | 15 | 14 | 9 | 8 | 9 | 6 | 10 | 8 | 17 | 15 |
| R | 8 | 8 | 19 | 17 | 13 | 13 | 8 | 7 | 19 | 14 | 25 | 24 |
| Ci | 1 | 1 | 1 | ... | 1 | 1 | 3 | 3 | 8 | 9 | 13 | 18 |
| G | 11 | 11 | 28 | 30 | 19 | 20 | 8 | 8 | 10 | 10 | 12 | 12 |
| U/g | ... | ... | ... | ... | 1 | 1 | 2 | 1 | 2 | 3 | 4 | 1 |
| P | ... | ... | ... | ... | ... | ... | ... | 1 | ... | 6 | ... | ... |
| S | 4 | 3 | 1 | 1 | ... | 1 | 1 | 1 | 2 | 1 | 2 | 1 |
| B/m | ... | ... | ... | ... | ... | ... | 3 | 2 | 1 | 1 | 1 | 1 |
| A | 4 | 4 | 1 | 1 | 2 | 1 | 4 | 1 | 3 | 1 | 1 | 1 |
| S/h | ... | ... | ... | ... | ... | ... | 1 | ... | 1 | ... | ... | ... |
| Unk | 1 | 1 | 1 | 1 | 1 | 1 | 1 | 1 | 1 | ... | 1 | 1 |
| Total | 8,712 | 7,127 | 11,458 | 10,190 | 16,618 | 16,024 | 7,590 | 8,507 | 29,281 | 25,902 | 22,372 | 21,551 |

NOTE. Cg = congenital; Ct = contagious; Cs = constitutional; N = nervous system; R = respiratory; Ci = circulatory; G = gastrointestinal; U/g = urinary/genital; P = pregnancy; S = skin; B/m = bone/muscle; A = accidental; S/h = suicide/homicide; Unk = unknown.

25. Ministero di Agricoltura, Industria e Commercio, *Statistica delle cause delle morti: anno 1882* (Rome, 1884), pp. 102–7, gives the following breakdown for 24,348 recorded deaths in Sicily for 1882. The data parallel, though in less concentrated form, findings for Nissoria.

| Cause of Death | Jan | Feb | Mar | Apr | May | Jun | Jul | Aug | Sep | Oct | Nov | Dec |
|---|---|---|---|---|---|---|---|---|---|---|---|---|
| Cg | 36 | 38 | 27 | 26 | 22 | 50 | 49 | 47 | 51 | 54 | 54 | 77 |
| Ct | 410 | 363 | 338 | 340 | 439 | 624 | 745 | 628 | 539 | 490 | 441 | 490 |
| Cs | 397 | 420 | 366 | 377 | 372 | 426 | 413 | 327 | 355 | 366 | 345 | 353 |
| N | 196 | 199 | 191 | 192 | 170 | 164 | 178 | 136 | 109 | 127 | 164 | 194 |
| R | 395 | 493 | 428 | 361 | 324 | 231 | 178 | 157 | 163 | 201 | 236 | 417 |
| Ci | 105 | 100 | 90 | 67 | 82 | 63 | 57 | 48 | 46 | 49 | 70 | 85 |
| G | 338 | 297 | 282 | 307 | 379 | 665 | 782 | 599 | 532 | 509 | 436 | 382 |
| U/g | 40 | 31 | 17 | 31 | 26 | 25 | 21 | 25 | 30 | 29 | 33 | 34 |
| P | 14 | 24 | 17 | 13 | 12 | 5 | 7 | 5 | 10 | 11 | 7 | 15 |
| S | 28 | 18 | 15 | 13 | 20 | 21 | 18 | 19 | 15 | 25 | 23 | 19 |
| B/m | 11 | 7 | 9 | 13 | 16 | 11 | 8 | 8 | 14 | 13 | 9 | 17 |
| A | 25 | 26 | 21 | 23 | 28 | 41 | 29 | 21 | 23 | 18 | 31 | 30 |
| Su | 3 | 3 | 4 | 6 | 6 | 3 | 4 | 4 | 5 | 1 | 4 | 1 |
| H | 7 | 15 | 5 | 6 | 6 | 7 | 8 | 4 | 6 | 4 | 4 | 8 |
| Unk | 10 | 21 | 11 | 9 | 9 | 20 | 17 | 24 | 13 | 11 | 13 | 8 |
| Total | 2.016 | 2,057 | 1,822 | 1,785 | 1,911 | 2,359 | 2,515 | 2,053 | 1,911 | 1,910 | 1,874 | 2,135 |

NOTE. Cg = congenital; Ct = contagious; Cs = constitutional; N = nervous system; R = respiratory; Ci = circulatory; G = gastrointestinal; U/g = urinary/genital; P = pregnancy; S = skin; B/m = bone/muscle; A = accidental; Su = suicide; H = homicide; Unk = unknown.

26. This account is reconstructed from the vital records at the Municipio in Nissoria.

27. Pier Francesco Bandettini, *La popolazione della Toscana dal 1810 al 1959* (Florence, 1961), pp. 11–26; Giuseppe Melano, *La popolazione di Torino e del Piemonte nel secolo XIX* (Turin, 1961), p. 84; G. Muttini Corti, *La popolazione del Piemonte nel secolo XIX* (Turin, 1962), p. 146; Luigi Izzo, *La popolazione calabrese nel secolo XIX* (Naples, 1965), pp. 166–69.

28. The account that follows differs sharply from the conclusions of a number of scholars, working mostly on the eighteenth century, about the indifference of parents to their children's deaths. Since the cultures and times involved are quite dissimilar, differing conclusions may be in order. But one constant theme in work on the eighteenth century is that the sheer quantity of death must have caused an attitude of resignation or even indifference. For example, François Lebrun, *Les hommes et la mort en Anjou aux 17ᵉ et 18ᵉ siècles* (Paris, 1971), writes (p. 422) that *"la fréquence même des décès a une autre conséquence que la familiarité à l'égard du spectacle de la mort, c'est la résignation devant l'inévitable"* and later (p. 430) *"avec une résignation qui peut sembler parfois de l'indifférence."* Lebrun goes on to concede that epidemics were different because they represented a direct and personal menace. But from the data displayed earlier in fig. 2 it is evident that there was a good demographic basis for perceiving every summer death as part of an epidemic kind of time. Only after the fact can statisticians determine that some years were not so bad after all, or at least no worse than normal (a level itself determined by the high mortality rate). And the surviving record does not indicate that rural Italians were more resigned to deaths which occurred in such normal years.

Evidence on perception and response to death (including that which follows in the present text) is unlikely ever to be more than suggestive. Thus the problem of reading modern perceptions into the past becomes expecially severe. Perhaps an example will illuminate the problem. Lebrun cites the baptism (and sending to a wet-nurse) of a sickly infant (p. 423, esp. n. 32) and concludes, *"On ne peut s'empêcher de penser qu'après une naissance si difficile, sage-femme et parents auraient été bien inspirés en attendant plusieurs semaines avant de faire suppléer les cérémonies du baptême et de conduire le bébé en nourrice à six lieues d'Angers."* Perhaps Lebrun's opinion on wet-nursing is correct, but certainly the emphasis on baptism can be read as evidence of concern for the soul of the child rather than as an indication of indifference to its worldly health. Moreover, given how little was known in the way of effective treatment of "sickly" infants, there is no reason to assume that the baptismal ceremony worsened the child's condition. In my judgment, it would be failure to baptize a sick child that would constitute better evidence of indifference to infant mortality. Even in Lebrun's admirably documented study, the conclusion about indifference to infant death rests heavily on an implicit assumption that it must have been this way, else the constant grief would have been unbearable. Such an assumption reflects less an eighteenth-century *mentalité* than a twentieth-century psyche with a low capacity to grieve and to bear adversity. Mortality rates in Nissoria until the twentieth century were as high as in Anjou in the eighteenth, but there is no evidence to indicate that the Nissorini were therefore indifferent to death at any age.

Edward Shorter, *The Making of the Modern Family* (New York, 1975), pp. 57–58 and 214–15, notes the merrymaking aspects of funeral ritual and concludes, incorrectly I believe, that participants were therefore indifferent to or even amused by death. Shorter, at least in this instance, tends to interpret the evidence in too linear a fashion and without sufficient attention to the duality of peasant celebration and ceremony. Lawrence Stone, *The Family, Sex and Marriage in England, 1500–1800* (London, 1977), pp. 81–82, examines thoughtfully the relationship between high mortality and low levels of affection. The little evidence available, he notes, shows that it was in a century of particularly high mortality that affective relationships improved, a finding contradictory to Lebrun's hypothesis. Stone posits the need to examine "an important intervening variable: the cultural norms and expectations of society." This is what I have tried to do for rural Italy.

29. deMause, "Evolution of Childhood," pp. 17–19.

30. In Rogliano it is "expected" that a bereaved female, at the next burial she attends, will repeat this emotional display.

31. The foregoing account is based on interviews and memorabilia connected with funeral rites (which are "never" disposed of). Villagers uniformly insist that burial customs remain unchanged to the present day; therefore I have supplemented the account from personal observation in Nissoria and Rogliano.

32. For an even more extreme case of November clustering of marriages, see my "Transformation of a Rural Village: Istria, 1870–1972," *Journal of Social History* (Spring 1974), p. 249.

33. Although this is not the appropriate point to enter into a detailed critique of George Foster's famous concept of "limited good," it may clarify the present discussion to note that I share Jacob Black-Michaud's alternative idea of "total scarcity" or "the moral, institutional and material premise of a certain type of society in which everything felt by the people themselves to be relevant to human life is regarded by those people as existing in absolutely inadequate quantities" (see his *Cohesive Force: Feud in the Mediterranean and the Middle East* [New York, 1975], pp. 121–22 and 160–78).

34. Previous work on the question of birth patterns invariably revealed seasonal trends, but results may have been based on too few cases to be fully convincing. The notable exception is the massive study of Ellsworth Huntington, *Season of Birth: Its Relation to Human Abilities* (New York, 1938). Unfortunately, as the subtitle indicates, the author's primary concern was with figuring out when geniuses and other such elites were likely to be born. Leaving aside all the spurious statistical presentations on this subject, Huntington's study amassed a good deal of useful data on seasonality. Fig. 4 portrays large numbers of events (N=18,695 for Nissoria; 19,722 for Albareto; 27,075 for Castel San Giorgio; and 28,360 for Rogliano), and the patterns are statistically significant at the .001 level.

35. *Statistica delle cause della morti*, 1881–86.

36. Barnett and Einhorn, *Pediatrics*, pp. 4 and 26–27.

37. P. A. Lachenbruch, "Frequency and Timing of Intercourse: Its Relation to the Probability of Conception," *Population Studies* (July 1967), p. 30. Among studies showing little relationship between increased frequency of intercourse and conception, see C. F. Westoff, R. G. Potter, and P. C. Sagi, *The Third Child* (Princeton, N.J., 1963), which reports a correlation coefficient under .10 for conception and coital frequency. The same authors reported similar findings in "Knowledge of the Ovulatory Cycle and Coital Frequency as Factors Affecting Conception and Contraception," *Milbank Memorial Fund Quarterly* (January 1962), pp. 46–58. Also see Robert G. Potter Jr., "Length of the Fertile Period," *Milbank Memorial Fund Quarterly* (January 1961), pp. 132–62, and J. Richard Udry and Naomi M. Morris, "Seasonality of Coitus and Seasonality of Birth," *Demography* (1967), no. 2, pp. 673–79.

38. Bell, "Transformation of a Rural Village," p. 259; J. Knodel and E. Van DeWalle, "Breast Feeding, Fertility and Infant Mortality: An Analysis of Some Early German Data," *Population Studies* (September 1967), pp. 109–32; j. Knodel, "Infant Mortality and Fertility in Three Bavarian Villages: An Analysis of Family Histories from the 19th Century," *Population Studies* (November 1968), pp. 297–318; C. Tietze, "The Effect of Breast Feeding on the Rate of Conception," *International Population Conference* (New York, 1961), 2:129–36; E. Gautier and L. Henry, *La population de Crulai, paroisse normande* (Paris, 1968), pp. 149–54; J. Harripin, "La fécondité des ménages canadiens au début du XVIIIᵉ siècle," *Population* (January–March 1954), pp. 74–75; H. Leridon and P. Cantrelle, "Breastfeeding, Mortality in Childhood and Fertility in a Rural Zone of Senegal," *Population Studies* (November 1971), pp. 505–34; and A. Jain, T. Hsu, R. Freedman, and M. Chang, "Demographic Aspects of Lactation and Postpartum Amenorrhea," *Demography* (1970), pp.

255–71. Interviewees in all four communities generally asserted that the desire to reduce family size was the primary reason for extending lactation.

39. A. Perez, P. Vela, R. G. Potter, and G. S. Masnick, "Timing and Sequence of Resuming Ovulation and Menstruation after Childbirth," *Population Studies* (November 1971), p. 497.

40. E. Shorter, J. Knodel, and E. Van DeWalle, "The Decline of Non-marital Fertility in Europe, 1880–1940," *Population Studies* (November 1971), pp. 375–93, assigns only a small role to the kinds of long-established methods discussed here in reducing both legitimate and illegitimate fertility.

41. Beaver, "Population, Infant Mortality and Milk," p. 244.

42. On this point, see the moving account of Carlo Levi, *Christ Stopped at Eboli* (New York, 1947).

43. Bourdieu, "The Attitude of the Algerian Peasant toward Time," pp. 55–72; Fred Gearing, "Preliminary Notes on Ritual in Village Greece," in J. G. Peristiany, *Contributions to Mediterranean Sociology* (Paris, 1968), pp. 65–72; Sydel Silverman, *Three Bells of Civilization: The Life of an Italian Hill Town* (New York, 1975), pp. 150–67; Julian Pitt-Rivers, *The Fate of Shechem, or The Politics of Sex: Essays in the Anthropology of the Mediterranean* (Cambridge, 1977), pp. 134–45; Juliet Du Boulay, *Portrait of a Greek Mountain Village* (London, 1974), pp. 41, 51, and 95 ff.; Ernestine Friedl, *Vasilika: A Village in Modern Greece* (New York, 1963), pp. 75–78; and Ernesto deMartino, *Sud e magia* (Milan, 1959), passim.

44. The index of strength of seasonal concentration is calculated as

$$\left[ \sum_{i=1}^{12} \left( X_i - \frac{100}{12} \right) \right]^{1/2}$$

45. Edmund Leach, *Rethinking Anthropology* (London, 1961), pp. 124–25.

46. Ibid., p. 131.

## Chapter 5

1. The account of the six Zeccas is based on family reconstitution from birth, marriage, and death registers kept in the Municipio at Albareto.

2. François Lebrun, *Les hommes et la mort en Anjou aux 17ᵉ et 18ᵉ siècles* (Paris, 1971), p. 430.

3. That the major exception is in diagrams of royal ancestry is well worth pondering.

4. Edward Banfield, *The Moral Basis of a Backward Society* (Glencoe, Ill., 1958), p. 85.

5. For a devastating analysis of this shortcoming in a variety of historical explanations, see David Fischer, *Historians' Fallacies: Toward a Logic of Historical Thought* (New York, 1970), pp. 166–72. For specific and detailed critiques of Banfield's concept of amoral familism, see Alessandro Pizzorno, "Familismo amorale e marginalità storica, ovvero perchè non c'è niente da fare a Montegrano," *Quaderni di sociologia* (1960), and translated in *International Review of Community Development* (1966), pp. 55–66; Sydel Silverman, "Agricultural Organization, Social Structure, and Values in Italy: Amoral Familism Reconsidered," *American Anthropologist* (February 1968), pp. 1–20; and John Davis, "Morals and Backwardness," *Comparative Studies in Society and History* (July 1970), pp. 340–53, followed by Banfield's reply.

6. Peter Laslett, ed., *Household and Family in Past Time* (Cambridge, 1972), p. 31.

7. Lutz Berkner, "The Stem Family and the Development Cycle of the Peasant Household: An Eighteenth-Century Austrian Example," *American Historical Review* (April 1972), pp. 398–418. Also see Berkner's wide-ranging critique of Laslett, "The Use and Misuse of

Census Data for the Historical Analysis of Family Structure," *Journal of Interdisciplinary History* (Spring 1975), pp. 721–38.

8. The best example, one that demonstrates that the problem is more than one of definition and classification is Philip J. Greven, Jr., "The Average Size of Families and Households in the Province of Massachusetts in 1764 and in the United States in 1790: An Overview," in Laslett, *Household and Family*, pp. 545–60.

9. Although Laslett's discussion makes clear that he is fully aware of this problem, his evidence and conclusions nonetheless stress static questions and a "snapshot" approach. See, e.g., Laslett, *Household and Family*, esp. table 1–3 and pp. 58–62.

10. Eugene Hammel, "The Zadruga as Process," in Laslett, *Household and Family*, esp. pp. 370–73. Compare this with the essay immediately following by Laslett and Marilyn Clarke, which asks only the questions Hammel concludes are not very useful and potentially misleading.

11. See Lutz K. Berkner, "Recent Research on the History of the Family in Western Europe," *Journal of Marriage and the Family* (August 1973), pp. 395–405, for a thorough bibliography of work to that point. I am also influenced by Arlene Skolnick, "The Family Revisited: Themes in Recent Social Science Research," *Journal of Interdisciplinary History* (Spring 1975), pp. 703–19; Tamara K. Hareven, "The Family as Process: The Historical Study of the Family Cycle," *Journal of Social History* (Spring 1974), pp. 322–29; and E. Anthony Wrigley, "Reflections on the History of the Family," *Daedalus* (Spring 1977), pp. 71–85. Mark Poster, *Critical Theory of the Family* (New York, 1978), became available too recently to allow me to make full use of it in the text. Poster's critique of a wide range of theory of the family is brilliant and devastating, so much so that the alternative models he offers seem rather timid, almost déjà vu. He concludes by suggesting that other researchers "test the value of the critical theory in concrete studies of the family." It is my judgment that Poster's four models of family structure (time-specific bourgeois, aristocratic, peasant, and working-class) are inadequate for the study of families in Mediterranean societies. His aristocratic, peasant, and working-class models share so many internal similarities that they merge more easily than he would wish into the "traditional" type treated by Shorter and other Parsonians as linear antecedents of the modern (read "bourgeois") family. Nor does Poster escape the cultural and ethnic centrism he so rightly condemns in Freud when he posits as "bourgeois" cultural characteristics peculiar to northern Europe, the United States, and Canada. The models he sets forth are Marxist in structure, divided according to mode of production, and in theory such an approach should be applicable to the Mediterranean or, for that matter, to non-Western areas. But virtually all the particulars Poster uses to flesh out his four models, cultural and psychological, make sense only within the narrowly defined limits of historical experience in a particular capitalist region. Repression of infant sexuality and early, rigid toilet training, for example, may be "bourgeois" in England, but no such practices flourished among Sicilian bourgeoisie. Poster clearly respects the importance of historical experience, and he indicates at one point that "ethnic" or other such models may be as useful as the ones he proposes. Such eclecticism, however, leads less to critical theory than to anarchy, a problem well known to Italians on both practical and theoretical levels extending beyond politics. Theory of the family indeed is needed, and let it be critical theory, but let it also facilitate comparative historical understanding beyond the North Atlantic.

12. For parallel and much more detailed findings on landholding women, see John Davis, *Land and Family in Pisticci* (New York, 1973), pp. 73–145. On inheritance disputes I owe particular thanks to Dino Talarico of Rogliano for allowing me to observe and learn from his experience as a lawyer involved in such matters.

13. Although this model differs from the specifics presented in Clifford Geertz, *Person,*

*Time, and Conduct in Bali: An Essay in Cultural Analysis* (New Haven, 1966), pp. 18–22, I am very much influenced by his analysis.

14. Giunta per l'Inchiesta Agraria, XIII, tomo 1, pp. 66–67. Also see Leopoldo Franchetti and Sidney Sonnino, *La Sicilia nel 1876* (Florence, 1925), 2:346–58.

15. For mean nuptial age patterns in several European nations since 1830, see Etienne van de Walle, "Marriage and Marital Fertility," *Daedalus* (Spring 1968), p. 492. The differences between the Rogliano and Castel San Giorgio curves and those presented by van de Walle stand out. The Rogliano and Castel San Giorgio curves begin at an earlier date and include a rise in female nuptial ages that is only hinted at in van de Walle's data. The second advance in nuptial ages in Rogliano and Castel San Giorgio (1920–60) is absent in van de Walle's material due, in my judgment, to a delay in rural Italy in adopting alternative means of conception control.

16. For a listing of occupations and how they are classified, see app. D. The son of a landowner was listed as a landowner whether or not he had received title to some land, unless it was already certain that he would not inherit.

17. Coefficients of variation in Rogliano, for example, in age of marriage for males and females, respectively, were .25 and .27 for the landless, .32 and .32 for propertied couples other than the wealthiest, and .40 and .52 for the big holders.

18. See Feliks Gross, *Il Paese: Values and Social Change in an Italian Village* (New York, 1973), pp. 8–13, on cultural and ecological stratification. Sydel Silverman, *Three Bells of Civilization: The Life of an Italian Hill Town* (New York, 1975), pp. 107–12, finds the *cittadini/contadini* distinction to be of major importance.

19. The reader will note that these figures reflect averages for the entire period under consideration and, therefore, understate the percentage engaged in agriculture in the nineteenth century. For decennial breakdowns of occupational structure, see the next chapter.

20. Among sixty businessmen, only one listed his father as a *contadino* and only two as a person here classified as "better rural."

21. The volatility of these figures is due partially to the small number of cases involved; nonetheless, the direction of variation is consistent with the hypothesis that changes in nuptial age reflected economic conditions.

22. Eric J. Hobsbawm, *Laboring Men: Studies in the History of Labour* (London, 1964), pp. 272–315.

23. This finding suggests that comparisons of mean nuptial age over time and among different regions and nations should take into account the portion of the population engaged in agriculture and similar measures of economic activity and diversity.

24. For evidence that the peasantry's lot worsened everywhere in southern Italy at this time, see Anton Blok, *The Mafia of a Sicilian Village, 1860–1960: A Study of Violent Peasant Entrepreneurs* (New York, 1974), esp. 39; Denis Mack Smith, *Modern Sicily after 1713* (New York, 1968), pp. 396–402; F. Catalano, R. Moscati, and F. Valsecchi, *L'Italia nel risorgimento: dal 1789 al 1870* (Verona, 1964), pp. 305–19 and 395–401; and Ottavio Barié, *L'Italia nell'ottocento* (Turin, 1964), pp. 409–18.

25. *Formulario dello stato civile* (n.p., n.d., but apparently 1865), p. 69.

26. Eugenio Menna, *Norme per il matrimonio* (Bologna, 1941), p. 32.

27. *Istruzioni sull' uso dei modelli e delle formole per la compilazione degli atti dello stato civile* (Rome, 1874), pp. 47–48.

28. The law provided that sons over the age of twenty-one whose parents were dead needed no familial consent to marry. If under twenty-one with both parents dead, a son or daughter needed the consent of all living grandparents or, if these had died, of a *consiglio di famiglia*.

29. Parallel figures for female ages at first marriage between 1840 and 1900 are as follows:

| | NISSORIA | | CASTEL SAN GIORGIO | | ROGLIANO | |
| AGE | N | % Change | N | % Change | N | % Change |
| --- | --- | --- | --- | --- | --- | --- |
| Under 16 | 132 | ... | 4 | ... | 32 | ... |
| 16 | 108 | -18 | 10 | 150 | 7 | -78 |
| 17 | 152 | 41 | 18 | 80 | 22 | 214 |
| 18 | 126 | -17 | 38 | 111 | 42 | 91 |
| 19 | 130 | 3 | 44 | 16 | 104 | 148 |
| 20 | 122 | -6 | 140 | 218 | 124 | 19 |
| 21 | 126 | 3 | 94 | -33 | 178 | 44 |
| 22 | 66 | -48 | 184 | 96 | 192 | 8 |
| 23 | 68 | 3 | 178 | -3 | 164 | -15 |
| 24 | 54 | -21 | 144 | -19 | 174 | 6 |
| 25 | 46 | -15 | 148 | 3 | 152 | -13 |
| 26 | 30 | -35 | 144 | -3 | 126 | -17 |

30. The figures are as follows:

| | Rogliano | Castel San Giorgio | Albareto |
| --- | --- | --- | --- |
| Mean male nuptial age, 1915–18 | 24.0 | 29.9 | 27.7 |
| Number of marriages, 1911–14 | 142 | 144 | 110 |
| Number of marriages, 1915–18 | 35 | 30 | 13 |
| Number of marriages, 1919–22 | 263 | 228 | 202 |

31. For comparative data on age at menarche, see Peter Laslett, *Family Life and Illicit Love in Earlier Generations* (New York, 1977), pp. 214–32.

32. In Castel San Giorgio, for reasons that no one could explain, couples who elope always go to nearby Pompei to marry.

33. Undoubtedly the reader recognizes that recollection by interviewees of such incidents does not imply that they were "typical" or usual. Nevertheless, it is noteworthy that among Nissorini stories of familial tension over nuptial choices are related with regret and a strong conviction that they occurred rarely, and then most often in some other town. In Rogliano and Castel San Giorgio, on the other hand, virtually all interviewees related such stories as part of their family history, usually with a sense of pride in the independence of the young couple.

34. See Edmund Leach, *Rethinking Anthropology* (London, 1961), p. 131.

35. Gideon Sjoberg, *Pre-industrial Cities Past and Present* (New York, 1960), pp. 175–77. Also see S. N. Eisenstadt, *From Generation to Generation: Age Groups and Social Structure* (Glencoe, Ill., 1956), pp. 43–87.

36. Massimo Livi-Bacci, *A History of Italian Fertility during the Last Two Centuries* (Princeton, N.J., 1977), p. 34. For a thorough technical discussion of the age at marriage statistic, see S. N. Agarwala, *Age at Marriage in India* (Allahabad, 1962).

37. E. A. Wrigley, *Population and History* (New York, 1969), pp. 82–83 and 138. Also see Sherburne Cooke and Woodrow Borah, *Essays in Population History: Mexico and the Caribbean* (Berkeley, 1974), 2:341–57; and Livi-Bacci, *Italian Fertility*, pp. 90–92.

38. One very significant variable related to nuptial ages and various measures of fertility and population growth is the percentage of females who remain unmarried, at least until after their childbearing years. Unfortunately, the local archives for Albareto, Castel San Giorgio, Nissoria, and Rogliano do not contain the data needed to calculate accurately the number of unmarried women at any given point in time or over a span of years. Therefore, I am not able to estimate how much the factor of celibacy reduced potential fertility. Livi-Bacci, *Italian Fertility*, pp. 101–6, provides summaries of census data showing percentages of single females in various regions. For some years the census volumes include breakdowns at the province or district level as well. It is reasonable to assume that

the percentage of single females in a particular community is best approximated from data for the next largest subdivision, in this case from the province or district rather than the region or the nation as a whole. Below I have tabulated the available data for Albareto (Parma), Castel San Giorgio (Principato Citeriore), Nissoria (Catania), and Rogliano (Calabria Citeriore). The figures are congruent with Livi-Bacci's finding that since 1861 the percentage of females who do not marry within their fecund years has been declining.

| | PARMA | PRINCIPATO CITERIORE | CATANIA | CALABRIA CITERIORE |
|---|---|---|---|---|
| | | 1861 (Towns under 6,000 Population) | | |
| Females age 46–55 (%): | | | | |
| Never married | 6 | 15 | 18 | 15 |
| Married | 73 | 64 | 56 | 55 |
| Widowed | 21 | 21 | 26 | 30 |

| | BORGOTARO | SALERNO | NICOSIA | COSENZA |
|---|---|---|---|---|
| | | 1881 | | |
| Females age 46–55 (%): | | | | |
| Never married | 12 | 14 | 12 | 15 |
| Married | 72 | 71 | 58 | 58 |
| Widowed | 16 | 15 | 30 | 27 |

| | | 1901 | | |
|---|---|---|---|---|
| Females over age 50 (%): | | | | |
| Never married | 9 | 12 | 9 | 14 |
| Married | 53 | 55 | 48 | 48 |
| Widowed | 38 | 33 | 43 | 38 |

| | BORGOTARO | SALERNO | ENNA | COSENZA |
|---|---|---|---|---|
| | | 1931 (Towns under 10,000 Population) | | |
| Females age 46–55 (%): | | | | |
| Never married | 9 | 11 | 6 | 10 |
| Married | 77 | 74 | 78 | 73 |
| Widowed | 14 | 15 | 16 | 17 |

39. Steven E. Beaver, *Demographic Transition Theory Reinterpreted: An Application to Recent Natality Trends in Latin America* (Lexington, Ky., 1975), pp. 1–60.See also Joseph Spengler, *Population Change, Modernization, and Welfare* (Englewood Cliffs, N.J., 1974), and Frank Lorimer, *Culture and Human Fertility* (New York, 1958).

40. Mikhail Bakhtin, *Rabelais and His World* (Cambridge, Mass., 1968), pp. 221–25.

41. The cheese and tripe associations exist in all four villages in very explicit form, including rough but humorous assertions that the best cheeses are made by nuns and postfecund women. The mountain oyster dish came to my attention through the culinary efforts of the widow who cooked for us in Nissoria; it has ritual significance elsewhere in Italy as well. When we were there in 1974 our seven-year-old daughter, at that time an only child, accompanied us. The widow was especially pleased, therefore, when we returned in 1977 with our infant second daughter in tow. To father a son would require eating yet another plate of mountain oysters, she assured me. A variety of aphrodisiacs are also known and used. When, in the course of discussing these with several Nissorini, I mentioned that modern medical science had in its array of drugs an aphrodisiac derived from the urine of pregnant women, one person stated that that particular "cure" had always been used in the village. What this implies about modernity and tradition I leave to the reader.

42. Wrigley, *Population and History*, pp. 131–35.

43. The Nissoria data are excellent until 1865, when new forms were introduced which dropped entries for parents' ages. Clerks then ceased recording, except in the most haphazard fashion, whether parents were alive. This arises from the customary Italian usage of preceding reference to a dead person with the word *fu*. Regulations called for the names of parents, but clerks in Nissoria only haphazardly entered this word to indicate that they were deceased. In Rogliano after 1865 similar forms were in use but clerks quite consistently entered *fu* when writing the name of a dead person. But consistently does not mean with 100 percent accuracy, and there may be some understatement of percentages of dead parents in Rogliano. With these caveats noted, the data are as follows:

| Decade | Four Parents Alive | Four Parents Dead | One Set Alive, Other Dead | All Other Combinations |
|--------|-------------------|-------------------|--------------------------|------------------------|
| | | Albareto | | |
| 1870 | 31 | 4 | 14 | 51 |
| 1880 | 32 | 4 | 14 | 50 |
| 1890 | 25 | 5 | 10 | 60 |
| 1900 | 28 | 4 | 10 | 58 |
| 1910 | 27 | 5 | 11 | 57 |
| 1920 | 44 | 3 | 9 | 44 |
| 1930 | ... | ... | ... | ... |
| 1940 | 34 | 4 | 12 | 50 |
| 1950 | 49 | 2 | 7 | 42 |
| 1960 | 62 | 1 | 4 | 33 |
| 1970 | 70 | 0 | 0 | 30 |
| | | Castel San Giorgio | | |
| 1900 | 32 | 3 | 13 | 52 |
| 1910 | 24 | 4 | 16 | 56 |
| 1920 | 23 | 3 | 10 | 64 |
| 1930 | 31 | 2 | 11 | 56 |
| 1940 | 35 | 2 | 8 | 55 |
| 1950 | 48 | 2 | 6 | 44 |
| 1960 | 55 | 1 | 5 | 39 |
| 1970 | 54 | 0 | 0 | 46 |
| | | Rogliano | | |
| 1870 | 24 | 6 | 9 | 61 |
| 1880 | 27 | 6 | 13 | 54 |
| 1890 | 26 | 8 | 15 | 51 |
| 1900 | 24 | 4 | 19 | 53 |
| 1910 | 23 | 5 | 11 | 61 |
| 1920 | 38 | 3 | 16 | 43 |
| 1930 | 42 | 3 | 4 | 51 |
| 1940 | 43 | 3 | 11 | 43 |
| 1950 | 53 | 2 | 4 | 41 |
| 1960 | 50 | 3 | 6 | 41 |
| 1970 | 62 | 0 | 5 | 33 |

44. Estimates were derived in the following manner. Expectations of life at age $x$ were taken from Louis Dublin and Alfred Lotka, *Length of Life: A Study of the Life Table* (New York, 1936), pp. 366–68 for Italy, 1876–87. These figures, which are repeated in several sources, originate with the Istituto Centrale di Statistica del Regno d'Italia; their applicability to Castel San Giorgio throughout the nineteenth century is somewhat problematic,

although mortality rate calculations displayed earlier in fig. 5 allow some confidence that they are approximately correct. Moreover, the correlation between estimated and observed figures in table 11 is close enough to give assurance that the estimation procedure is reasonably accurate. In any event, the next step required choosing a life table giving age-specific survivor rates for a population with "expectation of life at age $x$" experience similar to Italy's between 1876 and 1887. William Farr, *Tables of Lifetimes, Annuities, and Premiums* (London, 1864), provided figures which match almost exactly known portions of the Italian experience from the age of ten on. (Expectation of life at birth is five years greater for males and seven for females in the Farr tables on English mortality than the Italian data show, but after age ten expectancies are the same. The differences reflect accurately greater infant and child mortality in Italy, but this is not immediately relevant to the question of survival prospects among those who reached adulthood.) From birth certificates in Castel San Giorgio I have calculated that mean age of motherhood (the average of all births, not of the firstborn only) was thirty and of fatherhood, thirty-three. A more precise breakdown of these figures is as follows ($N=12,681$):

**Percentages of Births in Castel San Giorgio at Various Ages**

| AGE | FATHERS | | | | MOTHERS | | | |
|---|---|---|---|---|---|---|---|---|
| | 1811–49 | 1850–99 | 1900–1929 | 1930–73 | 1811–49 | 1850–99 | 1900–1929 | 1930–73 |
| Under 20 | 2 | 1 | 1 | 1 | 3 | 1 | 3 | 3 |
| 20–29 | 27 | 24 | 23 | 23 | 43 | 45 | 41 | 45 |
| 30–39 | 42 | 44 | 33 | 52 | 47 | 46 | 40 | 43 |
| 40–49 | 22 | 24 | 30 | 20 | 7 | 8 | 16 | 9 |
| 50–59 | 6 | 6 | 10 | 4 | ... | ... | ... | ... |
| Over 59 | 1 | 1 | 3 | 0 | ... | ... | ... | ... |

Adding mean parenthood figures to mean ages at first marriage—twenty-five for females and twenty-eight for males—I estimate that the average bride's mother was (or would have been had she survived) fifty-five, her father fifty-eight, the groom's mother fifty-eight, and his father sixty-one. The appropriate survivor rates from age thirty for females and thirty-three for males to ages fifty-five, fifty-eight, fifty-eight, and sixty-one are 71 percent for bride's mothers, 66 percent for brides' fathers, 66 percent for grooms' mothers, and 60 percent for grooms' fathers. These rates fall between mortality levels 6 and 7 for southern European life tables calculated in Ansley Coale and Paul Demeny, *Regional Model Life Tables and Stable Populations* (Princeton, N.J., 1966), pp. 661–62. It is then a matter of simple multiplication to calculate the life table estimates shown in table 11 (.71 × .66 × .66 × .60 for all alive, .29 × .34 × .34 × .40 for all dead, and so forth). There may be some tendency to question the need for such a complicated estimation procedure when the documents are at hand to show exactly how many parents of brides and grooms were alive. The point is to provide a means for analyzing the ways in which marriage varied within the constraints of demographic rates. For example, the assertion in the text that death of both sets of parents encouraged marriage by the children rests not only on observed data but also on comparison with an implicit null hypothesis: many more marriages reflecting this situation occurred than would have resulted from a random distribution situation in which deaths of parents had no consistent impact on children's marriage decisions.

45. Edward Shorter, *The Making of the Modern Family* (New York, 1975), pp. 29–39, comments perceptively on the debate. Also see Lawrence Stone, *The Family, Sex and Marriage in England, 1500–1800* (London, 1977), pp. 23–26.

46. These figures are summarized from table 11 as follows: 48 percent = rows 1–4; 41 percent = rows 1, 5, 9, and 13; 36 percent = rows 5–12; and 39 percent = rows 2, 3, 6, 7, 10, 11, 14, and 15.

47. That is, two sets of parents produce six marrying children who form three possible households, one of which cannot contain a set of parents.

48. Laslett, *Household and Family*, p. 31; Berkner, "The Stem Family," p. 407; and Wrigley, *Population and History*, pp. 131–34.

49. *Cartella di casa* folders for the 1951 census for *case sparse* in Rogliano located at the Municipio.

50. *Cartella di casa* folders for the censuses of 1901 and 1931 for Albareto located at the Municipio. These folders are kept "up-to-date" by municipal clerks who register formal entries and exits from the village. Therefore, the number of persons moving in and out of a house can only have been greater than those formally recorded.

51. Peter Laslett, *The World We Have Lost* (New York, 1965), p. 91.

52. The same point is raised for the Mediterranean generally in the discussion of M. J. Lineton's work by John Davis in *People of the Mediterranean* (London, 1977), pp. 174–76.

53. Although it is tempting to ascribe the narrower role of *la famiglia* in the northern village of Albareto to vague cultural distinctions between north and south, the matter of land inheritance and population pressure also seems to be consequential. See chap. 8 for an analysis of the impact of *la famiglia* on migration patterns and goals.

54. The view that I am questioning is ably presented by Leonard W. Moss, "The Passing of Traditional Peasant Society in the South," in Edward Tannenbaum and Emiliana Noether, *Modern Italy: A Topical History since 1861* (New York, 1974), pp. 147–70.

## Chapter 6

1. Rosa Runco, *Per una pace* (Bari, 1974).

2. For a typical statement of overall optimism in the face of massive data to the contrary, see Douglas Lamont, "Il Mezzogiorno: Southern Italy," in *Mediterranean Europe and the Common Market: Studies of Economic Growth and Integration,* ed. Eric N. Baklanoff (University, Ala., 1976), pp. 155–76.

3. See the multivolume findings of the *Commissione parlamentare di inchiesta sulla miseria in Italia e sui mezzi per combatterla* (Rome, 1953–54).

4. Richard Gambino, *Blood of My Blood: The Dilemma of the Italian-Americans* (Garden City, N.Y., 1974), pp. 68–69.

5. Anton Blok, *The Mafia of a Sicilian Village, 1860–1960: A Study of Violent Peasant Entrepreneurs* (New York, 1975), p. 48.

6. I use this term in a way parallel to Robert Redfield's usage in "The Primitive World View," *Proceedings of the American Philosophical Society* (1952), p. 30.

7. On *la miseria* and peasant/artisan antagonism, see Frederick Friedmann, "The World of 'La Miseria,'" *Partisan Review* (March 1953), pp. 218–31. Also excellent is Feliks Gross, *Il Paese: Values and Social Change in an Italian Village* (New York, 1973), pp. 24–30. For a related typology, see Willaim Mangin, "Similarities and Differences between Two Types of Peruvian Communities," in *Peasants in Cities,* ed. Mangin (Boston, 1970), pp. 20–29.

8. The "night of the knives" (see chap. 9) is the most formidable instance of class antagonism in Nissoria, and although the event itself may be viewed as episodic or even exceptional, its continuing cultural and social significance cannot be denied. For an astute analysis of the relationship between peasant unrest and societal change, see Henry Landsberger, "Peasant Unrest: Themes and Variations," in *Rural Protest: Peasant Movements and Social Change,* ed. Landsberger (London, 1974), pp. 28–33.

9. Joseph Lopreato, *Peasants No More: Social Class and Social Change in an Underdeveloped Society* (San Francisco, 1967), pp. 123–30; and Oscar Lewis, *Life in a Mexican Village: Tepoztlán Restudied* (Urbana, Ill., 1951), p. 429.

10. Robert Redfield, *Peasant Society and Culture* (Chicago, 1960), p. 66.

11. Jane Schneider and Peter Schneider, *Culture and Political Economy in Western Sicily* (New York, 1976), pp. 10–14 and 149–72; and Immanuel Wallerstein, *The Modern World System: Capitalist Agriculture and the Origins of the European World-Economy in the Sixteenth Century* (New York, 1974), p. 103.

12. Emilio Sereni, *Storia del paesaggio agrario italiano* (Bari, 1961), esp. pp. 305–78, and his contribution "Agricoltura e mondo rurale," in *Storia d'Italia* (Turin, 1972), 1:231 ff.; Giorgio Giorgetti, *Contadini e proprietari nell' Italia moderna: rapporti di produzione e contratti agrari dal secolo XVI a oggi* (Turin, 1974). On the relationship between agrarian and industrial capitalism, see Guido Baglioni, *L'ideologia della borghesia industriale nell' Italia liberale* (Turin, 1974), pp. 79 ff.

13. See app. D for a full list of occupations and how they are categorized. The number of cases is as follows: Albareto, 663; Castel San Giorgio, 1,102; Nissoria, 1,089; and Rogliano, 2,392.

14. Fig. 14 summarizes exactly what the death registers showed, but these figures are somewhat misleading for the period after 1960, when pensioners began to be listed as such rather than by their former occupations. For the recent period census figures are more accurate. For 1971 these are 63.5% in Albareto, 12.2% in Castel San Giorgio, 39.2% in Nissoria, and 17.9% in Rogliano. For a comparative analysis of agricultural/nonagricultural portions, see Jaginder Kumar, *Population and Land in World Agriculture: Recent Trends and Relationships* (Berkeley, 1972), esp. pp. 46–99.

15. Located in the Municipio at Albareto. Among 1,664 persons called to serve, 24 listed themselves in nonagricultural positions, 40 as landowners, and 1,600 as peasants or cultivators. For material on Albareto's economy, see sources cited in chap. 2, n. 2; also see Giunta per l'Inchiesta Agraria, II (Rome, 1881), fasc. 2, pp. 326–40, and fasc. 3.

16. Data summarized in tables 12–19 are from published census volumes on population in 1871, 1881, and 1936, and on industrial and commercial activity in 1927, 1951, and 1971.

17. For a good beginning on the study of women's work, see Joan W. Scott and Louise A. Tilly, "Women's Work and the Family in Nineteenth Century Europe," *Comparative Studies in Society and History* (January 1975), esp. pp. 43 ff. on rural economy.

18. Schneider and Schneider, *Culture and Political Economy*, pp. 19–56 and 113–38.

19. *Inchiesta parlamentare sulle condizioni dei contadini nelle province meridionali e nella Sicilia*, VI (Rome, 1910), tomo 2, p. 17.

20. Blok, *Mafia of a Sicilian Village*, pp. 245 ff., and assuming that I have properly identified the *comune's* actual name. On latifundism in eastern Sicily, see Jane Hilowitz, *Economic Development and Social Change in Sicily* (Cambridge, 1976), pp. 22–27. On the interior and southern regions, see Leopoldo Franchetti and Sidney Sonnino, *La Sicilia nel 1876* (Florence, 1925), 2:24–77, 153–204, and 270–336. The communities surrounding Nissoria reported the following percentages of total hectarage in *latifondi*: Assoro, 39.7%; Agira, 25.2%; Leonforte, 28.8%; and Nicosia, 31.5%.

21. *Inchiesta parlamentare sulle condizioni dei contadini*, VI, tomo 1, pp. 169–70.

22. Ibid., p. 368.

23. Giunta per l'Inchiesta Agraria, XIII, fasc. 4, p. 93.

24. *Inchiesta parlamentare sulle condizioni dei contadini*, VI, tomo 1, p. 298.

25. Ibid., tomo 2, pp. 106–7.

26. Ibid., pp. 23–25. The owners overlooked very little; a deduction from wages was made if a worker's spouse or child followed along to glean.

27. Blok, *Mafia of a Sicilian Village*, notes the peasant origins of many *gabellotti*, but I believe that his accounts of hostility between peasants and intermediaries suggests that even in western Sicily there was not a single latifundist culture.

28. For material on Rogliano's economy, see sources cited in chap. 2, n. 13.

29. Detailed percentages (pensioners excluded) are as follows for males in marriage and death registers over time:

| | Peasant | Wage Labor | Landowners | Nobles | Townsmen |
|---|---|---|---|---|---|
| **1810–59:** | | | | | |
| Marriage | 67 | 5 | 5 | 1 | 22 |
| Death | 40 | 8 | 16 | 5 | 31 |
| **1860–1909:** | | | | | |
| Marriage | 19 | 53 | 1 | 1 | 26 |
| Death | 14 | 51 | 7 | 3 | 25 |
| **1910–45:** | | | | | |
| Marriage | 26 | 34 | 2 | 1 | 37 |
| Death | 33 | 26 | 3 | 2 | 36 |
| **1946–73:** | | | | | |
| Marriage | 19 | 2 | 1 | 0 | 78 |
| Death | 36 | 9 | 2 | 1 | 52 |

30. On developments throughout Calabria, see Luigi Izzo, *La popolazione calabrese nel secolo XIX: demografia ed economia* (Naples, 1965).

31. *Inchiesta parlamentare sulle condizioni dei contadini*, V, p. 220, gives detailed figures on latifundism in Calabria.

32. In Albareto and Nissoria the term "bracciante" or other words indicating proletarianization of the labor force and complete alienation from traditional land rights never gained as strong a foothold as in Rogliano. In all four communities a multiplicity of terms were used in any given year and by the same clerk, indicating that shifts in terminology were not merely responses to bureaucratic directives.

33. *Inchiesta parlamentare sulle condizioni dei contadini*, V, p. 615, reports that *braccianti* found work only for 138–63 days annually.

34. See Gideon Sjoberg, *The Preindustrial City: Past and Present* (New York, 1960), pp. 182–219, for comparative data.

35. For the early period, see Ruggiero Romano, *Prezzi, salari e servizi a Napoli nel secolo XVIII (1734–1806)* (Milan, 1965); and for post-1860, see Giuseppe Santoro, *L'economia della provincia di Salerno nell' opera della Camera di Commercio, 1862–1962* (Salerno, 1966).

36. Giunta per l'Inchiesta Agraria, VII, pp. 146–66.

37. See Ministero di Agricoltura, Industria e Commercio, *Statistica delle cause delle morti: anni 1881–1887* (Rome, 1882–90), and *Risultati dell' inchiesta sulle condizioni igieniche e sanitarie nei comuni del regno* (Rome, 1886).

38. For parallel findings, see Raimondo Luraghi, "Wage Labor in the 'Rice Belt' of Northern Italy and Slave Labor in the American South: A First Approach," paper presented at Rochester University, New York (October 1974).

39. Comparative statistical data may be found in Vincenzo Bruno, *Evoluzione della mortalità per cause di morte nella prima metà del secolo XX in base alle tavole di mortalità del 1899–1902 e 1950–1953* (Pisa, 1960); and Giorgio Mortara, *La salute pubblica in Italia durante e dopo la guerra* (New Haven, 1925).

40. The number of cases is 3,283 for Rogliano births, 3,239 infant and child deaths for Nissoria, and 2,132 infant and child deaths for Castel San Giorgio.

41. For example, 81 percent (344 of 425) children under age 20 who died in Nissoria in the 1870s were the sons or daughters of peasants, whereas 79 percent (93 of 118) marriages recorded for this decade involved peasant males. The point plotted in fig. 15 is $[(344/425)/(93/118)] \times 100$.

42. Under an assumption that deaths were randomly distributed within families, a score of 120 and a mortality rate of 625/1,000 by age twenty yields a 10 percent likelihood that a peasant father of eight children would have no survivors beyond age twenty; this is over twenty-six times greater than the same probability for a townsman: for the peasant $(.625 \times 1.20)^8 = .1001$ versus for the townsman $(.625 \times .80)^8 = .0039$ when, as in Castel San Giorgio, these comprised approximately equal portions of the total population.

43. An extensive literature on the subject of occupational sociology, although not always fully applicable to the rural Italian situation, informs the discussion that follows. Two particularly useful introductions are Lee Taylor, *Occupational Sociology* (New York, 1968); and Richard Hall, *Occupations and the Social Structure*, rev. ed. (Englewood Cliffs, N.J., 1975).

44. The number of cases is much reduced for Castel San Giorgio due to the local practice of not recording an occupation for fathers who predeceased their sons. Adult males include those age twenty or older.

45. Hubert Blalock, Jr., *Social Statistics*, rev. ed. (New York, 1972), p. 285.

46. This conclusion, of course, rests not on the percentages shown in table 23 but on calculations of ratios of observed to expected frequencies which in effect control for the varying size of agricultural and nonagricultural sectors in each community. On kinship and rural-urban reciprocity, see Andrei Simić, *The Peasant Urbanities: A Study of Rural-Urban Mobility in Serbia* (New York, 1973), pp. 108–25.

47. Blok, *Mafia of a Sicilian Village*, p. 48.

48. Emilio Sereni, *La questione agraria nella rinascita nazionale italiana* (1946; reprint ed., Turin, 1975), p. 83. Also see Pasquale Villani, *Feudalità, riforme, capitalismo agrario* (Bari, 1968), and his *Mezzogiorno tra riforme e rivoluzione* (Bari, 1974), pp. 155–212; and Alberto Caracciolo, "La storia economica," in *Storia d'Italia* (Turin, 1973), vol. 3, esp. pp. 640 ff.; and Rosario Villari, *Mezzogiorno e contadini nell' età moderna* (Bari, 1961). For one view of the ideological and political difficulties of the PCI in the south, see Sidney G. Tarrow, *Partito comunista e contadini nel Mezzogiorno* (1967; reprint ed., Turin, 1972), pp. 221–26. For a critical view of Gramscian historiography on the failure of agrarian revolution, see Giuseppe Are, *Economia e politica nell' Italia liberale (1890–1915)* (Bologna, 1974), p. 149 ff. For a non-Marxist sociological analysis, see S. J. Acquaviva and M. Santuccio, *Social Structure in Italy: Crisis of a System* (Boulder, Colo., 1976), pp. 117–25.

49. On *braccianti* in these regions, see Luigi Preti, *Le lotte agrarie nella valle padana* (Turin, 1955), pp. 54–60.

50. Emilio Sereni, *Il capitalismo nelle campagne (1860–1900)* (1947; reprint ed., Turin, 1968), pp. 158 ff. and 166 for the extended quotation. Also see Charles Tilly, Louise Tilly, and Richard Tilly, *The Rebellious Century: 1830–1930* (Cambridge, Mass., 1975), pp. 271–300, for an attempt to grapple with these issues in a meaningful comparative framework.

51. A good summary on the "southern question" is Corrado Vivanti's "Lacerazioni e contrasti," in *Storia d'Italia* (Turin, 1972), 1:931–48.

52. Giunta per l'Inchiesta Agraria, VII, p. 166.

53. On walking home, see *Inchiesta parlamentare sulle condizioni dei contadini*, VI, tomo 2, p. 21. On peasant attitudes, see Giunta per l'Inchiesta Agraria, XIII, tomo 2, pp. 403–16. On the dual nature of the Jacini inquiry, into agricultural production as well as into social conditions, see Alberto Caracciolo, *L'inchiesta agraria Jacini* (Turin, 1973; orig. 1958), p. 5. On the failure of law and government regulation, see Franchetti and Sonnino, *La sicilia nel 1876*, 1:239–83. On owners' fears of peasant violence, see Salvatore Carbone and Renato Grispo, *L'inchiesta sulle condizioni sociali ed economiche della Sicilia (1875–1876)* (reprint ed., Rocca San Casciano, 1968–69), 1:42, 2:734–878 (esp. 751–78) for some remarkable testimony.

54. Enzo del Carria, *Proletari senza rivoluzione: storia delle classi subalterne italiane dal 1860 al 1950* (Milan, 1966), pp. 31–150, makes clear that such occasions were by no means trivial.

## Chapter 7

1. Printed in A. V. Savona and M. L. Straniero, eds., *Canti dell' emigrazione* (Milan, 1976), p. 170.

2. That such structures are not limited to southern Italy is shown in Sydel Silverman's "Patronage and Community-Nation Relationships in Central Italy," *Ethnology* (April 1965), pp. 172–89.

3. The practice of recording hamlet names continued in Albareto until 1921, only six years before Albareto itself was absorbed administratively within the large *comune* of Borgotaro.

4. These names occasionally find their way into legal land records located in the various municipal archives.

5. George M. Foster, "What Is a Peasant?" in *Peasant Society: A Reader*, ed. Jack Potter et al. (Boston, 1967), p. 10.

6. Ibid., pp. 11–12.

7. The discussion that follows draws upon the same local sources cited in chaps. 2 and 6.

8. The sample size here is small—twenty-four interviews in which the question was answered in a reliable way—but there is no reason to believe that the more reticent women who did not wish to talk at length with us had traveled widely in the past.

9. In this regard *campanilismo* is congruent with and reinforces other factors that encourage emigrants to cluster. See the following chapter.

10. For methodological problems bearing on the study of intermediate market centers, see G. William Skinner, "Marketing and Social Structure in Rural China. Part I," *Journal of Asian Studies* (November 1964), pp. 3–43, an essay of primary importance even for non-Asian specialists.

11. For a provocative application of Alfred Kroeber's fundamental work on cultural areas, centers, and donation, see Robert T. Anderson, *Traditional Europe: A Study in Anthropology and History* (Belmont, Calif., 1971), pp. 77–82.

12. A good introduction to the question of regional and local variation will be found in the essays of Giorgio Giorgetti, Stefano Somogyi, Rosita Levi Pisetzky, and Emilio Faccioli in *Storia d'Italia* (Turin, 1973), 5:701–58, 841–87, and 939–1030.

13. On the multiple communication roles of church and priest, see Anna Anfossi, *Socialità e organizzazione in Sardegna* (Milan, 1968), pp. 85–95.

14. Giunta per l'Inchiesta Agraria, XIII, tomo 2, pp. 416–19. See also Giovanni Verga's "I Malavoglia."

15. On peasant opposition to Mussolini after 1940, see Emilio Sereni, *La questione agraria nella rinascita nazionale italiana* (1946; reprint ed., Turin, 1975), pp. 356–74.

16. The data summarized in tables 24 and 25 do not distinguish consistently among the ability to read, the ability to write (which always assumes the ability to read), and *analfabetismo* (illiteracy). I have counted those able to read but not to write among the literate in order to allow meaningful comparisons between one census year and another. Those able to read but not to write constituted, for the 1881 census, 3 percent of literate males and 11 percent of literate females for all Italy.

17. Eugen Weber, *Peasants into Frenchmen: The Modernization of Rural France, 1870–1914* (Stanford, Calif., 1976), pp. 318–38, describes a parallel process.

18. John W. Briggs, *An Italian Passage: Immigrants to Three American Cities, 1890–1930* (New Haven, 1978), pp. 37–64.

19. These conclusions may be seen in tables 24 and 25 and are confirmed for Italy as a whole in Luigi Faccini, Rosalba Graglia, and Giuseppe Ricuperati, "Analfabetismo e scolarizzazione," in *Storia d'Italia* (Turin, 1976), 6:756–81.

20. Giunta per l'Inchiesta Agraria, XIII, tomo 1, pp. 480–81, 671; tomo 2, p. 90.

21. *Inchiesta parlamentare sulle condizioni dei contadini nelle province meridionali e nella Sicilia*, V (Rome, 1910), p. 688.

22. Luciano J. Iorizzo, "The Padrone and Immigrant Distribution," in Silvano Tomasi and Madeline Engel, eds., *The Italian Experience in the United States* (New York, 1970), pp. 43–75; and Alberto Giovannetti, *L'America degli Italiani* (Modena, 1975), pp. 155–81.

23. A number of studies on communication and the Italian peasantry exist. These generally ignore the problem of how rural folk get their messages out, assume that penetration by official cultural centers (Rome above all) is always a good thing, and take a far more positive view of the impact of television than I do. See esp. Mario Cataudella and Pasquale Coppola, *Spazio geografico e formazione culturale* (Naples, 1970), pp. 21–22; and Charles Wright, *La comunicazione di massa* (Rome, 1965), pp. 13–14, on television. Even more extensive claims are made in Lidia DeRita, *I contadini e la televisione: studio della influenza degli spettacoli in un gruppo di contadini lucani* (Bologna, 1964), wherein the author links television to emigration, consumerism, and voting behavior. On printed communication, see Ignazio Weiss, *Politica dell' informazione* (Milan, 1961), pp. 173–83, and "Il quotidiano ed i suoi lettori," *Nord e sud* (1966), p. 66, for data showing that, although most newspaper readers are northern and urban, enough are southern and rural to support the conclusion that even illiterate peasants eventually are affected by things written. For a critique of the failure of all segments of the political spectrum to allow the masses to communicate, see Roberto Faenza, "La comunicazione orizzontale," in Gianpaolo Fabris, *Sociologia delle comunicazioni di massa* (Milan, 1976), pp. 271–72. Policy-oriented research on the role of communication in facilitating "development" and/or "modernization" flourished between the Second World War and the late 1960s. Beginning about a decade ago, however, scholars began to question the optimistic and western-oriented character of such studies. See, e.g., Inayatullah, "Toward a Non-Western Model of Development," in Daniel Lerner and Wilbur Schramm, eds., *Communication and Change in the Developing Countries* (Honolulu, 1967), pp. 98–102; and Everett M. Rogers, "Communication and Development: The Passing of the Dominant Paradigm," in Rogers, ed., *Communication and Development: Critical Perspectives* (Beverly Hills, Calif., 1976), pp. 121–48.

24. In this formulation I am much influenced by Jean Labasse, *L'organisation de l'espace: éléments de géographie voluntaire* (Paris, 1966).

25. On continuing internal migration during the fascist era, see the persuasive analysis of Anna Treves, *Le migrazioni interne nell' Italia fascista: politica e realtà demografica* (Turin, 1976).

26. Edward R. Tannenbaum, *The Fascist Experience: Italian Society and Culture, 1922–1945* (New York, 1972), pp. 213–47, claims that the popular culture of fascism had only a negligible impact on the mass of southern peasants. He cites Carlo Levi, which is rather ironic since Levi's very presence as an exile in a southern village is good evidence of at least one aspect of fascism that rural folk understood well. To rest, as Tannenbaum does, with the dubious assertion that even when peasants were forced to listen to Mussolini, Il Duce's words "went over their heads, leaving no trace" misses a great deal about both peasants and dictators. It is one thing to conclude, as most scholars do, that neither the rise nor the fall of fascism depended on southern peasants, but quite another to assume that one had no impact on the other. In fairness to Tannenbaum, it must be noted that leading Italian scholars have not taken up the question of fascist popular culture and the peasantry in a rigorous way. Perhaps the profound antifascism of the present generation of Italian scholars has led them to emphasize instead the rather isolated instances of peasant resistance to Mussolini. Whatever the reason, neither Renzo deFelice's monumental volumes on Mussolini nor Enzo Santarelli's otherwise estimable three-volume *Storia del fascismo* consider in any detail the impact of fascism—for example, the campaign to "ruralize" Italy in the early 1930s—on peasant culture. Sereni, *La questione agraria*, pp. 212–99, does at least open the issue in his analysis of the fascist rise to power. Consistent with findings discussed in the previous chapter of the present study, Sereni shows that more fully proletarianized rural workers resisted fascism longer than did peasants prompted by petty private holdings or feudal residuals to defend landlord interests. This suggests that the parallelism between peasant traditionalism and fascist nationalism is more than coincidental, that Il Duce tapped a very real and potentially dangerous and regressive aspect of rural culture, an aspect worthy of further study.

27. For parallel findings in a different setting, see Morris Opler, "The Extensions of an Indian Village," in Potter et al., *Peasant Society*, pp. 42–47. On the much greater geographic mobility of English villages, see David Levine, *Family Formation in an Age of Nascent Capitalism* (New York, 1977), pp. 35–44.

28. For the national census of 1871 people had to state whether they had been born in the *comune* in which they currently resided. Figures at the provincial level confirm local results based on marriage registers. These percentages indicate clearly that marriage was the primary occasion for relocation.

| | NICOSIA<br>(Nissoria) | COSENZA<br>(Rogliano) | BORGOTARO<br>(Albareto) | SALERNO<br>(Castel San Giorgio) |
|---|---|---|---|---|
| Males: | | | | |
| Born in *comune* | 92 | 87 | 88 | 87 |
| Born elsewhere in Italy | 8 | 13 | 12 | 13 |
| Females: | | | | |
| Born in *comune* | 94 | 90 | 87 | 89 |
| Born elsewhere in Italy | 6 | 10 | 13 | 11 |

29. Skinner, "Marketing and Social Structure," n. 32, criticizes use of a "walking distance" approach as inapplicable to determination of sizes of marketing areas. The present analysis does not insist on "walking distance" as a determinant of marriage patterns but simply asks how many marriages remained within this limit.

30. Distance calculations were made for each place of birth mentioned in marriage registers by the shortest roadway from one communal center to another. The number of different *comuni* appearing in each register is as follows: Albareto, 169; Castel San Giorgio, 260; Nissoria, 137; and Rogliano, 231.

31. For each of the 797 places of birth recorded in the marriage registers (or the appropriate legal *comune* if a *frazione* was listed), I calculated density levels from 1871 population and land area data summarized in ISTAT, *Comuni e loro popolazione ai censimenti dal 1861 al 1951* (Rome, 1960).

32. Doreen Warriner, *Economics of Peasant Farming* (London, 1939), pp. 61–78, suggests that the best measure of population pressure in an agrarian economy is density and that one hectare per person (equals $100/km^2$ density) of arable land is the minimum amount that guarantees subsistence. The Albareto data indicate that an appropriate density ceiling in a pastoral economy is approximately two hectares per person. Space requirements for populations only partially devoted to agriculture are far more difficult to determine. Perhaps some indication or relative density for Castel San Giorgio may be gained from the following figures located in Witt Bowden, Michael Karpovich, and Abbot Usher, *An Economic History of Europe since 1750* (1937; reprint ed., New York, 1969), pp. 1–23.

| | | YEAR | |
|---|---|---|---|
| REGION | 1800 | 1825 | 1846 |
| Tuscany | 129 | 148 | 186 |
| Naples (Kingdom) | 142 | 162 | 186 |
| Sicily | 157 | 160 | 164 |
| Lombardy | 222 | 270 | 310 |

For the period since unification, see Teresa Isenburg, "Densità e distribuzione della popolazione," in *Storia d'Italia*, 6:700–705. On the continuing significance of density as a factor in migration, see Lodovico Meneghetti, *Aspetti di geografia della popolazione: Italia, 1951–1967* (Milan, 1971), pp. 112–22.

33. In order to keep these maps manageable, each place of birth has been assigned to the region in which it is located. Places of birth within the same provinces as the respective "base" communities are excluded. For example, the map for Albareto excludes all places located in the province of Parma.

34. On the impact of Naples, see Cataudella and Coppola, *Spazio geografico*, p. 89.

35. The national census of 1861 provides the following data on relocation and occupation at the provincial level. Figures represent percentages born in the *comune* in which they reside.

|                        | PARMA | | PRINCIPATO CITERIORE | | CALABRIA CITERIORE | | CATANIA | |
|------------------------|-------|-----|------|-----|------|-----|------|-----|
|                        | M     | F   | M    | F   | M    | F   | M    | F   |
| Agricultural workers   | 68    | 71  | 92   | 96  | 97   | 98  | 92   | 95  |
| Mining                 | 66    | ... | 94   | ... | 99   | ... | 74   | ... |
| Manufacturing          | 41    | 61  | 92   | 96  | 70   | 91  | 83   | 93  |
| Commerce               | 59    | 66  | 87   | 89  | 90   | 97  | 83   | 84  |
| Liberal professions    | 62    | 81  | 86   | 94  | 95   | 99  | 81   | 86  |
| Religious vocations    | 31    | 24  | 76   | 49  | 83   | 75  | 76   | 88  |
| Public service         | 43    | 40  | 62   | 92  | 85   | 96  | 78   | 80  |
| Military and police    | 9     | 75  | 2    | ... | 1    | 1   | 33   | ... |
| Landowners             | 69    | 53  | 92   | 90  | 95   | 92  | 90   | 89  |
| Domestics              | 36    | 44  | 71   | 68  | 87   | 85  | 79   | 83  |
| Destitute persons      | 55    | 66  | 96   | 96  | 97   | 97  | 90   | 94  |
| Without occupation     | 81    | 73  | 97   | 94  | 97   | 96  | 96   | 95  |

36. This finding conflicts with the generalizations offered in Anderson, *Traditional Europe*, pp. 83–93 and 135–51. The differing conclusion, it seems to me, stems from the ambiguous character of "landowners"; certainly they were not peasants in Anderson's sense, but neither were most of them aristocrats.

37. A very useful contribution on this subject is Aldo DeJaco, ed., *Gli anarchici: cronaca inedita dell' unità d'Italia* (Rome, 1971), and his earlier *Brigantaggio meridionale* (Rome, 1969). On the specific participation of at least one resident of Rogliano in instructing delegates to the First International at London, see Pier Carlo Masini, *Storia degli anarchici italiani: da Bakunin a Malatesta (1862–1892)* (Rome, 1969), p. 205.

*Chapter 8*

1. The classic example is Oscar Handlin, *The Uprooted* (Boston, 1951). See the critique by Rudolph J. Vecoli, "Contadini in Chicago: A Critique of *The Uprooted*," *Journal of American History* (December 1964), pp. 404–17. Two exceptional studies among these earlier works are Robert F. Foerster, *The Italian Emigration of Our Times* (Cambridge, Mass., 1919); and Phyllis H. Williams, *South Italian Folkways in Europe and America* (1938; reissued, New York, 1969). For an uncompromisingly critical view of the early work, see Mario Chiari, "Assimilation of Immigrants in Current Italian Literature," *International Migration Digest* (Spring 1966), pp. 26–39.

2. See esp. John W. Briggs, *An Italian Passage: Immigrants to Three American Cities, 1890–1930* (New Haven, 1978); Joseph J. Barton, *Peasants and Strangers: Italians, Rumanians, and Slovaks in an American City, 1890–1950* (Cambridge, Mass., 1975); Virginia Yans-McLaughlin, *Family and Community: Italian Immigrants in Buffalo, 1880–1930* (Ithaca, N.Y., 1977); Constance Cronin, *The Sting of Change: Sicilians in Sicily and Australia* (Chicago, 1970); Carla Bianco, *The Two Rosetos* (Bloomington, Ind., 1974); Silvano M. Tomasi and Madeline H. Engel, eds., *The Italian Experience in the United States* (New York, 1970); Betty Boyd Caroli, *Italian Repatriation from the United States, 1900–1914* (New York, 1973); and Brigitte Nuemann, Richard Mezoff, and Anthony Richmond, *Immigrant Integration and Urban Renewal in Toronto* (The Hague, 1973).

3. In addition to the works cited in n. 2, see Virginia Yans-McLaughlin, "Patterns of Work and Family Organization: Buffalo's Italians," *Journal of Interdisciplinary History* (Autumn 1971), pp. 299–314, and "A Flexible Tradition: South Italian Immigrants Confront a New York Experience," *Journal of Social History* (Summer 1974), pp. 429–45;

Samuel L. Baily, "The Italians and the Development of Organized Labor in Argentina, Brazil, and the United States, 1880–1914," *Journal of Social History* (Winter 1969–70), pp. 123–34; Robert F. Harney, "The Padrone and the Immigrant," *Canadian Review of American Studies* (Fall 1974), pp. 101–18; Lydio Tomasi, "The Italian American Family: The Southern Italian Family's Process of Adjustment to an Urban America" (mimeograph, 1971); and Rudolph J. Vecoli, "Prelates and Peasants: Italian Immigrants and the Catholic Church," *Journal of Social History* (Spring 1969), pp. 217–68.

4. See Caroli, *Italian Repatriation;* Massimo Livi-Bacci, *L'immigrazione e l'assimilazione degli italiani negli Stati Uniti* (Milan, 1961), pp. 27–35; and *Storia d'Italia* (Turin, 1976), 6:731–34.

5. Based on military conscription records and migration registers discussed below.

6. The enumeration in 1921 for Italy generally was not accurate, which makes the results for 1911–20 tentative. Moreover, the calculations provide an average net emigration rate for the period between two censuses. Intracensus fluctuations are not shown, which is obviously a shortcoming in a decade such as 1911–20.

7. The census counts before unification for Nissoria and Castel San Giorgio are not sufficiently accurate to justify extending the calculation to the period before 1861. I estimate that net emigration rates from these two communities were lower than from Rogliano.

8. Foerster, *Italian Emigration*, pp. 51–53.

9. Emmanuel Le Roy Ladurie, *Times of Feast, Times of Famine: A History of Climate since the Year 1000* (Garden City, 1971), p. 66.

10. M. Emma Alaimo, *Proverbi siciliani* (Milan, 1970), pp. 43–62, 125–38, for agriculture and meteorology.

11. Temperature and precipitation data from *World Weather Records* in *Smithsonian Miscellaneous Collections*, vols. 79 (1927), 90 (1944), and 105 (1947); U.S. Department of Commerce, Weather Bureau, *World Weather Records* (Washington, 1959); and U.S. Department of Commerce, *Monthly Climatic Data for the World*. Figures are not available for Catania prior to 1892; to estimate Catania data I applied the 1892–1924 ratio of Rome to Catania data to pre-1892 Rome figures, thus arriving at Catania figures reflecting Rome fluctuations. The procedure is highly accurate for temperature but less so for rainfall, which varies greatly even in places as close as Messina and Catania. On the unity of Mediterranean climate, see Air Ministry, Meteorological Office, *Weather in the Mediterranean* (London, 1962), 1:3–8 and 186–89. All data were detrended.

12. On weather and migration generally, see Grazia Dore, "Some Social and Historical Aspects of Italian Emigration to America," *Journal of Social History* (Winter 1968), pp. 110–11. On the early nineteenth century, see B. H. Slicher Van Bath, *The Agrarian History of Western Europe, A.D. 500–1850* (London, 1963), pp. 221–324. For seasonal migration as late as the 1940s, see C. J. Robertson, "Geographical Planning of International Migration: A Note on a Franco-Italian Project," *Population Studies* (December 1950), pp. 345–48.

13. As many as 90 percent of emigrants to other European nations returned. See the excellent analysis of various types of migration in Stefano Passigli, *Emigrazione e comportamento politico* (Bologna, 1969), pp. 3–84.

14. Fernand Braudel, *Capitalism and Material Life, 1400–1800* (New York, 1973), pp. 66–158.

15. Polish wheat and Prussian rye prices in Dutch guilders (annual average) at Amsterdam from N. W. Posthumus, *Nederlandse Prijsgeschiedenis* (Leiden, 1964), 1:7–8 and 22–23.

16. White cheese and meat price relatives at St. Bartholomew's Hospital from ibid., 2:379–81 and 364–67.

17. Wheat price relatives (1802–73 base) for England and France from C. E. Labrousse, *Aspects de l'évolution économique et sociale de la France et du Royaume-Uni de 1815 à 1880* (Paris, 1955), p. 28; also includes data from Ernest Labrousse, *Le prix du froment en France au temps de la monnaie stable (1726–1913)* (Paris, 1970), pp. 9–16; Abbott P. Usher, "Prezzi

del grano e indici prezzi dei beni di consumo in Inghilterra dal 1259 al 1930," in *I prezzi in Europa dal XIII secolo a oggi,* ed. Ruggiero Romano (Turin, 1967), pp. 3–24; and Alfred Dieck, "I prezzi dei generi alimentari nell'Europa centrale e nel Medio Oriente dal XII al XVII secolo," ibid., pp. 142–50.

18. Even though England was cereal-sufficient in good years and depended on American grain to supplement poor harvests, its role in finance and transportation brought it partially into the Mediterranean economy. On this link, see Eric J. Hobsbawm and George Rudé, *Captain Swing* (London, 1969), pp. 23–37.

19. Traian Stoianovich, "Material Foundations of Preindustrial Civilization in the Balkans," *Journal of Social History* (Spring 1971), p. 259, calls attention to the wider cultural implications of this division.

20. See, however, the important contribution of Giovanni Vigo, "Real Wages of the Working Class in Italy: Building Workers' Wages (14th to 18th Century)," *Journal of European Economic History* (Fall 1974), pp. 378–99.

21. The fraction of a quintal of wheat purchased by an hour's wage for male workers; from *Annuario statistico, 1904* (Rome, 1905) and reprinted in Shepard B. Clough, *The Economic History of Modern Italy* (New York, 1964), p. 382. My figures invert the original data, which were in terms of hours needed to purchase a quintal. This was necessary to obtain correlation coefficients with signs consistent with wage indices below.

22. S. B. Saul, *The Myth of the Great Depression, 1873–1896* (London, 1972), esp. p. 31 on improved conditions generally in the 1880s and 1890s. Also see Clough, *Economic History of Italy,* pp. 57–98.

23. Nominal wages as a fraction of the cost of living index with 1913 as the base year; from Cesare Vannutelli, "Occupazione e salari dal 1861 al 1961," in *L'economia italiana dal 1861 al 1961,* pp. 570–71, and reprinted in Clough, *Economic History of Italy,* pp. 382–83.

24. The hard wheat purchasing power of daily wages of *braccianti* in Sicily from 1905 to 1960 with 1878–79 as the base year; from Andrea Saba and Sebastiano Solano, "Lineamenti dell'evoluzione demografica ed economica della Sicilia dall'unificazione ad oggi," in *Problemi dell'economia siciliana,* ed. Paolo Sylos-Labini (Milan, 1966), pp. 42–43.

25. This phenomenon was by no means restricted to Italy; see Roger Price, "The Onset of Labour Shortage in Nineteenth-Century French Agriculture," *Economic History Review* (May 1975), esp. p. 265. For Europe generally, see Philip Taylor, *The Distant Magnet: European Emigration to the U.S.A.* (London, 1971), pp. 22–23; and Julius Isaac, "European Migration Potential and Prospects," *Population Studies* (March 1949), pp. 379–412.

26. On the impact of railroads in Sicily, see Denis Mack Smith, *Modern Sicily after 1713* (New York, 1968), p. 475.

27. J. F. Carr, "The Coming of the Italian," *Outlook* (February 24, 1906), p. 421, and cited in Andrew F. Rolle, *The Immigrant Upraised* (Norman, Okla., 1968), p. 31.

28. Marie Hall Ets, *Rosa: The Life of an Italian Immigrant* (Minneapolis, 1970), pp. 163–64. For a detailed survey of steerage conditions, see Taylor, *Distant Magnet,* pp. 131–66. The passage is still not an easy one; see Constantino Ianni, *Il sangue degli emigranti* (Milan, 1965), pp. 195–223.

29. Supplements to annual death registers in Rogliano for the period 1876–1910 contain frequent and poignant testimony about the efforts of family members (left behind while others went to work in mines in Pennsylvania) to locate burial places and obtain assurances that they were suitably marked.

30. Carroll Wright, *The Italians in Chicago: A Social and Economic Study* (1897; reprint ed., New York, 1970), pp. 52–273, presents valuable statistics on earnings.

31. On the padrone system, see the material cited in chap. 7, n. 22; and also Humbert S. Nelli, "The Italian Padrone System in the United States," *Labor History* (Spring 1964), pp. 153–67; and Harney, "The Padrone and the Immigrant." On migration chains, see John S. MacDonald and L. D. MacDonald, "Chain Migration, Ethnic Neighbourhood Formation, and Social Networks," *Milbank Memorial Fund Quarterly* (January 1964), pp. 82–97;

Rudolph J. Vecoli, "Chicago's Italians prior to World War I: A Study of Their Social and Economic Adjustments" (Ph.D. Diss., University of Wisconsin, 1963), pp. 71–234; and Harvey M. Choldin, "Kinship Networks in the Migration Process," *International Migration Review* (Summer 1973), pp. 163–76. In Nissoria, which is somewhat east of traditional strongholds of the mafia, several interviewees claimed to remember well the role of local associates of the mafia in financing initial migration costs between 1900 and 1910. The mafia offered lower interest rates than either landlords or banks (which were completely ineffectual before 1919); moreover, they were more flexible about repayment. See Francis A. J. Ianni, *A Family Business: Kinship and Social Control in Organized Crime* (New York, 1972), pp. 66–67, for an excellent account of mafia banking operations.

32. National rates calculated from tables in *Annuario statistico dell' emigrazione italiana dal 1876 al 1925* (Rome, 1926).

33. On Italian legislation, see Vittorio Briani, *L'emigrazione italiana ieri e oggi* (Rome, 1959), pp. 41–50.

34. Ibid., pp. 53–75.

35. Clough, *Economic History of Italy*, pp. 114–24.

36. J. S. MacDonald, "Agricultural Organization, Migration and Labour Militancy in Rural Italy," *Economic History Review* (1963), pp. 61–75.

37. On the *fasci* movement, see Salvatore F. Romano, *Storia dei fasci siciliani* (Bari, 1959).

38. Records of sales and land values stated in connection with disputes over water rights are located in the minutes of the municipal council.

39. At this density the land is underutilized. The pastures must be cut mechanically because of a paucity of grazing animals, chestnuts fall to the ground, and mushrooms go unpicked.

40. Based on census figures disaggregating population living in *nuclei* from those in *case sparse*.

41. On work days needed for various tasks and crops, see Maria Clara Tiriticco, "Occupazione e salari nell'agricoltura e nell'industria," in Sylos-Labini, *Problemi dell'economia siciliana*, pp. 218–21. For an excellent discussion of labor elasticity and owners' ability to dispense with tasks, especially in olive cultivation, see Juan Martinez-Alier, *Labourers and Landowners in Southern Spain* (London, 1971), pp. 56–78. Also see René Dumont, *Types of Rural Economy: Studies in World Agriculture* (London, 1957), pp. 229–61 and esp. p.251 for an estimate of 145 work days per year.

42. Mortality rates and seasonal distribution of deaths indicate chronic malnutrition and occasional starvation as late as 1900. As many as 20 percent of adult males left the village between 1810 and 1900 to work in sulfur mining.

43. A moving example is Richard Gambino, *Blood of My Blood: The Dilemma of the Italian-Americans* (New York, 1974), pp. 39–70. But the causal assertion also slips into works claiming a more scientific base. For example, without presenting any evidence, Edward Banfield asserts that "if they could do so, the people of Montegrano would migrate to the United States *en masse*" (*The Moral Basis of a Backward Society* [Glenco, Ill., 1958], p. 59). Data for Nissoria, which is equally poor, indicate that villagers can and do migrate, albeit with difficulty and sacrifice, but that they do not do so "*en masse*"; rather, individuals and families make rational choices about their future.

44. See the military conscription records described in the Note on Demographic Sources. Calls came at age twenty-one between 1821 and 1832 and at age eighteen after 1882.

45. Some of the cases of no response involved entire families that had emigrated, but these are excluded from table 36.

46. Between 1748 and 1892 Albareto produced at least forty-seven priests and many more who entered a seminary but were not ordained.

47. *Cartella di casa* folders located in the Municipio. These are kept "up-to-date" as long as any member of the household remains. Title to the land often remained with several

siblings, but only the one who stayed home worked the land, and he did not pay rent or share proceeds with the others.

48. Remittance registers (scattered) and interview with the retired director of the Cassa di Risparmio at Albareto.

49. If standard chi-square tests are applied to these differences, the possiblility that they might occur by chance alone is less than 1 percent.

50. Carpenters, masons, and general construction workers were hired as such in Belgium, whereas in the United States, in part due to the *padrone* system, skill tended not to be recognized.

51. Based on counts of family surnames, entries for godparents, and length of retention of the *Cartella di casa* folders.

52. Based on emigration permits and on interviews. Many persons now resident in Albareto were born in London, Paris, or New York, but none in Latin America.

53. This was not entirely a traditional contract based only upon a man's work. The local notary drew up a promissory note which the tenant then signed.

54. Responses to a questionnaire asking Albaretesi in America to rank occupations (on a 1–10 scale) according to how pleased they would be to have their children enter into these jobs. The statistical results were far less revealing than the subsequent discussion of reasons for particular rankings. The questionnaire did not indicate ranking criteria (income, security, prestige, or whatever); on the contrary, a major purpose was to elicit a choice among such criteria. Unlike immigrants from Castel San Giorgio, Nissoria, and Rogliano, the Albaretesi in the United States almost without exception ranked consistently according to their estimates of the income potential of each job.

55. Entries in the *Cartella di casa* folders indicate that a majority of emigrants in England and France did this for at least some period of their working careers.

56. The books indicate where immigrants came from (or emigrants were going), date of entry (or exit), place of residence, ages, numbers of persons in the group, and, since 1955, sex composition of the group. The emigration permits indicate year and place of birth, year of marriage, previous emigration, destination, schooling, and occupation.

57. The factory finally came in 1976, but it employs only thirty-two workers, and many Nissorini wish to see it closed because the air pollution (from smelting of lead) is a health hazard.

58. On Italian migration to Australia more generally, see Cronin, *Sting of Change;* C. A. Price, *Southern Europeans in Australia* (Melbourne, 1963); and John S. MacDonald and Leatrice D. MacDonald, "Italian Migration to Australia," *Journal of Social History* (Spring 1970), pp. 249–75.

59. This subject has aroused considerable scholarly interest. See R. P. Sergi Bonnet, "Political Alignments and Religious Attitudes within the Italian Immigration to the Metallurgical Districts of Lorraine," *Journal of Social History* (Winter 1968), pp. 123–55, on the tendency of Italian emigrants to vote for the PCI; also Manuel Castells, "Immigrant Workers and Class Struggles in Advanced Capitalism; The Western European Experience," *Politics and Society* (1975), no. 1, pp. 33–66. On motivation of migrants, see Kurt B. Mayer, "Postwar Migration from Italy to Switzerland," *International Migration Digest* (Spring 1965), pp. 5–13; and G. Gerarci, "Aspetti del movimento migratorio con i paesi europei nel periodo 1946–60," *Rivista italiana di economia, demografia e statistica* (July–December 1964), pp. 203–37. Hossein Askari, "The Contribution of Migration to Economic Growth in the EEC," *Economia internazionale* (May 1974), pp. 341–46, assesses only the direct impact of migration on economic growth and still concludes that it is significant. For a masterful treatment of the demographic structure of an immigrant population, see Anne M. Faidutti-Rudolph, *L'immigration italienne dans le sud-est de la France* (Gap, 1964).

60. Some of these moves were nontemporary only in the sense of applying for a particular category of emigration permit.

61. On the plight of these workers, see Goffredo Fofi, *L'immigrazione meridionale a Torino* (Milan, 1964); and on housing, see Lucio Libertini, *Capitalismo moderno e movimento operaio* (Rome, 1965), pp. 87–88.

62. Giuseppe L. Monticelli, "Italian Emigration: Basic Characteristics and Trends with Special Reference to the Post-War Years," in Tomasi and Engel, *Italian Experience*, pp. 20–22; also see Charles B. Keely, "Effects of U.S. Immigration Law on Manpower Characteristics of Immigrants," *Demography* (May 1975), pp. 179–91.

63. *50° Anniversario della vittoria* (Enna, 1968), "cenni storici."

64. Centro Studi Emigrazione, *L'emigrazione italiana negli anni '70* (Rome, 1975), provides an excellent series of analyses of the problems created by the "new" migration.

65. On rural depopulation, see Carlo Aiello, "L'aménagement de l'exploitation agricole dans les zones d'exode rural: Italie," in *Emigration and Agriculture in the Mediterranean Basin*, ed., C. A. O. Van Nieuwenhuijze (The Hague, 1972), pp. 27–49.

## Chapter 9

1. The foregoing account, except for factual details drawn from death registers and the like, is based on the collective versions of the Nissorini we interviewed. I have tried to capture their sense that the event was unique to them. For the wider context, however, see Salvatore Romano, *Breve storia della Sicilia: momenti e problemi della civiltà siciliana* (Turin, 1964), pp. 289 ff.; Giacinto de' Sivo, *Storia delle due Sicilie dal 1847 al 1861* (Trieste, 1868), 2:92–116; Denis Mack Smith, *A History of Sicily: Modern Sicily after 1713* (New York, 1968), pp. 438–441; Renzo del Carria, *Proletari senza rivoluzione: storia delle classi subalterne italiane dal 1860 al 1950* (Milan, 1966), 1:31–56, which specifically includes these events in Nissoria as class struggle rather than purely local feud; and esp. Romano's earlier work, *Momenti del risorgimento in Sicilia* (Florence, 1953).

2. As with the account of the "night of the knives," I have relied here heavily on interviews in order to portray the meaning of the event for its participants. In addition to Guido Varacchi, I am indebted to all the *Centocrocisti* who allowed me to join their reunion on April 25, 1977, to hear their story. One of the members wrote a detailed account of their experience; see Luigi Canessa, *La strada era tortuosa: sedici mesi di guerriglia sugli Appennini Liguri-Emiliani* (Rapallo, 1947). For the wider context, see Giorgio Bocca, *Storia dell' Italia partigiana, settembre 1943–maggio 1945* (Bari, 1966); and Roberto Battaglia, *Storia della resistenza italiana, 8 settembre 1943–25 aprile 1945* (Turin, 1964), which contains an excellent bibliography. Battaglia's *Story of the Italian Resistance* (London, 1957) is a good popular account.

3. On the crisis in Italy today, see S. S. Acquaviva and M. Santuccio, *Social Structure in Italy: Crisis of a System* (Boulder, Colo., 1976), esp. pp. 215–19 and the extensive bibliography.

4. Returns on the popular referendum of May 12, 1974, ranged from a low of 46 percent in Castel San Giorgio to a high of 55 percent in Rogliano against repeal of the divorce law.

# Index

Age at marriage: and birth rate, 99–105; and courtship practices, 89–94, 98–99, 104; and differences in spouses' ages, 94–99; and economic factors, 78, 80–87; and endogamy/exogamy, 168–72; of females, 70, 78–82, 89, 99–100, 102, 232–33, 247–48 n. 14; and geographic mobility, 83, 91; of males, 79–89, 232–33; and military conscription, 89; and parental consent laws, 87–89; and premarital pregnancy, 89–90; and town residence, 83–87; and war, 89, 248 n. 30
Age stratification, 76, 94–99
Agira, 48
Agriculture: arboreal, 16, 131, 184; capitalism in, 116–17, 121, 123, 126–27, 131, 148; on communal land, 119–20; and crop rotation, 13, 18; and emigration, 181–89, 197–201; exchange mechanisms in, 118–19; feudal vestiges in, 87, 116–17, 126, 131, 135–36, 147–48; and labor systems, 11, 14, 16, 19, 116, 120–21, 126–28, 134–36, 150; and land reform, 17, 84, 193, 201; and land tenure, 11–12, 14, 16–20, 120, 123–24, 128, 134–36; pastoral, 10, 16, 118–22; and seasonality of conception, 53–55, death, 40–43, marriage, 49–50; truck farming, 13–14, 136; viticulture, 14, 184; wheat, 18–20, 123–28, 186–88. *See also* Bracciantì; *Gabellotti;* Jacini Inquiry; Latifundism; Peasantry; Women's work
Aiello, 13
Albareto: birth in, 51–52, 55, 61, 100, 103–4; communications in, 154–56; death in, 40–41, 56–57, 60–61, 64, 138; economy of, 10–11, 28, 83–84, 117–22; emigration from, 180, 185–86, 189–91, 193–201, 207–9; family in, 67–72, 109–11; hamlets of, 9, 238 n. 1; historical myths of, 28–29; housing in, 9–10, 109–11, 209; location of, 5; marriage in, 47–50, 61, 65, 68, 79, 81–84, 95, 100, 103–4, 163–77 passim; and *la miseria,* 114–15, 128; and partisans,

212–15; physical setting of, 10–12; population, 9; status mobility in, 142–46
Anthony of Padua, Saint, 45
Artisanal activity: in Castel San Giorgio, 14, 133; in Rogliano, 16, 65, 130; and specific occupations, 234–35. *See also* Town life
Assoro, 26, 48, 211

Bakhtin, Mikhail, 105–6
Banfield, Edward, 72–73, 77
Berkner, Lutz, 74, 107
Berzolla family, 109–11
Biagio, Saint, 30
Birth: and age of mother, 250–51 n. 44; and class differences in birth rate, 139–40; and emigration, 208–9; and premarital pregnancy, 89–90; rate of and ratio to marriages, 100–104; seasonality of, 51–53, 55, 61–64; and Zecca case study, 68–72. *See also* Children; Conception; Illegitimacy; Infanticide
Blok, Anton, 114, 124, 147
Borgotaro, 10, 28–29, 120
*Bracciantì,* 16–17, 90, 123, 131–32, 135–36, 187, 194, 198–99. *See also* Agriculture; Peasantry
Braudel, Fernand, 186
Breast feeding, 40–41, 54
Briggs, John, 159–60
Butterfield, Herbert, 21

Cadastral survey of 1929, 14, 16, 18–19, 123
*Campanilismo. See* Village chauvinism
Castel San Giorgio: birth in, 51–52, 55, 62, 100, 102–4; communications in, 153–54, 156; death in, 42, 56–57, 60, 62, 137–41; economy of, 13–15, 85–87, 117–18, 133–37; emigration from, 181, 185–86, 190, 194–95; family in, 109; hamlets of, 11, 238 nn. 3, 4; historical myths of, 25–26; housing in, 11; location of, 5; marriage in, 47–50, 62, 65, 68, 79, 85–88, 92, 94,

265